# Oldham
## BRAVE OLDHAM

# OLDHAM
## BRAVE OLDHAM

*An Illustrated History of Oldham*

**BRIAN R. LAW**

Oldham Council

First published in 1999 by
Oldham Council,
Civic Centre, West Street,
Oldham, Lancashire OL1 1XJ.

Telephone: (0161) 911 3000

Copyright © Oldham Council 1999.

All rights reserved. No part of this publication may be reproduced, stored in a retrieval system, or transmitted in any form or by any means, electronic, mechanical, photocopying, recording or otherwise, without the prior permission in writing of the publisher, except in accordance with the provisions of the Copyright, Designs and Patents Act 1988, or under the terms of a licence issued by the Copyright Licensing Agency.

A CIP catalogue record for this book is available from the British Library.

ISBN O 902809 49 0 (cloth).
ISBN O 902809 50 4 (paperback).

Designed by Roger Birch.
Artwork and reprographic production by Carl Fisher Design & Marketing.

Printed and bound in Great Britain by Balding + Mansell.

*Frontispiece:* Yorkshire Street, mid-morning on the day of the Jubilee of Oldham's Incorporation, June 1899.

# Contents

| | | |
|---|---|---|
| *List of Tables* | *page* | 6 |
| *List of Maps, Plans and Figures* | | 6 |
| *Introduction by John Battye, Leader of the Council* | | 7 |
| *Author's Preface* | | 8 |
| *Note on the Value of Money* | | 9 |

**The Rise to Prominence: Oldham Before 1849**

| | | |
|---|---|---|
| I | The Beginnings | 13 |
| II | Oldham and the Industrial Revolution | 18 |
| III | Life in Early Victorian Oldham | 36 |

**Ascendancy: Oldham 1849 - 1919**

| | | |
|---|---|---|
| IV | Cotton Spinning Capital of the World | 80 |
| V | A Manufacturing Town | 113 |
| VI | Local Government | 133 |
| VII | Education for All | 172 |
| VIII | Life in Victorian and Edwardian Oldham | 187 |
| IX | Leisure and Sport | 220 |
| X | Oldham Politics to 1914 | 237 |
| XI | Fortunes made in Oldham | 244 |
| XII | Epilogue - The Great War | 254 |

**Decline: 1919-1945**

| | | |
|---|---|---|
| XIII | Oldham between the Wars | 259 |

**Renewal and Modernisation: Oldham since 1945**

| | | |
|---|---|---|
| XIV | Oldham: 1945 - 1974 | 288 |
| XV | Modern Oldham: 1974-1999 | 319 |
| XVI | Oldham's Future | 349 |

| | |
|---|---|
| *Appendix I: Mayors of Oldham* | 354 |
| *Appendix II: Members of Parliament for Oldham* | 355 |
| *Appendix III: Leaders of Oldham Metropolitan Borough Council* | 356 |
| *Sources and Further Reading* | 357 |
| *Acknowledgements* | 359 |
| *Index* | 360 |

## List of Tables

| I | Profile of the Cotton Industry: Oldham Parish 1841 | 26 |
|---|---|---|
| II | Oldham Parliamentary Borough: Main Occupations | 34 |
| III | Oldham Townships: Population Growth 1801-1851 | 36 |
| IV | Northern Industrial Towns: Population Growth 1801-1851 | 36 |
| V | Estimated Church Attendance March 1851 | 59 |
| VI | Sunday Schools: Registered Scholars 1851 | 61 |
| VII | Population Change 1851-1861 | 84 |
| VIII | Growth of Oldham's Cotton Industry 1851-1913 | 96 |
| IX | Estimated Cotton Mill Earnings (shillings per week) | 111 |
| X | Employment in Cotton and Engineering Manufacturing 1911 | 122 |
| XI | Oldham District: Population Growth 1851-1911 | 126 |
| XII | Oldham: Registration District: Population Change 1851-1901 | 126 |
| XIII | Oldham: Registration District: Birth and Death Rates | 127 |
| XIV | Composition of Oldham Town Council | 135 |
| XV | Oldham Corporation: Capital Spending to 1899 | 141 |
| XVI | Oldham Corporation: Financial Position | 166 |
| XVII | Oldham Corporation: Net Expenditure by Department | 167 |
| XVIII | Development of Elementary Education 1871-1911 | 177 |
| IXX | Oldham District: Population 1911-1939 | 268 |
| XX | Oldham District & Metropolitan Borough: Population 1939-1991 | 291 |
| XXI | Oldham Metropolitan District: Housing Stock | 302 |
| | Annex to Chapter XI: Leading Oldham Dynasties and their Wealth | 252 |

## List of Maps, Plans and Figures

| Location Map of Oldham | 10 |
|---|---|
| Settlement Map of Oldham | 11 |
| Butterworth's Map of Oldham, 1817 | 22 |
| Greenbank Mill complex, c.1850 | 25 |
| Mills and Coalworkings, c.1850 | 31 |
| Baines Map of Oldham, 1823 | 37 |
| Oldham District: Settlement Map c.1845 | 40 |
| Oldham Cotton Mills: Construction Dates | 95 |
| New Mill Building in Oldham | 96 |
| Spinning Results | 108 |
| Wage Movements: Oldham Cotton Spinners, 1868-1909 | 108 |
| Mills and Mill Lodges, 1880s | 152 |
| Oldham District: Townships | 167 |

# Introduction

The Centenary of the County Borough in 1949 saw the publication of Hartley Bateson's book *The History of Oldham*. In 1974 the book was re-published with an additional chapter to mark the formation of the present Metropolitan Borough. During the past 50 years no other comprehensive history of the Borough has been published.

Since that book was first published, Oldham has moved on at a rapid pace. It's principal industries declined, to be replaced by new ones. The composition of its population has changed, with families migrating from all parts of the world. Many of the social problems and legacies of the industrial revolution have been eliminated, making the Borough a much more pleasant and healthy place to live. It's retail base has altered beyond recognition with further exciting developments under construction.

Local Government reorganisation in 1974 brought the present Borough into being with the joining together of the County Borough of Oldham and the Urban District Councils of Chadderton, Crompton, Failsworth, Lees, Royton and Saddleworth.

So much has changed since 1949 that it was felt a new history was needed, not only to look at the past but also to cover the "Oldham Story" over the past 50 years.

1999 – the 150th Anniversary of the Granting of the Charter in 1849 and the Silver Jubilee of the present Borough, seemed the ideal time to look again at Oldham's past, present and future and in this book Brian Law has covered all that – and much more.

I hope that this book will prove as popular as the previous history and, likewise, will still be well-read in 2049.

John Battye,
*Leader of the Council*

# Author's Preface

My interest in Oldham was stimulated by the research which culminated in my book, *Fieldens of Todmorden: a Nineteenth Century Business Dynasty*. John Fielden, the main personality of that dynasty, was Radical MP for Oldham from 1832 to 1847. It was suggested to me that I should write a similar illustrated history, not of a business dynasty, but of a town, Oldham, to mark the 150th anniversary of that town's incorporation in 1999.

Oldham's history is a paradigm of that of many industrial towns in the United Kingdom. It has several distinct phases and themes, the first being a slow rise to prominence from humble beginnings in the early nineteenth century. There followed a phase of ascendancy, an extraordinary epic expansion when Oldham became cotton spinning capital of the world. Great wealth was created in that period but the town acquired a reputation for its smoke and drabness, "a dirty picture in a golden frame", as one of its famous sons was to say. Rapid growth in the economic base resulted in a huge increase in population that had be housed and serviced; local government developed to cope with the many resulting challenges; other social institutions, religious, educational, cultural, recreational evolved to meet the needs of a community finding itself and growing in affluence. The town was immensely proud of its achievements; the phrase Brave Oldham marked the way in which the enterprise and industry of its people had overcome local disadvantages to bring remarkable success.

That success was relatively short-lived and Oldham suffered a period of harsh decline in the inter-war period. But the last fifty years have seen renewal and modernisation of the economic base and the physical fabric of the town. The Oldham community itself has changed in character with the extension of its boundaries and the introduction of Asian and other minority groups.

These phases and themes are common not merely to Oldham, but to Bradford, Blackburn, Wolverhampton and any number of nineteenth century manufacturing towns. The dramatic rise, decline and renewal of a boom town is of course a vast panorama; for the general reader a portrait rather than a detailed substantive account is more appropriate. Such a historical portrait lends itself to illustration which highlights its themes, places and personalities pictorially; text can be complemented with maps, paintings, photographs and documents. *Oldham, Brave Oldham* is thus a combination of prose and image, interesting and accessible to the general reader but also relevant to the scholar.

I owe a particular debt to my collaborator Roger Birch, who has researched all the illustrations and supervised the design of the finished book. None of our research would have been possible without the supportive and patient assistance of the staff of Oldham Local Studies Library and of Oldham Museum; they manage a remarkable repository of material on

Oldham's past. My work has been facilitated and stimulated throughout by Paul Barnett of Oldham Education and Leisure. Among many other individuals who have helped, I must mention Douglas Farnie who, more than anyone else, has recorded Oldham's epic role in the later nineteenth century Lancashire cotton industry; Professor W.D. Rubinstein who has researched nineteenth century wealth; and Phillip Hirst, fifth generation of his family to be associated with the Oldham Chronicle, who has generously provided access to past issues and illustrations. But there have been many others who have contributed to this story of Oldham and they must forgive me if they are not named.

I hope that this book is worthy of the town and its people. I have enjoyed researching and writing it.

## *Note on the Value of Money*

Many of the money values expressed in this book relate to the nineteenth century. Throughout this period and indeed up to the First World War, the purchasing power of money was comparatively stable; if anything prices tended to fall. 1914-1920 saw a sharp inflation but the inter-war years saw prices falling again, although not back to pre-war levels. Inflation returned in the Second World War and has continued at a variable rate thereafter. As a general guide a multiple of sixty converts nineteenth century values to those of the present day. Thus a weekly wage of £1 would be £60 today; a rent of 5 shillings a week £15; a fortune of £900,000 left by Charles Edward Lees about £55 million in today's money.

Since the 1950s and 1960s, prices have risen more than tenfold, with much of that increase taking place in the middle and late Seventies.

Location Map of Oldham

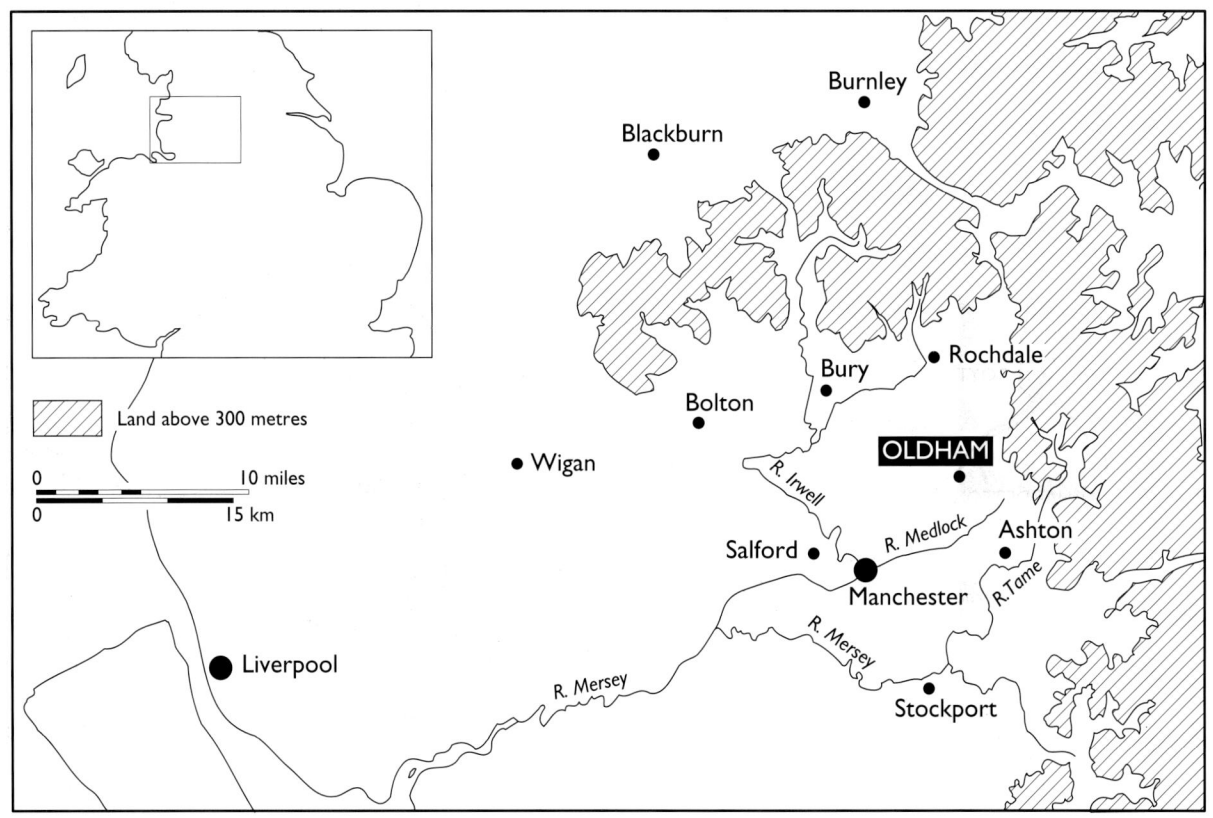

Location Map of Oldham

Settlements and Main Roads

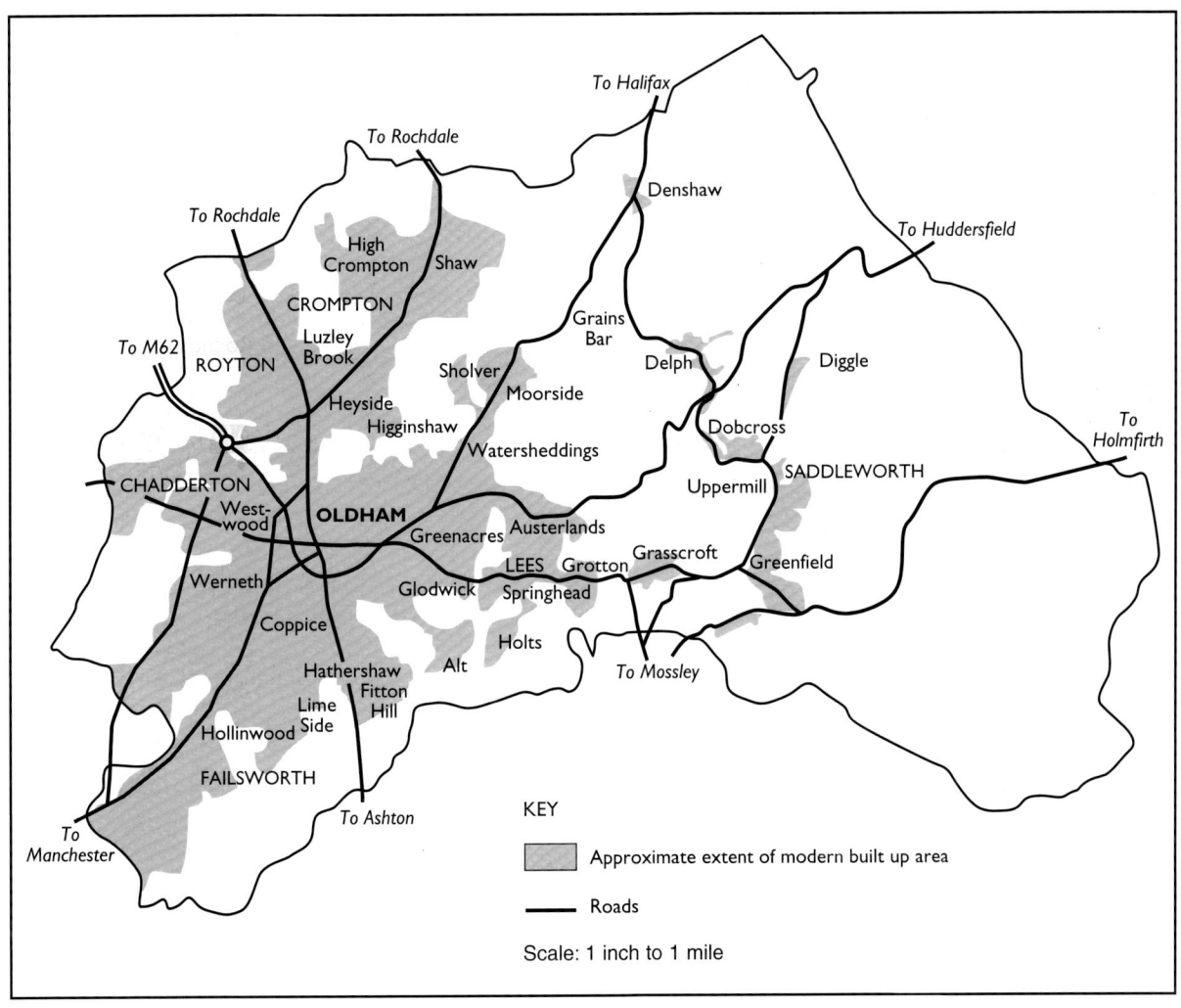

Oldham Metropolitan Borough: Settlements and Main Roads

# The Rise to Prominence: Oldham Before 1849

*Chapter I*

# THE BEGINNINGS

**The Setting**

Oldham is a town built on a hill. The modern Borough lies on the flanks of the Central Pennines; from high moorland to the north-east, rising to over 1,500 feet, the ground of the district falls, irregularly, around a series of hills and spurs divided by depressions and valleys before it reaches the flat Lancashire plain to the south-west. Oldham Edge, a bold spur around which the town of Oldham initially developed, rises to over 825 feet. Coppice and Glodwick Lows, Greenacres Moor and Copster Hill, were other outlying hills rising to 700-750 feet; their slopes were to be covered with streets and houses as the town grew in the nineteenth century. From these heights the ground falls sharply towards 300 feet, typical for the comparatively flat ground on the western side of the Borough; this was the setting for Failsworth, Chadderton and Royton. On the east side of the modern Borough lies the broad but steep-sided Tame valley; in this, "a wild and hilly country" to travellers in the past, the scattered settlements of Saddleworth developed.

The lofty, bare and often desolate moorland is based on coarse Millstone Grit, supporting a sparse vegetation of moor grasses, heather and extensive beds of peat, at best rough grazing, but important as gathering grounds for

**The setting of modern Oldham** as seen from Hartshead Pike. The Medlock valley is in the foreground; beyond, the ground rises to the spur of Oldham Edge and the outlying hill of Glodwick. In the distance is the moorland of Rossendale and, on the right, the Pennine hills.

*Facing:* **Royton Old Hall**, perhaps the largest of the several halls belonging to the minor land owning gentry of the Oldham district at the time of the industrial revolution. Dating from about 1620, the Hall was largely rebuilt in the eighteenth century. From 1662 it was the home of the Percival family, eventually passing by marriage to the Pickfords and then to the Radcliffes. Having sold their land they had ceased to live there by the early nineteenth century, no doubt influenced by the changing industrial character of the district. Over the years the Hall was then leased to various people and organisations and eventually was converted into flats. It was demolished in 1939.

*Facing:* **The old Oldham Church** looking along Goldburn from Mumps, about 1760. Goldburn, along what became Church Street and Bow Street, was the main routeway out of the town towards Yorkshire at the time.

urban water supply. Along its margins the high ground is frequently deeply indented by gullies or cloughs, formed by the surface drainage; bracken and many common trees grew along the sides of these moorland cloughs. The falling ground and lower parts of the district are formed on the overlying Coal Measures, shales, sandstones and seams of coal; much of this area is covered with Glacial Drift, thick layers of boulder clay, gravel, and sand. Here the natural landscape was woodland and pasture land, with trees especially a feature in the stream valleys. The local geology assured surface streams of soft lime-free water, and provided abundant building stone, clay for brick making, and accessible coal seams, some being thick and of good quality.

The whole Oldham district is drained by several rivers which eventually join the Irwell or the Mersey. Chief of these is the Tame, its headwaters in the high moorland. Smaller rivers are the Medlock and to the north the Irk and the Beal and their several insignificant tributary streams; one of these, Sheepwasher Brook, like many others now lost in the urban area, took the drainage of Oldham Edge. Rising ground, facing across the Lancashire plain, and exposed to mostly westerly winds, could expect a humid atmosphere and a cool damp but bracing climate. Rainfall is high averaging more than 55 inches on the high ground and 40 inches in the town, distributed throughout the year; extremes of temperature are rare. Oldham has always complained about its weather being "an overcoat colder" than Manchester but this has bred hardiness among its inhabitants.

## Pre-Industrial Oldham

Throughout the centuries, like the adjoining districts on either flank of the Central Pennines, Oldham was poor and thinly populated. Such a condition was reflected in the huge size of the mediaeval parishes, Prestwich with Oldham, Whalley (in which Saddleworth lay), Rochdale to the north, Halifax to the east. The terrain and climate could not support any significant agriculture nor was there any circumstance that would encourage town development. The district was crossed by routes that linked Lancashire and Yorkshire over the Pennines; the Romans had built such a road from Manchester to York with a fort at Castleshaw and there were mediaeval trackways and bridle roads serving the same purpose.

Poor farming, chiefly livestock on reclaimed pasture and enclosed marshy meadowland, but here and there augmented by arable growing thin crops of oats, seldom wheat, but later potatoes, gave only a frugal livelihood. The loom was a better source of income and thus from the sixteenth century at least the district became associated with the woollen industry pursued in rough stone-built farms and cottages. Coal was widely available from outcropping seams and there are mentions of coal working in the sixteenth century. Among the sparse scattered population, there was a numerous but changing local gentry owning small estates and living in larger houses or halls in grander if still modest circumstances; the Hortons of Chadderton Hall, the Pickfords (who adopted the name of Radcliffe) of Royton Hall, or the Cudworths of Werneth Hall were among the several examples. There were no large aristocratic landowners. Apart from the Lees family which acquired the Clarksfield estate in 1625, or the Cromptons and Milnes of Crompton, few

of those old families played any part in the later development of Oldham, but they formed the local elite in the eighteenth century. In due course, as it was said, they were "driven by manufacturers from the country".

That part of modern Oldham which lay within the large parish of Prestwich was divided into the townships of Oldham, Royton, Chadderton and Crompton. Meeting their religious needs there was a chapel of ease at Oldham certainly from the fifteenth century, possibly as early as the fourteenth. The site was probably chosen because of its accessibility as the crossing point of a number of the old routeways from Manchester, Rochdale, Ashton towards Halifax or Huddersfield over the Pennines. Oldham and the out-townships, as they came to be called, became a separate parish in the sixteenth century. It may be supposed that there would then be some kind of market place near Oldham church, a few inns and perhaps thirty or so houses, the beginnings of a town. A grammar school was founded at Oldham in 1606. The extensive Saddleworth district had a chapel, St. Chads, and an abbey in Friarmere, as early as the thirteenth century; never part of Oldham parish, whatever its church affiliation - and this was to the diocese of Chester - it fell within the county of Yorkshire. A chapel at Shaw, another modest centre in Crompton township, existed before 1552 and was rebuilt in 1739. At least from Elizabethan times, what government there was in all these townships or chapelries came through the vestry which elected churchwardens each Easter, appointed constables, overseers of the poor and surveyors of the highways with powers to assess a rate to meet their purposes. It is doubtful whether the

**St. Thomas's Church, Friarmere,** known locally as 'Heights Chapel', built in 1765-68 to meet the religious needs of the growing but scattered population of the upper Tame valley.

entire district had 6,000 people in the seventeenth century.

A simple placid frugal life began to change after 1700, principally under the influence of an expanding textile trade. Defoe's famous account of his visit to the central Pennines in 1724, although referring to the parish of Halifax, would certainly be descriptive of much of Oldham and Saddleworth as activity quickened. He describes a country "infinitely full of people" and "the people all full of business.... the clothing trade, for the convenience of which the houses are scattered and spread upon the sides of the hills." Defoe found the houses,

> "full of lusty fellows, some at the dye vat, some at the loom, others dressing the cloths; the women and children carding or spinning; all employed from the youngest to the oldest, scarce anything above four years old but its hands were sufficient for its own support. Not a beggar to be seen, not an idle person, except here and there in an almshouse, built for those that are ancient and past working. The people in general live long; they enjoy a good air, and under such circumstances hard labour is naturally attended with the blessing of health, if not riches."

Defoe goes on

> "Then, as every clothier necessarily keeps one horse at least, to fetch home his wool and his provisions from the market, to carry his yarn to the weavers, his manufacture to the fulling mill, and when finished, to the market to be sold; so every one generally keeps a cow or two for his family. By this means the small pieces of enclosed land ...... are occupied ........... and further improved by the dung of cattle. As for corn, they scarce grow enough to feed their poultry."

While the domestic woollen industry as thus described, pursued by farmer-weavers, remained the mainstay of Saddleworth and to a lesser extent of Crompton throughout the eighteenth century, other parts of the district took up fabrics based on the new material, cotton, that was then being introduced into Lancashire. Oldham and Royton townships especially became associated with fustians combining linen warp and cotton weft, and, to a growing extent, heavy all-cotton cloth, calicoes, checks and velvets. Silk weaving took hold in the adjacent Middleton district from where it spread to Failsworth and Chadderton. However tiny compared with what was to follow, the scale of the new textile activity, even before the introduction of machine spinning, is indicated by the national consumption of raw cotton, mainly imported from the West Indies and the Levant, which grew from about 1 million lbs at the start of the century to about 5 million lbs by the 1770s. The local trade in fustians and cottons, unlike that of woollens, was oriented towards Manchester where the materials would be purchased and the finished cloth sold. Local dealers or middlemen began to emerge who would engage the farmer-weavers, supplying them with materials, but many weavers would themselves make the journey to Manchester to sell their pieces and return with linen warps and raw cotton to card and spin.

Expanding activity in textiles had various consequences. The district was increasing in wealth and could support more people. While many still lived on the small farms, where spinning and weaving would supplement the income produced from sale of milk and butter from a few cows, increasing numbers now lived in cottages, landless and depending entirely on textile activity. Cottages were built in twos and threes close to the farms, or in small clusters which, as they grew in size, formed folds and hamlets. Oldham itself became a village, not yet a small town. Coal was worked on a greatly increased scale, from adits or levels and from early shallow pits, not merely for local use but for carriage and sale in Manchester and elsewhere. Felt-hat making was another activity pursued on a modest but growing scale in small workshops in the Bent neighbourhood of Oldham from the early eighteenth century. Increased population and above all increased trade and movement of goods required new or improved roads and provision for their maintenance. Turnpike trusts met the need and the district was to be crossed by several of these, the first linking Manchester, Austerlands and on to Huddersfield being authorised by Act of Parliament in 1734.

By the 1770s, the eve of the introduction of power-driven machinery to the textile processes, the townships of Oldham probably had about 8,000 people, Saddleworth perhaps 6,000. But the extensive district was still sparsely populated, rural in character and not different to the adjacent areas of east Lancashire. It was machine carding and spinning, factory scale production and the associated urban development, eagerly pursued by local enterprise, that were to transform its prospects over the next century.

*Below:* **High Kinders**, near Greenfield, a typical example of a building where the Saddleworth domestic woollen industry flourished. It is believed that as many as seven families occupied the building at one time, carding and spinning wool, or weaving cloth; there was also a small dyehouse in a separate building. At least one of the families was also engaged in farming, keeping cows, sheep, poultry and probably one or two horses on about 20 acres of pasture; there would also be grazing rights on nearby moorland. The external steps gave access to the workroom or loom-shop, which may also have been a "takin-in" shop for pieces of woollen cloth woven by weavers on other farms or cottages.

A lintel over one doorway is dated 1642. Parts of the building became unoccupied as early as 1841. Today the improved building, accessible by car, is divided into five houses.

*Facing, below:* **Coaching:** Oldham was on major coaching routes between Lancashire and Yorkshire. Increasingly its business orientation was to Manchester and regular coach services met this need to attend the Manchester markets. When the railway came in the 1840s they were quickly discontinued.

spinning mills were owned by manufacturers; others who put-out bought their weft and warps from the local mills or in Manchester. In Oldham town fustians were given up and heavy cotton calicoes, cords, velveteens, shirtings became the staple cloths.

Development in Saddleworth where the woollen trade persisted followed a different pattern. There had always been small fulling mills on the Tame or its tributary streams. Machines were introduced towards the end of the eighteenth century to perform different processes, formerly carried out in the clothiers' homes: opening up, cleaning and loosening raw wool; scribbling or straitening the fibres; and carding and slubbing, that is forming the fibres into slivers from which they could be spun into yarn. Water power was applied to these machine processes and small scribbling and carding mills were built, generally by the better-off more enterprising clothiers, wherever a suitable fall of water was available. At the same time household spinning and weaving expanded enormously and the district moved its speciality from coarse narrow cloths to finer broad cloth for which it was to acquire a national reputation. A contemporary account reported 36,637 pieces of cloth manufactured in Saddleworth in 1792, compared with under 9,000 pieces fifty years earlier. There were then 2,000 hand looms in the chapelry and as many as seventy-two small mills on the Tame and its tributaries.

The swift exploitation of available water power by a prospering woollen industry inhibited the spread of machine cotton spinning into the Tame valley. Neither cotton nor linen had been much used in Saddleworth, except perhaps

in those neighbourhoods closest to Oldham township, that is Austerlands and Lydgate. Early cotton spinning mills now started in these localities, steam-driven with the advantage of local coal.

Whatever the extraordinary vigour that accompanied the introduction of machine processes, attracted by exceptional profits, the long period of the Napoleonic Wars was one of difficult trading conditions, spasmodic depression and, especially when food was scarce, social unrest. The growth of the cotton industry, dramatic since the 1770s, continued, although more cautiously, as the increase in raw cotton consumption shows; if it had risen

## Cotton and Wool

**Pingle Mill** in Delph was typical of the many small water-powered mills on the River Tame. Built about 1780 by a local clothier it was scribbling, carding, and slubbing in 1800, in effect preparing raw wool for spinning and weaving at local farms and cottages. In 1800 there were as many as forty similar mills along the upper Tame and its tributaries as well as twenty fulling mills where water-powered hammers were used to felt and thicken woollen cloth woven nearby. Practically all the fall of the Tame was taken up by these many mills. Water power was cheap but had its disadvantages. In dry years mills could be idle for two to three months; in 1826 they clubbed together to build a reservoir at Readycon Dean to store water and attempt to regularise the flow of the Tame. In the end, to survive, most of them introduced steam power.

ten-fold to an average of 55 million lbs in 1800-1804, about 80 million lbs annually was being used in the five years through 1815. The industry in Oldham continued to expand with larger more spacious mills becoming feasible with the use of steam power. When Samuel Crompton carried out his census in 1811 he identified nineteen mills in Oldham township, with 130,000 spindles, almost entirely mules; he found another nine mills in Lees, small affairs averaging less than 4,000 spindles each and one at Waterhead Mill. A mere 20,000 spindles were recorded in Royton and 14,000 in Crompton/Shaw. The whole Oldham district accounted for about 4 per cent of the capacity of the British industry at the time. These mills would be employing at most perhaps 2,000 people, men on the mules assisted by youths and children, young men and girls in the preparation, carding and intermediate processes. In contrast by 1815 there were probably about 10,000 hand-loom weavers in cotton, fustian and silk in the Oldham townships and perhaps 3,000 in Saddleworth, the latter almost entirely in wool.

New turnpikes were built towards the end of the old century, new roads to Saddleworth and Standedge, to Ripponden and Halifax, to Rochdale and Ashton. Oldham became a stopping-place for coaches running from Manchester to Wakefield in 1790. And important at the time, the opening of the Rochdale Canal at the edge of the district in 1804 and extensions of the Ashton canal completed in 1795, provided waterway facilities to Manchester and beyond. The intersecting turnpikes on the firm higher slopes of Oldham Edge and their line over Greenacres encouraged development there, and gave good accessibility. The canal extensions, using the Medlock valley to Hollinwood, got no closer than two miles distance to the middle of Oldham as it then was; they were, nonetheless, especially important to the coal industry.

### COACHES.

HULL, the Cornwallis, from the Union-office, King's Arms Inn, every morning at seven, through Huddersfield, Leeds, Wakefield, and York; the True Briton, every day at twelve, and the Regulator, every day at a quarter-past two, through Huddersfield, Leeds, and York.

LEEDS, the Royal Umpire, from the Angel Inn, every day at a quarter before one; & the Commercial Union, every afternoon at a quarter before three.

MANCHESTER, the Royal Umpire, from the Angel Inn, every morning at half-past ten; the Commercial Union, every afternoon at a quarter before four; and the Sovereign, every morning at half-past eight, to the Hare and Hounds, Shudehill, and leaves for Oldham every evening at half-past five: the Royal Independent, every Tues. and Saturday morning at half-past eight, and leaves for Oldham at six the same evening; the Oldham Lark, every morning at half-past eight, and leaves for Oldham at six in the evening.

MANCHESTER, the Regulator, from the George Inn, every afternoon at a quarter-past three; and the True Briton, every afternoon at half-past five.

MANCHESTER, BOLTON, PRESTON, LANCASTER, KENDAL, CARLISLE, & GLASGOW, the True Briton, from the Union-office, King's Arms Inn, every afternoon at five.

MANCHESTER, WARRINGTON, LIVERPOOL, NORTHWICH, NANTWICH, WHITCHURCH, & SHREWSBURY, the Cornwallis, from the Union-office, King's Arms Inn, every morning at eleven.

### MARKET COACHES.

MANCHESTER, from the Union-office, King's Arms Inn, every Tues. Thurs. and Sat. morning at eight; from the Spread Eagle, every Tues. Thurs. and Sat. morning from eight to nine; and from the George Inn, every Tues. Thurs. and Sat. morning at eight.

MANCHESTER, the Accommodation, from the Coach and Horses, Shaw, every Tues. and Sat. morning at half-past seven in the summer, and eight in winter, to the Hare and Hounds, Shudehill; the Industry, from the Coach and Horses, Shaw, every Tues. and Sat. morning at eight, to the Lower Turk's Head, Shudehill; the Royal Defence, from the King's Arms, Shaw, every Tues. Thurs. and Sat. morning at eight; the Duke of York Packet, from the Jubilee, Shaw, every Tues. and Sat. morning at eight, to the White Swan, Shudehill; a coach, from Waterhead-mills, every Tues. and Sat. morning at eight; a coach, from the Coach and Horses, Lees, every Tues. and Sat. morning at eight; a coach, from the Red Lion, Lees, every Tues. and Sat. morning at eight; and a coach, from Royton, every Tues. and Sat. morning at eight.

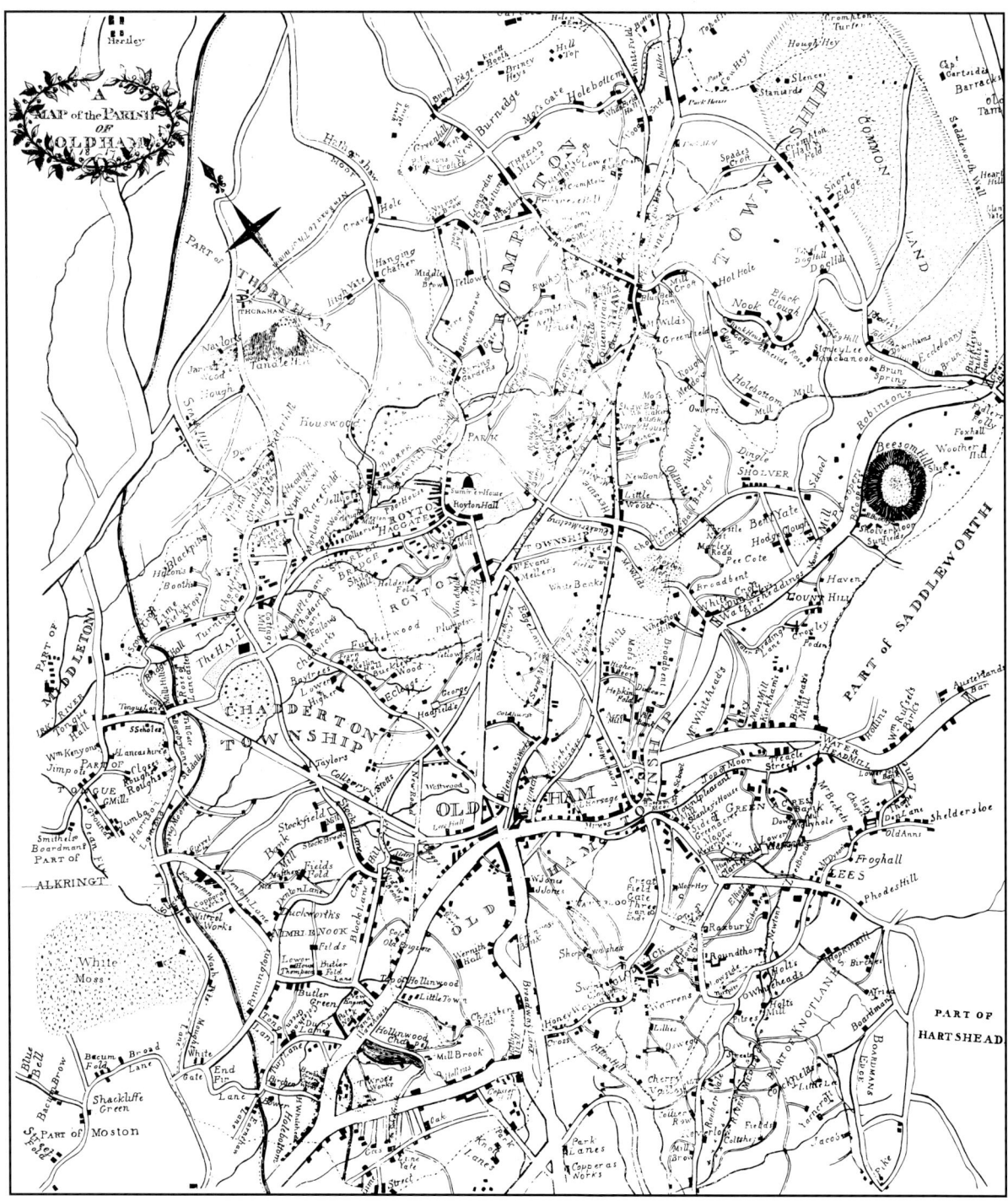

**Cotton takes off**

The return of peace in 1815 brought dramatic expansion; it was in the period after Waterloo that the enterprise, machine innovation and commercial skills of Lancashire together with the rapidly increasing supply of low cost raw cotton from the American South, created a new increasingly global market for cotton cloth. Raw cotton itself fell in price as did the costs of spinning and weaving, and cotton cloth, attractive for its lightness, became dramatically cheaper year by year. Raw cotton consumption remains the best index of the expansion of the industry; in the period between 1815 and 1850 this was to increase more than seven-fold or by an annual rate of growth of more than 5 per cent compound.

What happened in Oldham was representative of what was happening elsewhere, but perhaps more dramatic. A large increase in spinning capacity was accomplished by enlarging the early mills and building many new mills, especially in the town itself. These were all driven by steam engines, and the abundance of cheap local coal gave the locality an advantage at the time. Its proximity and easy access to Manchester by turnpike and canal was also of crucial importance. Confidence, energy and a spirit of enterprise and speculation supplied the aggressive drive. "Weavers and mechanics are daily springing up into manufacturers, commencing business with their accumulated savings", an Oldham magistrate said in 1822. Baines in 1825 could ask the question, "at what place in Lancashire in proportion to its size were cotton mills rising most rapidly? The answer is at Oldham". The number of mills had risen to sixty-two by 1831 but the number of separate enterprises was far greater. The practice of renting "space and turning" was well established by the 1820s whereby the owner of a mill would let space by the yard and make a separate charge for use of the steam engine. Many mills would have as many as four, six or even ten occupiers, each with a few carding engines, roving frames and perhaps up to ten hand mules and 2,000-2,500 spindles, and each employing perhaps twenty or thirty people. Such a situation made it easy to enter the industry, limiting the capital requirements and permitting a couple or three enterprising men, scraping together a little capital, perhaps borrowing money from relatives or shopkeepers, probably buying cotton with credit or even working on a commission basis, to start on their own in a quick small way and try their skills at the great adventure that the cotton trade then represented. Oldham, more than other Lancashire towns, in this early stage, thus became characterised by a large number of small spinning firms, new entrants as they may be described, some of them taking off and growing dramatically, others falling by the wayside.

Another important characteristic of the Oldham industry developed at this time, namely its association with coarse spinning, using American cotton. Bolton, using other types of cotton, went the other way and specialised on fine spinning. Why Oldham went in this direction is not clear; probably because this is where the largest growth and opportunity, using American cotton, was occurring at the time. At all times the business of Oldham was market led. For the most part its yarn was sold on the Manchester Exchange, mainly to merchants and agents, mostly to be woven into cloth in Lancashire, but some exported to Europe.

Sustained expansion of the industry did not guarantee success and prosperity to its participants. Competition was intense. Stimulated by periods of buoyant trade and the lure of fortunes to be made, capacity expanded as fast or faster than the needs of markets. Margins between the cost of cotton and the selling prices of yarn and cloth were lean or inadequate for much of the time. The recurrent characteristic was of trade and capacity being pushed too far in a period of boom, and for business and margins subsequently to

*Facing:* **Butterworth's Map of Oldham** in 1817 reveals a thickening population, still scattered among the many folds and hamlets or in straggling settlements along the turnpike roads. Oldham Town and Bottom of Moor stand out as more significant concentrations of buildings at the meeting place of several roads. The Rochdale Canal and the Hollinwood Branch of the Ashton Canal are shown on the western side of the Parish.

collapse. Over-capacity and competition among manufacturers with precarious resources led to weak selling as goods were pressed on an oversupplied Manchester market. To many, the Manchester Exchange was "the slaughterhouse."

Rapid changes in technology, in the size and speed of mules, or in improved steam engines and mill construction and design lowering fuel consumption in relation to the work load, for instance, while steadily reducing costs, resulted in a high rate of obsolescence. Loss of competitive status followed if a firm could not keep abreast by replacing or modernising its machinery and sources of motive power. Frequent destructive mill fires of under-insured buildings and machinery took their toll.

Finally there were other hazards; participants in the industry had to manage their exposure to the huge risks inherent in a highly volatile raw cotton market, a market that worked in a fog of uncertainty regarding crop prospects, shipments, arrivals, consumption and speculative participation. At this period news from America could take four to five weeks to cross the Atlantic. With raw cotton representing a large proportion of the value of yarn and cloth, the violent ups and downs of the cotton market were at once a source of huge risk and opportunity, a peril and a temptation, especially when the margin from trading with a balanced position was meagre or inadequate. Even if the spinner got his own position right, sharp movements in cotton prices could lead to supplier or customer default. These were the inescapable hazards of the trade.

Fluctuating raw cotton prices imposed their own cycle on demand and activity within the industry. When prices were high, traders were inhibited in expectation of a fall. When prices began to fall no-one would make purchases until some kind of confidence returned. Such had been the bitter experience in the period 1825-1826 when at the top of a four year boom, raw cotton prices peaked at over 19d a lb to fall to a low of below 6d a lb in 1826. A similar fall took place in 1836. On top of the cotton cycle, there was the general trade cycle: the recurrent phenomenon of exaggerated boom followed by commercial panic. At times of panic business was usually at a standstill. Early in 1826 the Manchester Chamber of Commerce reported that "many spinners and manufacturers were overstocked with goods for which no market could be found, and that even the goods for which there was a demand were being sold at a ruinous loss." But at this stage in the industry's history such setbacks, or "treacherous whirlpools" as they were described, tended to be short-lived; very brisk conditions had returned by 1827. As Butterworth put it, "the cotton manufacture seems to exceed all others for the extraordinary fluctuations to which it is subject."

Given these general circumstances however, and the fact that many new entrants had limited means and relied on debt for finance, it was not surprising that there were many more business failures than successes. "Three men fall for every one that rises", it was said. Butterworth noted the high turnover of firms in Oldham with few of the early entrants surviving. But while many firms failed as each boom collapsed, new enterprise moved in during the next upswing to carry the industry forward.

If Oldham had a large number of small spinning businesses, and many failures, there were some firms which achieved significant growth from

## Cotton takes off

humble origins, partly through good fortune but mainly, it may be supposed, due to the industry, single-mindedness and commercial acumen of the principals; these were the means of success together with frugality and thrift, financing growth by putting profits back into the business. John Lees who died in 1828 had established himself at Greenbank on the lane to Glodwick in 1816; his son, James, developed a large factory complex there, Greenbank Mills, employing close to 400 people in 1841 and this became the base of one of Oldham's leading business dynasties, the Greenbank Lees. Almost opposite on Glodwick Lane, James Collinge and John Lancashire had started at Vineyard in 1817, building the larger Commercial Mill a few years later. The first to introduce power looms into Oldham, by 1841 they had a workforce of 968 in two mills, one of the largest firms in Lancashire at the time. Other emerging large cotton firms in the second quarter of the century were the Radcliffes at Lower House Mill, and James Greaves, the son of a Saddleworth clothier, who had started renting space at Derker but then took over and enlarged the Mill employing over 500 people in the 1840s. Away from Oldham town, small enterprises were still the general rule with the exception of Travis and Milne in Crompton who were reported to employ 770 people at their mills in 1833; also in High Crompton the brothers Joseph and John Clegg had established a large business before they split up in 1855. In Failsworth, Thomas Walmsley had 700 employees at Firs Mill in the 1840s.

Many of the larger successful firms, having started as spinners, had invested their profits not merely in enlarging and continuously modernising their operations, but also extending them into power loom weaving. Introduced in the 1820s, the power loom made continuous progress, initially in the heavier coarser types of cloth. This suited Oldham with its established commitments to velveteens and corduroys. Although there were few specialist weaving concerns, by 1840 Oldham had thirty-two concerns combining spinning and weaving, employing on average more than 200 persons each. These large combined firms, together with the large spinners, were employing most of the workforce, notwithstanding the large number of small concerns. Although not to the same extent as in Manchester or Ashton where there were several firms employing more than 1,000, in Oldham most people were working in a large mill for a large employer, as the profile of concerns summarised in Table I shows.

The power loom, with its greatly increased productivity, inevitably undermined the market for hand-loom cloth. The brief golden age of the hand-loom weaver had passed long before the power loom was well established. Probably because too many people took up hand-loom weaving for a living, the prices paid for weaving had been under pressure for many years, with only brief periods when they rallied to provide relief. Complaints of poverty grew in the 1820s and were then greatly aggravated by the

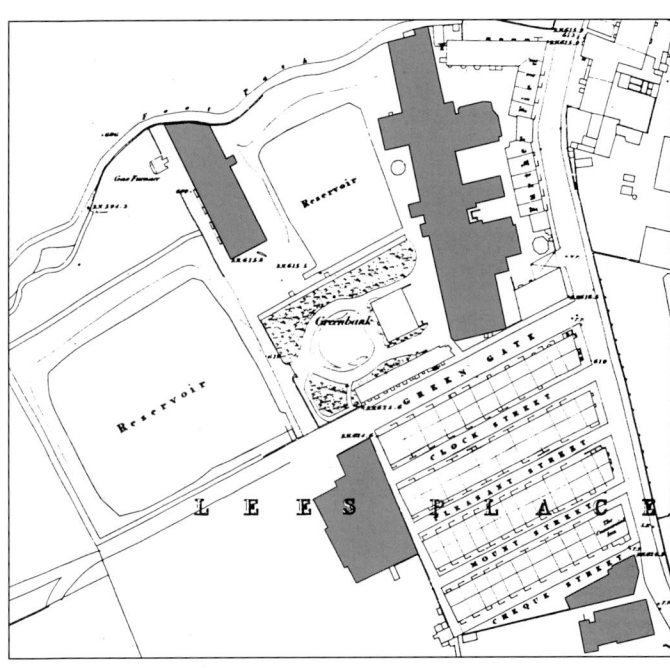

**The Greenbank Mill colony** on Glodwick Road in 1850. John Lees (1759-1828) built the first spinning mill here in 1816. The business was carried forward with great success by his son James (1794-1871). About 100 people were employed in 1830 but by 1846 when this map was drawn there were 550 operatives, working 47,000 spindles and 339 power looms, making this one of the largest concerns in Oldham. James Lees, who was Mayor of Oldham in 1852-53 and a prominent Tory, built Greenbank House as his residence beside the mill. To house his workforce he built the adjacent streets of back-to-back terraces. The Census of 1851 shows 480 people living in the ninety dwellings in the five streets. The Commercial Inn and street-end shops, also part of the complex, would have a busy trade. James Lees, the master, would be visible, accessible and approachable and no doubt had a first-name relationship with most of his workpeople. Their attitude in this paternal situation would be one of deference and gratitude. The growing wealth of men of drive and enterprise such as James Lees was not resented at the time by those to whom they had provided work.

TABLE I: PROFILE OF THE COTTON INDUSTRY IN OLDHAM PARISH: 1841

|  | Number of Concerns | Employment | Concerns employing over 100 people Number | Employment |
|---|---|---|---|---|
| Fine Spinning | 10 | 635 | 2 | 351 |
| Coarse Spinning | 85 | 7,160 | 25 | 4,977 |
| Spinning & Weaving | 32 | 7,137 | 25 | 6,599 |
| Doubling | 21 | 230 | - | - |
| Specialised Weaving | 6 | 406 | 1 | 218 |
| Cotton Waste | 47 | 1,045 | 1 | 180 |
|  | 201 | 16,613 | 54 | 12,328 |

*Source:* Factory Inspectors Report, BPP 1842, XXII.

competition of low cost factory cloth. In circumstances of acute distress, people left the trade, most easily where alternative work was available and where they were young enough to adapt to the discipline and work practices of the factory. Those who remained were increasingly aged, living in miserable circumstances, "scattered in cellars or perched in garrets", as Reach reported from the town of Oldham in 1849. Some found a better living by adapting their hand-looms to more sophisticated cloths or to other materials. Thus silk weaving was more profitable and continued to flourish as a cottage or loom shop operation. At Chadderton Fold, for instance, in 1851, of 224 residents, 103 declared themselves to be occupied in silk manufacture. Within Oldham and its townships in 1851 there were 1,372 workers in silk, probably none in Oldham itself but chiefly in Chadderton. There would have been many more in Failsworth, as in Middleton, neither part of Oldham at the time. But the silk weavers apart, hand-loom weaving declined rapidly and from as many as 10-11,000 at their peak in the early 1820s, throughout the Oldham townships, the number of weavers had probably fallen to about 1,000 by the mid-century. The decay of the hand-loom and the concentration of the newer steam-driven factories in the township of Oldham, at this stage, accounts for the check to population growth evident in Chadderton, Royton and Crompton especially after 1831, compared with continued rapid growth in Oldham (Table III).

The enterprise and drive now so strongly established in Oldham carried cotton spinning and weaving forward during the generally prosperous 1830s and through the acute depression of the period 1839-1842. Short time working, mill closure and business failure characterised that period; the slump in cotton manufacturing would affect coal, engineering, indeed, all types of commercial activity. But trade began to recover at the end of 1842. *The Economist* at the end of 1844 was to write of "better prospects than for several years past". Renewed mill building began in Oldham; empty mills again found tenants. 1847 and 1848, the year of revolutions in Europe, brought severe checks but there was a further strong recovery in 1849.

By the early 1850s the 200 or so cotton concerns in what was then Oldham Borough, were employing about 16,500 people; adding those working in a further twenty-two concerns in Crompton, thirteen in Royton and six in Chadderton, and the few remaining hand-loom weavers, the total workforce in cotton spinning and weaving approached 21,000. Oldham and its three townships, but not including Lees or Saddleworth or Failsworth, had about 1.5 million spindles and 10,000 looms in 111 mills at mid-century: about 7 per cent of Lancashire's spinning capacity, less than 2 per cent of its weaving. The place was by no means the spinning capital it was to become, vast as the energy had been, but it was one of the principal centres of the industry.

The factory cotton spinning established early in the century in those parts of Saddleworth closest to Oldham, and in the lower Tame valley, encroached on the hitherto specialised woollen district, encouraged by the boom conditions of the early 1820s and 1830s. Thus by 1840 there were thirty-nine mainly steam-driven cotton mills in Saddleworth (including parts of Mossley) employing 2,201 people, a larger total than the 1,718 working in forty-nine woollen mills, still relying to a large extent on water power. Four of the cotton mills, including a large mill at Waterside, Greenfield, had 618 power looms. There were only 165 power looms in the local woollen mills at the time; the majority of those working in wool were still working at home, still "spinners, weavers and farmers", with perhaps as many as 2,000 people still weaving on the hand-loom. Thus by mid-century, even before the coming of the railway, cotton was beginning to match wool in importance in Saddleworth, and traditional domestic manufacture of wool, if still important, was dying away.

Meanwhile, another cotton activity had taken a specialised hold in Oldham over this period, namely dealing in cotton waste, originating in spinning mills not just locally but in the adjacent cotton manufacturing towns - Manchester, Ashton, Stockport and elsewhere. Many Oldham firms not merely dealt in the waste; they sorted it, worked the best grades up for spinning and wove the loose yarn into candlewicks and other fabrics; the poorer waste was made into flocks for mattresses, and the worst, not much better than dust, was sold as shoddy for mixing with night soil. Most of the cotton waste dealers were concentrated in the Mumps and Bottom of Moor district; most of the operations were very small, with fewer than twenty people. Oldham with its waste business especially, but also with its commitments to spinning coarse yarn and weaving heavy cloths, the bottom end of the trade to some, thus came to be described at the time as "the pariah of the cotton trade".

## Engineering

The building, equipment and supply of cotton mills had encouraged a range of ancillary activities in this early period, concerns making ropes, skips or baskets, cops and bobbins, for instance, but none approached the significance of textile engineering. Almost as soon as factory operations began, Oldham men began to improve the existing machines. Some went into machine-making before 1800 and by the 1830s there was a cluster of iron and brass foundries, roller and spindle makers and machine shops in the Bottom of Moor area, perhaps as many as fifty enterprises. Most were at this stage small. That of Samuel Lees (1773-1845) had started to make rollers and spindles in 1816 adopting the name Soho, after the famous Birmingham establishment; one of Samuel Lees' sons, Asa (1816-1888), in partnership with Samuel Barnes, established a separate foundry and machine shop on an adjacent site; the two were eventually combined and one of Oldham's most

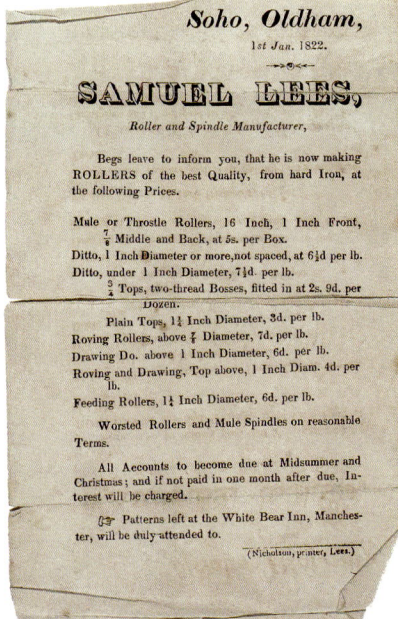

**Henry Platt**, born in Dobcross in 1793, came to Oldham and went into business in 1821 as a maker of carding machines at this house and workshop in Huddersfield Road, close to Bottom of Moor. Although a diffident man, he was a gifted practical engineer with an ability to improve any machine. His subsequent partnership with Elijah Hibbert in 1824 was the foundation of the huge Platt textile machinery enterprise. By 1843 when Henry Platt died, Hibbert and Platt's Hartford Works at Bottom of Moor was employing about 500 people; in 1844 with the start of the Hartford New Works in Werneth, the firm began its major expansion under his two sons, John and James.

notable engineering concerns emerged. Eli Lees (1815-1892), another son of Samuel, was to enter cotton spinning successfully at the nearby Hope Mill.

The most famous of all Oldham engineering businesses was started by young Elijah Hibbert (1801-1846) in 1821 in premises adjacent to the Soho works. Joined in partnership by Henry Platt (1793-1842), then precariously established in a small way as a carding machine maker, the firm of Hibbert and Platt grew dramatically. In 1829 they established the extensive Hartford Works at Bottom of Moor and began making a wide range of machines used in cotton manufacturing. In 1844, having outgrown the Hartford site, and with their business opportunity significantly enlarged by the removal of restrictions on the export of machinery in 1843, they erected a larger separate foundry and machine shop encompassing all steps in machine making and erection in Werneth, the other side of town, intentionally adjacent to the new railway, to be called Hartford New Works. The two works were soon employing about 900 men and boys. Both Henry Platt and Hibbert died prematurely in the 1840s, when ownership of the business passed to the next generation, effectively to the brothers John (1817-1872) and James (1823-1857) Platt. Although by no means the only textile machinery firm in Lancashire, Platts as it generally became called, quickly established an ascendancy, especially in cotton preparation, carding and spinning machinery, not least because of the quality of its machinery and its durability, the result of good materials and good workmanship. Many of Platts' workpeople came from other districts to Oldham to join the firm which began to enjoy a wide reputation for high wages and good working practices. Wherever possible men were paid on a piecework basis and the firm was always looking for improved ways of doing work to raise productivity: by the 1840s wages as high as 40s or 50s a week were not uncommon. Provided the work was done,

Platts were not strict about time-keeping, about men going out for ale in the middle of the morning, or even going absent from time to time on a drinking and gambling spree as many did. Platts was regarded as a good place to work. Not surprisingly it attracted and held good people, many of whom were subsequently to rise to high positions.

On one matter of principle John and James Platt took a firm stand in 1852. When the Amalgamated Engineers sought to restrict the numbers of unskilled men and boys in the trade and control the running of each machine, the Platts rejected such "unreasonable interference". They went further and required all those they employed to sign a declaration that they would leave or never join the Amalgamation. Those refusing to sign were locked out: they stayed out in many cases for as long as twenty weeks and some never rejoined, but the firm kept working throughout as many, old and new, accepted the terms. Their firm's dramatic success placed John and James Platt in the most prominent position by the late 1840s in a town that was already full of successful entrepreneurs. Of the close to 2,500 men and boys engaged in engineering in 1851, the great majority would work for Platts or Asa Lees. Already by 1851 this activity, although linked closely to cotton, was providing an important alternative occupation for men.

## Hatting

The Oldham of this period was not wholly dedicated to cotton. Hat making had taken root early in the eighteenth century and the numbers of hatting concerns grew steadily to reach a peak of twenty-four in the 1820s, mostly small family concerns but including five which worked on a factory rather than small workshop scale. At its peak the industry, specialised to felt hats, made from mixing wool and fur, may have employed as many as 2,500 people, men and women, partly in the workshops, but partly finishing hats in their own homes. Most were close to the town centre although there were plenty of home-workers as far away as Failsworth. Many processes were involved requiring skill and judgement, creating the hat body from the blend of wool and fur, shrinking or felting, shaping the particular style, dyeing, and finally finishing by creasing, ironing, lining and trimming.

Some particular families were prominent in hat making and dealing, especially successive generations of Cleggs, who lived in Bent, and the Henshaw brothers. The Cleggs of Bent became significant landowners and leading figures in the town, as did the Henshaws, said to employ over 300 people at their factory at Hargreaves, north of the parish church, and accumulating property to the value of £154,000 by 1807. The eldest brother, Thomas Henshaw, became an important benefactor whose wealth endowed Oldham's Bluecoat School.

The industry, although it flourished for a time, withered away. Cotton spinning was probably a more attractive and rewarding enterprise, both to capital and labour. The Oldham concerns may not have adapted well to changes in fashion, style and materials, in particular the shift to silk hats, which were more elegant in appearance and much cheaper to make. A damaging strike over wages in 1841 encouraged business to move to Denton in the Tame Valley, already an established centre, and although the industry revived in Oldham, Denton became far more important. There was much

**Oldham's Hatting industry** was significant in the early and mid-nineteenth century before it withered against competition from other centres, and from Oldham's flourishing spinning and engineering trades. The essential processes were carried out in small workshops. This much later photograph illustrates the wet-end, namely the felting and shaping of the mixture of wool and fur which made up the hat.

distress among the Oldham hatters after the strike and many drifted to other occupations but in 1851 there were still 842 people engaged in hat making, perhaps a third of the numbers at the peak thirty years earlier, but not greatly reduced from the 1,144 so employed in 1841. If many of the older companies had disappeared by that time, there were still significant employers: the Nelsons in Waterloo, the Gees in Hollinwood and the prominent Oldham Radical, William Knott, with a workshop in King Street; these or their successors were to continue for many years.

## Coal

Growing population and steam-driven mills provided a vastly increased local market for Oldham's easily won coal resources. That market was significantly widened by improved communications, the local turnpikes but especially the canal links which gave low-cost access to Manchester from the late 1790s. Oldham's coal entrepreneurs were swift to support both the Ashton Canal and the Rochdale Canal.

Development of the coal industry is especially associated with a few families. Prominent were William Jones and John Evans, said to be poor Welsh labourers, who came to Oldham sometime before 1770. They had the foresight to anticipate the growing demand for coal and with great energy and determination acquired rights to work coal and began sinking pits on Oldham Edge and elsewhere. William Jones was supported by his son Joseph whose daughter became the second wife of James Lees of Clarksfield (1759-1828), a man described by Butterworth as a "spirited capitalist", involved not merely in cotton spinning but in extensive land ownership, and with Jones, in coal, the turnpike trusts and canal companies. Another John Lees, no relation, became Lord of the Manor of Oldham when he bought Werneth Hall for £30,000 in 1795; he, with the Jones and Clarksfield Lees and others, took the initiative in promoting the enclosure of the remaining common land

*Facing:* **Coal Workings**: the Ordnance Survey of 1848 marked about 180 coal workings, shallow pits or deeper collieries, in the Oldham district. Most of these are identified on the map, together with the principal mills at the time, the latter still close to the crowded town centre and Bottom of Moor.

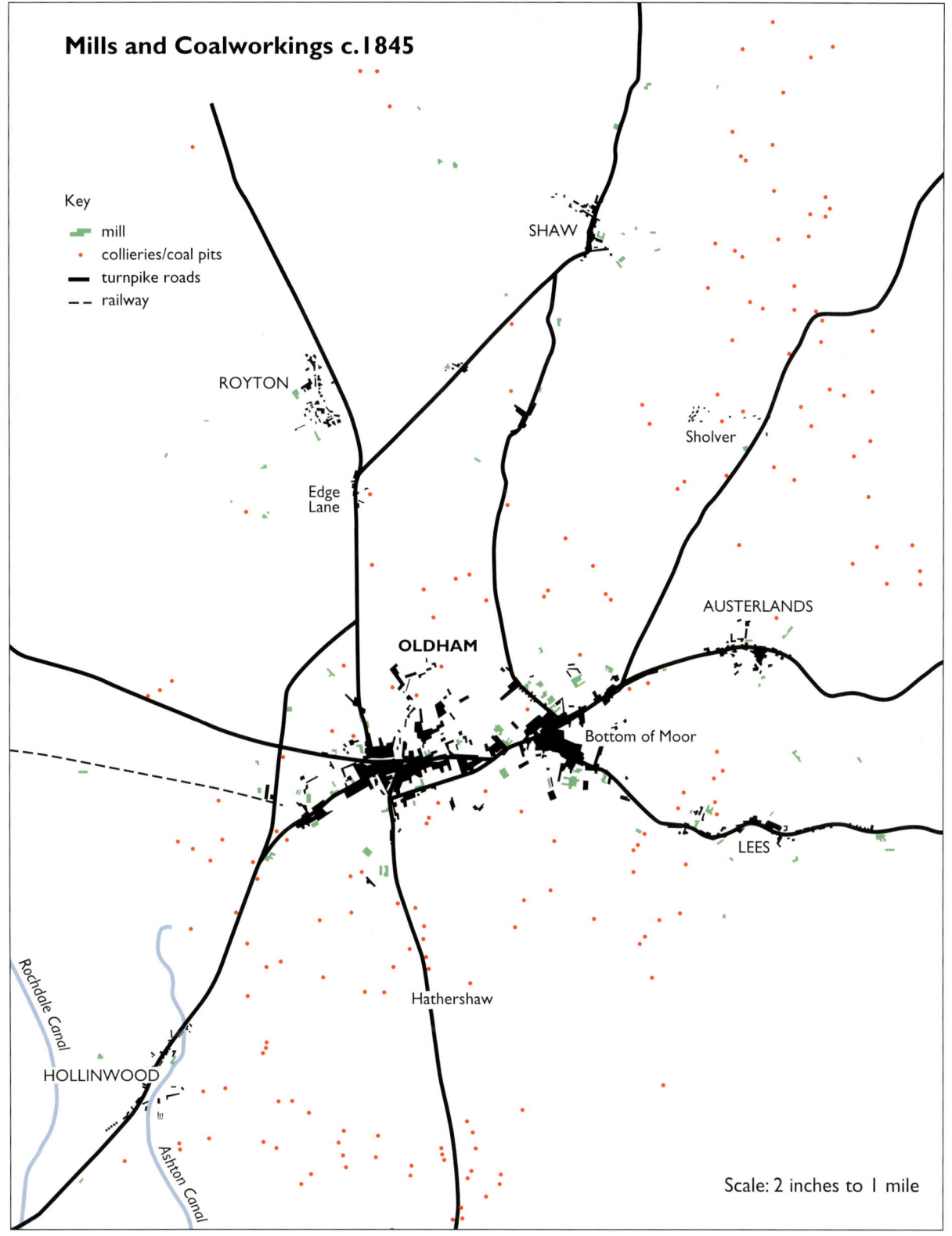

**Holebottom Colliery**, in the heart of Oldham, off Yorkshire Street, was worked for much of the nineteenth century. It probably employed no more than twenty men and boys. All its output would go to local mills or to coal merchants selling from house to house in nearby St. Mary's. There were other collieries close to the town centre at mid-century, notably at Rhodes Bank with its two shafts. The large building in the background is the Working Men's Hall, built in Horsedge Street in 1844. For many years this was Oldham's largest public hall, capable of holding 2,000 people; it subsequently became the Theatre Royal.

- the so-called moors - of Oldham in 1803, securing extensive mineral rights. Thus a few families, in association with each other, and with other parties, among them Booths and Duncufts, owned or acquired land or leases which gave them the right to work coal all over the district and control of most of the mining enterprises. The Jones and Lees families in particular achieved great wealth from their involvement in coal and timely ownership of much land in Oldham.

There were some particularly good seams to be worked in the district, the Lower Mountain Mine in the Lower Coal Measures, the Black Mine and the Royley Mine, each with four feet of good engine coal, and the Great Mine, eight feet thick although with bands of dirt; most of these and other seams outcropped but the fact that they dipped one yard in four added to the difficulty of working as did wet conditions. The early coal workings had been adits or levels on the hillsides or bell pits working coal within a small radius at shallow depth. By the late eighteenth century typical workings were from unlined shafts that went as deep as 100 yards. Much of the best coal could be worked at this kind of depth, and since the cost of such small shafts was comparatively low, typical practice was to remove the coal by long-wall methods within a radius of perhaps 200 yards from the shaft, an inexpensive haulage distance, and, rather than extend the workings further, abandon the shaft and sink a new one a short distance away. Initially the coal would be

raised by horse-powered wheels; steam power was first used for this purpose in 1792 and subsequently to drive drainage pumps. Many of the early shafts were worked for less than a year; rarely did they last three years; these were very small undertakings employing as few as five to ten men and boys. The consequence was a profusion of coal workings and a multitude of disused shafts. A mining concern at the time worked a district, rather than a particular pit or mine. As the easily won coal was exhausted, fewer deeper more permanent mines became the rule; coal was being mined at Royton from a depth of nearly 300 yards in 1832. Oldham's best known colliery, Chamber in Werneth, owned by Joseph Jones, was employing 211 men in 1841 and another Jones colliery at Hurst Lane in Chadderton in that year had 134 men. In these deeper mines coal was worked at greater distances from the shaft, perhaps as far as 1,000 yards.

Coal shafts for a period, however, were everywhere, including the middle of the town; a proposal to sink a shaft in Oldham churchyard was mooted at one stage. Some of the more concentrated workings were linked to the canal wharves by wooden tramways; otherwise horse and cart moved the coal. Hauling coal became a common every day sight in Oldham. Upwards of 200,000 tons was sent into Manchester yearly but the greater market was the local one for engine coal; some of the collieries were owned by local mills, Collinges and later Platts, for instance. The coal was cheap, perhaps 7s-8s per ton at the pit, but haulage quickly added to its cost; nonetheless the individual concerns expected to make at least 3s per ton profit, perhaps on an output of 20-30,000 tons.

Coal mining became a specialised occupation, sons joining their fathers at the age of seven or eight to work hauling the coal underground as "drawers" or "thrutchers", before becoming hewers as their strength developed. Some of the boys were employed to manage the wheel and rope at the top or the shaft. Women never worked in the Oldham pits, unlike other parts of Lancashire. Conditions of work were appalling and dangerous; there were frequent accidents, many fatal, usually due to fire damp, falls of stone or falls down the shaft; in one of the worst, locally, seventeen men were killed at Bent Grange Colliery in 1850.

The miner's wage depended on his output and the realised value of the coal; he paid his own assistants. The normal shift was eleven to twelve hours; as with cotton, activity was very unstable and work varied from short time, which might be three or four days only, to periods of boom when a second shift might be engaged to work through the night. At times there were many unemployed miners, scavenging a living, moving from pit to pit looking for work, walking long distances from home to work if the need arose. Disputes were frequent, especially about pay but also about measurement of output and working conditions. If a rough uncouth group, "inferior, morally and intellectually to the mill population", as one observer put it, the miners on full work were well paid by the standards of the time so long as their strength held. When old, they became coal carters. They lived throughout the community although no doubt they had their own neighbourhoods. They were notorious for swearing and cursing, heavy drinking, brutal sport, gambling and fighting among themselves. But they had a good feeling for mutual help and ran their own sick and burying clubs to cope with casualty and death. From a few hundred in 1800, by the mid-nineteenth century the number of miners in Oldham approached 2,000.

**Occupations in 1851**

The character of Oldham, creature as it was of the industrial revolution, is revealed by its work structure in 1851. Overwhelmingly working class, well over 80 per cent of the occupied population were engaged in manual labour. Cotton was employing over 50 per cent of those at work, with as many women and girls as men; and of all women and girls, that is those not classed as children or scholars, two out of every five worked in a cotton mill. There were few employed in service occupations, beyond the pubs, the shopkeepers, market traders, hawkers and pedlars. Domestic service was there, meeting the needs of the middle class for servants, gardeners and grooms, but the numbers were small in relation to the total, much smaller than in Manchester, and Salford, for instance. Professional and business services likewise were weakly developed. This was an area where the community looked to Manchester; the large city, for instance, had 2,922 commercial clerks and 770 travelling

TABLE II: OLDHAM PARLIAMENTARY BOROUGH: MAIN OCCUPATIONS 1851

|  | Male | Female |
|---|---|---|
| Total Population | 35,430 | 37,027 |
| Unoccupied |  |  |
|     Children, scholars | 10,415 | 12,156 |
|     Housewives, widows |  | 9,566 |
|     Other | 380 | 148 |
| Occupied Population | 24,635 | 15,157 |
|     Cotton and Fustian | 10,851 | 10,258 |
|     Metal Working & Engineering | 2,481 | - |
|     Coal | 1,859 | 7 |
|     Silk | 615 | 757 |
|     Hatting | 637 | 205 |
|     Building Trades | 1,172 | - |
|     Labourers | 976 | - |
|     Carters and Transport | 784 | - |
|     Farming | 868 | 202 |
|     Government, Professional and Clerical | 546 | 80 |
|     Domestic Service | 126 | 1,608 |
|     Others: shops, public houses etc. | 3,780 | 2,040 |

*Source:* Census of 1851. The Parliamentary Borough included the Borough of Oldham and the townships of Chadderton, Royton and Crompton.

salesmen in 1851, whereas Oldham had 148 in both occupations. Builders, labourers, carters were numerous in Oldham providing services supporting the main activities. Frederick Engels, writing at the time of towns like Oldham which surrounded Manchester, described them as "purely industrial conducting all their business through Manchester upon which they are in every respect dependent, hence they are inhabited only by working men and petty tradesmen".

Saddleworth, also, had well over 50 per cent of its occupied population in textiles: 3,333 in its cotton mills but 3,438 in wool. Many of these were still working in their homes. There were more farmers in Saddleworth, relative to its size, than in Oldham as would be expected. While very much a manufacturing community at the time Saddleworth was assuming a different character to the body of Oldham, a difference that was to grow wider as the century progressed.

*Chapter III*

# LIFE IN EARLY VICTORIAN OLDHAM

**Population growth and the spread of settlement**

Cotton, the early machine making industry, hatting and coal were the economic base of Oldham in the early nineteenth century, wool and cotton in Saddleworth. Their growth supported a rapidly increasing population although much greater in Oldham township than the other parts of the district. Indeed the out-townships stagnated somewhat, as did Saddleworth, after 1831, as hand-loom weaving declined, but Oldham township continued to grow dramatically, from 12,000 people in 1801 to 52,000 people by 1851. Such hectic growth was comparable with that of other Lancashire and Yorkshire towns of the period, although Bradford had grown far more rapidly and closer at hand Manchester and Salford, with over 350,000 people in 1851, dwarfed the surrounding manufacturing towns.

TABLE III: OLDHAM TOWNSHIPS: POPULATION GROWTH 1801-1851

|  | 1801 | 1811 | 1821 | 1831 | 1841 | 1851 |
|---|---|---|---|---|---|---|
| Oldham | 12,024 | 16,690 | 21,662 | 32,381 | 42,595 | 52,818 |
| Chadderton | 3,452 | 4,133 | 5,124 | 5,476 | 5,397 | 6,188 |
| Royton | 2,710 | 3,910 | 4,933 | 5,652 | 5,730 | 6,974 |
| Crompton | 3,482 | 4,746 | 6,482 | 7,004 | 6,729 | 6,374 |
| Failsworth | 2,622 | 2,875 | 3,358 | 3,667 | 3,879 | 4,433 |
| Lees [1] | (1,000) |  |  | (1,300) |  | (2,000) |
| Saddleworth [2] | 10,665 | 12,579 | 13,902 | 15,986 | 16,829 | 17,779 |

*Notes:* 1. Lees, eventually part of Oldham, was within the Knott Lanes district of Ashton Parish for most of the nineteenth century. Its population can only be estimated at various dates.
2. Saddleworth at this time included parts of Mossley, subsequently a separate district.

TABLE IV: NORTHERN INDUSTRIAL TOWNS: POPULATION GROWTH 1801-1851

|  | 1801 | 1831 | 1851 |
|---|---|---|---|
| Oldham | 12,000 | 32,000 | 53,000 |
| Ashton | 6,000 | 14,000 | 30,000 |
| Bolton | 18,000 | 42,000 | 61,000 |
| Preston | 12,000 | 34,000 | 70,000 |
| Blackburn | 12,000 | 27,000 | 47,000 |
| Bradford | 13,000 | 44,000 | 104,000 |
| Manchester & Salford | 89,000 | 223,000 | 367,000 |

## Population growth and the spread of settlement

More births than deaths, that is natural increase, undoubtedly contributed most of this population growth. As livelihood became easier, people married earlier, many before the age of twenty, and had larger families. High and recent natural increase meant a preponderance of young people; in 1851 nearly half of Oldham township's population was younger than twenty, 25 per cent younger than ten. But natural increase apart, large numbers of people, usually young unmarried men, moved into the district, hoping to better themselves, attracted by the work and business opportunities and the promise of higher living standards. Generally they came from adjacent areas in Lancashire and Yorkshire rather than from far-afield. Thus many Oldham families originated in Saddleworth, in Middleton or in Rochdale, where, perhaps, life was not moving so fast. A high proportion of the incomers succeeded, reflecting the spirit and enterprise that prompted their initiative in the first place. A small but distinctive minority of the incomers were Irish born, marked by their accent, their poverty and their religion, perhaps 2,500 in the town of Oldham in 1851, about 5 per cent of the population.

The town of Oldham grew round the meeting of roads that formed its centre. The Manchester to Huddersfield turnpike road became the main street through the town, variously named Manchester Street and Yorkshire Street; it replaced the older narrow winding Goldburn. Turnpike roads to Rochdale and Ashton also made new streets and other old roads became West Street and Henshaw Street, leading from the centre. A narrow High Street was the central portion of the main street, close to the old church, and here was the

**Baines Map of Oldham, 1823** shows Yorkshire Street replacing Goldburn (Bow Street and Church Street) as the main route through the town for traffic from Yorkshire. Union Street is a recently made but incomplete by-pass of the town centre. Bottom of Moor and Oldham Town are still separate. The town centre has already taken the shape it would retain. A large population was living in congested streets and courts off the principal streets within easy access of Market Place and High Street where shops and street-stalls were concentrated.

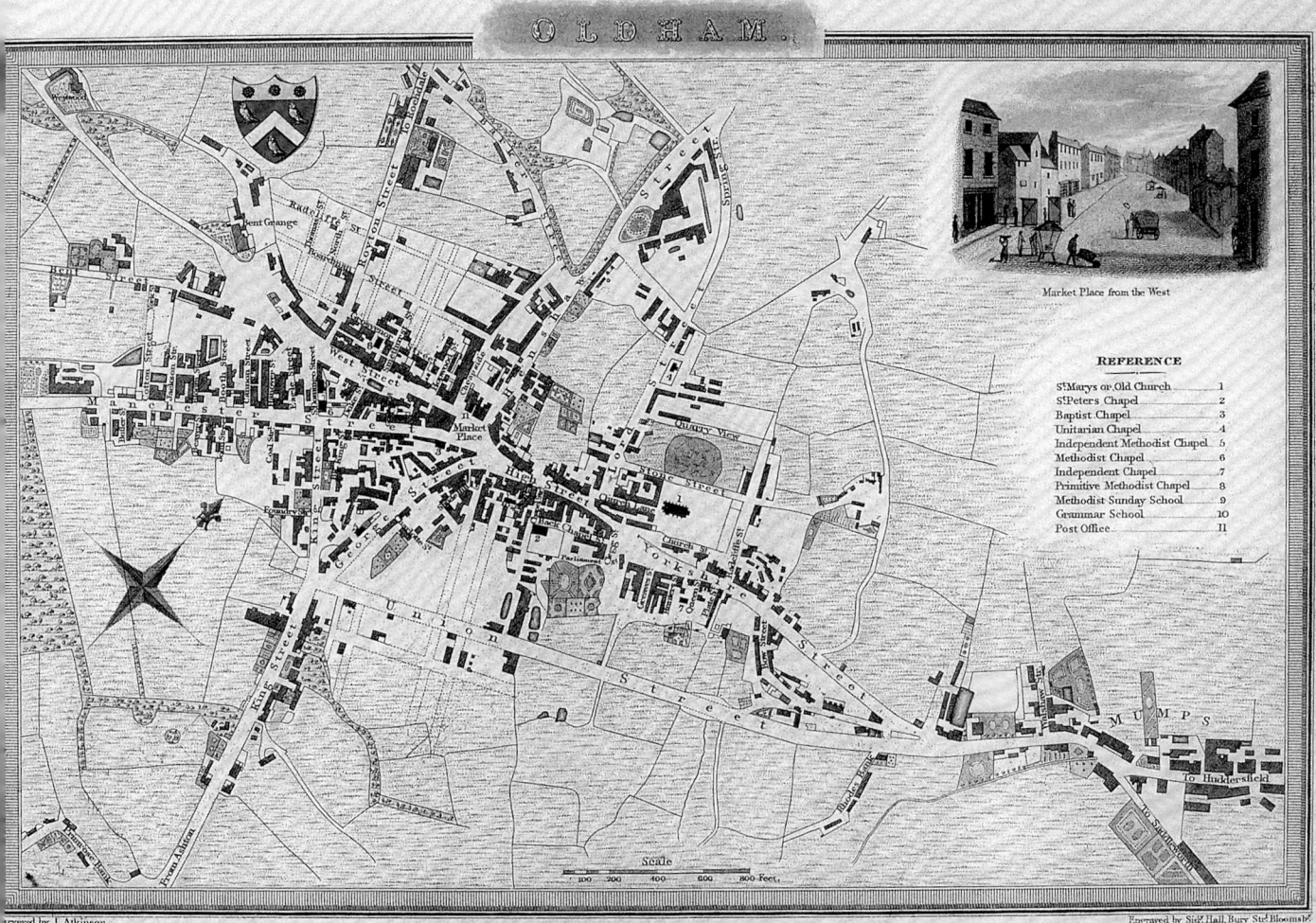

**Church Street**, climbing rapidly from Yorkshire Street, typical of the old streets around the town centre. This street, with Bow Street, was the old Goldburn.

more spacious Market Place where a street market was held from 1804. An open space to the north, Curzon Ground, became known as Tommyfield, a place for fairs, public meetings and by the 1830s for market stalls. Factories, houses, shops, public houses, chapels were built along the roads spreading out from the town centre. New streets were formed off these principal roads; courts and narrow back streets added to the maze of buildings which became a chaotic constricted cluster. Union Street, started about 1810 but incomplete for many years, was seen as a means of diverting traffic to and from Manchester round the town centre, namely a bypass of the time which avoided a steep climb to the Market Place from either direction.

If the centre, around the High Street and its radiating roads was the main nucleus, a second major concentration had developed at the neighbourhood of Bottom of Moor. Here, the enclosure of the old common, Greenacres Moor, in 1804 had made land available for cotton mills, foundries and machine shops, alongside the turnpike roads leading to Yorkshire. Many of the houses in this rapidly growing part of the town were built by the millowners for their own workpeople. James Lees followed by James Collinge, built streets around their mills along the Glodwick Lane in what became known as Mount Pleasant; the Radcliffes and the Greaves did so to a lesser extent. By 1830 Bottom of Moor and the adjacent Mount Pleasant development was half as large as the principal part of the town. Other commons had also been enclosed after 1804. Especially at Hollinwood and at Northmoor the availability of land encouraged some new building activity, but not on the scale of Greenacres.

All the town development was sudden and unregulated. One contemporary observed, "here we build as we like and do as we like." Butterworth found the providers of houses as eager in speculation as the manufacturers of yarn. Given such an enterprising spirit, streets were run up as fast if not faster than tenants could be found. Small builders, perhaps a

**Bent Hollow**, Lower West Street before demolition. These were early nineteenth century workshops and houses built around the town centre as Oldham began to grow rapidly. An unmade unlit road was typical for the time.

bricklayer and a carpenter working together, leased land at ground rents of perhaps 2d a square yard, borrowed money, hired labour and threw up houses to meet the demands of the market, rarely singly but usually "by the dozen or score, a single contractor building one or two streets at a time." Completed groups of houses were bought as an investment by tradesmen or others with accumulated wealth and let at rents expected to yield 5 per cent. People had to live near their work; they wanted to be near the markets and life of the centre; they could not afford much rent, typically 2s to 3s a week. This was the market and housing provision had to reflect these circumstances.

Cheap affordable house accommodation was best achieved by building to high density, a large number of small houses to the unit of building land, as many as sixty or more to the acre. A common arrangement in Oldham might have a front street of four roomed houses with a back door and even a small yard, giving onto a narrow back street of smaller houses, one room up, one down, back-to-back with similar houses that formed half of another street; the rents would reflect these different circumstances. The standard of construction was low, thin walls, poor foundations, no proper floors, no protection against damp. For the most part houses were built of locally made

**Oldham from Glodwick Fields (1831)**: J. H. Carse's painting (in Oldham Art Gallery's collection) catches the rapidly growing small town, built on a hill, surrounded still by meadowlands. The Gas Works of 1827 stands apart; the newly re-built Parish Church and the chimney of Church Mill are prominent as is Bluecoat School; the line of Union Street can be seen; there is no railway. This view can be compared with the panorama of 1879 (page 82). Oldham was changing rapidly from a country village to a crowded industrial town.

Oldham Brave Oldham

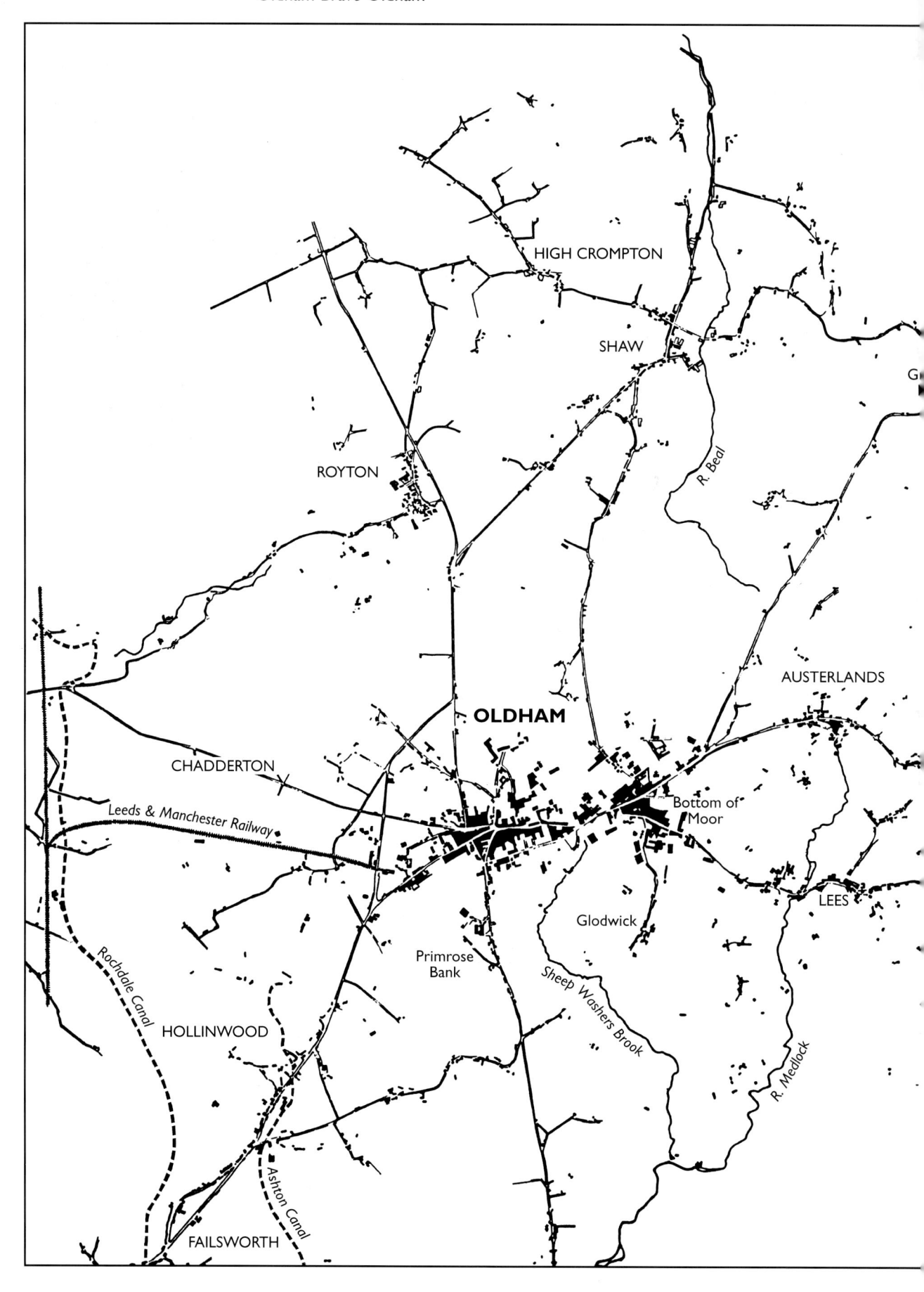

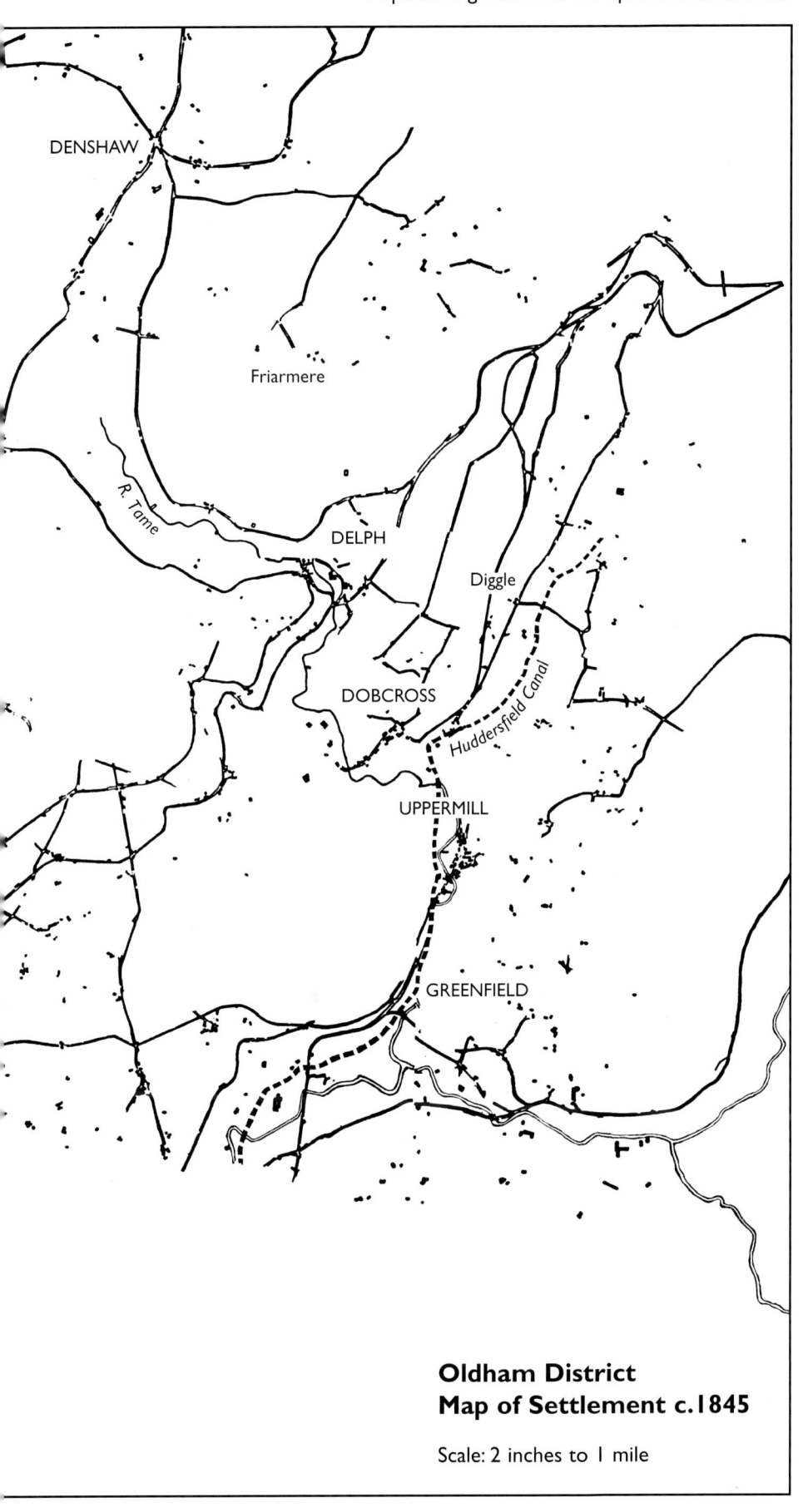

# Population growth and the spread of settlement

When the first Ordnance Survey was made in the late 1840s, the town of Oldham had taken shape with the main centre around the Market Place and the secondary concentration at Bottom of Moor. There were the beginnings of manufacturing villages at Royton, Shaw, Austerlands, Lees and Hollinwood although these were mainly straggling settlements along the turnpike roads. Elsewhere people were still dispersed in small farm and cottage clusters (folds) or in isolated farms, as they had been for two or three centuries. Scattered small settlements remained especially characteristic of the Tame valley; Delph, Dobcross, Diggle and Uppermill were still little more than hamlets.

**Oldham District
Map of Settlement c.1845**

Scale: 2 inches to 1 mile

brick; building clays were freely available as was coal and shifting small brick works were an early feature of Oldham. Whether in narrow back streets or in crowded courts people shared what primitive sanitary facilities were available. The streets and courts were unmade, unlit, undrained and uncleaned, typically in wet weather ankle deep in slutch.

Tradesmen, shopkeepers, parsons, the handful of professional men, small employers lived side by side with the general population in Oldham, although avoiding those streets and courts which had already, long before the mid-nineteenth century, acquired the lowest reputation. As early as 1817 Butterworth described some of the streets as "extremely loathsome". West Street and the streets and courts leading from it, Cheapside, Priesthill, Smethurst Street, Grimshaw Street among others, the district known as "The Bent", became notorious and turbulent, the locale of lodging houses, low pubs, brothels, filthy courts inhabited by those in the most wretched circumstances, for whatever reason. Most of Oldham's Irish were living in this neighbourhood in 1851, often as many as fifteen or twenty men, women and children to each house. The more respectable had their own streets, offering better accommodation at a higher rent, cleaner, safer, quieter, however humble; there were no segregated superior residential districts at this time, but already there were discrete neighbourhoods.

Those families who had inherited wealth, or already acquired it as large millowners or coal proprietors, were generally living in larger houses surrounded by gardens or even small parks but very close to their mills and the cottages of their workpeople. The colony of mansions at Greenhill, occupied by the Collinge and Lancashire proprietors; Greenbank, the home of James Lees; Derker House for James Greaves and Westwood House belonging to the Duncufts were examples, but there were many others. There was the grandeur of Higher and Lower Clarksfield, with their splendid views, the seats of the two older sons of James Lees. Most recently, at mid-century, Werneth Park, where John Platt, the Radcliffes of Lower House Mill, and Eli Lees of Hope Mill, had built mansions for themselves and their families in extensive private grounds, were the most striking examples of the successful class setting itself apart, not yet by distance, but dramatically in style. Nonetheless, to most of those working in Oldham, their employers would be visible, accessible, and indeed approachable. In the small "space and turning" spinning concerns or in the small engineering workshops there would be little to set master and employee apart. These men, according to Angus Reach maintained "in great degree their operative appearance, thoughts and habits"; they were "just the same as if they were fellow workmen of those they employ", living in the same kind of houses, drinking and singing in the same taverns.

There are contemporary accounts of the town from visitors. In 1849 Angus Reach found Oldham "a mean-looking straggling town" where "airless little back streets and close nasty courts are common" with dismal waste ground separating "confined and crowded mills'. Samuel Bamford in 1844 had been even less flattering; "a multitude of human dwellings crowded round huge factories, whose high tapering funnels vomit clouds of darkening smoke." Engels, writing in 1845 likened Oldham to the other towns round Manchester,

**John Platt's house** in Werneth Park, an ugly millowner's mansion reflecting the taste of the nouveau-riche at mid-nineteenth century. Similar houses were built by the Radcliffes and by Eli Lees. The old Park of Werneth Hall afforded privacy and amenity to this new elite, while their places of business were near at hand.

## Population growth and the spread of settlement

"almost wholly working-peoples districts, interspersed only with factories, a few thoroughfares lined with shops and a few lanes along which the gardens and houses of the manufacturers are scattered like villas. The towns themselves are badly and irregularly built with foul courts, lanes and back alleys, reeking of coal smoke, and especially dingy from the original bright red brick, turned black with the time."

Crowded, smoky, unhealthy as it was, the growing town of Oldham still retained one redeeming feature. It had its extensive and attractive views of moorland or the Lancashire plain, and everywhere within short walking distance were still meadows, wild flowers, streams that carried fish, and woodland.

The map of building development based on the first ordnance survey shows how, away from Oldham town, settlement remained dispersed. Indeed within Oldham township, the compact contiguous built-up area, the town with its two centres, only accounted for two-thirds of the population. Expanded hamlets like Primrose Bank, Glodwick, Waterhead Mill or Moorside with cottages grouped around a mill or mills and maybe a coal mine, were important scattered nuclei at mid-century; subsequently the spread of the built up area brought them within the town. When the Congregational Minister, R.M. Davies, came to Oldham in 1843, he thought Oldham "but a collection of scattered hamlets, with no roads, no proper system of local government".

Crompton, Shaw and Royton stand out as straggling manufacturing villages but elsewhere the pattern was still one of a multiplicity of isolated farms with their associated cottages, folds and hamlets, thicker perhaps than they had been but still separated by meadow land. The communities of the upper Tame valley, the old settlements of Dobcross and Delph and the

**The Tame Valley**: Carse's painting of 1858 looking towards Uppermill from Dobcross, shows the viaduct of the recent London and North Western Railway. It communicates the open pastoral character of the Tame valley, picturesque and still unspoiled by urban development.

beginnings of Uppermill and Greenfield remained small and compact, villages rather than towns, around them scattered "a thick population of small farmers and hand-loom weavers" in their picturesque valley and moorland setting. This was not a district given over substantially to mills and streets; the traditional open rural character, the landscape of domestic industry, still prevailed. When Charles Dickens visited Saddleworth he spoke of "an oppressive sense of loneliness. At every turn the hills shut out the world". Those who lived there enjoyed the solitude.

**Life in early Victorian Oldham**

There are many surviving accounts which describe life in the rapidly growing mill town, notably those of Benjamin Grime (1824-1895), the Oldham Accountant and Councillor, whose columns "Memory Sketches" were a feature of the *Oldham Chronicle* in 1884 and in subsequent years. Samuel Bamford in his *Walks in South Lancashire* (1844) and Angus Reach in his letters to the *Morning Chronicle* in 1849 were others whose observations at the time were recorded. It was particularly in Oldham itself that new lifestyles were emerging rather than in the out-townships where change was slower and on a far smaller scale; many places remained comparatively isolated and the people, though their own individual village community might be reasonably large, were living among their families in much the same way as they had for generations.

Governing all was the mill; over half Oldham's occupied population worked in a cotton mill of one kind or another. A high proportion of these were children from the age of eight upwards, youths of both sexes and older married or unmarried women; adult men were a comparatively small part of the workforce. The early mills had little regard for amenity: they had been quickly built to accommodate machinery; typically they were cramped on several floors with low ceilings; they were badly lit with candles or flaming gas; excessively hot and airless for much of the time; dirty and noisy; and, with unfenced belting and moving machinery, appallingly accident prone. Reach thought the cotton waste factories of Oldham were "the most repulsive working places in Lancashire."

Work was not merely unpleasant and unhealthy; for the most part it was tedious monotonous drudgery, but not necessarily arduous given the slow machines and frequent stoppages. It was not uncommon for men to relieve the monotony and slip out to a nearby alehouse in mid-morning or the afternoon. Until 1850 the normal working week was not less than sixty-nine hours, more than that in the earlier period. The mills worked from six o'clock in the morning until seven or eight in the evening with limited breaks for meals. Meals or "baggins" would normally be brought to the mill, perhaps twice a day, not much more than porridge, butter-cakes or occasionally potato pie. Saturday was a shorter day ending at four in the afternoon. There were few holidays, perhaps four or five days a year. Working hours and conditions were no different in the coal workings, in the machine shops, or brickyards and building sites, or even in the shops and stalls of the market place; indeed their hours may have been longer. Nor were conditions different for the elite. Weekday life for the great majority was mainly all bed and work;

# Life in early Victorian Oldham

**A Carding Room** in the 1830s: the successive processes of carding, drawing and roving which transformed laps of cotton into loose thread to be spun into yarn on mules or throstles were common to all spinning mills. Invariably the operatives were girls or young women, earning wages of 7 - 9 shillings a week.

**Mule Spinning** in the 1830s: hand mules were in general use, only partly driven by steam or water power. They were much smaller and slower than the self-acting mules that were introduced from mid-century onwards. The spinning room was not entirely a male domain, with the skilled spinner or minder here supported by a female piecer and little piecer.

as one contemporary wrote "for the most part, master and man, millionaire and the poorest of his hands, eat to live and live to work".

Each concern would have its own culture. The smaller employers, if little removed from their workmen were the hardest to get on with; they had the roughest style, not without cuffs and kicks, abuse and arbitrary dismissal, "squeezing the very existence out of their operatives". These people, it was said, were not "in cultivation or in character, persons to produce an ameliorating influence on the vast mass of people whom they employ". The larger employers were the most respected, their mills better regulated, their concern for their workpeople often genuine, and however firm the discipline it would be applied in an honourable and fair way. This was true of the Platts,

growing number of friendly societies and sick and benefit clubs. The friendly societies also provided for insurance against the costs of a burial. Even as early as 1817, the Oddfellows and Foresters had several lodges in Oldham while small benefit clubs were associated with many of the pubs and Sunday Schools. In 1846 there were twenty-five Oddfellows Lodges in the Oldham District of the Manchester Unity, with 1,510 members, meeting each four weeks in a local public house; Shaw District had eight Lodges, Saddleworth also had eight. The Rechabites, a temperance friendly society, came to the town after 1835.

Total household income varied significantly according to family size and age structure. On the same wage and at the same trade one man might be comfortably housed and well fed, and another wretchedly housed and half starved. A young couple before marriage could save, and on marriage, two active working partners could be well off. As children were born their circumstances would deteriorate. Four or five small children with only one earning parent would bring hardship. As many as one-third of all households took lodgers to create extra income. It was not uncommon for two families to share a house, sleeping four or five to a bed, especially in hard times; lodgers and house-sharing were especially found among the Irish. Child-minders, and these could be aged parents, growing children, neighbours, might enable a mother to go back to work; plenty of babies were carried to suck at the mill.

When children began to earn circumstances improved and were at their best when a household had perhaps four or five wages coming in; when work was brisk 40s or 50s a week would not be unusual for many such families. Then, as children left home, and old age and infirmity approached, fear of poverty would haunt many people. Men would cling to their work as long as they could and would usually be found a less demanding task at lower earnings. Generally the old, unable to work and without income, relied on children for support. For the destitute, usually several hundreds, squalid and comfortless small local workhouses were the last resort; the larger Union workhouse was built at Northmoor in 1851.

The narrow streets and courts where people lived were intimate places. There was little room for privacy; this was communal living in its varied forms. Residential density was extremely high. Close to the town centre, the short and narrow Bow Street, for example, in 1851 had 463 people living in eighty-three houses; Greaves Street, by the new Town Hall, had 273 people in fifty-two houses. With cramped uncomfortable homes, typically the two-roomed back-to-back holding on average five persons, and frequently many more, and doors opening directly onto the street or court, much of life was on the street when leisure was available. This was the playground for children or a place for adults to meet, relax, laugh and gossip, a convivial place however ugly and grim. The streets and courts were filthy, not least because of the middens and ashpits, open piles of all kinds of household refuse, decaying, stinking, swarming with flies, abominable. Somewhere, perhaps at the end of a row of houses, were a few shared privies often leading to a cesspool. Middens and privies were rarely cleaned; the tenants would have to pay or persuade a farmer to remove the contents and spread them on his fields; emptying them during daytime, moving the contents through the streets, was another source of offence. Sometimes it was left to heavy showers of rain to sweep refuse into a sewer, at the time an open drain. But people were indifferent to their surroundings; they had been used to these conditions, to the smells and the filth, all their lives. There was nothing they could do about them nor were they the subject of protest; the hazard they presented to public health was scarcely recognised by the people at large.

However bad the worst streets and courts, conditions in the lodging houses, and there were as many as eighty of these, charging 2d or 3d a night, catering for the needs of itinerant labour, the recent Irish arrivals or the most destitute and homeless, were often worse; in the lowest of these people were sleeping ten or twelve to a room, men, women and children, sharing a few bug-ridden beds and filthy bedclothes. Generally, however, the worst streets and courts, like the lodging houses, were well hidden, and the respectable community did not go near them.

What of other facilities for most people in Oldham at the time? Piped water at this period was expensive adding perhaps another 3d to the weekly rent, and reached only the better homes, at best a third of the whole. For the majority there was heavy reliance on rain water. A street, a court, may have had a well or a tap but frequently, especially during dry periods, water was brought in large kits or cans from wells, pumps, or streams some distance away; queuing for water was then commonplace. Much of it was polluted and unwholesome, a carrier of disease, nor were supplies reliable. In drought

**Potters Yard** was between Union Street and Bow Street. The Yard was unmade and a few hens were kept but no pigs are in evidence. This was typical early nineteenth century housing close to the centre of the town.

there was often resort to water from disused coal workings, described as "alive with wick red things" that could, at least, be used for washing. Not surprisingly families economised their water, using it over and over again. Few people would bathe, most would only wash their hands and face on a regular basis. For many households the weekly wash was a limited affair.

Gas was not generally available. Rooms would be lit by candles and long winter nights were spent in semi-darkness. Few people had clocks or watches; they were knocked up at five in the morning. Walls were whitewashed, floors flagged and sanded, furniture plain and sparse. Every house used coal, bought from a cart, and often stored in a heap outside. With a coal fire in the principal room most houses were stuffy and over warm; people did not believe in opening windows or in the virtues of fresh air. Kindling the fire could be a major problem for there were no matches, paper or firewood. Thus fires were banked up and kept overnight; otherwise people went to their neighbours in search of a flame or a piece of burning coal. Borrowing from the neighbours, food, water, utensils was regular practice.

As for food, oatmeal porridge with black treacle, oatcake, home baked jannock or oatmeal bread, potatoes, cheese, bacon and cheap meat costing 7d a pound, at best once or twice a week, perhaps made into potato pie, or hotpot, were the staple fare. Now and then on Sunday there might be a fowl. Spice cake or parkin were occasional luxuries as were expensive tea or coffee with sugar. Seasonally there would be vegetables, onions, swedes, fruit such as gooseberries and apples. Cheap blue (skim) milk and butter milk or new milk (2d a quart) were widely used, but often adulterated or thinned with water, delivered to the door step or fetched from a milk seller, much of it brought in from Saddleworth or Oldham's meadowland farms during the summer-time. As Jackson Brierley, Mayor in 1897, was to recall looking back over fifty years, many families kept hens or a pig, in the court, in a pig cote near the midden. The scream of a pig being killed was a common sound in the Oldham of the time, a butcher being hired for the purpose; nearly every part of the pig found a use, the immediate delicacies being the pluck and the liver, and blood pudding, but trotters, ham and bacon would be valuable variants to the diet. The slaughterhouse attached to a butcher's shop was a familiar neighbourhood nuisance with live animals being driven through the streets an accepted diversion; when animals were slaughtered their entrails were thrown on the nearest midden.

Most households would drink beer with their meals, in the evenings round the fire, and at the weekend, Saturday after work or Sunday. Special occasions such as a christening, wedding or funeral would certainly be marked in this way. In a great many cases the beer was home brewed, malt and hops and yeast being available at every grocer's shop and housewives took pride in the quality of their home brew, prepared once a week, with some expertise. Alternatively beer was brought in from a beer house or from a hush-shop, the illegal beer sellers who flourished at the time in the poorer districts. Among women, rum and tea was a popular drink, or more cheaply, "small drink", as it was called, a mixture of treacle, water and ginger.

In the early days of factory and mine employment workpeople were paid in shop notes or tokens, redeemable only at particular shops, or by the detested truck system when wages had to be exchanged for provisions at the

# Life in early Victorian Oldham

**Oldham Market Place at mid-century**: apart from the shops and public-houses, there were dozens of open stalls along the road side selling produce of all kinds as well as fast food such as black peas, tripe and Yorkshire Ducks. Friday and Saturday nights after the mills closed were exceptionally busy; the market would continue until Blind Joe rang the bell at 11p.m. Shopping from stalls in the street was a wretched experience on dark cold winter evenings; the first covered market in Curzon Street was opened by a private company in 1855. The horse-drawn milk cart with two churns delivered milk house-to-house, fresh from the farm, if often watered or polluted. This early photograph was probably taken to mark the provision of the drinking fountain in 1859 by the Oldham Industrial or King Street Co-operative Society.

so-called "tommy shop" connected with a particular mill or mine. Certainly by mid-century that was in the past; weekly or fortnightly payments in cash were the rule. Oldham did not lack competing shopkeepers, badgers as they were called, near at hand throughout the streets, most of whom gave credit fairly freely. Thus many households bought on trust as the system was called, settling "the score" as wages came in. Perpetual debt was often a consequence with many working men not free agents, while widespread credit added to the trader's risk and inflated his margin. Provisions from local shops were typically sold in very small quantities, "one or two pennyworths only", an amount, as Bamford wrote, as "would just suffice for the meal about to be prepared". There were plenty of hawkers and pedlars but most of the town was within walking distance of the Market Place and Tommyfield and here, from dozens of stalls, significant weekly purchases were made, of food, much of it of miserable quality, adulterated or unwholesome, cheap clothing and hardware. The Saturday evening market would be a lively scene with the shops and stalls trading late until the market bell was rung at 11pm.

Working people were modestly dressed, fustian jackets, cord trousers, beaver hats, and for women shawls, blouses and skirts; Samuel Bamford at the time thought the factory hands at Crompton were "decently and cleanly attired", no rags or squalor. But not many at this time would have a respectable get-up, a Sunday best. Much of the clothing would be made at home or by a neighbourly dressmaker or small tailor. Shoes were unusual among the poorer classes, typically bought on credit; clogs were the normal wear.

There were over twenty doctors or surgeons in Oldham and the townships at mid-century or one for every 3,500 people; at least one dentist visited the town one half-day weekly providing his services at one of several haircutters' shops and charging one shilling to extract a tooth and up to £15 for an entire set of artificial teeth. Those who wanted a bath had a choice of two establishments, each provided by enterprising haircutters, the cost being 6d cold or 9d warm. For the great majority who would never consult doctors, there were plenty of druggist's shops, and market quacks, selling a great range of pills, elixirs, tonics and salves that claimed to cope with most complaints. Childbirth would be a local affair with plenty of neighbourly help. The dead, often unburied for a week, lay with the living in crowded homes.

Funerals could be a formidable expense; perhaps £2 for an adult, 30s for a child but most families sought to be respectable on this occasion, and, at least for the better-off, that meant appropriate clothing (crepe, sashes, hat bands, white or black gloves), and for all classes meat and drink as well as grave and coffin. Whenever possible among the working class the dead were buried on Sunday to avoid loss of a day's wages; the coffin was invariably carried by bearers from the house to the grave with the mourners following on foot.

Not surprisingly, given these living circumstances, expectation of life was low. Death rates are a matter of conjecture in the second quarter of the century but in Oldham town would be close to 30 per 1,000 per year, more in the poorest quarters. About two to three in ten children born live would die within the first year of life; only about half of all children would survive beyond the age of five. If there were epidemics of infectious disease, smallpox, typhus, scarlet fever, these were not recorded when there was no medical authority, few doctors. Consumption was probably the most common cause of death among adults. Oldham, it has to be said, avoided the cholera epidemics that caused panic in London, Liverpool, Manchester and elsewhere in the 1830s and 1840s. Grim as conditions in Oldham seem, in retrospect, they were not different from those in other similar new towns.

**Leisure**

Leisure was scarce, given the long hours of work and few holidays. For most of the population, theatres, concerts, music saloons were hardly known. Treats, parties, teas were provided by churches and chapels and some employers, especially at Christmas or New Year. For their members the lodges of friendly societies met monthly, invariably at public houses, for a convivial evening of drinking and singing. Apart from Christmas, Easter was an occasion for some to visit Knott Mill Fair in Manchester, and Whitsun had Kersall Moor races, or the Sunday School walks for the more respectable.

Streams of people, men, women and children, would be walking through Failsworth and Miles Platting to Manchester on these occasions, but the majority would not go beyond five miles from their home in their lifetime. There were events such as Pancake Tuesday, or Bonfire night in November to break the routine. Christmas was celebrated in a traditional way: bands and singers in the streets, family get-togethers with plenty of home brew and currant loaf.

As for many years previously, the Wakes were the major annual event celebrated throughout the district at different dates in August. Rival rush carts, laboriously but skilfully made from bunches of rushes to an ark shape and decorated with borrowed ornaments, were paraded through the villages, neighbourhoods or streets of Oldham town, accompanied by troops of gaily dressed dancers and crowds of supporters. In the centre of Oldham, on Tommyfield, there were other travelling shows and entertainments, swing-boats, freak shows, card-sharpers, ballad-mongers and the like, a source of excitement and diversion. What may be called fast food stalls, were selling potato pie, black peas, black puddings, Yorkshire duck, tripe, gingerbread, sweets and there were plenty of mountebanks selling cheap cutlery, pottery and the like. Oldham Wakes would draw many into the town from the surrounding villages with the young walking long distances, as they did at the time. A popular country wakes was held in September each year at Grains Bar, "on the tops", when sparrow shoots, dog trails, foot races and pigeon flying were featured. The Wakes, as with seasonal fairs whether in Saddleworth, Failsworth or Shaw and elsewhere, as well as Oldham town, were always a time for carousing, heavy drinking, rowdiness, brawling and for street fights between rival gangs; they acquired a reputation for intemperance and folly which increased as the century progressed.

These seasonal occasions apart, the main leisure outlet for many of the population was the public house. There were at least three categories of drinking place at the time. Firstly, the inns or taverns, licensed by the magistrates, of which there were about 190 in Oldham and its townships in 1850; these were in the town centre and main streets in prominent positions. Then there were about 200 beerhouses, mainly in the back streets, uncontrolled by the magistrates and needing an excise license only under the Act of 1830. Finally, in the poorer districts, a large number of illegal unlicensed hush-shops, perhaps 300 or so, were competing in the same trade by selling very cheap drink. Most of these establishments at the time would brew their own beer, of very variable quality, and it would be sold for consumption on or off the premises, off-sales in a jug or pot for consumption at home being very important. The extent of public patronage and demand was such that about one public house, whether inn or beerhouse, but excluding hush-shops, could survive for each 200 people in Oldham at mid-century. Most people had a pub within a hundred yards.

Public houses were open most of the time, from five or six in the morning to eleven or twelve at night. There might be restrictions on Sundays, at least during the hours of religious services in the morning and early evening, but not every place observed these. There were no restrictions regarding age. Women and youths were as welcome as men. Working clothes were not minded. Clearly this was a place to relax; the pub was warm, light, convivial, a social centre, a relief from a drab crowded cottage after work, but especially on Saturday evening or on Sunday. There might be music and singing, an occasional newspaper for those who could read, company, gossip and games such as dominoes or cards; cheap plain food was available but above all there was cheap beer, typically 3d a quart. For some, resort to the pub resulted in habitual drunkenness as was evident throughout the streets, full of staggering drunks every weekend, and resulting in a regular procession of offenders before the magistrates. Busy as the pubs were in the good times, this was an unstable trade, the first to suffer when trade was bad; many of the hush shops would then close.

Public houses offered facilities for many organisations, friendly societies, building clubs, trade unions, political groups and even local government. Many of the inns had rooms for dinners, parties and dances, entertainment after weddings and funerals. Business men in various trades would congregate in hostelries at Bottom of Moor. Some pubs were respectable, some were sordid; it was in the low parts of the town that they acquired the worst reputation. Thus here they had no proper sanitation; a vertical flagstone by the front door served the needs of men and boys to relieve themselves. As a resort of prostitutes some were little better than brothels.

Outside the lowest pubs, street fights, late on Saturday night or Sunday afternoons, were an accepted part of the scene. There was no authority to curb them. The Oldhamer relished a free fight whether individually or in gangs; not for nothing was he called a "roughyed". Pelting and otherwise insulting strangers was another feature, especially if they were Irish, for few people had a good word for Paddy. Such was the town's reputation, but it must be said that the ruder, coarser violent side of Oldham life was not different from what occurred in all the new industrial towns of the time; Rochdale had its "mashers", Pudsey its "blacks".

There were other pastimes for the respectable if not the poor. For the church and chapel goers, choral singing developed. Some groups such as the Society of Singers of Shaw Chapel achieved high standards and wide renown, but Oldham had several well known vocalists and keen musicians; there were both musical and choral societies from the eighteenth century onwards. Favourite oratorios, notably the Messiah, but also from a wider repertoire, were performed regularly in church or in chapels. Music from brass bands and small orchestras attracted some, playing and listening, and this participation increased as the nineteenth century progressed. Music's popularity should not be

**Shaw Chapel**, built in the eighteenth century, acquired a reputation for its singing, especially of sacred music. Here is a programme of 1824; the charges for admittance and the day and time would restrict the audience to the well-to-do.

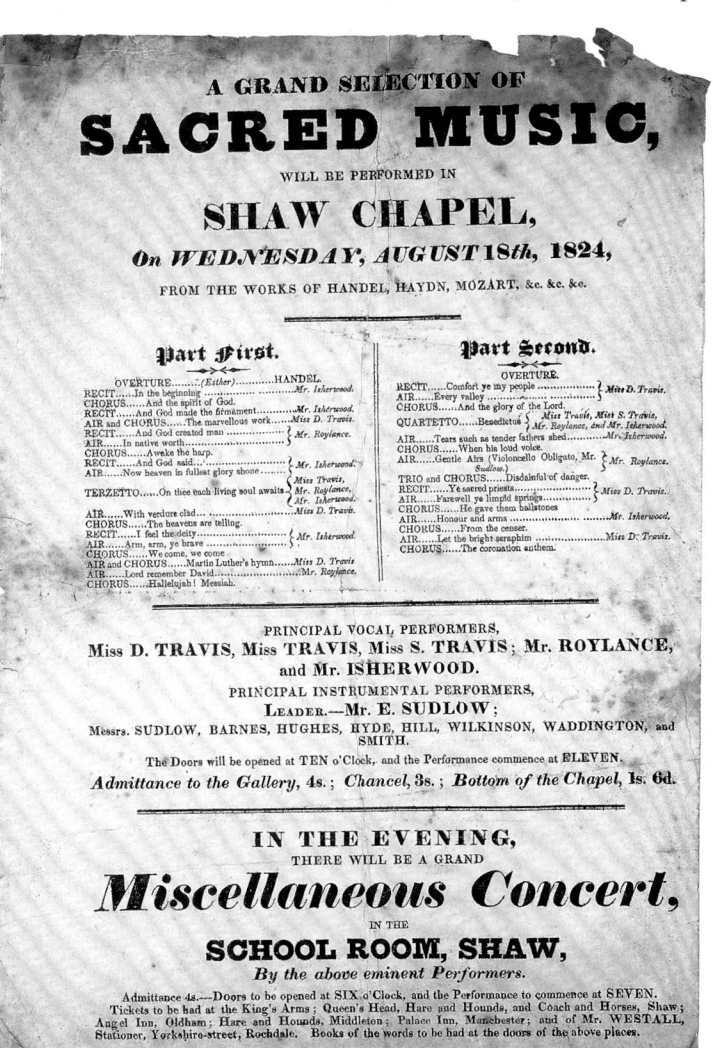

overstated, however; in 1851 there were no shops selling music and only five music teachers recorded in the Census of that year. There were small theatres in Manchester and Eagle Streets at which travelling companies performed occasional plays, and in 1845 Oldham acquired a regular theatre when a license to use the newly constructed Working Men's Hall was granted to the Theatre Royal. Public meetings, debating groups and lectures were generally well attended, out of interest and curiosity, an agreeable diversion.

Elections, when they occurred, processions on special occasions, were exciting events, welcome breaks to a drab routine. There seem to have been major gatherings or celebrations to mark the victory at Waterloo, at the opening of the Standedge canal tunnel with a crowd of 10,000 in 1811, the coronation of George lV, the passing of the Great Reform Bill in 1832, the accession of Queen Victoria and finally Repeal of the Corn Laws. Certainly on the Royal occasions, Sunday Schools, the Friendly Societies, the Masonic Lodges and members of the Orange Order, gentlemen and tradesmen of the town, accompanied by a band, would parade the streets watched by huge crowds of people; in some places an ox would be roasted, while the children would be given spice cake and ale. A funeral or a wedding, certainly a grand one, would always attract a crowd. Absalom Watkin described the throngs of people in 1845 who stood to watch four carriages drawn by grey horses with postillions in scarlet jackets, carrying his family to an elite Oldham wedding.

All the time for the multitude of children there were the traditional games played in the street or court. Boys and young men gathered at street corners or in public places, insulting passers-by and especially young women; they had other street diversions, kicking people's doors on dark nights, calling nicknames, putting slates on chimney pots, throwing stones. For working men there was sport, often brutal sport: bull baiting, cock fights, dog fights, rat fights, and wrestling, boxing and vicious clog fights, all attracting wagers. More placid but eagerly pursued by some were whippet racing and pigeon homing, games like knur and spell, and illegally, because it was gambling, pitch and toss. The coming of the railway in the 1840s introduced an exciting new opportunity, the cheap trip, limited so far as Oldham was concerned until the railway reached the centre of the town at Mumps. Most popular and most affordable were short excursions to places like Hollingworth Lake or Belle Vue, both rapidly developing their attractions and facilities to meet the new demand. But a far greater adventure was a trip to the seaside and by 1850, for a fare of 3s, a three hour journey in open carriages was taking a few hundred from Oldham

---

### ZOOLOGICAL GARDENS, BELLEVUE, HYDE ROAD, MANCHESTER.

**Mr. JENNISON, PROPRIETOR,**

Trusts that the Importance of this Place of Public Resort, equal in reference to the Capital expended in bringing the GARDENS to their present State of Perfection—the Novel and Attractive Style in which they are disposed—their Unparalled Extent—the Vast Assemblage of OBJECTS OF INTEREST, Natural and Artificial which they present—the Facility and Cheapness of Access—the Succession of PUBLIC ENTERTAINMENTS, introduced during the Season, and his determination to maintain the Strictest Decorum and Propriety in their Management, may induce many to avail themselves of a means of Recreation, so Cheap, Healthful and Improving, and confirm the resolution still further to render BELLEVUE Worthy the Support of the Community of Manchester and the Neighbourhood by **The Frequent Introduction of Additional Features of Attraction.**

*Since Last Season, the Improvements and Additions have been on an Extensive and Varied Scale, amongst these may be named the Erection of a*

**SPACIOUS BUILDING**
FOR THE BETTER CONVENIENCE OF THE

**MUSEUM OF CURIOSITIES, STUFFED ANIMALS AND BIRDS,**
And other Objects, to which *Great Additions* have recently been made, including Two VERY FINE SPECIMENS of the

**LION AND LIONESS.**

A NEW MONKEY HOUSE,
*Has also been Constructed, in which is placed a* MONSTER CAGE, 21 *Feet in Height and Covering an Area of upwards of* 600 *Square Feet.*

**A GYMNASIUM,**
Complete in every detail, has been introduced for the Healthful Recreation of frequenters to the Gardens. To the previous Extensive ZOOLOGICAL COLLECTION may be mentioned, **The Addition of Remarkably Fine Specimens of the Leopard, Striped Hyæna, Ocelot or Tiger Cat, Wolf, Bear, Zebu Bull, Ostrich, Vulture, and innumerable other varieties.**
In the Grounds the Numerous SERPENTINE and other ORNAMENTAL WALKS and PROMENADES have been entirely renovated and a Large Variety of Exotic and other Plants added.

**THE EXTENSIVE SHEET OF WATER,**
On which Float many Small PLEASURE BOATS for the further Accommodation of the Public, continues to be a source of Great Attraction; and the

**ELIZABETHAN MAZE,**
Affords much Amusement, especially to Juveniles.
To the Admirers of HORTICULTURAL and DECORATIVE GARDENING, the Hot Houses and Green Houses, Ornamental Parterres, Fountains, Shaded Walks, Rockeries, Grottoes, Caves, Arbours, &c., present a Pleasing Assemblage of Objects for contemplation. The

**SPACIOUS DANCING PLATFORM,**
Has been enlarged to an Area of upwards of 15,000 Square Feet, and in the event of Unfavourable Weather, Accommodation is provided in the Gardens for the shelter of thousands. *Three Floral and Horticultural Shows are held Annually in the Gardens, at stated intervals.*
BELLEVUE is Situated Two Miles from MANCHESTER, on the Road to HYDE; it also adjoins the LONDON and NORTH-WESTERN Line, at the Newly-Erected LONGSIGHT STATION, which renders it easy of approach from MANCHESTER, STOCKPORT, MACCLESFIELD, and the STATIONS on the Line to CREWE; it is also within Half a Mile of the GORTON STATION on the SHEFFIELD and LINCOLNSHIRE Line.
*Visiters can be Accommodated with Wines and Spirits of the Finest Qualities, Guiness's Bottled Stout, Breakfasts, Dinners, Tea and other Refreshments, at a Moderate Charge.*
**A Powerful Brass Band in daily attendance during the Summer Season.**
N.B.—The Gardens are open every day throughout the year, as in Winter they are very appropriate for SKATING, the Waters being very extensive and less than three feet in depth, which renders this amusement perfectly Safe.

**Belle Vue** became a popular attraction in the 1840s. Subsequently cheap railway fares brought it within reach of a mass market for the time, not least people from Oldham. It was to retain its attraction for at least a hundred years.

to Blackpool or New Brighton for the day. Oldhamers, it has always been said, worked hard and they also played hard: for the rest of the nineteenth century they were to prove the truth of that statement.

## Church and Chapel

Growing population in the eighteenth century required increased provision for religious worship. Further chapels of ease had been built at Hey in 1744, Royton in 1754 and in Hollinwood in 1769; there was also one at Friarmere at the head of the Tame Valley in 1768. The need was greatest in Oldham town itself and there, financed by voluntary subscriptions, St Peter's was opened in 1768, a plain building with its own graveyard, but in a central position and not far from the Parish Church of St Mary's.

Meanwhile dissent had established itself within the district. Robert Constantine, minister of St Mary's, was ejected in 1662 and began to attract an Independent congregation at Greenacres in 1672; an Independent Chapel was built in Delph in 1746. Wesleyan preachers came to Oldham in the late eighteenth century; their visits and that of John Wesley himself led to a modest Wesleyan Chapel being established in Manchester Street in 1776, superseded by a larger one opened in 1790. There was a Methodist chapel at Delph in 1781.

The nonconformist chapels broke the monopoly of the Anglican church.

**St. Paul's, Royton** was originally (1754) a chapel-of-ease and became a Parish Church in 1835. Its accommodation was limited and, with most of its pews appropriated, many local people in a growing population could not find room to worship. The church was enlarged in 1854 to be rebuilt in the 1880s.

# Church and Chapel

The bonds of traditional society were in any case being weakened by the rapid development of the town and the new ways of working and living. Existing facilities for religious worship could easily be overwhelmed in these circumstances. In Oldham itself, for instance, Anglican seatings hardly changed over the first thirty years of the nineteenth century while population doubled; the same happened in Saddleworth. Entirely new districts like Bottom of Moor lacked immediate places of worship for many years. Both the Anglican church and the non-conformists struggled to meet the needs of the new community; they were also in competition with each other, and, within nonconformity, the multiplying sects added to the variety of forms of worship that became available.

Funds to build new churches, as well as leadership and will, were the constraints. After much controversy, not least as to meeting the costs, the old church of St Mary's in Oldham was demolished and rebuilt, on a larger scale, in 1827-30. Generally Anglican initiatives were stimulated by patronage and state aid. The Church Building Act of 1818 provided the money to build St James at Greenacres in 1827-1829 with James Lees of Clarksfield the principal patron. Later Peel's Ecclesiastical Commission led to new parishes being formed throughout the new towns of Lancashire; in the Oldham

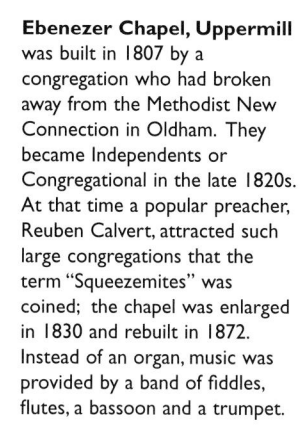

**Ebenezer Chapel, Uppermill** was built in 1807 by a congregation who had broken away from the Methodist New Connection in Oldham. They became Independents or Congregational in the late 1820s. At that time a popular preacher, Reuben Calvert, attracted such large congregations that the term "Squeezemites" was coined; the chapel was enlarged in 1830 and rebuilt in 1872. Instead of an organ, music was provided by a band of fiddles, flutes, a bassoon and a trumpet.

**St. James, Greenacres** was built in 1827-29 at a cost of £9,651 to meet the needs of the growing local population. Government money (the Church Building Act of 1818) met most of the costs while James Lees of Clarksfield, its principal patron, provided the site, then worth £300. Surrounded as it became by mills and iron-works the church has survived to the present day, as this contemporary photograph records. When built, the church was the largest in Oldham with over 1,800 seats of which 1,200 were free and not subject to pew rents, an important deterrent to the poor. The living in 1832 brought an income of £72 a year; W.F. Walker, the first vicar, was one of many influential Oldham clergymen.

**The Independent Chapel, Greenacres**: there had been a Presbyterian chapel at Greenacres late in the seventeenth century. The building of 1784 was the second and by then the cause had become Independent or Congregational. It was enlarged and improved in 1822 and replaced in 1854 by the third and larger chapel which seated 800 people. As one Minister said, "here the word of God was read, expounded and applied, to many who we trust were seemingly interested and benefited by it."

townships eight such Peel Parishes were formed, with new churches to serve them, financed by government. Five were in Oldham town, and the others included St John's at Chadderton in 1845, and St James at East Crompton in 1847; Failsworth got St John's in 1845, under the same provision.

A typical pattern of nonconformist initiative was a small group of people renting a humble meeting room, hearing a charismatic preacher, and gathering strength and conviction to lease land and build a modest chapel, incurring debt in the process. As numbers grew and debt was cleared by voluntary effort, a larger more ambitious building followed, with stronger patronage but usually a further burden of debt that was gradually cleared by fund-raising initiatives. Some of the new chapels were the outcome of missionary activity from an established chapel of the same denomination; they were seeking to make provision in a new district of the town. In other cases - and Hope Chapel built at Bottom of Moor in 1824 is an example - the initiative and the resources came from a person of means, in this case Samuel Lees of Soho Ironworks, to provide his workpeople with a place of worship of his own faith; to provide continuing income for the Chapel he endowed it with ownership of several streets of workmen's cottages nearby. These were the processes by which, belatedly, churches and chapels proliferated, side by side. By 1850, for instance, in Oldham Borough there were over forty places of worship.

The nonconformist chapels may have had a special appeal to the new middle class, millowners, shopkeepers and aspirant respectable working people. The Anglicans retained their hold, however, with the older families and attracted adherents among the new. People were spoiled for choice in the centre of the town and where they worshipped was partly a matter of convenience, congeniality and parson appeal rather than deep conviction.

The Religious Census of March 1851 gives a basis for judging the strength of the different denominations and the scale of religious attendance. The Census data may be interpreted in various ways: Table V summarises the figures developed by Smith in his book on religion in Oldham. The Anglican congregations had fallen to little more than a third of the total, below 30 per cent in Saddleworth, and the Anglican churches were clearly filled with empty pews. Independents, or Congregationalists as they were now called, were important in Oldham with prominent well-patronised chapels throughout the town appealing strongly to shopkeepers and artisans, but Methodists formed the largest group, divided as they were into several sects drawing from different social groups. Smith estimates that 37 per cent of Oldham's eligible population (for instance excluding the very young) and 32 per cent in Saddleworth attended church or chapel on Census Sunday. Almost certainly these figures understate the scale of religious involvement; the returns were incomplete and the Census was held in March on a cold day of driving rain; there was also an influenza epidemic at the time. Smith concludes that around 45 per cent of the eligible population were attending church regularly at the time. But a majority of townspeople, the poorer group, with the exception of the Irish, remained outside religious observance. The non-attenders were deterred by a variety of motives, indifference, the expense of pew rents, a lack of suitable clothing and reluctance to mix with the respectable. As one observer wrote at the time, "the poor man is made to feel that he is a poor man, the rich is reminded that he is rich, in the great majority of our churches and chapels". Many working men, not going to church on Sunday, loitered at the corners of the street, and frequented the public houses as soon as they were open for there was nowhere else to go.

**The Independent Methodists at Smith Street, Greenacres** were bolder than many in their programme of fund raising events in 1856, all to pay for building a new and larger chapel.

## TABLE V : ESTIMATED CHURCH ATTENDANCE: MARCH 1851

|  | Oldham | Saddleworth |
|---|---|---|
| Anglican | 5,872 | 1,357 |
| Methodist |  |  |
|     Wesleyan | 1,555 | 961 |
|     Primitive | 1,051 |  |
|     New Connection | 1,791 | 70 |
|     Others | 1,187 |  |
| Independent | 3,145 | 1,408 |
| Baptist | 898 | 30 |
| Roman Catholic | 675 | 120 |
| Other | 1,480 | 852 |
| Totals: | 17,042 | 4,798 |
| Percent of Eligible Population | 37.2% | 31.5% |

*Source:* Mark Smith, Religion in Industrial Society, Oxford, 1994, p. 251.

Whatever the vitality of religious life by the mid-century, there can be no doubt that the influence of the Sunday School reached practically every home and at some stage of their life, almost every person. Almost every Oldham child went to Sunday School, once, twice, each Sunday and perhaps on weekday evenings too; this was the prevailing habit. Baines in 1831 reported about 6,000 in the Sunday Schools in Oldham town, 3,000 in the rest of the Parish. These numbers had more than doubled by 1851 when 24 per cent of the total population of the Borough and more or less three-quarters of those aged between five and fourteen years, more girls than boys, were registered at one or other of forty-three Sunday Schools. In the townships - Chadderton, Royton, Crompton - the position was much the same with the Sunday School engaging over one quarter of the population.

**The Independent Sabbath School at Greenacres**, built in 1837, at the time not merely a place of religious instruction and social activity but provider of the main basic education - reading and writing - to the majority of children in its district.

Simple religious teaching, bible stories and childrens hymns, an exhortation to morals and manners, were basic to the Sunday attendance, but the Schools provided, for many, their only instruction in reading, spelling and writing. Some of the Schools had evening classes, especially for writing and arithmetic, but reading, together with religious instruction, was "principally the labour of the Sabbath". Most of the Schools had a library of books. There were some, in all the faiths - George Grundy, the long serving Vicar of Hey, or the Superintendents at Queen Street Congregational Church in 1825 being examples - who were insistent that there was no room for secular instruction in a place of worship. But they were exceptional. The Sunday Schools supplied an unsatisfied need. Children had to be able to read the bible and their teachers took pride in what was achieved; the Schools were regarded as "the legitimate and sufficing source of all knowledge". Many children went there, or were sent there, to learn, rather than for religious reasons.

TABLE VI: SUNDAY SCHOOLS: REGISTERED SCHOLARS 1851

|  | Schools | Scholars |
|---|---|---|
| Oldham - Borough | | |
| Anglican | 10 | 3,484 |
| Methodist | | |
|    Wesleyan | 4 | 1,300 |
|    Primitive | 4 | 765 |
|    Others | 5 | 1,501 |
| Independent | 8 | 2,886 |
| Others | 12 | 2,555 |
| Total | 43 | 12,491 |
| Royton | 6 | 1,620 |
| Crompton | 7 | 1,867 |
| Chadderton | 8 | 1,853 |
| Saddleworth | 20 | 3,457 |

*Source:* Census 1851.

Every Parish Church and Chapel had a Sunday School, perhaps a modest building at first, but often larger and grander than its parent building. Philanthropy - gifts of land and building costs - were often important but as a rule the enterprise relied on voluntary effort and assiduous fund raising. People, it was said, would give to Schools when they would give to nothing else. Finding teachers could be a problem but generally these became available from the better-off classes. Many of the Sunday Schools were also to serve as voluntary denominational day schools.

The place and pride and rivalry of the Sunday Schools was demonstrated each Whitsuntide in the Walks. Thousands of children, specially dressed, often in clothes bought new or made for the occasion, paraded the streets of Oldham and each village behind their banners, accompanied by bands as the century grew older. The occasion usually ended in an outing, races and games in a field, buns and tea; more ambitious outings came later in the century. This was the most memorable annual Sunday School occasion although at every opportunity for a parade, the Sunday Schools of Oldham more than any other group showed their strength.

The new churches were concerned with public morals, with Sunday observance, with sober recreation in place of vulgar and brutal sports, and especially with the conspicuous menace of drink. Many nonconformists, but some Anglicans like Grundy of Hey, preached total abstinence. That message was put from the pulpit, it was inculcated in the young through the Band of Hope movement and it was proclaimed in the open air. It was mainly church and chapel people who supported the Oldham Temperance Society founded in 1833; by 1841 this organisation was to claim over 1,500 members, total abstainers. At first the Society met in school rooms but eventually acquired the public hall, built in 1844 as a "Hall of Science" by a group of working men, in Horsedge Street; this had acquired a mixed reputation and subsequently failed as a concert room and was available cheaply, at £450, half

**George Grundy**, graduate of Brasenose College, Oxford, was vicar of Hey from 1838 to 1901. He made an immediate mark for his firm stand against secular teaching, of writing in particular, in his Sunday School, but his formidable reputation derived from his inspirational preaching, stern leadership and devoted service to his congregation. A strong Tory, he loved his people and was careful to maintain a modest lifestyle. That was not always apparent; here he stands with his curate, wife and servants, outside Hey vicarage, built in 1854 at a cost of £1,135, about ten times the cost of a workman's cottage at the time.

its cost. The Temperance Society held two meetings weekly in Temperance Hall over many years, apart from their speakers on Tommyfield. Strong feelings were involved, especially regarding the desecration of the Sabbath. "The working people", James Platt wrote, when advocating a public park in 1846, were "driven to dissipating scenes for the Evening and Night of the Week, and by the same circumstances, compelled to continue therein during the sacred hours of the Sabbath, until, from force of habit, they look upon it as a right." Drink and religion were to be bitter rivals throughout the century.

### Education

Apart from what was provided by the Sunday Schools there was not much education for the ordinary people in early nineteenth century Oldham. There were the so-called Dame schools where, for 3d or 4d a week, children of caring parents might learn the rudiments of alphabet and reading from some woman, or perhaps an aged man, probably in the evening in a cottage kitchen. The 1833 Factory Act restricted children's hours of work to nine daily, and obliged cotton mills to provide limited education; probably there were a few factory schools as a result, good or bad according to the wish of the employer who met their expense, but it was reasonable to assume that Act was weakly enforced. While most children went to the Sunday Schools and received some instruction there, the standard of attainment is not clear. Leonard Horner, the Factory Inspector, found the district, like nearby Ashton "quite destitute of any day-school for the humbler ranks". He questioned whether "in any part of the civilised world a parallel case could be met with". Strong words indeed, but it is likely that at the time a high proportion of the working class in Oldham, adults and young people, were illiterate, uneducated, still clinging to many primitive beliefs and customs, and speaking an unpolished Lancashire language, full of idiom and vulgarisms.

**St. Peters School**, advertising itself in 1845. This was a fee-paying school that would be beyond the means of most people. Factory children were offered cheaper terms for half-time attendance.

Voluntary or denominational schools, as these were established, began to make a difference to literacy, manners and speech. By 1851 there were seventeen with 2,499 scholars in Oldham and its out-townships, and 922 attending such schools in Saddleworth. Especially the Anglican churches with their National Schools, and to a much smaller extent the Wesleyans and the Congregationalists, took the lead in providing schools, financed by their own resources and by modest charges for attendance but assisted by a small government grant towards the initial cost of buildings, and subsequently towards furniture and the like. Very cautiously the government also appointed inspectors, primarily to report on conditions in the schools. Thus St Mary's National School received a grant of £1,000 when it was founded. Sometimes the voluntary schools used Sunday School buildings; sometimes generally inadequate crowded separate buildings. Teaching staff would be ill-paid and virtually untrained; teaching method would rely heavily on monitors, the older more forward children teaching the younger. For much of the time the children attending would be doing nothing; the curriculum would be very narrow. The 1851 Census recorded sixty-nine teachers for over 70,000 people in the Parliamentary Borough. At St John's School in Hey, as an example, up to 300 children were taught, with strict discipline, in one room, by one schoolmaster, Ambrose Harrop, assisted by a mistress, Betty Platt.

There was of course no obligation to attend these schools; as the population grew, large numbers would not do so either because no convenient place was available, or because of expense or indifference. Probably fewer than one quarter of the children of the less well-off were going to the voluntary schools, and for many who enrolled, attendance was spasmodic for whatever reason, falling away drastically during periods of short time working. A high proportion of those going to school were boys, young girls being needed at home as baby minders. School provision in Oldham at mid-century was clearly grossly inadequate, probably worse than in any comparable town of its size.

The half-time system, applicable after the Factory Act of 1844, required children between the ages of eight and thirteen to attend school three hours daily, morning and afternoon in alternate weeks, but except at the largest concerns, which set up factory schools, the new law was still weakly applied. Many half-timers went to the voluntary schools but the half-time system did not really take effect until more comprehensive public schooling became available later in the century.

Finally, attracting the children of the better off, there were many small private day schools in Oldham charging fees; some took infants; some, the Academies, older children. Thus at the 1851 census, 3,660 children were attending over sixty private schools, these numbers suggesting that all the children of the better-off were receiving formal education. The very wealthy were already sending their sons and daughters away to boarding establishments and again there was a choice among these, at a convenient distance in the pre-railway age, charging fees up to twenty guineas a half year, and teaching basic subjects as well as music, drawing and dancing.

So far as education was concerned, the middle classes felt that they were able to take care of themselves; they were not greatly concerned about those whose future was work in the mill or the mine. The poorer classes felt that the Sunday Schools were enough; they did not interfere with work or cost anything. Generally they wanted their children at work as soon as possible, "to nurse a child, push a coal-tub, or perform the least service, in the eagerness to profit by their labour in good times, to meet the necessities of a family in bad ones". Certainly there was no popular demand for the state to intervene in providing education.

By mid-century the ancient grammar school close to the centre of Oldham

**The Old Grammar School** in School Croft, immediately behind the High Street, was in what had become one of the poorest Irish neighbourhoods. In 1843 one teacher taught seventy local boys, mainly the sons of tradesmen, in a single classroom. Twenty years later the school was hardly used.

in what had become one of the poorest parts of the town, adjacent to a slaughterhouse in one of the Irish quarters, was sadly run down. However distinguished its patronage, it was poorly resourced with an endowment of £30 annually. A single teacher was teaching seventy boys, mainly the sons of shopkeepers, in a single room without a playground when Leonard Horner, the Factory Inspector, visited in 1843. Twenty years later the number had fallen to a dozen and the school, described as filthy, was sinking into disuse. There was also a grammar school at Hollinwood, founded in 1786, but in much the same condition; it closed in 1869.

The Oldham Bluecoat School had been endowed by the wealthy hatter, Thomas Henshaw, as a charity school; its site was given by Joseph Jones, Junior of the coal family, and with the aid of a public subscription, the school was built over the period 1829-33. When opened, 50 poor boys from the district were admitted, this number rising towards 120 by mid-century, drawn not merely from Oldham and Saddleworth, but from Ashton, Rochdale and Manchester. The buildings were described as spacious and handsome, the school well run, and those fortunate to attend well provided for, unlike the great many of the town.

Butterworth, in 1826, thought Oldham "sadly defective" compared with other towns in the "lack of encouragement to the rising generation in the study of general literature or that of the arts and science". He was referring to the lack of a Mechanics Institute or a Library: a small subscription library in the town charged entrance and required a standard of dress and appearance which "precluded all the labouring classes". If young men wanted to read a newspaper they had to go to a public house. The first attempt to set up a Mechanics Institute failed in 1830 after a year. In 1837, under the leadership of the hatter, Horatio Nelson, a new initiative was taken to meet some of these needs with the foundation of the Lyceum. At first it met in

Henshaw Street and then in Queen Street, establishing a newsroom, library, and evening classes in a variety of subjects. Membership fees were charged, 8s a year, intentionally cheaper than those typical of Mechanics Institutes, and the Lyceum had some initial success with 576 members after three months; at the census of 1851, membership was reported as 408, predominantly, but not entirely, young men.

Perhaps more importantly, patronage of the Lyceum became a hallmark for Oldham's emerging elite, an indication of commitment to the "overthrow of ignorance and the advance of enlightenment". In 1847 the first "brilliant soiree" for the Lyceum was held in the new Town Hall, a grand reception and ball for the town's most prominent citizens and their wives. The Manchester press described the event as "quite unequalled in Oldham at any former period …….. and exceeding any similar celebration in second-rate towns". Not surprisingly, the Lyceum would shortly require its own prestigious building.

At the other end of town a Mechanics Institute, serving broadly similar purposes to the Lyceum, had been set up at Greenacres Moor with sixty eight members in 1851. Butterworth reported as many as twenty mutual improvement societies, literary institutes or similar bodies in the town and district early in the 1850s. One in Henshaw Street had 110 members; the Stockbrook Literary Institute in Chadderton had eighty members. A number of young men in Royton formed the Temperance Seminary, one of the most successful of all Lancashire working class ventures in self-improvement. In Saddleworth, Mechanic Institutes were set up at this time in Uppermill, Delph

**The Bluecoat School** on Oldham Edge was an Oldham landmark. Built in 1829-1833 as a charitable foundation, it provided residential education to poor boys not merely from Oldham but from a wider district extending to Rochdale and Manchester. This early print shows the school and the town with its smoking chimneys behind.

and Dobcross. Many of these organisations had a chequered history, lapsing for lack of support and then reviving under different leadership. The counter attraction of the pub was a strong one and fatigue at the end of a day's work another deterrent, as, for some, was the cost. But there were young men with the urge to extend their reading proficiency, acquire knowledge and develop skills in debate and argument. They, generally clerks and mechanics but also piecers, were determined to improve themselves and their prospects, whatever the obstacles. There was no public provision, and while the different voluntary initiatives had only a limited impact, a high proportion of Oldham's leaders and successful men in subsequent years were enabled to rise from poor origins by these means.

**Radical Oldham**

The new industrial community, or at least the town of Oldham itself particularly, soon acquired a reputation for radical behaviour. Whether the incidence of social protest and turbulence in Oldham over the period was different from that in other rapidly growing industrial towns is conjectural. In the 1790s the background of revolution on the Continent, the new political ideas of Tom Paine and the Rights of Man, subsequently the demand for the vote, were common throughout the country. During and after the Napoleonic Wars social distress and perceived injustice were widespread in a growing changing unstable economy, plagued by bad harvests and, at times, extreme food shortage and subject to powerful new influences. All the incidents of disaffection, disorder and riot are well recorded, for Oldham as for other communities in Lancashire and elsewhere, each of them proud of their involvements. Oldham may have acquired its particular reputation because it has attracted more comment and analysis by historians - "an almost excessive burden of interpretation" as one writer put it - rather than that radical protest was more frequent or more serious than elsewhere.

Much of the turbulence of the time was, as Rayner Stephens, the fiery Tory and radical preacher of Ashton said, "a knife and fork" question. Rowbottom never tired of describing the situation over the years in his diary; his general complaint is summarised thus:

> "The poor of this neighbourhood and country in general experience the most tortuous misery owing to the dearness of every necessary of life and the scarceness of work and uncommon low wages."

Responding to grievances of this kind, William Cobbett could tell an audience in Royton in 1832 that

> "the reform you want is to make you better off, to mend your wages, ........ to give you good clothing instead of rags and to send you beer and meat instead of miserable potatoes."

The riots of the early Napoleonic war in the Oldham district and across the country, were in large part motivated by very high prices of food, indeed, at times, almost famine conditions. The prices quoted in Rowbottom's diary, for example, show that the basic items in the general diet, oatmeal, flour and potatoes rose by over 40 per cent between 1792 and 1795, while between the

# Radical Oldham

This group of **Peterloo Veterans** records the significance of the events of 1819. Huge numbers of people from the Oldham district walked to Peterloo. Many years later they were proud to commemorate their involvement in what became an epic event in working-class history.

spring of 1799 and that of 1800 they increased by not less than 150 per cent, following harvest failure; this was the time when nettles were sold at Oldham for 2d a pound. The disturbances of 1812 began with food riots in Oldham, Ashton, Manchester and elsewhere.

Many of the thousands who walked across south Lancashire to Peterloo in 1819 were hand-loom weavers, whose livelihood at the time was being so harshly crushed. Such was the tension at this period that the Home Office's correspondent in Oldham could write, in 1818, that "the grand struggle is approaching"; the following year, before Peterloo, he reported that "the minds of the lower orders in these parts are exclusively occupied .......... with the expectation of an approaching explosion which is to produce a complete change in the present order of things". This was not to be but a few years later men of property were again deeply concerned. 1826 was a year of acute distress following the boom of 1825, and it was these circumstances which occasioned loom breaking throughout the textile districts. The most severe depression, as already mentioned, occurred between 1839 and 1842 with high food prices aggravating the consequences of severe unemployment, not merely in the Lancashire towns but across the country. This was the period of the Chartist agitation, and in 1842, more locally, the dramatic Plug Drawers riots which in the end, by stopping so many mills across Lancashire, brought about the recovery of trade.

These periods of general distress and political agitation apart, intermittently, slowly, life was improving, and with its relatively high-paying occupations, it was probably improving in Oldham more than in other places; the poor rate was among the lowest in England. If not in Crompton or Chadderton or Saddleworth, there were probably few hand-loom weavers left in Oldham after 1830. That being said, for the great majority life, if getting better, remained a struggle; wages had to be earned and hours of work were long and exhausting. Much of the argument and agitation of Oldham's radical activists was remote from the day-to-day concerns of ordinary working people. There was not much energy or motivation for protest except when men were idle or starving. Generally, even then, and at election times at the hustings and at the poll when street rowdiness, demonstrations and intimidation often approached a condition of riot, the street crowds, the mob if it can be so described, was predominantly made up of the "roughyeds" - rough lads, youths and young men, a few girls, bored, immature, mischievous, excitable, and seeking escape from crowded homes after work. They were a numerous group at the time, 5 to 10,000 strong, living in the poorer districts round the town centre, and easily roused. Stimulated by freely available cheap drink they were generally looking for a row, and would join any group on the rampage; otherwise they would fight among themselves, as they frequently did. To groups, such as these may be added the many who swelled their numbers out of mere curiosity, to see what was going on rather than to participate. Throughout nineteenth century Oldham it was never difficult for determined leaders to raise a large street crowd, or gather an audience on Tommyfield or Oldham Edge or in one of the few meeting halls, for a rousing speaker or an agitator. But demonstrations of this kind should not be confused with widespread popular participation.

After Peterloo, Samuel Bamford wrote of "the best and truest supporters of the radical cause, a small but firm band of patriots at Oldham". The district did perhaps have more than its share of determined activists, people interested in political ideas, and especially Reform, the right to vote. If the Reform issue was paramount in the period up to the Act of 1832, when Oldham, by vigorous representation, secured a two-member constituency, it remained lively thereafter in the Chartist movement. There were other issues which involved the activists, as elsewhere in Lancashire, namely the movement for shorter hours of work in factories, opposition to the new Poor Law of 1834, successfully postponing its implementation for many years, and the Anti-Corn Law campaign. Saddleworth, which certainly had a radical tradition through Peterloo seems to have gone quieter; the Chartist Feargus O'Connor was to speak of its "dull spirit," a "destitute parish" made up of "sleeping men".

For the most part the Oldham activists were middle class, tradesmen, men of property. That was true of William Knott, a hatmaker, of Alexander Taylor of Mumps, a prosperous provisions dealer, of James Quarmby, a bookseller or James Holladay, a successful cotton spinner. William Fitton, active for many years in Royton, claimed to be a surgeon. The issues that most concerned these men were their right to participate in political decision taking, locally and nationally, oppressive taxation and wasteful expenditure; they wanted to make government more accountable to the people. Many of them were Nonconformists. Their successful challenge to the church rates levied to pay for the rebuilding of St Mary's was a popular victory. These concerns were not uppermost to John Knight, described as "the most fervent and aggressive stalwart of local radicalism after the turn of the century". Knight remained a leader of radical protest in Oldham to the time of his death in 1837; some of his spoken opinions reflected a consciousness of class and underprivilege which was less characteristic of his contemporaries.

Oldham did have some distinctive incidents which, while not exactly manifestations of class war, indicate a tension and militancy in industrial relations in the town, especially between the well-paid skilled spinners, crucial to the mill operation, not too numerous, and easily organised, and their employers. A loose association of mule spinners had led to bitter strikes against wage reductions in the winter of 1826-27 and again in the summer of 1831. On each occasion, the use of strike breaking labour, knobsticks as they were called, to keep the mills in production had led to violence. This practice led to a more serious dispute in 1834 at Bankside Mill when a strike by spinners led the employer to engage new hands. There was violence between the strikers and the strike breakers; the police, feeble as they were, intervened and seized two of the protesters. The sequel, demonstration by a great body of people, strikers and their supporters, led to an assault on the Mill, extensive damage and looting, and the fatal shooting of someone in the crowd. Eventually the riots were quelled by the arrival of the militia who were then quartered in the town for several weeks. Meanwhile many factory operatives refused to work, hoping for support from other communities. After a fortnight the affair petered out although not without a great crowd honouring the funeral of the person shot.

The state of hostility continued and there was another spinners' strike over wages at the end of 1836 with a turnout at many of the Oldham mills lasting four months. Eventually the spinners went back to work on the employers' terms; they had not the resources, the discipline or the leadership to engage these disputes successfully at this time. Unsuccessful stoppages involving local weavers, hatters and miners took place in the depression year of 1841 while Oldham cotton operatives joined the mob from Ashton and Stalybridge in the Plug Drawing episodes of August 1842. The militia were again called to the town on this occasion before a general resumption of work took place, eighteen days after the first incident. When the cotton trade turned down again at the end of 1846 the spinners, concerned to avoid unemployment and wage reduction - the bitter experience of a few years earlier - urged their employers at large public meetings, with some success, to resort to short time, "eight or ten hours a day for a season." Short time working was to remain their preferred stance in subsequent periods of bad trade.

These early disputes, bitter as they probably were, and engaging intense feelings both on the part of those leading the operative spinners, and the employers and their friends, were well-remembered in Oldham. They did not measure up to the great Preston strike of the 1850s or the subsequent labour disputes in the Lancashire weaving districts or in Oldham itself later in the century. But they gave a stamp to the place. It shared its radicalism with other towns but in Oldham there was a particular edge; the tradition of militancy among the well paid spinners, established in this period, was to persist.

Meanwhile in the 1832 election the new constituency of Oldham elected two Radical MPs to the Reform Parliament. William Cobbett by the time he came to Oldham was an old man but, with his radical past, "idolised and deeply venerated" by many, although some activists had deeply felt differences with his views. John Fielden was a highly successful business-man who, with his brothers, had built "one of the richest houses in Lancashire",

**John Fielden,** MP for Oldham, 1832 - 1847.

**William James Fox,** (1786-1864) born a poor country boy, self-educated and then a Unitarian minister in London, emerged as a popular Radical pamphleteer and orator, full of eloquence and zeal, associated particularly with the campaign against the Corn Laws and in favour of popular education. Hardly a young man at the time, the Platts brought him to Oldham where he was successful against John Fielden in 1847, topping the poll. He lost his seat in July 1852 but fought again in the riotous by-election in December of that year when he was successful. Losing in 1857 he regained the seat in the same year and retired in 1862.

worth more than £300,000 in 1832. Described by the Manchester press as a "man of excellent character, ample fortune and liberal views", he must have commended himself to the Oldham men of property at the time. His particular Oldham supporters throughout were Jonathan Mellor, an active Tory - like himself a Unitarian, and wealthy man - and Joshua Milne, scion of an old Crompton family and a successful millowner. Fielden's election address committed him to "see the people restored their just rights, and especially the condition of the labouring portion of society greatly improved". He and Cobbett had no serious opposition at the 1832 election which suggested they were entirely acceptable to the voting elite of the time; Cobbett also stood as a Radical in Manchester where he was defeated. The new franchise gave the vote to the £10 householder but in 1832 the new Parliamentary Borough with a population of 50,000 people had no more than 1,131 electors.

John Fielden's subsequent views and behaviour - his successful resistance to the new Poor Law in Todmorden and particularly his leadership of the Ten Hours Movement - attracted the hostility of most millowners, resistant as they were to any form of state interference with their business activity and concerned with competition from overseas. To many of his class Fielden's radicalism was a paradox; he was selfish and hard in business, adamant in his concern for the rights of property, resistant to taxation of any form, and however paternal he was as an employer or publicly concerned with the plight of the hand-loom weaver, his own firm was one that led the way in the adoption of the power-loom. Of his popularity with the local radical activists and working men of Oldham for a time there can be no doubt. He was re-elected convincingly in 1837 in the bitter aftermath of the spinners' dispute, despite stronger local Tory opposition, and in 1841 he, and his fellow member, then General Johnson, were unopposed. These Radical election successes between 1832 and 1841, rather than the incidence of social protest and riot, are the strongest manifestations of Oldham's radicalism and the real basis of its reputation.

Fielden's support proved vulnerable and certainly by 1847 the men of business in Oldham were against him; all the significant cotton employers signed petitions against the Ten Hours Bill. The Platts and the Radcliffes, now prominent, turned to William Fox, a Unitarian parson, prominent dissenter, fluent writer and powerful speaker, described by a fellow Radical as "the bravest of us all" for his persistent advocacy of universal suffrage, church disestablishment, retrenchment, free trade and popular education. If Fielden had lost the support of men of property by his factory campaign, he split his radical supporters by the high handed way in which he insisted that John Morgan Cobbett, William Cobbett's son, and soon to marry his daughter, should be his fellow candidate. The younger Cobbett, rejected by the voters at the 1835 by-election following his father's death, was perceived to be insincere and conservative by many of Oldham's activists. Their instinct was probably right but Cobbett found his followers in the district, not least in the out-townships where he took a majority of the vote in 1835. He was subsequently to fight many Oldham elections, not without success.

Many of the radicals led by Alexander Taylor stayed with Fielden in 1847. Others who would not support Cobbett tried to promote James Holladay, one of their number, to stand. Eventually, led by Knott and Quarmby, they accepted William Fox with enthusiasm. With the radicals divided, the Tory elements in Oldham - families like the Jones, the Lees of Clarksfield and the Worthingtons of Hollinwood - themselves promoted a stronger local candidate, John Duncuft, a small but enterprising cotton-spinner and speculator in railway shares, a strong Anglican, living in Westwood. The stage was set for a bitter election, fought entirely over personalities because there were no large national issues in 1847. This was an occasion for frequent placarding, for intensive canvassing and for large scale intimidation. While the working men could not vote they could demonstrate at the hustings, as they did vociferously in favour of Fielden and Cobbett. Exclusive dealing, the threat to boycott tradesmen who did not support Fielden and Cobbett, was widespread and pernicious. On polling day a mob was roused to smash windows and break down doors of Fox supporters; the riot act was read, not for the first or last time. "At every time of political excitement here", it was later said, "life and property are in fearful insecurity". Fielden went down in 1847, bottom of the poll, "put out to grass" as he euphemistically said; bitterly disappointed, he died two years later. Two hundred millowners had voted against him. The election left Oldham with a new Radical MP, William Fox, and a Tory, John Duncuft.

The subsequent years were featured by much bad feeling, abuse and recrimination among political activists in the borough, Cobbettites on the one hand, followers of Fox on the other. This showed especially in the 1852 election campaign. Importantly, however, new middle class leadership in politics had emerged and these men, not least the Platts and Radcliffes on the one side, and the Clarksfield Lees and Greenbank Lees on the other, with their associates, and a greater degree of party organisation, were to control Oldham politics in the second half of the century.

**The By-Election of December 1852**, fought between Fox, the Radical, and Heald, the Tory, was the most acrimonious of all Oldham Parliamentary contests. Crowds and gangs of the rival factions roamed the town, accompanied by bands and flags, assaulting adversaries and damaging property, both at the hustings and at the ballot, creating turmoil and confusion in their attempts to influence and intimidate the small electorate. The Tory gangs, the so-called Bendigo Lambs named after their agent, inspired John Platt claimed "by ignorance and the beer barrel", were probably the most active, but the Radical side were not idle. On polling day, alarmed at the prospect of violent confrontation, the Riot Act was read and to calm a huge excited crowd a platoon of the First Dragoons took position in front of the Town Hall, as this early photograph shows. Various incidents followed before the poll was completed. Fox, who had kept away, won fairly comfortably, and life quickly returned to normal, that is mainly bed and work.

## Local Government

Since Elizabethan times what local government there was in each township was in the hands of the churchwardens, elected by the parish vestry each year. Other officers were also elected from recognised leaders in the community, overseers to provide for the poor - which they did in primitive workhouses or by outdoor relief - and to maintain the highways. To meet their costs, painstakingly minimised as they were, a rate could be raised on those holding land or property. A constable would deal with wrong-doing; in Oldham township there was a lock-up in Curzon Street and stocks in front of the Parish Church.

Inadequate as this structure was to cope with the problems and needs of rapidly growing communities there was little change up to the mid-nineteenth century, except in Oldham township itself. Here, to meet a number of concerns, collective or community action became imperative. Something had to be done to provide a public water supply, for instance, and as gas lighting began to be adopted throughout the country, provision had to be made for a public supply in Oldham. These purposes were met in some degree in 1825 with the formation of the Oldham Gas and Water Company; small reservoirs were built at Strinesdale and the first gas works started off Union Street, close to the town centre. The first manager of the new undertaking was George Emmott, a Quaker immigrant from Keighley; he founded a significant Oldham dynasty and began to build his own fortune, while still managing gas and water, by shrewd investment in land around Union Street and by successful involvement in cotton spinning.

The prime movers in the initiative for stronger collective action were the emerging new elite rather than the old gentry. Those prominent at the time include Joseph Jones Junior of the coal family; James Lees of Greenbank Mill; Nathan Worthington of the leading Hollinwood family, landowners and cotton manufacturers; Jonathan Mellor; and Horatio Nelson and Abraham Clegg of the hatmaking families. Most of this new elite were subsequently to become magistrates, recognising their standing. They were the people who pressed for the creation of a new institution for town government, the so called Police or Improvement Commissioners, securing an Act of Parliament in 1826. They were doing no more than following the example of other towns in a similar situation.

The preamble to the 1826 Act recognises the perceived problems of the day that called for new institutions and powers. The town had never "as yet been lighted or watched, except in a very partial manner, by private individuals", and this

**The Oldham Act of 1826**

*ANNO SEPTIMO*
## GEORGII IV. REGIS.

*Cap.* cxvii.

An Act for paving, watching, lighting, cleansing, and improving the Township of *Oldham* in the County of *Lancaster*, and for regulating the Police thereof.
[26th *May* 1826.]

WHEREAS the township of *Oldham* in the County Palatine of *Lancaster* is an extensive and populous township, a place of considerable trade and manufacture, a great thoroughfare for travellers, and in the vicinity of and in immediate connection with the most populous districts of the counties of *Lancaster* and *York*, and from its position and natural advantages hath of late much increased, and is rapidly increasing in population:

And whereas the said Township of *Oldham* hath never as yet been lighted or watched, except in a very partial manner, by private individuals, or by voluntary contributions, and the want of effectually lighting and watching has been productive of great inconvenience and danger to the inhabitants and others resorting to the said Township:

And whereas there are many streets newly laid out, and other streets, lanes, public passages, and places within the said township, the greater part whereof are not paved, or properly cleansed or repaired, but are subject to various nuisances and annoyances, endangering the health and comfort of the inhabitants:

And whereas there is no public building nor any suitable office or offices wherein to transact the public business of the said township:

And whereas it would tend to the safety, convenience, and advantage of the inhabitants of the said township, and all persons resorting to or travelling through the same, if the same were more effectually lighted, watched, and the Police thereof duly regulated; and if provisions were made for the paving cleansing,

was a source of inconvenience and danger. New streets and indeed most of the old streets and lanes "are not paved or properly cleansed or repaired and are subject to various nuisances and annoyances endangering health and comfort". Finally there was no public building or town hall "wherein to transact the public business".

Under the Act everyone owning property worth more than £50 a year, or paying a yearly rent of £30 or more could become a Commissioner; over 300 residents in the township were eligible. They were to meet monthly, appoint officers to discharge their responsibilities and could borrow up to £20,000 on mortgages and impose and collect a rate to meet their expenses subject to a maximum of 2s 6d in the pound on the annual value of each property. The Commissioners had extensive powers under the Act, to improve the town and regulate nuisances. Some provisions give the flavour of the time; thus the Act required householders to put sand on their foot pavements before eight in the morning at times of frost; pigs wandering the streets, a common nuisance, were to be seized and forfeited; beadles were to patrol the streets and apprehend those committing a broad range of offences ranging from drunkenness, singing ballads, insulting females, exposing the person indecently, playing games, and setting dogs to fight.

In short, a democratic body had very wide powers to improve Oldham and control its rowdy inhabitants. The results were completely unsatisfactory. Meetings of the Commission were a forum for argument between different factions in the town where prominent radicals in particular could air their views; they were little more than a talking shop. Rates were imposed but collected with some difficulty. Beadles and lamp-lighters were appointed, fire engines were purchased and firemen recruited and street scavenging started, but what was accomplished was quite inadequate. Policing for instance was left to three, later six beadles, helped by the town's five lamplighters whenever there was a threat of riot or disturbance; when serious riot threatened hundreds of special constables, mainly shopkeepers, were sworn in as in 1842. Poorly paid, the beadles were an unreliable force, prone to drunkenness and indiscipline, unpopular with the magistrates, and the town generally. At first they were augmented by night watchmen but dissatisfaction with this force led to its abandonment in 1831; thereafter those with property to safeguard had to appoint their own watchmen. The beadles appear to have done little about crime and were more concerned with sanitary nuisances and the traffic problems of the day.

Unsurprisingly, twenty years after the Commission was set up, a much larger town was in far worse condition, although costing about £7,000 a year to manage and having incurred a debt of over £11,000. Most of the streets were still unpaved and the source of loud complaint in wet weather; Union Street was frequently ankle deep in mud. Scores of horses and carts, carrying coal, iron, cotton, yarn as well as general supplies were a rapidly increasing traffic. On all sides there was evidence of foul sanitation and absence of cleansing; filth and foul smells were not confined to the courts and poorest streets but were conspicuous throughout the town. There was palpably insufficient policing. Market stalls obstructed the principal streets. The public water supply was inadequate and far too expensive for most of the population. Thick black smoke had become a new problem, from the

*Facing:* **James and John Platt:** the young Platt brothers became prominent following the death of their father. John (lower photograph) was the gifted ingenious mechanic with a keen eye for business opportunities and tremendous drive and energy; he took the growing machine-making business rapidly forward. James, the younger brother, more approachable and intellectual, looked after relations with the work-people and administration. Both became involved in local political activity, campaigning for the Charter, joining the new Council and establishing the Liberal party as the main political force in Oldham. They brought Fox to Oldham and James himself was elected to Parliament in 1857 before his premature death in a shooting accident the same year. John Platt became the first Liberal Mayor in 1854.

multitude of houses but especially from mill chimneys, where thousands of tons of coal weekly were being consumed; by 1850 most of the buildings were black, trees and shrubs in the town generally a thing of the past. The problem of burying the dead was now acute; the few church yards became completely full and decaying bodies were disturbed almost whenever a new burial took place.

Having no decent place to hold their meetings, the most visible evidence of the Commissioners' work was the Town Hall. The initial building, unpretentious but with an elegant portico, facing the Market Place and the Parish Church, was completed in 1841 at a cost of £4,810; the site had cost £1,700, subject to a ground rent of 2d per yard. Land was becoming expensive in Oldham but the town now had a recognisable centre. Inside the new Town Hall the rooms were modest but dignified, hardly providing adequate space for large public meetings. That need had to be met for many years by the Temperance Hall or the larger Working Men's Hall, also built in Horsedge Street by local Chartists who had been refused use of the Town Hall for a meeting; the latter was financed mainly by workers' subscriptions.

An unsuccessful attempt to incorporate the town was made in 1833; government recommendations to that effect were rejected at a public town meeting, largely because of radical objections led by the young William Knott. A further attempt to secure a charter of incorporation was made in 1840, largely to forestall the possibility of a larger police force, controlled by the county. Again there were strenuous objections on grounds of expense. Oldham might be a rough and dirty place but it was cheap to live in and many wanted to keep it so; getting a charter could cost £1,000. Many of the radicals were fearful of a small elite running an elected corporation; they enjoyed their large Commissioners' meetings.

But new men of influence and power now came on the scene, not least the Radcliffes and the Platts. They were less concerned with emotional debate and more with the well-being and progress of the town and its reputation. Writing of the millowners in 1844, Samuel Bamford commented "in politics

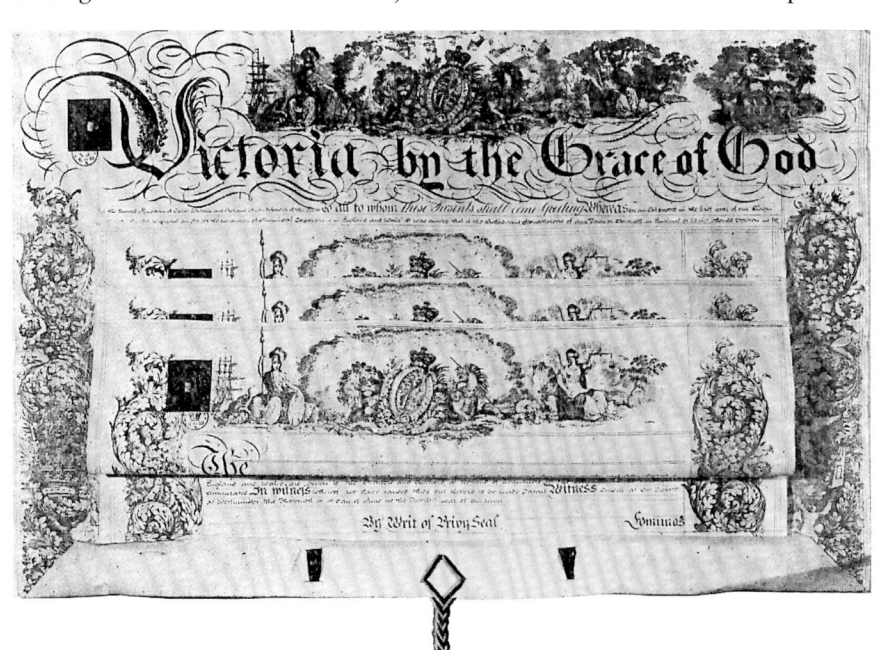

**The Charter of Incorporation**

they as a body are but new beginners and it is but lately that leaders of ability in their own rank have sprung amongst them". He might have been speaking of John and James Platt in particular, still young men but with a powerful inheritance following the death of their father, flushed with business success and quickly acquired wealth, who now assumed a prominent role. In subsequent years they were to give their time and their energy, if not their money, profusely, and now took the lead in urging that Oldham should become a Borough whose collective affairs could be managed by an elected Corporation rather than a town meeting, a body that would have more vigour and get better results and would also lend dignity and prestige to the town.

The Platts' initiative to seek a charter became a political issue; Fox Radicals or Liberals on one side, and these included many cotton manufacturers, led by the Platts, opposed dissident Radicals led by those who had supported the defeated John Fielden, allied with the Tory group, the Jones, the Clarksfield Lees, James Lees of Greenbank, James Collinge and the Worthingtons whose fears were that a Corporation would be a great deal more expensive. After extended controversy the Platt group got their way. A Charter of Incorporation was granted and a new Borough was formed. Bitterly contested elections to a new Council made up of three councillors from each of eight wards were held in July 1849. The voters' list then included 2,919 names. Perhaps to general surprise, the Tory and other factions who had opposed incorporation won the councillors' election, and appointed their own aldermen for each ward, some of them being defeated candidates, "men out of the street" as it was said, a highly unpopular move. One of their number, William Jones of the coal and land family, became the first mayor. The first Town Clerk, John Summerscales, was a political appointment.

The new Corporation was, of course, a tighter more focused body. Its powers were not greater than those of the old Commissioners but it was capable of stronger will and resolution. The tasks and challenges facing it were formidable and an indication of the difficulties it would face had emerged in an earlier incident. The Platts, Radcliffes, Worthingtons and many others joined by the Anglican Vicar, Thomas Lowe, and the emerging Nonconformist leader, Richard Davies of Hope Chapel, proposed that Oldham should have a public park. An earlier initiative to create two public walks, at Werneth Coppice and Greenacres Moor, had failed despite the offer of a grant of £1,000 from the Commissioner of Parks and Forests. Now, at the end of 1846, with the same government grant on offer and influenced by the example of Manchester where three parks had been built at a cost of £30,000, and by the new cause of "national recreation" to elevate "the physical, mental and moral condition of the people", a major effort to create a park was made through public meetings, petitions and vigorous attempts to solicit funds.

Alexander Taylor, in urging the scheme, regretted the earlier enclosure of Oldham's commons and the fact that a town of over 40,000 inhabitants "had not even an acre of ground which could be said to be public property for the purposes of healthful exercise of this great community". Revd. Lowe spoke of men "working twelve hours in an unhealthy atmosphere and going perchance to a miserable, comfortless home ..... tempted in too many instances by the allurements of the pernicious beer-house". John Platt spoke of a public park as a "truly noble monument to the public spirit of the people of Oldham". The Platts, from their bounty, promised £250; their workpeople £125; the Radcliffes £250, and John Fielden MP, worth at least £200,000, offered £100, and John Duncuft the same amount. But in total only £1,843 could be raised, an insufficient amount, and the scheme was quietly abandoned in 1847. Clearly the new elite, let alone the multitude of small masters, could not be persuaded to "open their pockets" on an adequate scale.

**Oldham at mid-century**

While the out-townships and Saddleworth continued their comparatively modest progress, Oldham township, now a Borough, seemed a dynamic entity. It had an established position in coarse cotton spinning with a multitude of enterprises, large and small, and its rapidly growing textile machinery businesses were creating a national, if not wider, reputation for innovation and quality in that field. A host of ancillary activities supported these pillars of the economic base.

By mid-century, although all classes were living close together, social differentiation was becoming more pronounced and would increasingly be reflected in respectable and poor neighbourhoods in separate parts of the town. There were already differences in income, in education, in habits and lifestyle, in religious observance, but these were to become much larger in later years. "There was no place in the world" it was said, "where so many working men had risen to be masters, men who could scarcely write their own name who were now in a respectable position in society". The presence of so many self-made men was itself a great motivator, fostering the belief that anyone could achieve success by energy and perseverance. Some of the new elite, the large employers, the more successful, had already set themselves apart following, for the most part, an ostentatious lifestyle. But they still lived in the town and through their various leadership and patronage roles, remained deeply involved in it; they had no feelings of guilt believing that those who had made fortunes, enriched the whole community. Below them there were the many small employers, professional men, shopkeepers and close to them the overlookers, skilled artisans, many of the spinners: these were described as:

> "well fed, becomingly clothed, moderately versed in educational attainments, grave and firm on devotional subjects, sober in their domestic habits, respectful in their demeanour."

These men and their families would be the pillars of church and chapel; they made up the growing intermediate class who aspired to be respectable and independent. Among them "an improvement in manner and intellectual cultivation is beginning to be visible", as one visitor said.

These respectable classes would not want to mix with the more numerous poor, "improvident, intemperate, gross in spirit, sensual in their dispositions, and vicious in their pleasures", as they were described, let alone the lowest group, the occupants of the Bent, the Irish, the class that was later to be identified as the residuum. Such was society in mid-century Oldham, overwhelmingly working class but increasingly differentiated. All were described as hospitable and warm hearted "gradely folk", persevering, diligent, honest, generous, always cheery, however rough and blunt their manners and speech.

The Committee advocating a public park in 1846 wrote of the people of Oldham:

> "All sections of society, from the richest to the poorest, have hitherto been so occupied in manufacture as to leave scarcely any room to think of the cultivation of the mind, or the due recreation of the physical powers, beyond the attainment of elementary instruction, or the acquisition of pleasure from social tavern converse".

But horizons were widening. The railway had reached Werneth in 1842, to be extended after prolonged argument and attempts to promote rival schemes, to Mumps in 1847; it gave much cheaper and faster accessibility to other places. Working people were slowly beginning to enjoy the benefits of an expanding economy; they had more to spend and more goods and services were becoming available. The days when their lives were little beyond "eating, drinking, working and dying" were passing. They had more leisure, if modestly at first as the Ten Hours Act gave earlier finishing in the evening. Life was going to become a great deal better.

Oldham as a town had a new Corporation and a rising energetic middle class that could address its problems, many as these were. With Lancashire and the cotton industry on the threshold of a great boom, Oldham could enter the period of its ascendancy in a mood of confidence and promise, sustained by the spirit of great industry and aggressive enterprise and speculation which had already been powerfully demonstrated. In due course the limited liability movement was to harness new sources of risk capital which would drive the town's industry forward. Oldham people, it was said, were "more indebted to art and industry than to nature, and they supplied by that industry what nature had denied them". What had been achieved was by their own efforts. But many believed that just as industry, and thrift, had brought about their individual success and the transformation of the place, so these qualities alone could sustain that success. Parsimony, or economy, a less harsh term, was to become a guiding principle for the new town government.

"Property has its obligations", James Platt wrote, "the chief of which is to provide sufficient means for the health and morality of the people from whom it springs, or among whom it is preserved". That was one view. But as the public park affair had shown, Oldham's many self-made men, succeeding by enterprise, hard work and thrift, were to prove extremely reluctant to part with their wealth to pay for public purposes. "There is such a desperation among the manufacturing community" one member of the class could say, "to save and to get, that they forget the comfort of those around them". In Oldham, as in other new towns, "the place and the staple trade had grown so much that there was no leisure to attend to much besides the production of wealth .... taste and comfort, and even health itself, must all give way to the one great necessity of productive work". If other places could "excel in splendour" that was not for Oldham; rather the town would prove itself by "the usefulness of its achievements". That was the prevailing mood at mid-century.

**Carse's water-colour** shows Oldham Town Hall at mid century. Facing the Parish Church, the building brought a modest dignity to the centre of the town; here was the natural place of assembly on all public occasions. The view looks down Yorkshire Street with the rising ground of Greenacres in the background.

# Ascendancy: Oldham 1849 - 1919

# Chapter IV

# COTTON SPINNING CAPITAL OF THE WORLD

**Mid-Victorian Boom**

The decade of the 1850s was a golden period for the Lancashire cotton industry. In absolute terms its growth was not exceeded in any comparable period. Numbers of mills, installed spindles and looms, the workforce employed, all grew by more than 50 per cent. Likewise cotton consumption rose from an average 613 million pounds in 1849-51 to an average of 1,023 million pounds in 1859-61. The world-wide demand for cheap cotton cloth seemed inexhaustible and Lancashire enterprise and skill, and expanding American raw cotton production, was able to supply it, without, at the time, significant competition.

Leonard Horner, the Factory Inspector, could write in 1852, "New mills were being built on all sides and machine makers are said to be overwhelmed with orders." Enterprise and capital were attracted by the exceptional profits on yarn and cloth which prevailed in 1852 and 1853. Profits came under pressure in 1854 and subsequent years, and especially in 1857, the year of the Indian Mutiny, when depressed demand aggravated by wide-spread bank and business failure coincided with a poor American cotton crop and high cotton prices. But the decade closed with a renewed extraordinary boom, fuelled by the huge surge in exports to India once the Mutiny was over, and by cheaper cotton. Profits in the industry rose throughout 1858 and 1859 and climaxed in 1860 when they were as high as in any comparable period in the period to the World War. As always the boom went too far. Markets were oversupplied in 1861, profits fell away and poor trade and short time working were checking the industry's expansion even before the onset of the American Civil War and the Cotton Famine.

Oldham and the townships took full advantage of the boom. By now the concentration of cotton spinning was yielding external economies of scale: a skilled experienced workforce; an adapted infrastructure of support; a wealth of ancillary manufacturing activities from manufacture of skips (baskets), bobbins, ropes, and spindles through to specialised sophisticated machine making, and perhaps to Platt's mules in particular. The strength of these benefits, exploited by driving competitive individualism, a go-ahead spirit and the urge to make money, easily enabled Oldham to overcome its comparative disadvantages. Important as the coming of the railway was, first to Werneth and then through the town, Oldham was ill-served by rail transport as it was to complain about forcefully over many years. But the town was only seven miles from Manchester where the Royal Exchange was becoming the greatest market for yarn and cloth in the world. Not surprisingly, Oldham's spinning capacity doubled in the decade of the Fifties to about 3 million spindles in

1862, by then about 9 per cent of the industry's total; many more looms were also added.

Older mills were rebuilt and extended during this period but a feverish phase of mill building started at the height of the boom; twenty-eight new mills were completed in Oldham between 1858 and 1863, sixteen in 1860 alone. By 1862 the district had 150 cotton mills of which 120 were in the Borough. The workforce employed in cotton in the entire district had grown from 20,614 in 1851 to 27, 273 at the Census of 1861, a much lower increase than that of capacity. There were huge gains in productivity resulting mainly from the larger and faster self-acting mules that were now being more widely adopted, and an increase in the number of looms worked by each weaver. The large wage increases that were achieved during the boom reflected these productivity gains.

Some of the mill enlargement and rebuilding took place around the town centre. But the new mills were mainly sited on accessible and cheaper flat land close to the main roads leading from the town. In particular Northmoor, Westwood and Busk adjacent to the Middleton Road, and the fringes of Chadderton, attracted new developments at this time. A cluster of new mills grew along the Ashton Road. A few were also built along Shaw Road and in Shaw itself, which was becoming the main centre of the Crompton township; this was to be helped by the completion of the railway link to Oldham and Rochdale in 1863. New steam driven cotton mills were also built in Greenfield and Uppermill in Saddleworth during the pre-Civil War boom, adding to the dwindling number of older woollen mills. Like the earlier mills, these new Oldham mills still relied heavily on timber in their construction, for beams, joists and lathes and for floors; given the inflammable material they handled, fire risks were enormous and mill fires, sometimes disastrous, now became a regular feature of the Oldham scene. Multiple-occupation, by many small concerns, of old and new mills remained a feature of the Oldham district. Between 1858 and 1861 many new firms were started in this way, as a rule by men who had been overlookers and were able to borrow, usually on a mortgage. But this was the period when the large private concerns that were

**Wellington Mill, Greenfield**, was Saddleworth's largest cotton mill, built in 1853 and enlarged in 1861 at the peak of the mid-century boom; in 1900 it had 85,000 mule spindles. The picture shows the new rows of terrace houses as Greenfield and Uppermill developed into industrial villages; at the same time the numbers living on the scattered hillside farms and cottages were falling sharply.

**Woodend Mill, Shaw**, built in the mid-century cotton boom as an extension of the older Park Mill. A & A Crompton were one of the large private cotton businesses in Crompton/Shaw. Along with the Cleggs at High Crompton they retained their prominence, even when Shaw came to be dominated by the large mills of the Limiteds later in the century.

prominent at mid-century, generally combining spinning and weaving, confirmed their position of leadership, laying the foundations of some of Oldham's largest family fortunes. To mention some examples, James Lees was in his prime at Greenbank Mills on Glodwick Lane; at the nearby Commercial Mills, "Collinges" as it was known, control had passed for a period from James Collinge to his nephew Edward Abbott Wright. These two

# Mid-Victorian Boom

large concerns greatly extended their operations in 1860. Eli Lees enlarged his combined spinning and velvet weaving Hope Mill in the 1850s, adjacent to his brother Asa's Soho Ironworks. James Greaves and his son Hilton expanded their business at Derker Mill off Huddersfield Road. There were new mill-owning dynasties emerging over these years: the Emmotts were steadily acquiring established spinning and weaving businesses in Oldham town; the Mellodews with a large combined mill were dominating the village of Moorside. In Crompton and Shaw, leadership lay with the several established family concerns: A. and A. Crompton at Park and Woodend Mills; James Cheetham at Clough Mill; and the brothers John and Joseph Clegg who went their separate ways with their own successful mills at Sandy Lane.

The Oldham industry was thus still one of a multitude of private businesses, large and small, paternal and individual, flourishing, stagnating or failing according to the acumen and drive of family members, their willingness to re-invest as distinct from withdraw capital, and their ability to find able successors from one generation to the next. Many private firms failed, gave up or sold out; some achieved high success.

Cotton aside, Oldham's engineering firms were quick to seize the opportunity of strong demand for textile machinery of all kinds across Lancashire. The numbers employed in metal working and engineering grew from 2,481 to 6,531 between the two Censuses of 1851 and 1861. Probably about two-thirds of the output of textile machinery went into Lancashire mills, but even at this stage a third was being exported, principally to Europe.

**Oldham Panorama, 1879**: more than any words, this photograph describes the heart of Oldham as it had then become, an ugly smoke-blackened clutter of factories, workshops, crowded streets with a few public buildings. The town centre around the Parish Church and Market Place is now linked by continuous development to the congested Bottom of Moor off the picture to the right. The first gas works and the railway are prominent in the foreground; Waterloo Road crosses the scene from the right foreground and Rhodes Bank Colliery with two shafts is in the right centre. "Lancashire towns" a contemporary had written, "are generally regarded ......... merely as places of business, as places endurable because they are money making." Alfred Emmott, later Lord Emmott, growing up in Oldham at this time, described the town as "a dirty picture in a golden frame", much the same statement as, "where there's muck there's brass".

*The Economist* could comment in March 1860 "that never before have the machinists found themselves so fully employed". Platts, in particular, flourished in this period, greatly extending their works in Werneth; John Platt claimed to employ 5,400 mechanics, labourers and boys, in 1861. Coal mining also retained its role, although supplying a diminishing part of local needs, and Oldham still had over 2,000 miners in 1861. The hat making business of Oldham however, continued to decline with only about 300 workers in the same year.

TABLE VII: POPULATION CHANGE 1851-1861

|  | 1851 | 1861 | Percentage Increase |
|---|---|---|---|
| Oldham Borough | 52,818 | 72,334 | 37 |
| Chadderton | 6,188 | 7,482 | 20 |
| Crompton | 6,374 | 7,032 | 10 |
| Royton | 6,974 | 7,489 | 7 |
| Saddleworth | 17,779 | 18,631 | 5 |

So large an expansion in activity supported a huge increase in population. Oldham's grew by 37 per cent in the decade to 72,334 people in 1861. It was in this period of the Fifties and early Sixties that the St Mary's and Bottom of Moor districts were completely built up with close packed streets and courts. New streets to a somewhat higher standard were built in Werneth and especially Westwood, close to Platts' New Hartford Works and the new spinning mills either side of the Middleton Road, still within easy walking distance of the town centre. Although more and more land was covered with mills and houses, there was still plenty of room on the slopes of Greenacres, Coppice and Glodwick; the Borough's population was to double from 1861 to the end of the century.

The growth of the townships had not really started. Except on the fringes of Chadderton, the drive of the cotton spinning industry had not yet reached the meadowlands that surrounded Oldham to the north and west; that was for later. Lees, not recognised as an administrative unit, remained a small place of about 2,500 people. Saddleworth, growing slowly, was being left behind by its aggressive neighbour.

**The Cotton Famine**

Oldham, in the early Sixties, could only take pride in its astonishing and phenomenal progress in activity and population, now surpassing other Lancashire towns; the name of Oldham, it was claimed, was known throughout the world. Townsmen and visitors were quick to attribute prosperity to the independent enterprising spirit and untiring industry of Oldham people. But a rude shock was imminent. The conflict between the North and the South in the United States developed into a fighting war in the course of 1861. Eventually shipments of cotton from the Southern ports was blockaded and the Cotton Famine developed. Shortage of cotton began to be felt in the summer of 1862 and frenzied speculation in Liverpool then drove cotton prices towards 30d a pound, six times the previous level. They were to remain above 20d for the next three years, rationing the limited supplies that were reaching the market, taken from stocks accumulated before the war that were now released at enormous profit, American cotton that evaded the Northern blockade, and increasingly imports from other sources such as India and Brazil.

The second half of 1862 was the worst period of the Famine, not so much because cotton was unavailable as because the profit for working it disappeared; the selling prices of yarn and cloth had not risen to anything like the same extent as raw cotton. "To manufacture cotton bought now into goods now sold can only entail a very heavy loss" wrote *The Economist* on 27 December 1862. This was the time when mills throughout Lancashire stopped, or went on sharply reduced working. UK cotton consumption fell to 452 million lbs in 1862 compared with 1,007 million lbs the preceding year.

Once reduced output of yarn and cloth took its effect, their prices rose and profits came back to more adequate levels. And in 1863 more and more cheaper cotton began to arrive from non-American sources, especially Surat, as Indian cotton was called. Surat was different in character; its fibres were short and difficult to work, but spinners learned to use it, as they also learned to use more cotton waste. These cheaper materials helped to restore the profit margin. The worst of the Famine was over by the summer of 1863. Cotton consumption began to recover and had reached 723 million lbs in 1865, about three quarters of the pre-war level. Throughout this period cotton was always available to those willing and able to pay the price but many small firms had not the resources to do so. Most firms, large and small, were inhibited by the enormous risks they were assuming. Not only were prices extremely high; they were dangerously volatile, lurching one way or the other as news and rumours reached the market of battles lost or won, of "peace scares" and the like. Business became a lottery, with profit depending much more upon catching the turn of the market than operational skill.

Oldham like other places took the shock severely in 1862. As mills stopped working thousands of people lost their incomes. As their circumstances became desperate, reluctant as they were to be regarded as paupers, they could only turn to the Poor Law Guardians who could not cope; new forms of relief had to be organised, as they were by Oldham's leading employers. At the end of 1862 over 27,000 people, at least a quarter of the population of the district, were getting relief, that is money to buy food and coal or pay the rent. That was the peak of hardship; the numbers on relief fell thereafter. The acute distress of this period, less in Oldham than in other Lancashire cotton towns, has been vividly described by historians. Also placed on record is the passive forbearance of those in distress, enormously reassuring to men of property at the time, ever fearful still of riot and disorder. Serious riots did occur in Ashton, Stalybridge and Hyde in March 1863 and fears that they would spread to Oldham occasioned the swearing in of many of the town's shopkeepers as special constables. If tense, Oldham remained quiet and a brief show of force as 150 cavalry of the 14th Hussars rode through the streets aroused no more than curiosity. Relief to Oldham came from many sources including a gift of 100 barrels of flour from a group of Oldham families who had established themselves in Philadelphia in the 1850s; they specified that Austerlands and Lees should share in the gift.

Especially in 1863 and 1864 many small and medium sized Oldham spinners failed, generally those renting space and in the older mills. They were the ones less able to adapt their machinery to use Surat or waste; they had no financial reserves to meet the burdens of closing down their operations for a while; they were more prone to get caught out by the dangerous cotton market in the later months of 1864 and early 1865. The larger established firms with the resources and skills to survive were happy to see such competitors go under. Their own view remained confident and optimistic; they could look forward to renewed expansion of the industry after the war in a market starved of cloth. Some of them, who had foreseen the huge rise in cotton prices and laid in stocks of cotton or yarn or cloth, were able to add hugely to their profits as values appreciated. Their overwhelming consideration was to keep their hands together, prevent workpeople drifting away or emigrating to places like Queensland or North America whose allure, enhanced by free passages, was advertised weekly in the Oldham press. Letters from Oldham people who went to Queensland in 1862, complaining of lack of work and accommodation, low wages as more emigrants arrived, and abominable flies, were prominently featured in 1864, and highlighted by John Platt.

A complementary consideration among employers was to avoid demoralisation and loss of self respect among the workforce, the perils of idleness and dependence, the possibility of social unrest. R. M. Davies, the parson of Hope Chapel, held in high regard in the town, could reassure the public with his message

> "the time may be long and while it lasts it will be dark and gloomy. Do not give way to despair and depression. After this calamity is gone, there's a good time coming, lads."

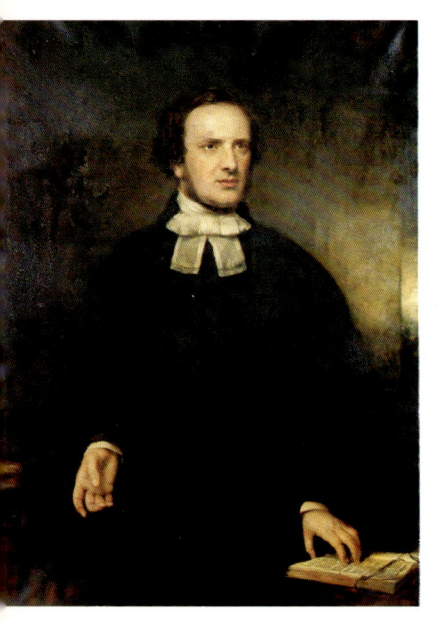

**Richard Meredith Davies** came to Oldham as minister at Hope Congregational Chapel, Bottom of Moor in 1843. He was to remain there for fifty years. Apart from his preaching gifts, which filled his chapel over his lifetime, he first assumed a prominent public role as Chairman of the Relief Committee in the Cotton Famine. He was later to be the long-serving Chairman of the School Board. No public occasion was complete without him; his wise words, eloquence and wit invariably caught the right sentiment. He would please his audience when he said of Oldham, "the stern unflinching, uncompromising independence of its working men, the ingenuity of its devising men, the enterprise of its commercial men, the philanthropy of all its men, have won my admiration".

Relief in the form of cash, clothing, clogs, coal and food was basic in the worst times. But above all the working man needed "summat to do". Sewing classes, elementary education, minor public works were not really the answer. In one way or another the mills had to keep working or get working again. And that was what Oldham accomplished.

Some of the large employers who had bought cotton in advance, worked full time throughout the Famine. Others were able to keep going by their skill in adapting and developing their machinery to use what cotton was available, especially Surat, augmented by cotton waste. In this endeavour they were ably assisted by the technical resources of Platts and Asa Lees. Thus the employment experience of Oldham, sharp as it was, was a great deal less severe than for other Lancashire towns; by the summer of 1863 most people were in work again, not full-time, maybe, but enough.

The Famine, of course, affected not merely the cotton spinning and weaving concerns, but the range of ancillary activities. All suffered loss of business as the mills closed or worked short time. Most of Oldham's collieries went on short time working. This was also the experience of the thirty or so engineers, foundries, boiler and spindle-makers and the like. But they recovered quickly and the fact that by July 1863 nearly 90 per cent of the engineering workforce were back to full-time working, indicates the competitive vigour of the Oldham enterprises and the fact that somewhere, even at the depths of the Famine, customers could be found for machines. Clearly some among the larger well-resourced businesses chose to use limited working as an opportunity to replace old machinery and modernise or even extend their plant, installing new carding engines and larger self-acting mules, in particular. Platts and Asa Lees were admirably placed to fill the need; John Platt was later to claim that Oldham actually increased its capacity by as many as 250,000 spindles during the Famine. Meanwhile the waste business, which Oldham people had made their own, flourished. Thus in terms of Oldham's economic drive, the Famine, while a shock, was no more than a temporary set back. It may indeed have been beneficial, eliminating weaker competitors in Oldham and elsewhere.

**Leaps and Bounds: Flotation Mania**

When the Civil War ended, cotton prices fell erratically for several years as supplies from America were restored; with falling prices the late 1860s were a difficult period in Lancashire, aggravated by commercial crises in the City of London. But as so often in Victorian England a new surge forward followed, the extraordinary boom of the early 1870s, started perhaps by the Franco-Prussian war, and encouraged by strong demand for goods in North America, across Europe, and in India and China. This was the period when Gladstone was to speak of the economy expanding by "leaps and bounds". In Lancashire, where the industry was now back to cheap American cotton, profits rose sharply, reaching or even surpassing those of the period immediately prior to the Civil War.

Characteristically the response to boom and high profit was to put down more capacity, build more mills. But now in Oldham there was a difference. If elsewhere in Lancashire it was private capitalists, whether the established concerns or new ones, who invested in expansion in the traditional way, the surge in Oldham was dominated by a new form of enterprise, limited liability companies floated by local promoters and financed by the savings of the populace at large. Oldham at this time, with its hardworking, thrifty and acquisitive population, gave birth to "popular capitalism", contributing money for investment that the old private employers could never have hoped to attract. Widespread involvement and participation in limited companies was an enormous stimulus to performance and a source of the extraordinary dynamic drive which now made the town the cotton spinning capital of the world.

The principle of limited liability, where an investor's risk was limited to the share capital he owned, had been established earlier. Before the Cotton Famine, many "co-operative" mills had been floated in Lancashire, with a large proportion of the shares being owned by working men, inspired by the dream of owning their own workplace and "becoming masters of themselves". Most of these ventures failed in the Famine; one that had started in Oldham in 1859, the Oldham Building and Manufacturing Company, initially as a weaving business but then going into spinning at the Sun Mill in Chadderton, equipped with Platt's self-acting mules, had survived.

With 60,000 spindles in 1865 the Sun was far larger and more modern than most other mills. The co-operative ideal of the "labouring class elevating

**Royton Spinning Company's first mill** was built in 1871, one of the earliest Limiteds. The idea of a co-operative mill in Royton had been debated in 1861 following the example of the Sun Mill. Deferred by the Cotton Famine, and then revived, the Company's swift success in the boom years of the early 1870s inspired the flotation of many other mill building companies. The new mill was built on Dog Kennel Meadow, a field that had housed kennels from nearby Royton Hall. Bricks were made from clay found on the site although this source proved inadequate; some 3 million bricks were needed in total. The mill took over a year to build, and was equipped with 50,000 mule spindles and the appropriate carding engines and preparatory machines on the first floor. Initially it employed only sixty operatives. The second mill was added in 1882. Both J. B. Tattersall and T.E. Gartside, leaders of the Oldham spinning industry as they subsequently became, learnt the business at Royton Spinning.

**The Directors of the Royton Spinning Company, 1871**: very typical of the Boards of the early Limiteds, they were mainly skilled working-men and local tradesmen, earnest and responsible in their intentions. George Holden, the Chairman, born of old Royton stock, educated in the village school and at night school, had worked in a cotton mill from the age of twelve. He advanced to management, became active in the co-operative movement and local politics. Such a Board at the time would have no difficulty in raising share and loan capital from the general public. Many of the Directors, like George Holden, would join the boards of other Limiteds.

itself commercially by owning shares in their place of work", which had inspired its formation, had withered away. By 1867 it had become "an association of small capitalists employing other workpeople", as Gladstone described it on his visit that year, when he was told that only four of its thousand shareholders were employees. From 1864, as well as share capital, it had been attracting savings from the public in the form of loan capital offering competitive rates of interest and easy access if the money was needed. Sun Mill began paying quarterly dividends on its share capital in 1867 which in 1871-73, reached an average of 25 per cent annually. It became a dramatic model, a corporate firm where working men, shopkeepers and the like could lend their savings, or buy shares without difficulty, and while taking larger risks as shareholders, augment their incomes with huge dividends paid from the profits that had traditionally accrued to private capitalists.

There were other striking early successes on the same lines, such as the Greenacres Mill Company, floated in 1871 by co-operative enthusiasts from the Oldham Equitable Society, and paying a 20 per cent dividend in 1874 and, in one quarter, at the rate of 42 per cent. Central Mill, another early Limited began to spin in 1872 and could pay out 40 per cent in 1874; Royton Spinning Company, set up in 1871 by Royton co-operators led by George

Holden, paid dividends from 1873 to 1875 that comfortably exceeded the paid-up cost of the shares. These and other examples deserved emulation, not least when business conditions and profits were right.

In a thrusting community obstacles and constraints could be put aside. Given a body of eager promoters, themselves bringing expertise of mill operation and commercial transactions, it was easy to set up and promote a limited company. Informal groups of enterprising individuals would decide impulsively over a potato pie dinner or a pint of ale, to float a company. Many schemes were hatched in the Black Swan Inn at Bottom of Moor, frequented by Oldham's cotton waste dealers. The Hey Spinning Company was started in 1875 by members of the congregation at Hey Church, encouraged by their long serving vicar, George Grundy. Legal, accounting, banking services quickly developed in the centre of Oldham, responding to the opportunity. Once the concept caught on, excited by the promise of high dividends, there was no problem selling shares to the public, nor in attracting savings in the form of loan capital. There were specialists who could design and build mills, equip and commission them, and there were pushing working men who could manage them, keep their accounts, buy their materials and sell their output, aspiring to become directors. All these contributory elements developed, evolved, came together, within a period of a few years, fuelled by the versatile competitive individualism and money-making zeal, already a feature of Oldham. This was the basis of the first great Oldham boom.

By 1872 there were fifteen "co-operative" spinning companies in Oldham. These early Limiteds, as they became known, still remained peripheral to the local spinning industry; by 1872 Oldham's spindleage had risen to over 5 million, but was still mainly in private concerns. The Flotation Mania of 1873-75 was to follow and change the situation. In total seventy limited companies were established in Oldham during these years, thirty-seven of which were formed to build new mills, the rest to buy out private concerns. Typically these early mill building companies had a nominal share capital of about £50,000, in £5 shares, only a proportion of which was called or paid on issue, and taken up by small shareholders. The Moorfield Mill Company in Shaw, for instance, floated in 1875, issued 14,000 £5 shares, £4 of which was called or paid by 1878; it had 772 initial shareholders of whom 629 had fewer than twenty shares each; only twelve shareholders had more than 100 shares.

It is difficult to describe the Mania which gripped Oldham between 1873 and 1875 or the extraordinarily eager demand for shares, a demand that frequently drove prices to a premium even before shares were allotted. There were cases in January 1875, the crest of the wave, where people fought to get hold of shares; where scuffles took place to secure application forms as in the so called "Shaw orgy", or at the launch of the Swan Mill Company at the Black Swan Inn when 11,666 £5 shares were taken up in 20 minutes. Many who bought shares in those circumstances did so not for the expected stream of dividends, but to speculate on a quick capital gain. Some of those who promoted the new Limiteds would contribute specialised knowledge, as overlookers, salesmen, engineers, builders, accountants, for example; some were prominent names, town councillors in particular; others were shopkeepers, publicans, coal merchants, adding common sense or horse sense

**Mill Flotation**: prospectuses for new companies, either to build new cotton mills, to take-over existing mills, or for all kinds of new enterprises, filled the Oldham press in the early 1870s, attracting a public eager to buy shares in the hope of quick profit or high dividends.

*Facing, above:* **Money Wanted**: the Limiteds needed loan capital and raised it in this way, much like a building society was to do later.

*Below:* **Share Dealing**: as more Limiteds were floated, the need to buy and sell shares developed. To conduct such transactions, some enterprising individuals set themselves up as brokers. Eventually, to do their business, they met regularly in the Lyceum, not built for such a purpose.

if not cotton know-how. There was money to be made in promotion, especially where shares went to a premium, and there were fees and prestige for the directors whose places were generally eagerly sought. The Mania was exploited by many who had no real interest or knowledge of the industry, not least those who owned land or had acquired it in anticipation of demand, whose only interest was to secure a good rental.

By the mid 1870s probably one in three Oldham households were owning shares or lending some of their savings to the Limiteds. If some of the new shareholders worked in the cotton industry, there were many others who were local tradesmen, shopkeepers, publicans and the like. Probably, those in cotton were the better paid overlookers, minders, mechanics; generally they tended as a matter of prudence not to invest in the mills where they worked but they were willing to assume risk "to make a bit of brass". Overwhelmingly in the early stages shareholders were from the Oldham district; to a lesser extent they came from "a distance", from Manchester and other nearby towns. They were diverting savings from the established institutions, co-operatives, building societies, savings banks. Small investors thus became an entirely new source of capital to the Oldham industry. Shareholdings and loans were so widely diffused among Oldham households, that one observer could say, "the whole town is rapidly becoming one huge joint stock concern, where day after day, night after night, the talk is of nothing but premiums, loans, shares and dividends". In the euphoria which gripped the community for a while, spinning mills lost their novelty and all kinds of ventures could be promoted. Companies that speculated in land or property development had some logic; other ventures promoted were in hen farming on land at Chadderton, where profits of 50 per cent were projected, or in a tailoring company to make clothing on a factory scale for Oldham people.

Sharebrokers, as many as forty, drawn from a variety of occupations, quickly came into business during the Mania, opening small offices in Clegg and Greaves Streets in central Oldham or in their houses elsewhere in the town. Brokers attracted buying and selling clients through their own networks and by advertising in the local press. They were quick to encourage investment but especially speculation which multiplied the number of transactions and the commissions that could be earned. Most of the business was carried out in particular public houses, the Market Hotel, or the Black Swan at Bottom of Moor, or the Kings Arms, in the centre of the town. Eventually an Association or Exchange was formed and a room rented in the Lyceum from 1883 in the hope that share activity could be confined there. But business continued in public houses along with gambling on likely dividend announcements, an alternative to horse racing which was also increasingly popular. The brokers themselves took positions in shares, often with the benefit of insider information; indeed it is probable that throughout the period of an active share market in Oldham, insider dealing was rife, with mill managers and directors profiting from their advance knowledge of results. An Oldham List had been published from May 1874 and share prices were printed in the weekly Oldham papers. Both the *Chronicle* and the *Standard* began to devote space to company information, rumours and gossip about business, personalities, forthcoming results. Needless to say the new shareholding public took an eager interest in the progress of their investments, not least through boisterous shareholder's meetings.

Between 1871 and 1876, fifty-four new mills were built, mostly by new Limiteds, seeking meadowland sites away from the congestion of the central area of the Borough. Local initiatives would influence much of the siting, but the cost and availability of land, access to roads or the railway, local clay for bricks which were often made on the site, and especially, availability of water for steam raising and condensation, were important considerations. Shaw and Royton best met these site considerations with flat land available on lease as cheaply as 1d a square yard, a third or less than rents in the Borough where 3d was general and which in some situations had reached 7d a yard. Generally the new mills had around 50,000 spindles, much larger than most of the older mills; if the old mills, even with fairly recent equipment were valued at 9s to 12s a spindle, typical new mills, built at the height of the boom, were costing 18s to 20s per spindle. Each new mill claimed to be "second to none" in Oldham. They typically had one syllable names, Park, Star, Earl, Oak, which became simple distinguishing brand names for their yarn. With the mills went new streets of terrace housing to attract and house the workforce and Oldham now began to sprawl, bringing a sharp increase in population in the townships. The spate of new mill building, needless to say, drove up land values, created a tremendous boom for the building trades, the machinery makers and for those involved in mill supplies of all kinds. It also led to intense if short-lived competition for workpeople. For a few years, with the "wild mad fever" of the Mania and the surge in activity, Oldham was an extraordinary place.

The new mills, their reservoirs or "lodges" to hold condensing water, and their associated streets, began to create a distinctive landscape. Mill architecture adapted itself to creating simple purpose-built "containers for machinery", to accommodate the larger spinning mules that were now becoming standard, as well as the preparatory processes, storage areas and steam engines and boilers. Floor areas were far wider and larger than the narrow mills of the 1850s or earlier. Good light in the working areas, higher ceilings, were sought after as well as large floor spaces undivided by pillars. Use of cast or wrought iron columns and girders facilitated those objectives as well as reduction of the fire risk, an all-important consideration; the modern mill could be described as "a simple curtain of brick cloaking the rigid fireproof structure within".

The promoters had pride in their mills and also required some features that would give distinction and differentiation. So the characteristic tall multi-storey Oldham cotton mill evolved, square, red brick built, large glass windows, indeed a facade that was more glass than brick, high chimneyed, the name boldly displayed. Several firms of specialised architects emerged, A. H. Stott, Joseph Stott, Edward Potts, to name the most prominent, competing between them to design the multitude of new mills. Each found that their specifications and designs lent themselves to easy repetition. Invariably the mills were built by local contractors, one firm in particular, S & J Smethurst, becoming prominent. Fiercely loyal to the locality, directors ensured that materials, machinery, engines, boilers, ropes, hoists, fire escapes and many other items came from the Oldham district.

### Money Wanted.

THE LANSDOWNE COTTON SPINNING COMPANY LIMITED.—LOANS received at 5 PER CENT. per annum at the Manchester and County Bank, or at the Mill.

JOHN & SAMUEL TAYLOR LIMITED.—This Company is prepared to receive LOANS, Interest at the rate of FOUR PER CENT. per annum. Deposits can be made at the Office, Primrose Bank, Oldham.

THE HIGGINSHAW MILLS AND SPINNING CO. LIMITED, Shaw-road, Oldham, are prepared to receive LOANS at FIVE PER CENT. Interest. Deposits may be made at the Manchester and County Bank, Mumps, or at the Mill.

EMPIRE SPINNING COMPANY LIMITED, HEYSIDE.—The above Company is prepared to receive LOANS at 4 PER CENT. PER ANNUM. Deposits may be made at the Oldham Joint-Stock Bank, or any of its Branches, or at the Mill.

OSBORNE MILL COMPANY LIMITED.—The LOAN ACCOUNT is now OPEN. Interest 4 PER CENT. Deposits may be made at the Oldham Joint-Stock Bank or Branches, or at the Mill, Cowhill, Oldham.
W. W. MILLS, Secretary.

THE OLDHAM BOILER WORKS COMPANY LIMITED.—LOANS, in sums of £50 and upwards. Interest, FOUR PER CENT. Deposits can be made at the Manchester and County Bank or at the Works.
WALTER F. SCHOFIELD, Secretary.

JOWETT, WATERHOUSE, & CO. LIMITED.—This Company is prepared to receive LOANS. Interest at the rate of 4 PER CENT. per annum. Deposits may be made at the Oldham Joint-Stock Bank Limited, or at the Registered Office, 8, Clegg-street, Oldham.

THE BOROUGH SPINNING COMPANY LIMITED is prepared to receive LOANS for a limited amount. Interest, 4 PER CENT. PER ANNUM. Present Loan Capital, £16,000. Uncalled Share Capital, £36,000. No Mortgage.—Deposits can be made at the Manchester and County Bank, or at the Mill.

CLOUGH COTTON SPINNING CO. LIMITED Springhead, Lees.—The above Company is prepared to receive LOANS. Interest at the rate of 4 PER CENT. per annum. Deposits can be made at the Union Bank, Oldham, and branches, or at the Mill.
JAMES KELSALL, Secretary.

WATERLOO BREWERY COMPANY LIMITED.—The LOAN ACCOUNT IS OPEN. Interest 5 PER CENT. per annum. Deposits to be made at the Oldham Joint-Stock Bank Limited, or any of its branches, or with the Manager, at the Registered Office, Waterloo-street.

OLDHAM AND LEES SPINNING COMPANY LIMITED.—LOANS may be deposited at the Oldham Joint-Stock Bank, or at the Mill, Waterhead. Terms, 4 PER CENT. twelve months, and 3½ PER CENT. one week's notice. Sums of over £500 by special arrangement.

ION SPINNING COMPANY LIMITED.—Registered Office: 301, Shaw-road, Luzley Brook, Heyside, Royton. The LOAN ACCOUNT is open. Interest, 4 PER CENT. per annum. Deposits to be made at the Oldham Joint-Stock Bank or Branches. Office open 6 to 9 p.m. Thursdays.

THE MAY MILL SPINNING COMPANY LIMITED, Pemberton, Wigan, are now open to receive LOANS. Interest 5 PER CENT. per annum. Bankers: Manchester and Liverpool District Bank Limited. County Alderman W. S. Barrett, J.P., Chairman.
HENRY H. L. FLETCHER, Secretary.

RUBY MILL COMPANY LIMITED is prepared to receive LOANS, which may be paid into the Oldham Joint-Stock Bank, or at the Registered Office, 125, Union-street, any day, or 204, Littlemoor-lane, on Thursdays, from 6 30 to 7 p.m. Interest, 4 PER CENT. per annum.
JAMES DAWSON, Secretary, pro tem.

WOODSTOCK MILL SPINNING COMPANY LIMITED, ROYTON JUNCTION, OLDHAM.—LOANS received at 4½ PER CENT. per annum. Special arrangements for large sums. Deposits may be made at Oldham Joint-Stock Bank, or at the Mill during office hours; also, First Saturday in the month, from One to Three p.m.

### OLDHAM SHARE MARKET.

The Share Markets held during the week have continued to show an improved tone in the price of shares. The upward tendency of last week has further developed itself, with the result that shares have enhanced in value from 1s. to 4s. This is in a great degree accounted for by the unanimity prevailing, both upon the short time question and the reduction of wages. That the better tone will continue there is much reason to believe, the impending strike being regarded as an occurrence which will increase the value of shares, as the stoppage of the production will, it is generally believed, improve the margin, and make spinning more profitable than it has been for some time. The better reports from the Yarn Market have also had a good effect upon shares. Compared with last week the official list shows a much higher level of prices; and, notwithstanding the substantial rise, buyers predominate. All round the inquiry is followed by good bids. Duke, Duchess, Dowry, Fern, Palm, Oak, Royton, Central, Oldham Twist, United, Werneth, Westwood, Star, North Moor, Boundary, Borough, and a few others, have been in strong request.

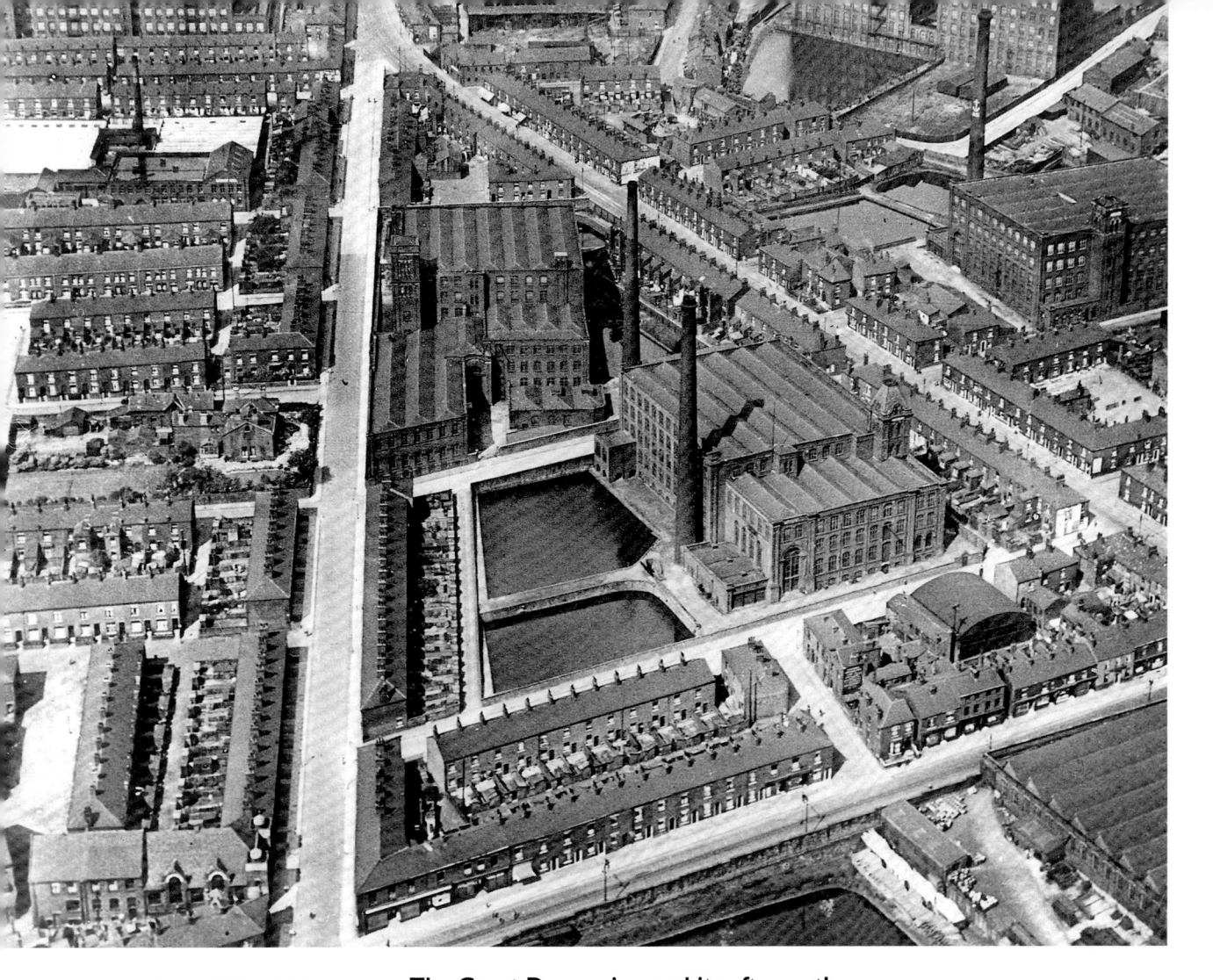

**Featherstall Road/Main Road:** the aerial photograph captures the new Oldham of the 1870s, multi-storey spinning mills, mill-lodges, surrounded by disciplined monotonous rows of terrace houses, two-up-two-down with a small yard and a passage-way at the back. Westwood Mill, built in 1875 is in the centre, Anchor Mill (1881) at the top right.

## The Great Depression and its aftermath

The Flotation Mania, as was characteristic of Nineteenth Century booms, added too many new mills, too much additional capacity that became available just when the trade was faltering. Profit margins began to fall early in 1875. It was then that Hugh Mason, head of the dominant private concern of nearby Ashton, and leader of the private spinners most threatened by the Limiteds, spoke out trenchantly against the folly of continued mill building and share speculation and the huge risks that thousands of people were assuming. His warnings were timely, sentiment changed completely, and new flotations abruptly ceased. The next few years brought bad trade, culminating in 1878, described as "a year of unparalleled commercial depression".

The profitability of the companies floated in the boom collapsed. Between 1877 and 1879 the Oldham Limiteds reported losses of £150,000. Dividends fell away or ceased, the interest paid on loans fell to 4 per cent. Share values shrank. The golden promise, the Eldorado, had been, it seemed, a mirage. Working men shareholders, at least those working in cotton spinning, gave up their illusions and in many cases sold their shares. Those who had loaned money also had their doubts but, despite many false rumours, no run on the Limiteds developed; the loanholders continued to feel they had good security, based in the end on "the business character of Oldham people", and the fact

# The Great Depression and its aftermath

that the mill to which money had been loaned was still there, with a good reserve of uncalled share capital. The continuing conviction of the loanholder that his money was safe was a crucial mainstay of the Oldham industry.

In the event, all the companies floated in the 1870s survived and Oldham's appetite for investment and speculation remained alive and alert. But investors now became more sophisticated, seeking out the better managed mills which could out-perform the rest, achieving better results that would be reflected in dividends and share prices. When profits revived, and dividends began to be paid again in 1880, new spinning concerns were again floated. Whether the industry needed new capacity was not the point; more relevant was whether the public, perhaps a different public, would buy the shares. The promoters in the second and later mill building boom, were perhaps less concerned with the potential profits from mill operation, more concerned with the profits to be secured from mill construction or company promotion itself. Land companies, architects, building contractors, machinery and mill-store suppliers were often the driving forces. A new mill and its machinery including steam engine and boilers would cost about £1 per spindle, in total between £50 and £100,000 depending upon size, important business for the many concerns employed in its design, building and fitting out. Thirty-one new mills were built between 1881 and 1887, larger again than their predecessors, typically 75,000 spindles.

Profits had fallen again in 1883 and subsequently; the markets for yarn, unstable as they were, were not expanding at anything like the rate of Oldham mill capacity. There were periods, as *The Economist* said in 1885, of "enormous and superfluous production of Oldham yarns". Intensified competition between a multitude of individual concerns, "a heavy dark cloud" as it was described, was the only result. Unquestionably the new mills with their Oldham made machinery and their highly driven keen young managers were much more efficient than the older capacity. They brought mill costs for spinning below 2½d per lb. If the new mills could live with this, and make profits, the old mills could not; their yarn needed prices as much as 1d a lb dearer than the level now set by Oldham. Some older mills re-equipped the better to compete, but a great deal of older capacity was driven from the business; much was in Oldham itself where old small mills near the town centre were closed, machinery sold and the buildings demolished to make way for new uses. With so many mill closures and re-equipment, Oldham had an active trade in second-hand machinery throughout this period. Across Lancashire, spinning was abandoned in many old mills that dated from the water-powered period, or in the so-called spinning and weaving "combined mills" that had once been state of the art.

As these changes took place, Oldham was establishing an unassailable supremacy as a cheap low cost spinning district producing yarn of reliable good quality. Meanwhile, reflecting its concentration on spinning, the town ceased to add to its looms in the 1880s. Across Lancashire, as a result of the rise of Oldham, spinning became divorced from weaving; Oldham's yarns found their market in the rapidly growing specialised weaving districts of North East Lancashire. As they claimed about Shaw, " this no other place surpasses, spinning yarn for Blackburn lasses". Supplier and customer met on the Manchester Exchange, either face to face or through agents; the deals

**Share Prices**, quoted weekly in the local press for the benefit of the thousands of local shareholders.

*Facing:* As the industry boomed the new mills were built on the meadow lands surrounding Oldham wherever cheap flat land with good access and local water was available. The map shows the outward spread of mill development in each phase of growth; Shaw, Royton and Chadderton attracted the large mills built in the later period.

were done there, manufacture and the movement of goods followed, all smoothly arranged.

The rise of the Limiteds enormously enlarged the demand for banking services, a demand that grew whether the industry was making profits or not. If Oldham had previously been served by branches of Manchester banks, a feeling that a more local and committed institution was needed led to the formation of the Oldham Joint Stock Bank in 1880. This was a huge success, opening several branches in the district. It built a large and prestigious head office on Union Street in 1892, now the home of the Midland Bank, with which the Oldham Bank was eventually to merge.

The industry remained unstable, feast or famine. There was a mini-boom in 1889-91 when profits again rose and twelve new mills were built, some of them, the Lion at Royton and the Pearl at Glodwick being larger than 100,000 spindles. This was followed by a long period of poor trade, poor margins and low profitability, exacerbated by the trade disputes of 1892-93. Samuel Andrew, long serving Secretary of the Employers Association was to complain, "we go on building mills and cannot make them pay." The industry "served increasingly, as a machine for the payment of wages, rent and loan interest, rather than profits." Many Limiteds paid no dividends during this "nightmare period of despair"; losses were financed by bank borrowings or by calling unpaid capital. Between 1891 and 1896 Oldham spinning company share prices fell continuously, on average by as much as 50 per cent; many small shareholders sold out during this period.

**The Last Great Mill Building Boom**

Trade eventually revived and with restored profits came the last great wave of company promotion and mill building in the mid 1900s. Fifty-five new mills were built between 1900 and 1908, thirty-seven of them between 1905 and 1907 when profits were exceptional and average dividends about 15 per cent. "Every loom and spindle that could be gaited is being worked at full stretch" wrote *The Economist*'s Manchester correspondent in 1906, "one of the best years in the history of trade". 1907 was described as a "a year of unbounded prosperity, the most remunerative ever experienced". This was Lancashire's last high period, when the industry's pride and confidence seemed to boil over. As one industry leader put it, "Lancashire clothed the world and its workpeople are unique. However many mills are built we cannot hope to satisfy the needs of expanding world population". In 1913, with over seventeen million spindles in 320 mills, owned by over 200 separate companies, the Oldham district had 30 per cent of the United Kingdom's spindleage. No other town approached its dominance: Bolton had a mere seven million spindles. Indeed Oldham had more spindles than any foreign country, except the United States, and in total one-eighth of the world's spindles. Truly it had become the cotton spinning capital of the world, "a town of spindles". More than £60 million of capital was invested in the industry, whether as shares or loan, overwhelmingly from local people. Nearly everyone in Oldham was directly or indirectly interested in the town's industry, working in it or for its suppliers, and either owning shares or lending it money, depending on the spending of millworker's earnings for their own livelihood as shopkeepers, publicans, or landlords.

# The Last Great Mill Building Boom

**Oldham Cotton Mills by Date of Construction**

Key
- Pre 1872
- 1872-1880
- 1880-1900
- 1900s
- Platts Engineering Works
- road
- --- railway

SHAW

ROYTON

CHADDERTON

OLDHAM

LEES

FAILSWORTH

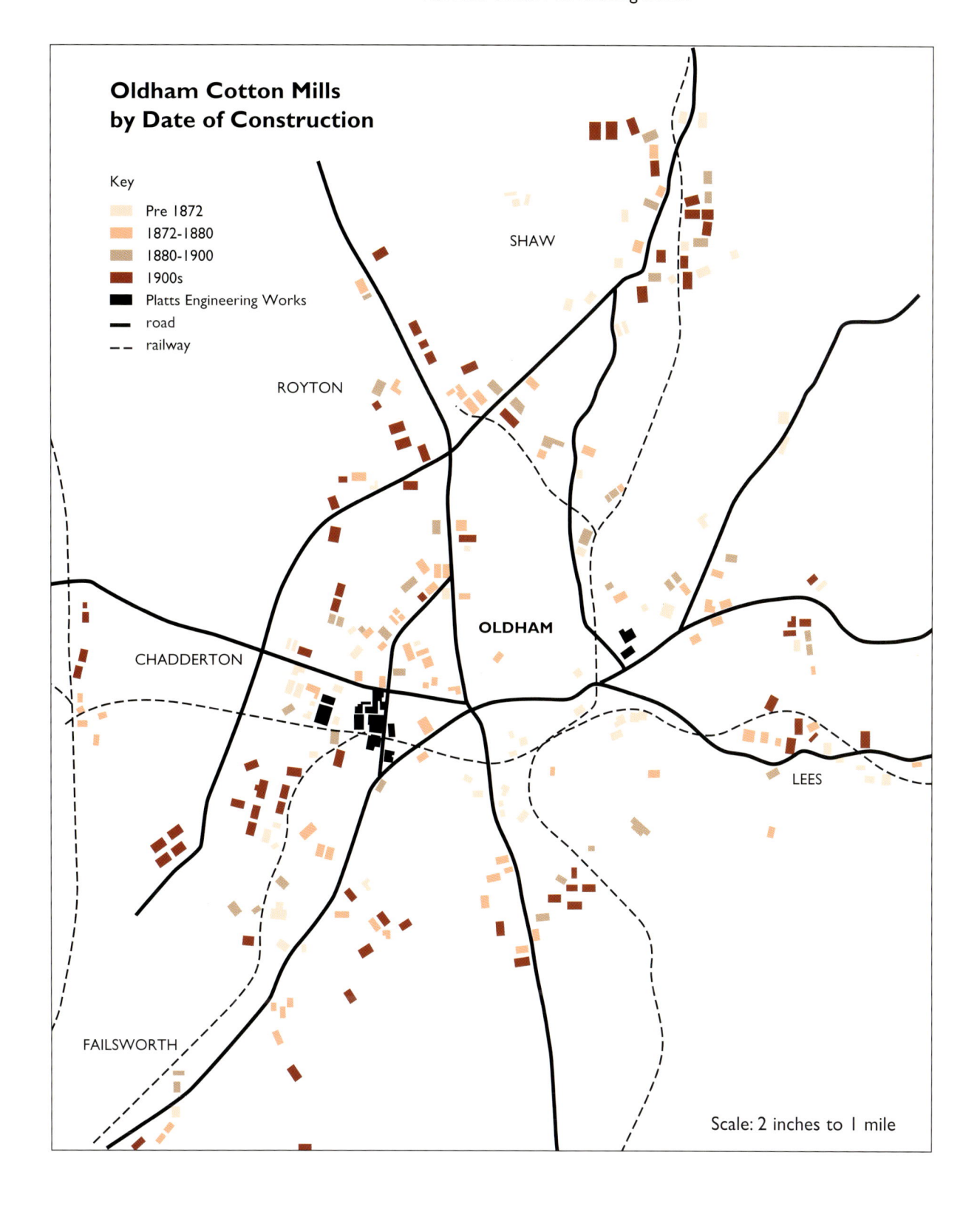

Scale: 2 inches to 1 mile

TABLE VIII: GROWTH OF OLDHAM'S COTTON INDUSTRY 1851-1913

|  | Number of new mills in period | Number of Spindles (million) | Share of UK Spindles (per cent) | Estimated Workforce Borough | Townships |
|---|---|---|---|---|---|
| 1851 | - | 1.5 | 7 | 21,000 | |
| 1861 | 29 | 3.0 | 9 | 28,000 | |
| 1871 | 15 | 5.0 | 15 | 33,000 | |
| 1883 | 63 | 9.3 | 24 | 29,000 | 14,000 |
| 1893 | 36 | 11.2 | 27 | 30,000 | 17,000 |
| 1903 | 15 | 12.2 | 28 | 30,000 | 20,000 |
| 1913 | 50 | 17.2 | 30 | 35,000 | 28,000 |

Nearly all the mills built after 1880 had been on the fringes of Oldham Borough, for instance in Hollinwood and Hathershaw, but especially now they were in the adjacent townships, Chadderton, Royton and Crompton. Shaw (part of Crompton) in particular seems to have taken to the idea of the limited liability company with great enthusiasm, led by a number of thrusting promoters of whom Thomas Henthorn (1850-1913) was the most prominent. Here, it was said, "boys were born with a cop or a bobbin in their hand"; by 1913 Shaw had one-sixth of the spindles in the district. By the end of the century as mills and houses spread, the townships had grown together; in almost any direction, clusters of mills were visible, five or six storeys high with their towering chimneys, perhaps forty or fifty to be counted in one view,

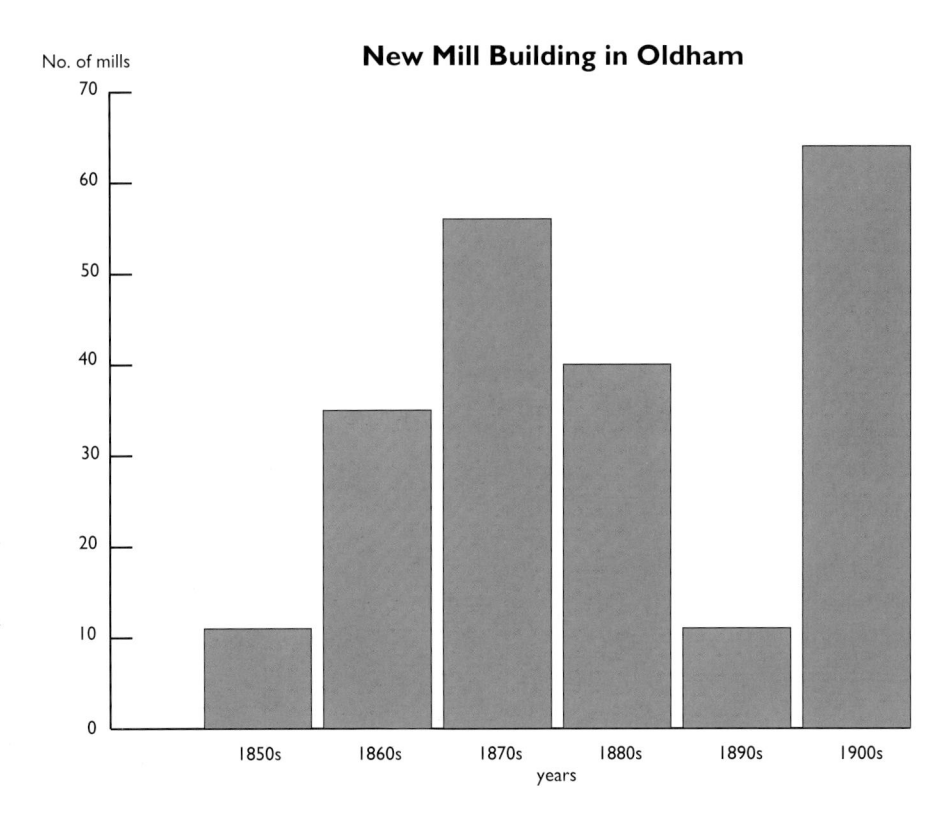

**New Mill Building in Oldham**

**Mill Building fluctuated** with the state of trade. The depression of the 1890s gave way to a brief period of euphoria in the first decade of the twentieth century. The mills built in this last boom phase had only a brief period of glory.

# The Last Great Mill Building Boom

a dramatic sight when the mills were ablaze with light on a winter morning or evening, or when the multitude of chimneys were belching grey or black smoke.

The dramatic increase in employment was in the townships rather than the Borough. The total numbers employed in cotton spinning and weaving in the entire district continued to grow to a peak of 63,000 on the eve of the Great War. Between 1871 and 1913 Oldham's spindleage had grown over threefold, the numbers employed less than twofold, such was the continued steady improvement in productivity that modern larger mills and larger more reliable faster machines, with fewer faults and breakages, permitted. The superior efficiency of the newest mills stimulated the re-equipment of older mills with the latest machinery, so as to be "equal to any in the district"; in this way higher productivity spread across the industry. If there were 4,500 or so weavers in Oldham in 1913, overwhelmingly the workforce was engaged in spinning and its preparatory processes.

Once a decision to build a mill was taken, usually in the context of expected high profits, speed of construction was paramount. The sooner a mill was in production the better. One of the new mills, the Iris, built in 1907, was in production four months after building started. It was said in one case that "machinery was being moved into the ground floor and started to work long before the top floor was finished." The later mills were bigger again than their predecessors, in particular much wider, and their design, more sophisticated; the average size of those built after 1900 was 90,000 spindles, many over 100,000. Sadly, these huge proud mills of the last phase, Rutland, Lily, Lilac, and Briar in Shaw, Monarch, Bee and Delta in Royton, or Durban, Heron, Rugby, Ram, Ace and Gorse in Chadderton and Hollinwood to name but a few, were to be quickly overtaken by the misfortunes of the industry which followed the Great War.

**Heron Mill 1905**, designed by P. S. Stott, completely typical of the large spinning mills built by Limited Companies in the last phase of Oldham's expansion, described by one visitor as "some of the finest and best-equipped factories in the county." Heron Mill had 105,000 spindles supplied by Asa Lees.

Oldham Brave Oldham

**Knocking-Up:** until 1919, Oldham's mills started work at 6 a.m., and those who were late lost earnings, or were often shut out. Not surprisingly, knocking-up became a recognised occupation for which thousands of households paid a few pennies a week.

**Dinner Time at Collinges Mill:** Collinge's Commercial Mill, Glodwick Road, along with the nearby Greenbank Mill, was one of Oldham's most successful spinning and weaving enterprises throughout the nineteenth century. At dinner-time, that is 12.15 p.m., many of the workpeople would go to nearby homes; others would send out for fish and chips or the like; others would have food brought in by children.

## Milltown Limited

Working hours in the cotton mills, if less than at mid-century, were still long through the 1860s; as many as sixty weekly, made up of days from 6.00 a.m. until 6.00 p.m. with breaks for breakfast and dinner, and a Saturday ending at 2 p.m. although it was often later before the overlookers let their operatives leave. Notwithstanding the Factory Acts, "time cribbing", or working beyond the defined shutdown was widely practised until trade unions became established. The willingness to start work at 6 am, which meant for many to be knocked up as early as 5 am, remained almost an institution, favoured by the workers themselves because it avoided any temptations from public houses which were generally not open so early. That is not to say that the multitude, adults and children, enjoyed trudging to work on a dark cold wet winter's morning. Most workers were punctual; at many mills the gates were shut at 6 and lateness meant loss of earnings, but the start-up was often ragged on Monday mornings.

A modest reduction in hours took place in the 1870s when Saturday became established as a half-day, ending at 1 pm and, following the Factories Act of 1874, the mills closed at 5.30 in the evening, establishing the ten hour day. From this position, fifty-six and a half hours weekly, save for the introduction of Saturday closing at 12 o'clock in 1902, there was virtually no change until after the Great War. Nor for many years did holidays change very much: a day at Christmas, Easter and Whitsun and a few days at the August Wakes. By the 1880s, however, the practice of taking seven days unpaid holiday at Wakes became established informally and was formally recognised by employers in 1890; this was a significant change in working class lives since it permitted, for those who could afford, a brief but complete escape from the humdrum working environment.

By the end of the century most of the workforce were in modern mills, much larger than their earlier predecessors. Except in doubling and cotton waste, few small cotton mills had survived. The modern mill's functional design was intended to accommodate the latest spinning machinery, efficient power transmission and easy movement of material between processes. There was little regard for the amenities of the workforce, no canteens or rest areas and probably limited toilet facilities; these became features of Oldham mills only a half-century later when workers were scarce and difficult to attract and hold. That having been said, the modern mills were better places to work than their predecessors.

Within the cotton mill there remained discrete operations for men and women respectively. Bale-opening, mixing, scutching (cleaning, separating the fibres) were activities for grown men, as generally was the supervision of the carding machines which straightened the fibres and formed them into band-like slivers. Women and girls were employed on the intermediate processes,

*Left:* **The Carding Room**, mainly operated by girls and young women, an essential operation in every Oldham spinning mill.

*Above:* Oldham was not merely the cotton spinning metropolis; by the end of the nineteenth century there were over 16,000 power looms and at least 4,000 weavers, mainly women. **Cotton weaving** in combined spinning and weaving mills was mainly the domain of the large private concerns, Collinges, Greaves of Derker, Mellodews and Emmotts among others. Oldham specialised in heavy cloths, corduroys, velvets and sheetings.

**A Minder with his piecers:** the photograph catches the relative ages of the three types of operative, their characteristic oil-stained light overalls and bare feet on slippery wooden floors. They are "doffing" the mules, that is replacing the full cops of spun yarn.

**An Oldham minder** typically worked a pair of mules with up to 2,000 spindles in the modern mills of the late nineteenth century. His earnings, derived from the complex Oldham List, were closely related to the volume of yarn his mules produced. With good work a skilled minder would take home at least £2 weekly in 1913 making him highly paid for the time.

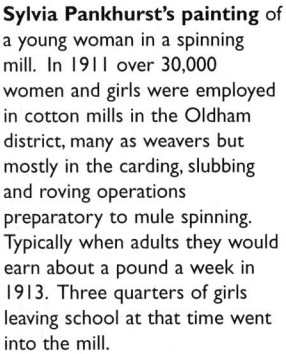

**Sylvia Pankhurst's painting** of a young woman in a spinning mill. In 1911 over 30,000 women and girls were employed in cotton mills in the Oldham district, many as weavers but mostly in the carding, slubbing and roving operations preparatory to mule spinning. Typically when adults they would earn about a pound a week in 1913. Three quarters of girls leaving school at that time went into the mill.

drawing, slubbing and roving, reducing the slivers to bobbins of rovings ready for the spinning mules. In the mule rooms, one minder and a big and a little piecer would operate a pair of mules, perhaps 2,300 spindles by the 1890s. The minder was as much a mechanic as a spinner while his team's tasks were to join broken threads, that is "piecing"; to remove the cops which received the spun yarn, that is "doffing"; to replenish the supply of rovings by replacing empty with full bobbins; and to oil and clean the machines. Working on slippery, oily wooden floors in high temperatures, walking as much as six or seven miles a day as the mules moved backwards and forwards, the minder and his assistants were barefooted and clad in little more than light overalls. The spun yarn on cops would be packed in skips or wooden boxes and moved to the warehouse or mill yard. Each mill would employ a few overlookers, an engineer, an engine tenter and perhaps a few general labourers. In Oldham's weaving sheds the workforce was predominantly women. The whole community at each mill would vary between 150 and 300 people, depending on size; only the very largest combined mills would employ more than these.

If the new mills were more spacious, cleaner, safer and well lit and if improved machinery, hoists and the like had reduced the bodily labour, the working environment remained smelly, hot and noisy. Dust and floating cotton fibre were hazards throughout the cotton preparation processes; pneumonicosis, bronchitis and

TB were common causes of death. Cancer of the scrotum, or mule spinners cancer, was another serious hazard among minders and piecers, caused by leaning at the waist over oiled machinery over many years of a working life. Working in a cotton mill was not seen as a healthy occupation. Meals were still brought to the factory by children or wives. Many workers hurried home for dinner, if home was nearby. Towards the end of the century fish and chip shops, small grocers shops selling pies, onion cakes, pastries and the like met the fast-food needs at mid-day.

Within the cotton industry the workforce was divided between the private and the limited mills, with their somewhat different cultures. In Oldham Borough the several large private concerns, mainly family concerns even though professional managers would be employed, continued to hold their

**Greenbank Mills, about 1900.** The illustrated billhead should be compared with the map on page 25. The back-to-back terraces are still there but the millowner's house has given way to a new spinning mill and the premises generally have been massively enlarged. Lees and Wrigley, successor to James Lees and Company, became Oldham's largest spinning complex. Eventually the workmen's cottages facing Glodwick Road were demolished to make way for more production space.

own. Collinges, Lees and Wrigley, Eli Lees, Greaves of Derker, Mellodews of Moorside, Emmotts, Shiers all remained prominent, many of them combining spinning with specialised velvet weaving. Some of the important concerns of the earlier period had failed, or been sold out, the most notable casualty being the Radcliffes of Lower House in 1892; the old firm of Worthingtons in Hollinwood was an early withdrawal, selling out to the Oldham Twist Company in 1867. But there were significant private newcomers, notably the concerns led by Alfred Butterworth at Glebe Mills in Chadderton which in 1900 had 152,000 spindles and 1,456 looms, and James Stott who made a significant beginning at Coldhurst Hall in the 1870s, and later added Werneth Mills and became one of the best remembered employers in Oldham. Crompton and Shaw, important as they became for the Limiteds, retained the long established private companies run by the old families, Cromptons, Cleggs, Cheethams, who maintained their own paternal traditions and loyal deferential work force. Together the private mills probably accounted for about one-fifth of Oldham's spindles in 1913 and practically all of its 16,000 looms. Their workforce would be about 16,000, approaching 25 per cent of the total in Oldham and district, and included all the 4,500 or so weavers, mainly women.

The great majority of cotton operatives then, were working in mills owned by limited companies. How far there was a difference to the family firm is a matter of conjecture. Sam Platt, Chairman of Platts, was to say "the limited company has no bowels." What he meant was that it lacked the presence and involvement of a committed family, giving the business an individual style and, as Sam Platt knew, carrying some kind of obligation and paternal relationship with the workforce, not being solely preoccupied with generating profits and dividends.

In mid-century Oldham the number of "self-made men" who became small employers was believed to contribute to social harmony. The boss and his workers had grown up together, they were accustomed to mix in the same public houses and clubs, and to speak plainly to each other. In the changed pattern of ownership, certainly in the 1870s, it was commonplace to claim a new high level of involvement by workers in the Limiteds, identifying with the performance and success of their particular mill, knowing "the ins and outs of trade". This, it was believed, derived from widespread share ownership and a more open democratic style where mill results, perhaps published quarterly in great detail, could be analysed, compared and debated publicly, often in heated shareholder's meetings where on a show of hands, chairmen and directors could be voted out of office. One co-operative idealist could write

> "The daily discussions which take place ... as to why dividends are small or otherwise have led almost every intelligent operative to become more economical with material, more industrious and to see what effect his individual efforts have upon the cost of the materials produced".

The demise of private spinners and the success of Oldham was attributed to the exceptional involvement of workers in the new spinning companies which they partly owned. On top of this involvement was the competition between the companies and their individual determination not to be left behind.

These somewhat idealistic views crumbled as the Limiteds, in a frequently oversupplied market, fell on hard times. As profits fell or gave way to losses and dividends shrank or were passed, a harder management style emerged, and with it the seeds of conflict. As managers were pressed for results the consequence was more aggressive handling of the workforce, stricter discipline, insistence on better time-keeping, "speed-up" as machine speeds were increased, resort to cheaper cotton with the consequence of "bad spinning" affecting the mule spinners output and earnings. Another tendency was a temptation to create margin by speculation whether by selling yarn ahead of buying cotton, or more usually buying cotton before making sales in anticipation of a rise in values. There were plenty of people in Lancashire and not a few in Oldham who had made their fortunes in this way. On a falling market, the maxim was "sell when you can, buy when you must". Buying cotton ahead of sales had disastrous results for many companies when prices fell in the early 1890s. Intensified competition and difficult trading, as well as an increasingly militant workforce, encouraged more and more of the Limiteds to hide their affairs from the public and cease to publish balance sheet information. Shareholdings, especially in the newer flotations, became more restricted, indeed almost private, the preserve of fewer wealthier investors, while working-men shareholders became fewer and fewer.

The Limiteds, far more than the private concerns, were wholly concerned with financial performance. Company directors, and especially mill managers, salesmen, secretaries and other officials were there to deliver profits and dividends. If they failed they were replaced. Mill management had become a profession in Oldham. Most managers had risen from half-timer experience, aided by night school and some technical instruction, but mainly on the basis of their own push, untiring industry, mastery of all aspects of the business, and supposed acumen. Some were very successful; many failed, their places quickly being filled by any number of eager aspirants for the responsibility, the comparative rewards and the status. Among the better known, as an example, was William O'Neill (1860-1934) manager of Sun Mill where he spent all his working life. Of him it was said, Sun came before everything else; he was at the mill every morning before work began and there

**Sun Mill Managers and Overlookers, about 1910**: the group would be typical of those managing any Oldham spinning mill at the time. Mill management was a serious occupation and good managers were sought after and highly paid; the poor performers rarely survived for long. William O'Neill, at the centre of the photograph, acquired a particular reputation for his skills and dedication which turned round the Sun Mill enterprise. Whatever its initial success when it was launched, the Company had a long period of bad results after the boom of the early 1870s.

long after the operatives left, every weekend inspecting the various departments of the mill, on Change in Manchester every Tuesday. Typically he had an arrangement with Platts whereby Sun Mill tried out every new machine they introduced. Oldham was full of hard-driving mill managers and sharp mill salesmen, well known in the town, personalities on the Manchester Exchange, earning £200 or £250 a year, a high salary at the time. Revealing the strength of the profession in Oldham, over 700 managers and engineers attended lectures analysing a boiler explosion at Stanley Mill in 1885.

Similarly a number of professional directors emerged, those who had demonstrated, by results, their business competence and judgement, and became involved in many concerns, receiving fees of about £50 a year. To quote a few examples, Samuel Ogden Ward (1834-1903), a tin plate worker and long serving Oldham councillor, active in the co-operative and building society movements, became chairman or director of ten concerns in the 1880s; William Wilson (1842-1921), who started as a warehouseman, was holding seven directorships in 1900. Three personalities in particular emerged as strong men in the difficult later period prior to 1914. In each case they achieved control of a group of mills as a dominant chairman, becoming a large shareholder in each mill, possibly having promoted some of them. They saw their role as making mill managers fully accountable, ensuring that good mill practice was implemented across their group. Subject to the strong chairman's close control, the individual mills remained separate profit centres, doing their own buying and selling; there was little, if any, sharing of common services, accounting, legal or technical between mills in a group.

Most notable was John Bunting (1839-1923), a former blacksmith who began investing in mill shares and went on to establish a successful business as a sharebroker. As his resources and influence grew, and he gathered a large faithful clientele of wealthy investors, he began to promote mill building companies and by this means, as by large share ownership or outright purchase, he acquired control of a group of twenty modern mills, the so-called Bunting Group, accounting for over 2.3 million spindles in Oldham and adjoining districts, approaching 10 per cent of local capacity. Bunting was a hard taskmaster towards those accountable to him, interesting himself closely and continuously in all the crucial aspects of mill performance and costs, machine speeds and downtime, waste, labour productivity, coal use, yarn quality, and the like. He would frequently turn up at his mills unexpectedly. Unlike many others he insisted that profits had "to be made in the mill" rather than by speculation in cotton. Non-performing managers were quickly disposed of, but those he valued were highly rewarded, as were his workpeople. Such was his confidence that he was able to borrow much of the capital his mills employed at low interest rates; by restricting his use of share capital he achieved outstanding dividends across his mills. At the Iris Mill at Hathershaw, for instance, he could pay an 80 per cent dividend with the aid of £103,000 loans and a paid-up share capital of only £6,250; Iris shares were unquoted and tightly held. His companies consistently outperformed the industry and through his mill promotions, his large shareholdings and share dealing, Bunting became one of Oldham's richest men, leaving £743,000 on his death in 1923. A strong individualist, he had little regard for the opinions of others; he pursued his own course with regard

**John Bunting**, once a blacksmith but later a local stockbroker, made a huge fortune as an investor in Oldham Limiteds. More than an investor, he acquired control of many companies which formed the Bunting Group where his management and leadership skills achieved high performance for shareholders in the years before 1914. Hugely rich and powerful as he became, he lived throughout his life in a modest house in Union Street and worshipped regularly at Henshaw Street Primitive Methodist Chapel.

to wages and working time, fearlessly ignoring reproaches from elsewhere. He remained throughout his life a Primitive Methodist and a teetotaller, occupying a simple terrace house in Union Street close to Oldham's commercial quarter in Greaves and Clegg Streets. His aim in life, as he often said, was to provide regular well-paid work and the security and comfort it brought, to a large number of his fellow Oldhamers.

Thomas Gartside (1857-1941) was another dominant personality in this later period. Like so many others he liked to recall his humble start in life, in his case at the counter of Royton Co-op earning 6s for a sixty-nine hour week, moving on to work as a warehouse boy in a Royton Mill. Becoming a clerk he was shrewd enough to extend his legal and administrative experience and entered mill-management as secretary of Royton Spinning Company. There and more importantly at the Shiloh Spinning Company, in trouble in the depressed 1890s, Tommy Gartside dramatically improved performance and, with the help of large borrowings, delivered a satisfactory stream of dividends. He then went on to create his own network or empire of companies, which, in effect he controlled, partly by ownership, but primarily by his grasp of the essentials of management, his leadership skills and his natural authority. He eventually became chairman of eight Royton spinning companies with over 900,000 spindles.

A third major personality among the Limiteds was John B. Tattersall (1845-1925), born the son of a Royton tailor and starting as a half-time little piecer in a local mill and in his early twenties becoming a minder of a pair of mules. As a young man with great energy and intelligence, sharpened at night school, he was well able to grasp the complex calculations of earnings on spinning mules, and he became prominent and active in the cotton spinners union. Having put modest savings in the successful Royton Spinning Co, and becoming a Director in 1872, his career changed course when he was made Secretary in 1874 and then Yarn Salesman and later General Manager. From that base he pushed himself to prominence, in Liberal politics as well as among the Limiteds. He promoted other companies in the district including especially the Lion Mill, floated in 1889 as the largest mill in Royton and exceptionally successful, paying a regular 10 per cent after 1900. Tattersall extended his influence during the last mill building boom and by 1910 he had directorships in a dozen or so Royton and Shaw firms; he was said to control between one-third and a half of Royton's spinning capacity. Once an aggressive and effective union official, he became President of the Oldham Master Cotton Spinners Association and Vice-President of the Federation which brought together the various local Associations within Lancashire. In these roles, and with his detailed knowledge of spinning mill practice, he was a strong negotiator and took a hard uncompromising employer's line on wages and the right to manage, much admired by his fellow mill directors but resented by his former union colleagues. Tattersall, competent as he was, had not many friends among the mill workers; he neither acquired the wealth nor did he receive the accolades of his contemporary, John Bunting.

**Industrial Relations**

The skilled male cotton minders in Oldham had a tradition of militancy. They had organised themselves, if loosely, since 1798 and there were well recorded disputes as the industry was growing in the first half of the century, notably in periods of bad trade, unemployment and wage reduction. But although the potential strength of the skilled spinner was considerable their organisation remained weak with incomplete membership and inadequate funds, hardly the conditions for successful resistance to employers. Circumstances changed with the rapid expansion of the industry after 1870. Nowhere else was there so large a concentration of cotton spinning as in Oldham; inevitably the issues that divided employers and their workmen would have to resolved here, if necessary by industrial action. This was to be the cockpit.

In 1868 the Oldham Association of Operative Cotton Spinners had only 2,282 members, almost all minders. They were divided into nine local "districts", their officers jealous of each other, and more concerned with organising benefits to out-of-work members, whether because of sickness, or work stoppages from various causes. What central organisation existed was rudimentary, meeting in a public house, with few records and little will for collective action. In changing this situation the appointment of Thomas Ashton (1841-1919) as General Secretary in August 1868 was crucial. Following another classical Oldham career, picking coal from pitbanks as a small child, half-timer from the age of nine, minder at twenty, self-taught through the Henshaw Street Mutual Improvement Society and the Lyceum, Ashton became a day-school teacher before his appointment. He led the Union, as General Secretary and then President until his retirement in 1913 when it had 19,731 members and operated from prestigious offices in Rock Street. Dogged, shrewd, independent and extremely well informed on mill practice, he was blunt and emphatic in speech and august in manner, a person of great authority, trusted by his members and respected by employers, one of the most popular people in Oldham in his later years.

Throughout this period as local rivalries were curbed and as membership, organisation and centralised funding were strengthened, the Association secured many improvements in working practices and conditions. Thus an earlier shutdown on Saturday, and subsequently reduction in weekday hours of work were achieved in the early 1870s and weekly rather than fortnightly payment of wages became standard. Notable was agreement after a seven weeks strike on the Oldham List in 1875, establishing, for the whole district, the complicated system of piece rates on which minders were paid in relation to the output of the mules they managed.

This was the first big Oldham strike, involving many thousands of people. Minders in the Association got strike pay, 10 shillings a week and 4 shillings for each child but most others employed in idle mills got nothing. Many companies could not afford to stop working and accepted the new List; others followed in the end. There was particular anguish at several Limiteds where the "co-operative" ideal was strongest; working men shareholders were apparently in dispute with themselves; the conflict between labour and capital had not, it seemed, been resolved by the new form of ownership. This experience, and the aftermath of the Flotation Mania, persuaded many working men to leave shares alone. The List removed a major source of dispute at individual mills when the basis of payment had hitherto been variable mill by mill across the district. There remained other causes of conflict, mill by mill, usually on matters relating to "speed-up", "bad

**Thomas Ashton**, born in Oldham in 1841, went into the mill as a half-time little piecer at the age of nine, and taught himself at night school and Sunday Schools. A minder at the age of twenty he left the mill to become a day-school teacher and then joined the Oldham Operative Cotton Spinners as General Secretary. In that position and later as President he led a huge increase in membership during the turbulent period of expansion from 1871 to the Great War. He became one of the best known and most widely respected men of Oldham.

spinning", or "time cribbing" as individual managements followed a harder style and looked for gains in productivity or savings in costs. But after the List, the central issue, the principal one, became the level of wages (or more properly piece rates) in an unstable industry where activity and profitability fluctuated significantly from one year to the next.

In years of poor trade and depressed profits the employer's response was to endeavour to reduce wages; in resisting this the minders called for short time working to reduce supply and raise yarn prices. "Reducing wages is no remedy for bad trade. If markets are glutted, put mills on short time", was the call. Co-ordinated short time working, even in the Oldham district, proved impossible to achieve. The employers' organisation, the Oldham Master Cotton Spinners Association, formed in 1866, mainly to resist demands for higher wages, did not cover all mills in the district nor could it enforce collective action among its members. Mill managements had to compare "the loss on running with the loss on stopping", taking into account the need to keep their workforce together and maintain their business transactions. The weaker concerns rarely worked short time; lacking resources they had little alternative but "to run themselves to death". Thus competing individual concerns, private as well as limited, usually went their own way, many continuing to work as others adopted short time; this in turn led to recrimination and reprisal. Some large employers, Alfred Butterworth at Glebe Mills, the Bunting Group in later years, maintained a staunchly independent position outside the Association, rarely working short time and joining disputes and settling their own rates of pay. Butterworth, an exceptionally religious man, but also very paternal, would settle disputes at his own mills by calling his workpeople to join him in prayer. A related problem was that employers in other spinning towns were happy to see Oldham fight the industry's battles, continuing to work when Oldham was in dispute and indeed taking advantage of the situation. It was only in the 1890s that an effective Federation of employer's associations in the different towns emerged.

But these difficulties apart, increasingly over the years, the employers Association would negotiate with that of the spinners over any matters in dispute, at individual mills or across the district. For most of the spinning companies, industrial relations ceased to be a concern of the individual employer, the master, and his workmen. The old paternalist style was generally abandoned; instead negotiations became

**This illuminated testimonial to Alfred Emmott**, son of a large private employer, on his marriage illustrates that feelings of gratitude and deference were still typical of many mill workers in the last decade of the century.

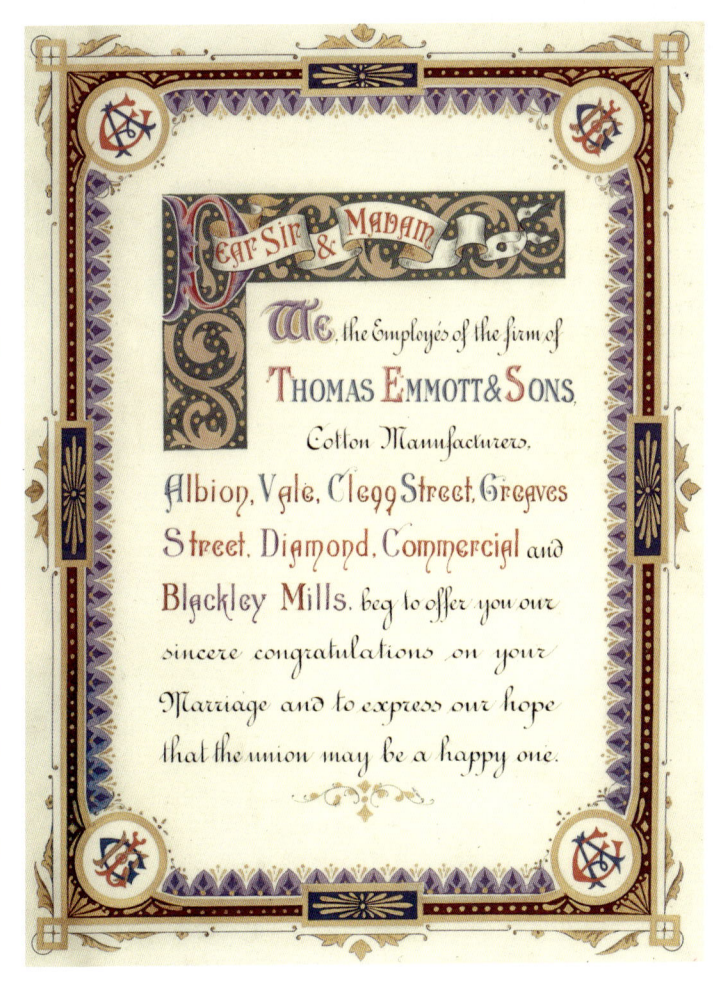

**Spinning Results:** the unstable character of the cotton spinning business is reflected in its very volatile financial performance. There were long depressed periods of poor trade, intense competition and inadequate margins together with comparatively brief years of very high profits. Dividend payments and share prices varied accordingly.

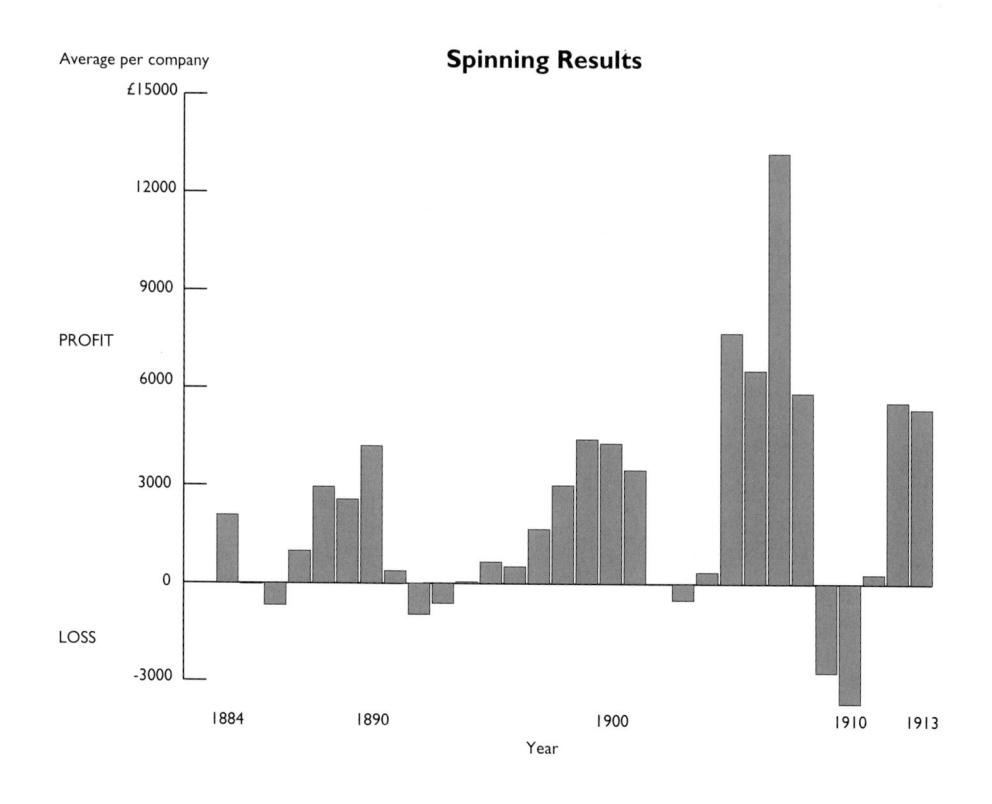

## Spinning Results

**Wage Movements:** payments as a percentage of the original Oldham List rose and fell with cotton spinning margins. Inevitably attempts to impose wage reductions were resisted by an increasingly well-organised Operative Spinners Association bargaining with the Employer's Federation.

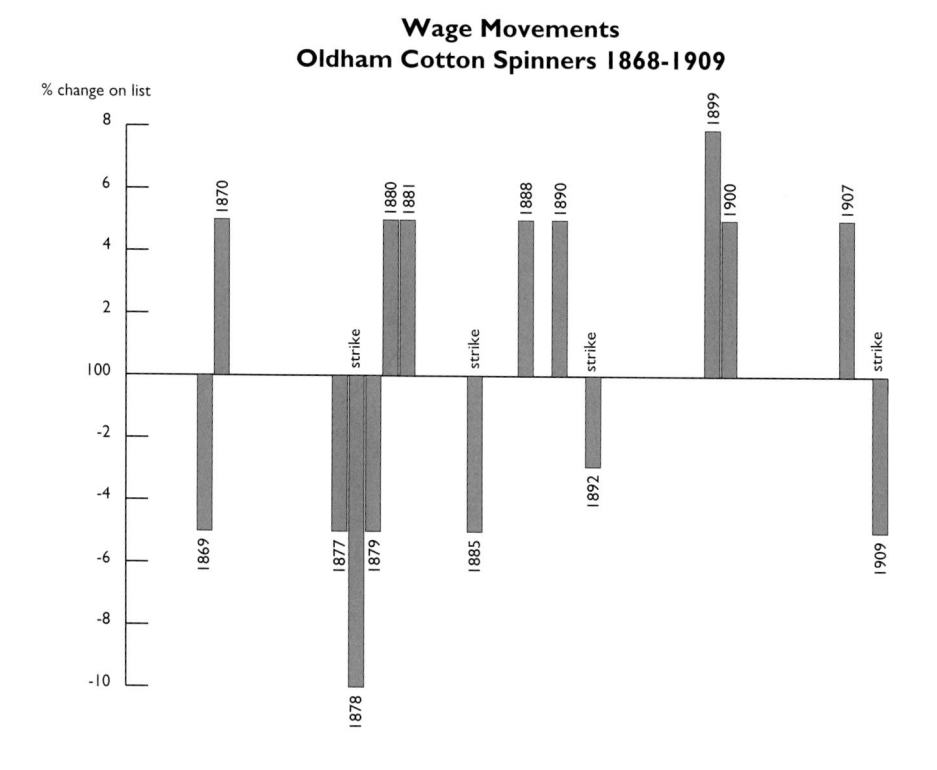

## Wage Movements
## Oldham Cotton Spinners 1868-1909

# Industrial Relations

institutionalised with both sides seeking solidarity to increase their bargaining strength, the employers trying to adopt and maintain a common position, the organised workforce the same.

The level of wages, determined as a percentage of the List, became the principal and constant source of tension as the spinner's profit, readily calculated from published prices of raw cotton and yarn, rose and fell. Everyone in Oldham knew the state of trade from the daily newspaper. Wages rose and fell frequently, sometimes through negotiation but often after a strike. When hours were reduced in 1874 wages remained unchanged. The period of depression in the late 1870s brought several cuts, culminating in a six week strike in October 1878 which ended in compromise. These reductions were partly restored in the next few years but 1885 brought another major Oldham strike lasting thirteen weeks; with their funds almost exhausted, union members returned to work accepting a 5 per cent reduction against 10 per cent, the employer's initial proposal. The aftermath was one of great bitterness; minders and others blamed the poor condition of the industry on excessive building of new mills and the inability of competing mills to agree on short time. Employers complained of clever trade union officers intensifying the old enmity between capital and labour, of "a growing tendency for labour to overbear capital, to want to be master and not servant;" there was concern that capital would desert the Oldham district. Capital, of course, was not rich individual mill owners but those who managed the Limiteds on behalf of their numerous small shareholders. However bitter, the Oldham disputes lacked a class-war implication.

Wages were increased in 1888 and 1891 but when bad trade and declining profitability, aggravated in many cases by companies taking a wrong view of the cotton market, returned in 1892, a major confrontation became inevitable. What was the most bitter dispute in Oldham's history started in October when the employers led by J. B. Tattersall failed to agree on short time working and insisted initially on a 10 per cent and then on a 5 per cent reduction. The Association refused these terms and the resulting lockout lasted over twenty weeks and brought great distress. The Operative's Association paid out over £182,000 to its members before a settlement was eventually reached with a compromise reduction of just over 2.9 per cent.

Never again, said the parties on both sides. Apart from the losses to spinning companies, the drain on the savings of operatives and their distress, the whole Oldham community suffered, shopkeepers, landlords, workers in other occupations. Oldham was getting a bad name. After protracted discussion the employers and the unions made the Brooklands Agreement which laid down procedures for settling disputes by extended negotiation before, as a last resort, strike action or lockout. Following Brooklands there was no major industry strike for many years. Disputes at individual mills, some serious, continued, reflecting an increasingly militant work force, more disposed to follow aggressive leaders at their mill, embryonic "shop stewards", rather than the conservative Association officers. In 1904 the employers reported "more strikes at individual mills and those of longer duration", than ever before.

Wages increased after the turn of the century and especially in the boom of 1905-07 but were reduced by 5 per cent after another long dispute in 1908-09. In 1913, so far as minders were concerned, they were approximately

---

**THE GREAT STRIKE IN OLDHAM.**

OPENING OF THE MILLS ON MONDAY.

NO RESUMPTION OF WORK.

THE STRIKE TO BE CONTINUED.

DISTURBANCES AT MILLS.

WORKPEOPLE ASSAULTED.

THE POLICE CALLED OUT.

**The 1885 Strike** against a proposed wage reduction of 10 per cent lasted thirteen weeks before the spinners went back. An even more bitter strike in 1892 lasted twenty weeks; the union could claim success here when the settlement provided for a reduction of only 2.9 per cent compared with 10 per cent initially proposed by the employers.

where they had been in 1877. The change in wage rates, over the period as a whole, was modest; earnings were a different matter. Related as they were to output from the mules, with the minder sharing improvements with the employer under the terms of the Oldham List, a significant increase, as much as 50 per cent, had occurred as a result of larger, faster and more productive mules; at the same time labour costs per pound of yarn also fell. Subject to the incidence of short time working, minders' earnings improved substantially from the 1870s: in the boom of 1906 and 1907 with no short time they were better off than ever before. Having made these gains the Oldham spinners were reluctant to see them reduced, as the major strike in 1908-09 demonstrated, Brooklands notwithstanding.

The minder's assistants, his two piecers, often relations, were traditionally paid from the minder's gross pay, typically in a public house when work finished on Saturday afternoon. The Oldham List provided that the piecers should be paid by the employer at rates related to the minder's earnings. Piecers identified with the minders whose high paying jobs they aspired to and frequently attained at a comparatively young age when the industry was growing so fast. Gradually the piecers joined the union, and by 1913 outnumbered the minders in the Association's membership. Promotion of piecer to minder, not an issue for the Union, remained an ongoing concern among young men in the mills, especially when the industry ceased its growth.

The other large group of cotton mill workers were those engaged in the preparatory processes, predominantly girls and young women, but including men for the most part working in the scutching room or as over-lookers, harder to organise, comparatively badly paid, and less stable as a group. They were the victims of the strikes called by the Operative Spinners Association.

**The Cardroom Workers**, mainly girls and women, were more difficult to organise. Without the support of any union funds, they suffered great distress in the big Oldham strikes. Eventually a Union was established, led by William Mullin and became as active and militant as that of the Spinners.

After many years of separate weak local initiatives, an organisation emerged early in the 1880s, the Oldham Card and Blowing Room Operatives Association led by William Mullin (1855-1920), also an Oldham man. During the first great Oldham strike of 1885, the Association had only 1,279 members whom it was barely able to help financially; the many thousands of workers outside its ranks had to fend for themselves, relying on charity, the pawnshop or the Poor Law Union.

The strike of 1885 led to a subsequent strong increase in membership in Oldham, where it quickly rose to 5,000, as well as elsewhere, and to a greater determination for the local associations to form a stronger General Amalgamation covering the whole industry. This Amalgamation was set up in April 1886 with Mullin first General Secretary. About 25 per cent of the relevant workforce were then members, compared to 90 per cent of the minders. Subscriptions were increased to cover sick and out-of-work pay as well as strike pay. Many

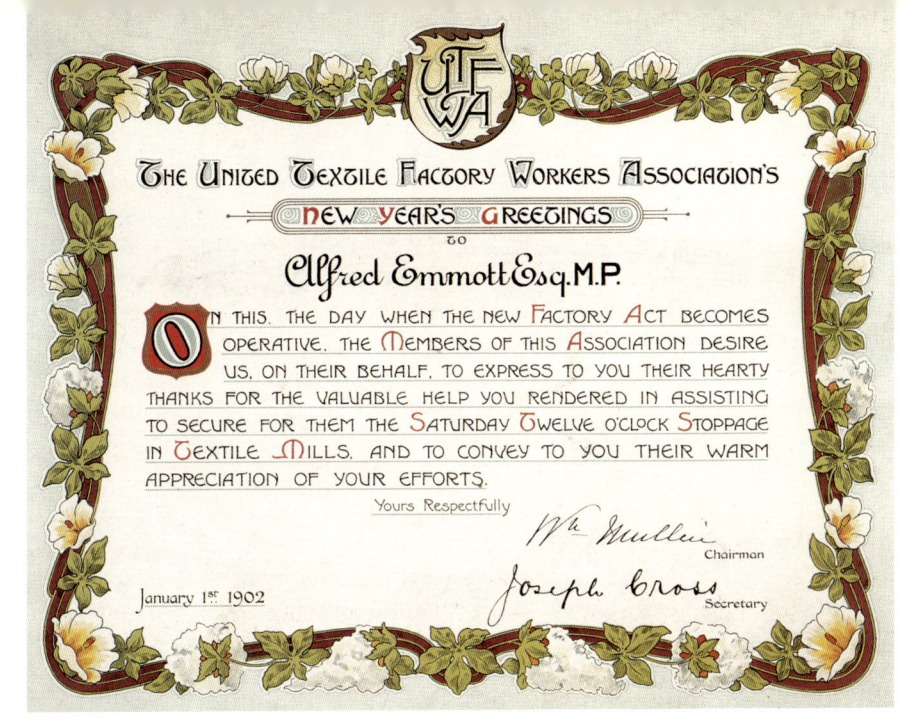

> **The United Textile Factory Workers Association's New Year's Greetings to Alfred Emmott Esq. M.P.**
>
> On this, the day when the new Factory Act becomes operative, the members of this Association desire us, on their behalf, to express to you their hearty thanks for the valuable help you rendered in assisting to secure for them the Saturday Twelve o'clock Stoppage in Textile Mills, and to convey to you their warm appreciation of your efforts.
>
> Yours Respectfully
>
> Wm Mullin, Chairman
> Joseph Cross, Secretary
>
> January 1st 1902

However bitter the Oldham strikes, the large Oldham private employers retained the respect of their workpeople. **Alfred Emmott**, by then well-established as the town's senior Liberal MP, mainly on the vote of working-men, is thanked for his part in securing a further reduction in the hours worked on Saturday. By then the "short Saturday" with all it permitted in the way of rest, recreation and sport, was well-established, as was a week's unpaid annual holiday.

problems were gradually overcome, not least the meaning of solidarity, implying sacrifice by those who might not be directly involved in industrial action. Robert Ascroft, the Oldham solicitor and prominent Tory, had been involved since 1881; he was a powerful support. The Oldham Association had success in securing wage increases in 1888 and 1890, and an Oldham standard wages list setting out relative rates for different tasks was agreed in November 1890. The Union acquired a reputation for militancy at this time, challenging various practices and conditions with employers, individually and across the district. Relationships with the Spinners Association became closer. By the time of the 1892 lockout an estimated 75 per cent of the card and blowing room operatives were in the union; strike pay was given but had to be reduced after a month and then proved difficult to sustain. The Amalgamation then had a difficult time during the poor economic climate of the 1890s, but gained strength and militancy in the new century, engaging in some bitter strikes at individual mills, not always successfully. Oldham had 12,423 members in 1907. By then wage rates were where they had been in the mid 1870s, as was the case with minders, but actual earnings were a great deal higher, as much as 25 per cent for many of the women and girls, much more for the strippers and grinders of the scutching room, again the result of huge increases in machine productivity in the preparatory processes.

TABLE IX: ESTIMATED COTTON MILL EARNINGS (SHILLINGS PER WEEK)

|  | 1850 | 1886 | 1913 |
|---|---|---|---|
| Overlookers | 25 | 40 | 50 |
| Strippers and Grinders | 12-13 | 20 | 30 |
| Drawers and Rovers | 7-9 | 15-16 | 19-20 |
| Minders | 20-24 | 30-35 | 40-45 |
| Big Piecers | 9 | 13-14 | 18-20 |
| Little Piecers | 3-4 | 10-11 | 14-15 |

Prior to the 1880s, the press, perhaps the public generally, were hostile to trade unionists. Certainly in Oldham, essentially a working-man's town, that position changed as membership grew, and so far as the local press was concerned, following the launch of *The Cotton Factory Times* in Ashton in 1884. Thomas Ashton, a JP, and James Mawdsley (1842-1902), his successor as General Secretary when Ashton became President of the Spinners Amalgamation in 1878, were held in such respect that for a time they were Liberal and Conservative candidates for Parliament. Both Mawdsley and William Mullin, also a JP, over many years wrote columns for the Oldham newspapers, the *Chronicle* and the *Standard*. As another indication of standing, their respective funerals were huge occasions when they were honoured by many of their townsmen; Thomas Ashton, who died in 1919, had thirty carriages in a quarter-mile procession, headed by 300 minders walking in front of the hearse; thousands lined the route to Chadderton Cemetery. By the end of the century, the trade unions were part of the Oldham establishment. Cotton was King, and these men, as leaders of a huge body of working people engaged in the industry, became principal figures in the community, accepted and honoured the more because they were conservative figures, not disposed to challenge the existing order, not believing that the working class needed its own separate political party in Parliament. They were typical of late Victorian Lancashire. Much was to change with their passing, in the state of the cotton industry and in the political behaviour of the working people of Oldham.

Chapter V

# A MANUFACTURING TOWN

By the end of the century cotton spinning had made Oldham ascendant and dominated the local economy. But the town had developed a broader manufacturing base; in particular it had become as famous for its textile engineering as for its cotton spinning mills.

**Platts and Lees**

Oldham's reputation in textile machinery had already been established by Platts, as by Samuel and Asa Lees, by the middle of the century. Both these firms, and the many other small engineers and foundries linked to cotton textiles, had benefited greatly from the boom of the 1850s; they were checked

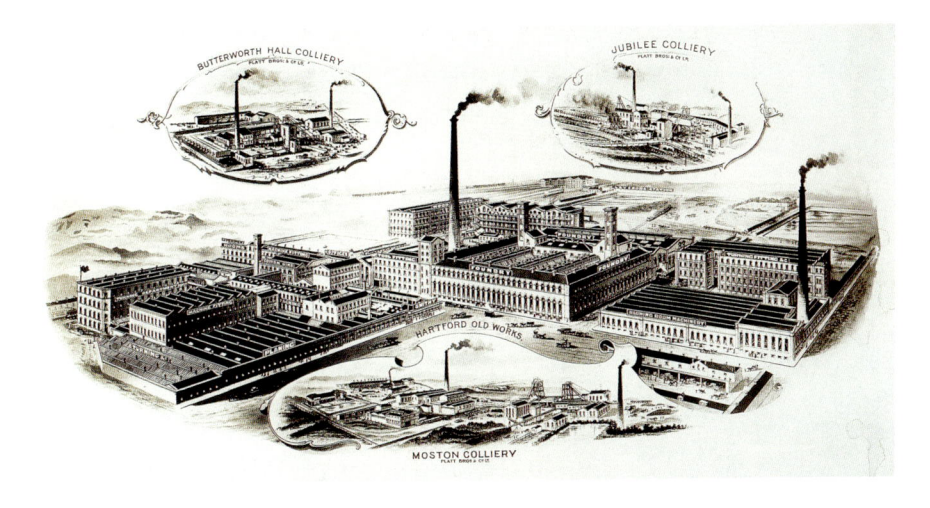

**Platt Brothers**: overstated as they are, these illustrations of the Hartford Old and New Works convey the vast scale of the enterprise at its peak in the late nineteenth/early twentieth century. Encompassing most if not all the processes of making textile machinery, the two sites, at Bottom of Moor and at Werneth, employed over 10,000 men and boys in 1911. To work at Platts was a matter of pride and superiority in Oldham at the time, as well as a well-paid and seemingly secure job.

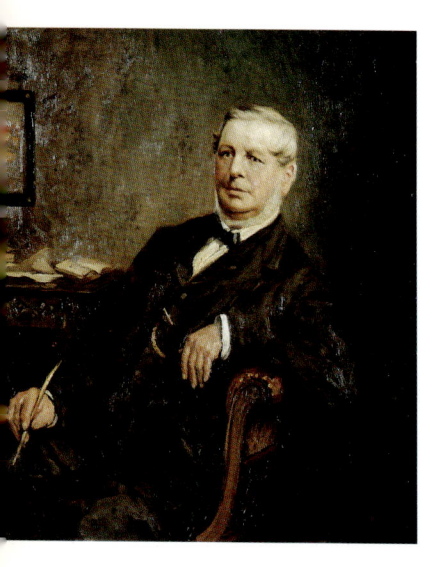

but not damaged by the Cotton Famine. Whether the massive subsequent surge in Oldham's spinning business was the result of Platts' leading position as makers of spinning machinery, or merely facilitated by the latter's presence in the town, is a point that can be argued. What is certain is that as the multitude of new mills were built and equipped, Platts, in particular, and others grew with them at an extraordinary rate.

With the death of his younger brother, James, in 1857, John Platt was undisputed master of the firm. Probably wisely, given the many involvements in the town and in national politics, which they chose to pursue, the brothers in 1854 had already made the business a partnership bringing in their most trusted senior associates. They had always paid good wages to all their workpeople but the chief managers were then earning as much as £1,500 yearly, a huge amount at the time. Now the new partners were given a share in the profits; they included William Richardson (1811-1893) who had worked his way up from apprenticeship to manage the old Hartford works, and Edmund Hartley (1810-1870), who came to Oldham from Rochdale to join Platts as a fitter and progressed to manage the huge new Hartford Works; he was regarded by contemporaries as "the lion of his day; when he gave an order those to whom he spoke felt compelled to obey". In 1868, extending the principle of involvement, the business became a limited company, capitalised at £1 million with 20,000 £5 shares, admitting managers and foremen throughout all departments, even down to the stables, as shareholders. When not all the foremen could afford to pay for their shares, they were given "assured" shares, receiving the dividends so long as they remained with the company; needless to say there were no lack of aspirants to be foremen. Such a system of co-partnership, far ahead of its time, brought its benefits. As a contemporary said, "thus the workmen were settled in their minds to do their best for the firm", and were completely loyal to it. The Directors could claim "that the men were part and parcel of themselves"; it was also said, however, that "you didn't get paid for nowt at Platts".

If John Platt remained the dominating leader until his untimely death at the age of fifty-five in 1872, his son, Sam Platt (1845-1902), as he was universally known in the business and the town, who succeeded him as Chairman, was a more genial, less driven individual. The architects of the firm's continued success were undoubtedly its senior managers, and foremen, for the most part life-long employees, technically expert, completely committed to preserving and enhancing Platts' standing and participating in its success. By 1876 the Platt family holding had fallen to 59 per cent of the share capital. Richardson, in particular, who became Vice-Chairman to Sam Platt, grew rich with the company leaving over £580,000, a huge fortune, when he died aged 82, still in his office every day, in 1883. John Dodd (1832-1912) who had started as a pattern maker was another notable servant, obsessively meticulous in inspection of important work down to the finest detail before it left Werneth; an imperious personality, he was to succeed Sam Platt as Chairman and also left a huge fortune, around £220,000. William Hilton (1834-1909) worked for Platts for sixty years rising to General Works Manager, a Director in 1895 and Vice-Chairman to Dodd in 1902; he was actively involved in the flotation of many spinning mills which were to take Platt machines. These were the prominent names but there were many other dedicated Platt stalwarts who gave all their working lives to the firm and rose to responsible positions within it.

The firm's operation remained based on certain strong principles. As far as possible they would be self-sufficient, even to owning their own coal mines. Platts did not make iron but worked it through all the processes from crude pig-iron purchases. All the component parts of Platt machines were made from the best materials worked to the highest standards, whether in its large foundries, or grinding, planing, turning and milling departments. Continuously the firm sought to enable their men "to do more and better work", by developing and introducing improved machine tools. They were concerned to facilitate the smooth progress of materials through the works, giving a lot of attention to layout and arrangement of the different departments. No machine left the erection department without careful testing of its performance. Platt technicians installed the machines in the customer's mill and were available to monitor performance and service them. Above all Platts were innovative, constantly improving their machines, making them larger, increasing their speed, reducing breakages, raising the quality of the yarn they spun. They aspired to make all kinds of textile machinery, but their strength lay in carding and spinning, rather than the other processes; especially they perfected and developed the self-acting mule. They were probably not the cheapest of the Lancashire machine makers; in fact, despite the impressive modern layout of the huge Werneth operation with its private sidings from the adjacent railway, their preoccupation with self sufficiency and high standards made them expensive. Their market position was based on quality, technical excellence and a carefully preserved reputation. John Platt's maxim was that "good work commands good prices and maintains an ever increasing trade", or, more succinctly, "quality first, quantity after". When William Richardson was dying, he told his successor, "remember there's always a best and it comes out on top; make sure it's Platts". These were strong Oldham principles. Asa Lees apart, their several competitors in spinning machinery had no comparable standing; only when ring spinning began to take a hold in Lancashire towards the end of the century did Platts see newer firms like Howard and Bullough begin to challenge their supremacy.

A very high proportion, certainly over two-thirds of the machinery installed in Oldham mills after 1870, came from Platts, in many cases because of the influence of Platt workmen among the shareholders. Their share of the market was less in the other spinning towns. They developed a large business in carding machines and mules with the Yorkshire woollen and worsted mills. But more than other firms they reached abroad, across Europe to Russia, within Asia to India, China and Japan, to Brazil and elsewhere, designing mills and sending their men out to equip them just as Oldham men then went out to manage them. The export demand had its ups and downs, but approached 1,000,000 spindles in the good years, falling to 400,000 in the lean; most of the power looms made by Platts were exported, mainly to Europe. Home demand, needless to say, was strongest in the mill-building years, falling away dramatically in the years of poor trade and pessimism, in the late 1880s and especially the 1890s, but reviving strongly for several years after 1899. In the result, if Platts total business expanded, like other

*Facing:* **Edmund Hartley** (top), **William Richardson** (centre) and **John Dodd**, all virtually life-long employees of Platts, held senior management positions immediately below the family. Each lacked formal education and although their particular strengths differed, each would probably have succeeded in any walk of life. Men like these, especially as John Platt and his sons became involved in other affairs, made the firm the success it was in the years up to 1914. Owning shares in the firm, they all left large fortunes when they died.

**Asa Lees** was second to Platts but its machinery had a similar world-wide reputation for outstanding workmanship and performance.

**Bottom of Moor.** The map shows St. James's Church, Greenacres, surrounded by a congested tangle of mills, foundries, engineering workshops and poor housing that developed in the nineteenth century. This was perhaps the busiest part of Oldham where many of the town's major enterprises had at least part of their operations.

engineering concerns, peaking in 1906, it was highly unstable from one year to the next. Profits varied accordingly. The company, its workforce and indeed Oldham had to cope with such enormous variations in the level of activity; there were many times when large numbers of Platts workmen were idle, or when the firm was sacking its employees.

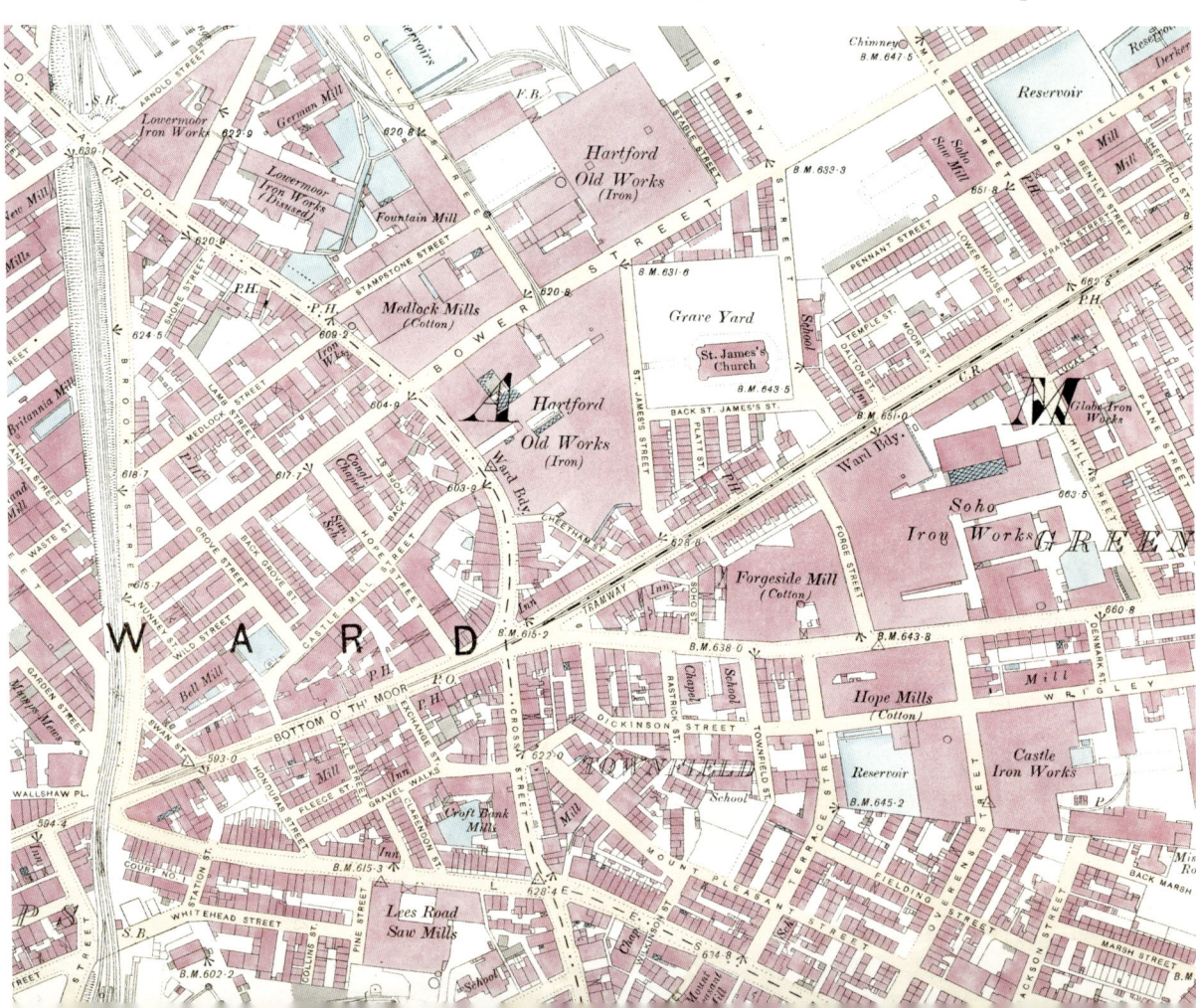

The success and prestige of Platts overshadowed that of Asa Lees Limited at the Soho works at Bottom of Moor. Specialising in spinning mules but trading more cautiously, its business grew solidly after the Famine, becoming the second supplier to the new Oldham mills. Its peak output was also in 1906; its workforce, at 3,000, compared with the 10,000 or so employed by Platts; its premises, large as they were, seemed modest compared with the bulk of Platt's old Hartford works and the vast sprawl that the Werneth site became by the end of the century. But Asa Lees (1816-1882), and his associate, Robert Taylor (1823-1912), had built a strong business, following similar principles and even more profitable than Platts. In the end Asa Lees had more staying power, but that was to become apparent at a later time.

**Many other engineers**

Platts and Asa Lees apart, Oldham in late century had a multitude of small concerns, as many as 150, mainly in the Bottom of Moor district, describing themselves variously as engineers, millwrights, iron and brass founders, and machine tool makers. They were normally centred round one or two gifted practical engineers with commercial skills, specialising in particular types of work, and finding a ready clientele in the cotton mills. Some achieved comparative prominence, particularly the makers of steam engines. Typical was Woolstenholme and Rye, started in 1821 as roller makers, moving to Lower Moor Ironworks in 1825 and expanding into general foundry work and spindle making. Employing about 250 workers by mid-century they were then making mules and power looms. William Rye (1809-1882), brought up in Ancoats, came to Oldham and worked as a mechanic with Radcliffes at Lowerhouse Mill before joining Woolstenholme in 1840; he subsequently became the main driving force, as the business changed to the manufacture of mill engines. Once its reputation was established there was a ready market in the district during the mill building boom of the 1870s, Rye, renowned for his through knowledge of any business he was involved with, and his courteous kindly manner, became a popular Mayor of Oldham; when he died in 1882 the firm went into liquidation in the subsequent period of bad trade.

The largest of the Oldham steam engine makers was Buckley and Taylor, started in a small way in rented space in 1861 but moving to new premises at

**Buckley and Taylor**, Castle Ironworks, Bottom of Moor, about 1870. The firm enjoyed great success in making steam engines for Oldham mills. Workmen are feeding bought-in pig iron into an outdoor furnace.

**Boddens** in Coldhurst were one of the more prominent and enduring of Oldham's engineering companies. Their speciality lay in making spindles, but they repaired, remodelled and "put in thorough working order" any type of spinning machine. Their all-male work force, encompassing young lads, apprentices and many older men, full of pride, is captured in this photograph.

Castle Ironworks, Bottom of Moor the following year. Both the partners were practical engineers. Samuel Buckley (1837-1911), the more prominent, had a classical career as an Oldham self-made man. He was born in Hey, the son of a mule spinner, starting work in the mill at the age of six, progressing to chief engineer at Radcliffe's Lowerhouse Mill at the age of twenty and then going into business with James Taylor. The new business had quick success, initially making valves for Oldham's waterworks, and then installing an engine at the Sun Mill in 1867. They went on to make scores of engines for the new Limiteds of the 1870s and 1880s, and also engaged in much millwright work. They were closely associated with the Oldham Boiler Works on Oldham Edge, where Buckley was a Director. Castle Ironworks was employing 400 workers by 1889. Samuel Buckley was three times Mayor of Oldham.

There were many other engineering firms serving the spinning industry. Bodden and Mercer, later William Bodden and Son, in Coldhurst, were the leading spindle manufacturers but ready to do almost any kind of work modifying, repairing or improving spinning machinery. William Bodden (1822-1897), another self-made man who had come to Oldham as a child with his widowed mother, in circumstances of utter poverty, also became an Oldham Mayor and leader of the Liberal Party in the Borough. Another successful entrepreneur was James Dronsfield (1809-1880), a migrant from Shaw. Working as a boy in the cardroom, he developed appliances for maintaining the teeth of carding machines. He came to Oldham, living and working in four back-to-back cottages in Atlas Street, close to the middle of town, in 1845. His sons joined him in the business which eventually became Dronsfield Brothers, creating and enlarging over the years their Atlas Works, from where patented card grinding machines were supplied all over the world. With their great success, the Dronsfields created a minor Oldham dynasty, active in local government and benefactors to the town.

Oldham was not a weaving town. If on a small scale, Saddleworth was and not all its able young practical engineers migrated elsewhere. Two thrusting young men, John Hutchinson and James Hollingworth, in business as iron founders, began making power looms at Dobcross in 1860. They developed a superior, faster and more versatile loom to others on the market, capable of weaving "fancy" worsted and woollen cloths. Their business grew rapidly as a result, the Dobcross Loom finding a large market in Yorkshire especially, and overseas. Theirs was another story of success and achievement.

**Dobcross Iron Works**, perhaps an unlikely location for a successful business which made a superior power-loom for woollen manufacture and enjoyed a strong market from the 1850s onwards.

*Below:* **Braddocks** were the leading firm making gas meters, needed in every home by the late nineteenth century but a finite market that dwindled rapidly once supplied. Oldham had no less than eight manufacturers of gas meters in 1880.

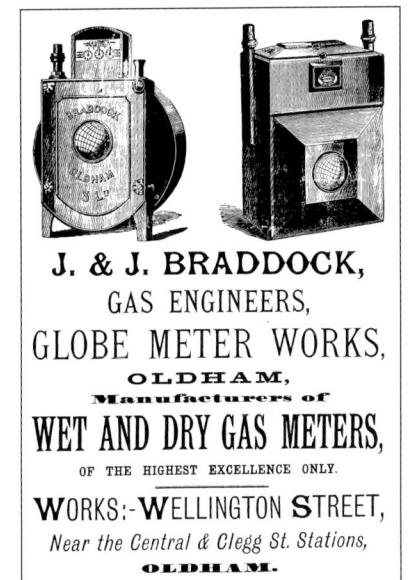

Not all Oldham's versatile and enterprising foundries and engineering concerns were concerned with the staple textile industry. The Town had at least three significant manufacturers of gas meters, the largest for many years being Braddocks of the Globe Meter Works, Wellington Street. Also in Wellington Street, Bradbury and Co., a limited company, had a long history since 1852 as makers of sewing machines and subsequently baby-carriages, motor-cycles and many other specialities. Fred and Tom Rothwell also started to make sewing machines in Gas Street in 1872; their business evolved to bicycles, bell punches for tram tickets, and knitting machines, and eventually to motor cars with their first successful model launched in 1903. They built 300 hand-made vehicles between then and 1914, "quality cars of no little repute". One quarter of all cars and lorries registered in Oldham up to 1910 were made by the Rothwells although the firm petered out when the Partners died a few years later. Other businesses specialised in central heating boilers and radiators, fireplaces, kitchen ranges, and in chip (and fish) frying ranges. Electrical engineering came to Oldham in 1896 when Sebastian de Ferranti started a small factory in Hollinwood, attracted by the low rent and good labour.

**J. & J. BRADDOCK,**
GAS ENGINEERS,
**GLOBE METER WORKS,**
OLDHAM,
Manufacturers of
**WET AND DRY GAS METERS,**
OF THE HIGHEST EXCELLENCE ONLY.
**WORKS:-WELLINGTON STREET,**
Near the Central & Clegg St. Stations,
OLDHAM.

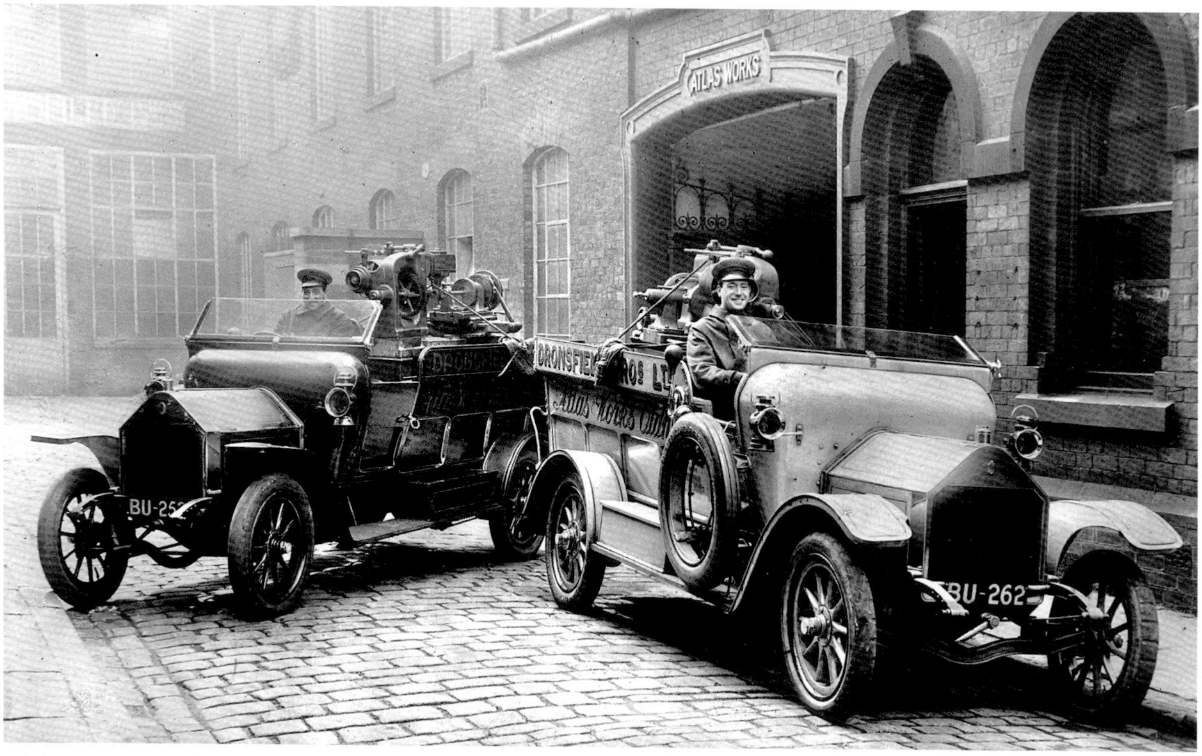
ATLAS WORKS
BU-262

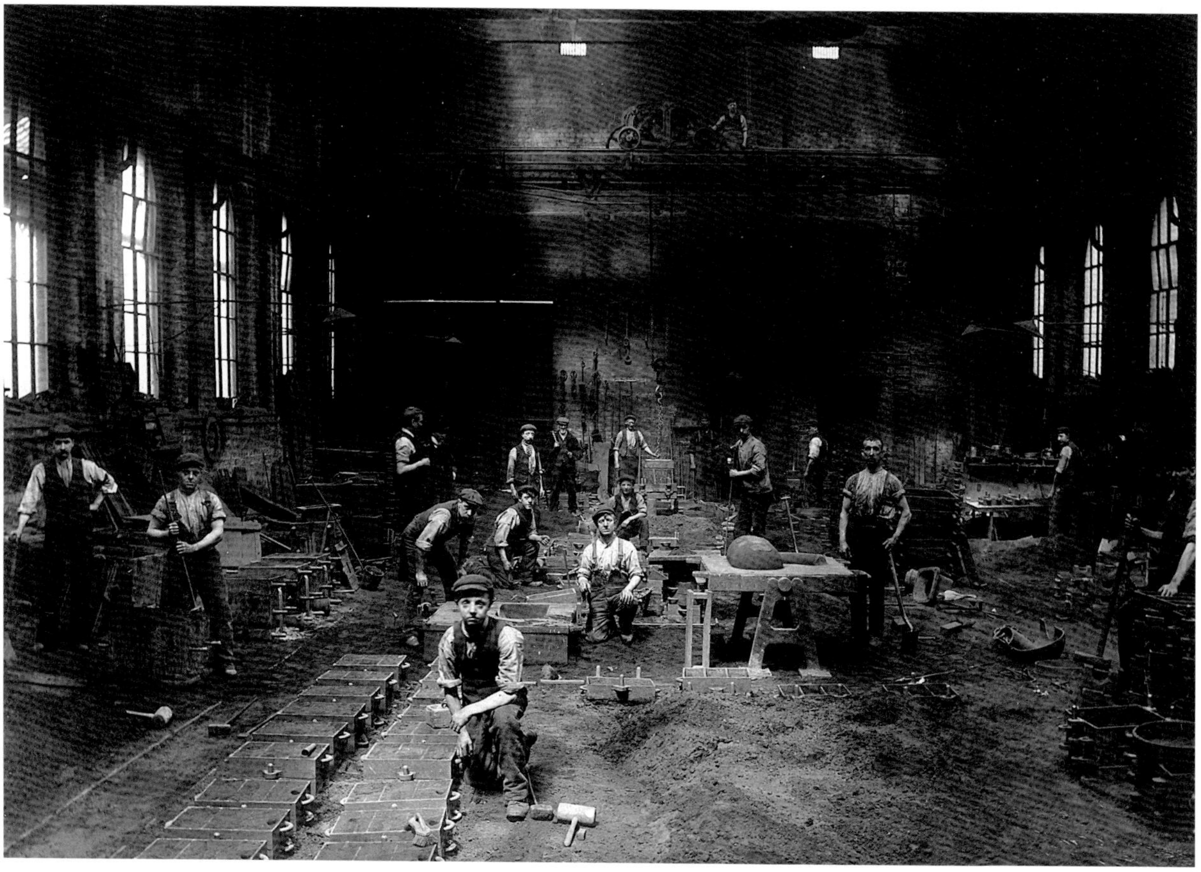

Not surprisingly the whole spread of foundry and mechanical engineering businesses provided a source of generally well paid work for men and boys. The downside lay in the fact that these businesses, for the most part, made capital goods and were vulnerable to the ups and downs of investment activity, frequently brought to a standstill in periods of depression. Many of their products were overtaken by rapid technical change and became obsolete, and all were vulnerable to intense competition. These were the risks of a dynamic economy to which all were accustomed at the time.

## The Chamber of Commerce

All Oldham's businessmen, whatever their trade, had many interests in common. One was running the town efficiently and economically, keeping down the rate burden. Another, was maintaining harmony between labour and capital; no-one disputed that long and bitter strikes hurt not merely the business but the reputation of the town. A third was cheap and efficient transport services. Oldham's confused railway system had long been a source of complaint, although geography was its main cause. What concerned businessmen as the town approached maturity was the level of railway charges, on coal and especially cotton and iron, and manufactures going out. There was a strong feeling that the Lancashire and Yorkshire Railway Company was exploiting its monopoly to the detriment of Oldham's trade.

The Chamber of Commerce concerned itself with these issues as with commercial matters generally, the legal obligations of companies, taxation, technical education in the town, accounting standards and the like. In particular it supported the Manchester Ship Canal, perceived as a means of lowering transport costs and breaking the railway monopoly on freight from Liverpool. Oldham businesses were leading shareholders in the Canal Company, while Sam Platt became a Director. When the Company had difficulties in raising enough money to complete the project in 1892, Oldham Corporation considered seeking powers to lend up to £250,000. In operation the Canal offered cheap rates for bulk commodities like cotton, timber and grain and, as a result, railway charges between Liverpool and Oldham fell. For a time there was even bold talk of extending the Canal to Chadderton and Royton; this came to nothing and in the event most of Oldham's trade with Liverpool stayed with rail. But there is no doubt the Canal helped Oldham.

## A World of Work

Whether in the cotton mill, the machine shop or other occupations, Oldham was a world of work; for the overwhelming majority of working age there was no alternative except the workhouse. Oldham's working population averaged about 60 per cent of the total population in the second half of the century, a higher proportion than in most other towns; the main groups not working were children, housewives and the comparatively few regarded as too old to work.

Distinctively, over half the women of working age, about 30 per cent of married but over 80 per cent of the unmarried, were at work. Children, following the 1844 Act, could not work full-time before the age of thirteen but half-time employment at the age of eight was permitted until 1874 when

*Facing, above:* **Rothwell's, Oldham's motor car company**, grew out of the enterprise of two brothers who went into business to make sewing machines in 1872. Their slogan was "All Others Eclipsed". They later made bicyles, tram ticket bell punches and, after several years copying German and French machines, motor cars from 1903. Two of their vehicles are shown here, proudly working for Dronsfields, another of Oldham's engineering success stories. When Tom Rothwell died in 1918 the firm lost its driving force and closed down.

*Facing, below:* **The Star Iron Works, Greenacres Road**, a typical Oldham iron foundry. There were over twenty similar concerns in the town in the late nineteenth century. Most of them were making cast-iron kitchen ranges but other staple items in almost universal demand for newly built homes were rain-water pipes, gratings, fenders, gas stoves, and mangles. William Toole, proprietor of Star Works, claimed to do "every description of castings."

**The half-time system** regulated the work of children in Oldham mills until its abolition in 1919. At the date this certificate was issued, 1892, a child could work in the mill after the tenth birthday, provided a particular but low level of educational attainment - Standard III - had been reached. In 1893 the minimum age was raised to eleven and again to twelve in 1899, and the educational requirement rose to Standard IV. There had been nearly 5,000 half-timers in Oldham in 1874, about 3,900 in 1892 but the numbers fell rapidly thereafter. Typically a half-timer would work in the mill from 6 a.m. to 12.30 p.m. and go to school in the afternoon; alternatively school from 9 a.m. to 12 noon was followed by work in the mill from 1.30 to 5.30 p.m.

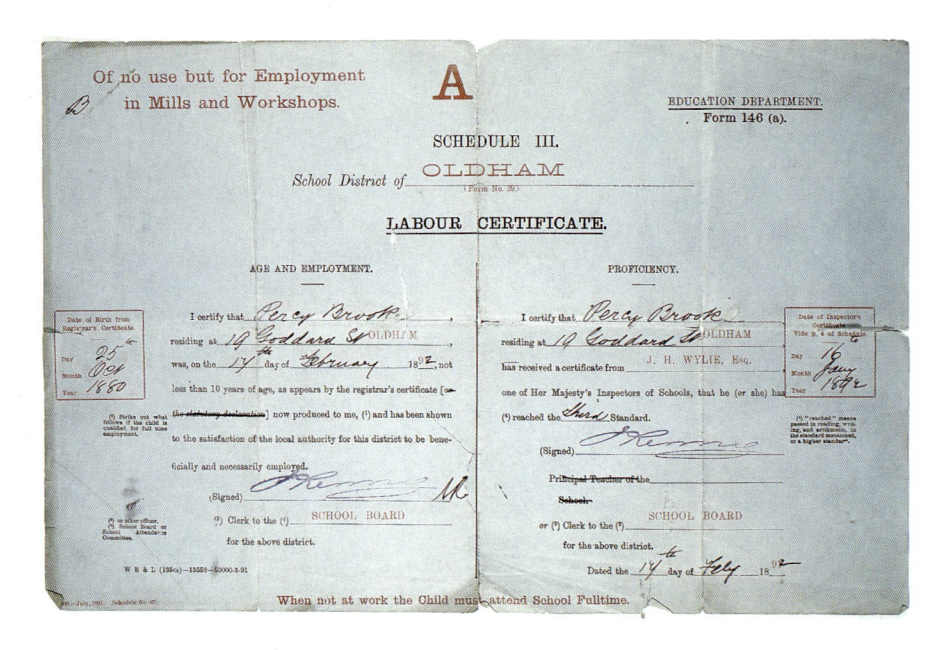

the half-time age went up to ten and the minimum full-time age was raised to fourteen; exemption could be secured at thirteen subject to attainment of basic educational qualifications. The minimum age for half-timers was raised to eleven in 1893 and to twelve in 1899; from over 5,000 in 1870 the numbers had fallen away sharply to no more than a few hundred in 1911. At that time there were still many children from poorer homes working at thirteen but for most children work began at fourteen; ninety per cent of fourteen year old boys were at work, nearly eighty per cent of girls, probably earning eight to ten shillings a week. The fall in the number of children at work was a subject of lively complaint by many cotton spinning companies who found themselves unable to recruit little piecers or girls to perform menial tasks for low wages; the education authorities were blamed for encouraging children to remain at school, but it was parents who, in the end, had made the choice.

### TABLE X: OLDHAM BOROUGH AND DISTRICTS: EMPLOYMENT IN COTTON MANUFACTURING & ENGINEERING 1911

|  | Occupied Population (thousands) |  | Employed in Cotton (thousands) |  | Employed in Metals and Machinery (thousands) |
|---|---|---|---|---|---|
|  | Male | Female | Male | Female |  |
| Oldham | 50.7 | 28.8 | 15.9 | 20.1 | 14.5 |
| Chadderton | 9.7 | 5.0 | 4.4 | 4.2 | 2.2 |
| Royton | 5.8 | 3.3 | 3.5 | 2.5 | 0.3 |
| Crompton | 5.2 | 3.1 | 3.2 | 2.5 | 0.1 |
| Failsworth | 5.3 | 2.6 | 1.7 | 1.8 | 0.8 |
|  | 76.7 | 42.8 | 28.7 | 31.1 | 17.9 |
| Saddleworth | 4.5 | 2.1 | 2.3 | 1.5 | 0.6 |

Notes: 1. Saddleworth employment includes wool textiles as well as cotton.
2. No data is available for Lees but its occupied population would be approximately 1,800 with about 1,100-1,200 in cotton.

# A World of Work

**Cardroom Workers at Belgian Mill, 1904**, girls and young women, and a few men. Clogs, clothing, faces and hair-style all tell a story, but, not one of poverty.

Overwhelmingly, of course, those at work were in cotton. An estimate prepared in 1914 indicated that over three-quarters of all girls leaving school, and more than half of the boys, went into a cotton mill. The position in Oldham relative to the Townships in 1911 is illustrated in Table X. Chadderton, Royton and Crompton were almost exclusively cotton communities with 54 per cent of occupied men and boys, and 81 per cent of women and girls so employed. In Oldham the position was not totally dissimilar for women but men had a substantially greater range of occupations, as they did in Failsworth. Although the numbers are small compared with the Oldham district, textiles still accounted for over 50 per cent of all jobs in Saddleworth, more in wool than in cotton, especially for women.

Other than cotton, engineering and machine-making had grown to be a huge sector, predominantly for men and boys; the numbers employed reached over 18,500 in 1911 compared with about 6,500 in 1861, in both years in the Borough and the Districts including Saddleworth. Significant numbers of those employed by Platts, in particular, would be living in Chadderton, Failsworth and even Royton in 1911, carried to work by early morning trams. There were still over 1,500 coal miners scattered throughout the district, many in Failsworth and 300 in Crompton where Platts had a large mine at Jubilee.

## Oldham Brave Oldham

**Mill Boilers**: the multitude of Oldham mills were powered by steam engines, mostly made in the town as were the steam-raising boilers. Thousands of tons of coal weekly were shovelled into the boilers; engine tenting was a recognised "good job", fairly secure and well-paid.

Among men, and also dependent on cotton or on engineering, there were large numbers, close to 5,000, employed in transport of one kind or another. As much as 20,000 tons of coal weekly were used in the district, in its mills and the 40,000 or so houses, some still local but most coming by rail from Wigan; 9,000 bales of cotton went through the mills weekly and the equivalent weight moved out in skips of yarn, beams of warp or woven cloth as well as waste. When all the movement associated with engineering and building is taken into account, Oldham's roads and streets were constantly filled with hundreds of horse drawn carts and wagons, serving a busy railway system, not to mention public transport, and services to shops or homes.

Beyond this, in a manufacturing town, work was in the building trades (over 4,000 men), in local government (over 1,000) and in the service trades, in shops and public houses, in public entertainment, and for women, in domestic service, although reflecting a predominantly working class community, the proportion in domestic service was far below the national average. Commercial occupations connected with the staple trades - banking, yarn agents, merchants, insurance agents, estate agents, sharebrokers and the like - were well-established while other white collar occupations of various kinds - teaching, the law, what could be termed medical - were there but on a limited if growing scale.

In so many of the commercial and professional areas and in specialised retailing, Oldham continued to look to Manchester, with its extensive and well developed services, not more than a few miles away with an improved railway connection, and after 1900, the electric tram. Thus in 1911 the Oldham district had about one in six of all workers in services, including local government; the proportion in Manchester, the commercial metropolis of the region, was about one in two, vastly different. If Oldham had 65 per cent in textiles and engineering, Manchester had less than 30 per cent. When Arthur Shadwell described Oldham in 1908 as "the most complete example of the purely manufacturing town that can be found anywhere", he was not far from the truth.

## Raising Men like Mushrooms

It was Arthur Young who observed that "the increase of employment will be found to raise men like mushrooms." So it was again in Oldham. The dramatic if irregular expansion of the local economy, checked in the 1860s and by bad trade in the 1890s, booming at other periods, supported the striking increase in population. The figures speak for themselves; notable is the huge growth in numbers in the two decades after 1871, rapid enough in the Borough but exceeding 75 per cent in Chadderton, Royton, Crompton and Failsworth, where land for mills and streets was more freely available. Inevitably the growth slowed after 1891, especially in the Borough, least so in Chadderton and Failsworth, with plenty of land and ready access to Manchester and all its work opportunities. Lees did not participate in the mushroom growth while the population of Saddleworth, like that of many other small textile communities, peaked in 1891. People were leaving the remoter scattered farms and folds of Delph and Dobcross; the more accessible Uppermill, Greenfield and Springhead continued to grow but only slowly compared to their more dynamic neighbours.

*Facing:* **Clegg Street Railway Sidings,** in the centre of Oldham 1879. Local coal quickly proved inadequate and most of Oldham's rapidly growing requirement was brought in by rail. Although coal wagons from the Barnsley district and from the Wigan area are conspicuous, much of the coal appears to be coming from collieries in Ashton-under-Lyne. Huge quantities would be carted through the town every weekday, both for the mills and in bags for weekly delivery to every household. Baulks of timber and building stone are also evident. Bradbury's sewing machine factory is in the background.

Table XI: OLDHAM DISTRICT: POPULATION GROWTH 1851-1911

|  | 1851 | 1861 | 1871 | 1881 | 1891 | 1901 | 1911 |
|---|---|---|---|---|---|---|---|
| Oldham Borough | 52,818 | 72,334 | 82,629 | 111,343 | 131,463 | 137,246 | 147,483 |
| Chadderton | 6,188 | 7,486 | 12,203 | 16,899 | 22,087 | 24,892 | 28,299 |
| Royton | 6,974 | 7,493 | 7,794 | 10,582 | 13,395[1] | 14,881 | 17,069 |
| Crompton | 6,374 | 7,032 | 7,302 | 9,797 | 12,901 | 13,427 | 14,750 |
| Failsworth | 4,432 | 5,113 | 5,685 | 7,912 | 10,425 | 14,152 | 15,998 |
| Lees | (2,000) | (2,700) | 2,919 | 3,511 | 3,877 | 3,621 | 3,650 |
|  | 78,786 | 102,158 | 118,532 | 160,044 | 194,148 | 208,219 | 227,249 |
| Saddleworth [2] | 17,779 | 18,631 | 19,923 | 17,920[2] | 18,238 | 17,018 | 17,654 |

Notes:  1. Boundary Change.
2. Saddleworth includes part of Mossley until 1881 (Population in 1881, 4,379). In 1901, the communities of Saddleworth included Delph 3,710, Dobcross 3,044, Greenfield 3,487, Uppermill 2,079 and Springhead 4,698.

Where did the huge increase in numbers come from? Primarily as in the earlier part of the century from natural increase; more people got married and at an earlier age and had large families when times were good and living easier. For the high period of population growth Table XII summarises the figures. Over a period of sixty years, excess of births over deaths account for 66 per cent of the growth. Clearly however a lot of people moved into the Oldham district especially in the 1870s and 1880s. This is hardly surprising given the work opportunities. All the evidence suggests they did not move very far, mainly from adjacent districts in Lancashire and to a lesser extent Yorkshire and Cheshire, where work at good wages was not so easily available. The only significant long distance migrants were from Ireland. In 1851 Oldham had 2,743 inhabitants who had been born in Ireland, probably

TABLE XII: OLDHAM REGISTRATION DISTRICT: POPULATION CHANGE 1851-1911

|  | Increase in population | Births | Deaths | Natural Increase | Net Migration |
|---|---|---|---|---|---|
| 1851-1861 | 24,488 | 38,174 | 25,130 | 13,044 | 11,444 |
| 1861-1871 | 15,705 | 44,131 | 30,452 | 13,679 | 2,027 |
| 1871-1881 | 41,479 | 55,653 | 37,077 | 18,576 | 22,093 |
| 1881-1891 | 33,547 | 62,495 | 42,100 | 20,395 | 13,152 |
| 1891-1901 | 13,616 | 59,301 | 43,815 | 15,486 | (1,870) |
| 1901-1911 | 19,957 | 57,557 | 40,566 | 16,991 | 2,966 |

Note: The Registration District includes Middleton.

with their English born children, about 3,500 Irish in total. The number recorded as Irish born peaked at the 1861 Census at 5,817. Saddleworth and the other out-townships, in contrast, had very few of Irish birth. In absolute terms and as a proportion, Oldham's Irish population was far lower than in Liverpool or Manchester, or even than in towns like Ashton or Preston.

With its huge natural increase, Oldham's experience replicated that of the rest of the country; both the birth rate and the death rate were very high, but the former greatly exceeded the latter. The figures in Table XIII tell the story.

## Raising Men like Mushrooms

TABLE XIII: OLDHAM REGISTRATION DISTRICT: BIRTH & DEATH RATES

|  | Birth Rate (per 1000) | Death Rate (per 1000) Oldham | Death Rate (per 1000) England & Wales |
|---|---|---|---|
| 1851-1860 | - | 25 | 22 |
| 1861-1870 | - | 26 | 22 |
| 1871-1880 | 38 | 25 | 21 |
| 1881-1890 | 34 | 23 | 19 |
| 1891-1900 | 29 | 21 | 18 |
| 1901-1910 | 26 | 19 | 16 |

Oldham had a stubbornly high death rate, well above the average for the country although comparable with similar industrial towns and significantly lower than in Manchester or Liverpool; the townships and Saddleworth were healthier places, close to the national average. The causes are not hard to find, a combination of poor working and living conditions and rudimentary health care. What can be said is that the death rate was falling, although at nineteen per 1,000 people at the turn of the century it compared with about eleven a century later. High infantile mortality, varying between 160 and 180 children per 1,000 live births dying in the first year of life, much higher in the poor wards such as St Mary's, made a significant contribution, while a large number of the children who survived their first year died before age five; deaths of children under five were usually 40 to 50 per cent of all deaths, such a common event that they were often unmarked. Infantile mortality was as low as six a century later in the 1990s. Longevity was also low, much lower than in the country as a whole. For most of the period, only about 5 per cent of Oldham's population was aged over sixty; there were only a handful of people aged over seventy-five.

Notwithstanding their high mortality, Oldham, like other Victorian towns swarmed with children, playing, running around the streets until they were schooled or went into the factory. 35 per cent of the town's population in 1891 was aged below fifteen. The population profile of the town began to

**King Street, Delph**, also, like any Oldham street, full of children, reflecting the huge natural increase in population.

change at the end of the century. A modestly falling death rate resulted in some increase in the numbers of elderly people, but still only about 6 per cent of the whole. More children were surviving but the birth rate fell dramatically and with it the numbers of young people aged below fifteen, down to below 28 per cent in 1911. Oldham became a somewhat older town, although strikingly youthful in comparison with later and the most recent periods when those aged below fifteen have been only about 20 per cent and those over sixty over 20 per cent of the whole. And for a given population, Oldham in the early years of the present century had fewer households; the average household of 1991 was no more than two and a half people, that of 1911 nearly five.

Why the birth rate fell is uncertain. The same change was taking place nationally but it was much more pronounced in Lancashire towns. Earlier tendencies were now being reversed; fewer young women were marrying, the age of marriage was rising and the married were restricting the size of their families. The reasons, more than anything, reflected rising living standards, improved education, greater concern for comfort and a modest affluence. The need for a large family to augment household income was perhaps diminished. If people had learned how to avoid having too many children, they had every incentive to practice family limitation. The birth rate, of course, continued to fall: from about thirty at the turn of the century, a hundred years later it was close to thirteen.

**People and Houses**

Coping with the huge increase in the number of households, whether from migration or population increase, led to a massive surge in house-building. In the boom periods there was an acute housing shortage, across the town, and locally as individual mills opened or expanded their employment. The consequence was doubling-up and house-sharing, young couples living with parents, a large number of lodgers, and significant overcrowding as large families occupied quite inadequate accommodation. To meet the need, 12,000 new houses were built in Oldham Borough between 1870 and 1890, no less than 5,000 in the busiest years 1876 to 1880. The scale of new building then fell away but remained volatile, surging again usually after years of prosperity when new mills were built or new districts opened up. Building in the townships followed a similar history.

Thus thousands of new terrace houses, in blocks of monotonous parallel streets, separated by small yards and back passages to their rear, or in ribbons along the principal roads, were built to sprawl over the still vacant hillsides of Oldham and the meadowlands to the north and west. Typically densities were high, about thirty houses to the acre, but that compared with close to sixty in the older crowded areas. The houses followed the mills and with them went pubs and shops, usually on street corners, but here and there in clusters along the main roads, as well as churches, chapels and schools, and, on a limited scale as the century progressed, new institutional buildings, council offices, baths, libraries and the like. The slopes of Greenacres Moor were developed in this way, along and between the roads to Ripponden, Huddersfield, Saddleworth and Lees. Hathershaw along the Ashton Road, Hollinwood, Chadderton, and, still detached by open fields, Royton and

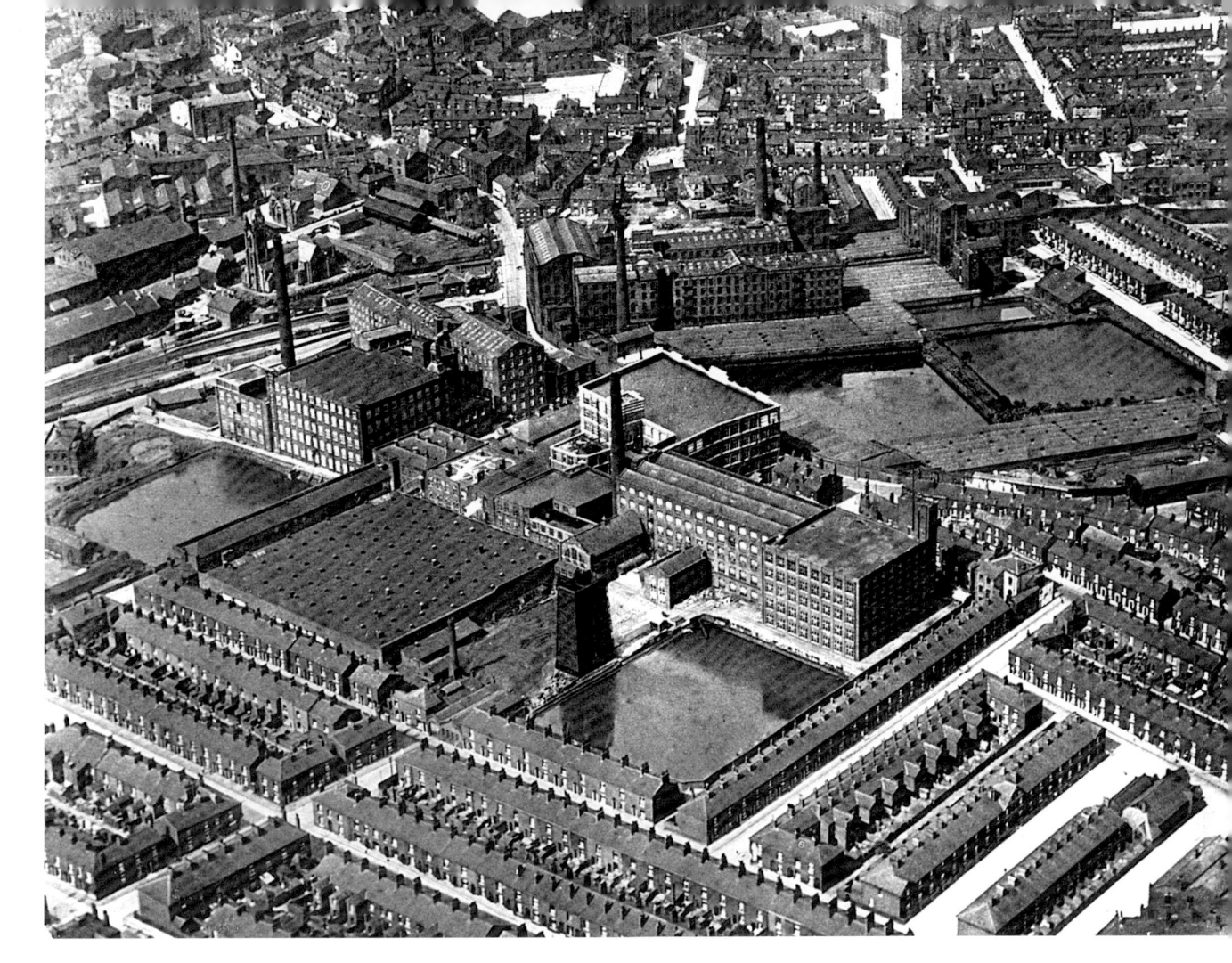

Shaw, followed the same pattern, the houses being clustered around the many new mills, with here and there terraces of better quality or villas with more room and more privacy and the occasional mill-owner's mansion. It was the multi-storeyed mills, each with their mill lodge, the forest of mill chimneys, and the associated rows of uniform red-brick houses, that gave the Oldham district its special character. Such a pattern of development may have been stigmatised by later writers, but it was an efficient arrangement at the time, low cost housing close to the place of work, and a vast improvement on the crowded older streets near the town centre, now increasingly left to the poor.

Until the end of the century only the more well-to-do could afford to live any distance from the place of work. They could also afford to pay for amenity, more space and light, better air, getting away from the immediate mill environment. Glodwick, convenient to Bottom of Moor, was developed as a purely residential district for the better-off working man after the 1870s; reflecting its respectable tone it had no public houses and no mills within its street plan. In particular, the convenient and attractive sites on higher ground at Coppice became Oldham's superior residential suburb, with its wider streets of larger terrace houses, some with small gardens, some even with stables for pony and carriage, typified by Werneth Hall Road, Windsor Road or Osborne Road, appropriate names for a genteel middle class neighbourhood. Coppice was described in 1875 as "dotted over with chaste

**Oldham's growing population** was housed in new suburbs such as Glodwick, with Bolton and Kersley Streets in the foreground in this later aerial view. Lees and Wrigley's Greenbank Mills and Collinge's Commercial Mills have reached their mature extent. In the distance is the less disciplined but more congested older housing of Mount Pleasant, close to Bottom of Moor.

**The home of Charles and Sarah Lees** in Werneth Park affords a sharp contrast to the old and new streets of small terrace houses where most of Oldham's population lived.

**Queens Road**, not quite an address in Werneth Park but only a step below, was one of Oldham's most exclusive streets. The building plots had been part of the land acquired by the Corporation for Alexandra Park. In selling their leaseholds for development, mainly to yield a useful much-needed income, the Council insisted on large plots and substantial villas, suitable for an emerging and affluent class of successful business and professional men.

and elaborate residences, the fashionable west end of the town". Grander enclaves still, close to the green open space of Werneth Park or the new Alexandra Park of the 1860s, were Frederick Street, Wellington Road, Park Road and Queen's Road, with their large villas, often in private grounds, the homes not perhaps of the few families who reached the town's grand elite, the Platts, Lees or Radcliffes, but of successful manufacturers, tradesmen and professional men.

The many thousands of houses were built by private enterprise, to plans approved by the Corporation in conformity with its bye-laws. Generally land was freely available from a large number of owners, for mills as for houses, invariably on a 999 year lease at ground rents of about 2d to 3d per square yard equivalent if capitalised at twenty years purchase to £800-£1,200 per acre. Those who owned the land, and many were small farmers, saw these values as a fortune; their land might have been worth £15-£30 an acre before Oldham began to explode. Few landowners imposed any conditions on the type of house that could be built, nor did they provide any estate development, roads or the like.

Many of the developers were speculative builders who had leased the land, borrowed money, and built a row of houses, paid for the street to be paved and drained, and sold the houses as a street or individually, hoping to make a profit. There were also the speculative property companies, Oldham Estate, County Land, Lancashire Land and others, whose shares were easily floated in the mania of the early 1870s, who bought leases on building land, or less frequently bought the freehold; they then went on perhaps to resell either the ground rent or the freehold; or alternatively contracted with a builder to throw up houses to be sold or let, they rather than the builder assuming the

**Albert Mount**, in Derker, now the property of a Housing Association, was built in 1862 by William Rye, partner of an Oldham engineering firm and Mayor of Oldham in 1868. The individual houses varied in size and comfort; Rye himself lived in the largest. At the time these were superior houses, occupied in 1871 by men pursuing a variety of occupations including three cotton waste dealers, a master brick-maker, and several cotton spinners and metal tradesmen.

**Houses built by the Royton Co-operative Society** for owner-occupation at the turn of the century. Their quality reflects the prosperity of the well-paid overlooker and minder of the time.

risk. For a while these companies were paying dividends of 25 per cent or more on their share capital; that was in the boom of the mid 1870s; when conditions deteriorated and land and house prices fell as they did in 1878 and subsequently, many of these companies failed. Some of the large private millowners continued to build houses for their workpeople, especially the Mellodews at Moorside and the Greaves at Derker, but generally this practice had ceased, although many of the enterprises retained ownership of houses built earlier in the century. There were also private individuals of whom Samuel Ogden Ward, Town Councillor and Director of many Limiteds was one, who became housing developers using money borrowed from building societies. To the extent that the Co-operative Societies, towards the end of the century, acquired land and had houses built to their own specification, usually of better quality, then to be let, they were also developers. None of the Limiteds were involved in house building, unlike the private mill owners earlier in the century. But the large building concerns who built the mills would frequently also build a few terraces nearby confident of a demand for the completed houses.

Thus did the new community, "the purely manufacturing town" develop, to serve and house those working in the huge specialised industry created by its acquisitive and go-ahead entrepreneurs, and financed by new forms of popular capitalism. It needed government just as its people had to be educated; slowly it offered its inhabitants a better life than any they had enjoyed before. These are the next chapters in the history of Oldham's ascendancy.

*Chapter VI*

# LOCAL GOVERNMENT 1849-1914

Oldham was incorporated in 1849 so that an elected council, limited in size, could provide more effective government of the rapidly growing town. In the out-townships, as in Saddleworth, local government still remained as it was, that is in the hands of the vestry; it was only when their populations began to grow more rapidly and sanitary improvement became more pressing that stronger institutions were formed, namely local boards, generally in the 1860s. When another local government milestone was reached in 1888 with the formation of county councils, Oldham retained its autonomy as a county borough while the local boards of the townships gave way to district councils which shared responsibility with the new Lancashire County Council, or in Saddleworth's case, with the West Riding of Yorkshire. Inevitably, since the growth of population and settlement in the townships was regarded, at least in Oldham, as an extension of the town, the relationship of Oldham Borough and the neighbouring local boards was an uneasy one, with amalgamation, or annexation according to the point of view, a regular agenda item as it was to remain indeed until its final resolution in 1974. The government of the townships and their relation to the larger "metropolis" will be described later: first the government of Oldham town requires review.

## Oldham Town Council

The first bitterly contested election in 1849, for twenty-four Councillors in eight wards, gave a narrow success to the Conservative and Fieldenite coalition who had opposed incorporation. They had defeated the Radical or Liberal group, led by the Platt brothers and their friends and associates, especially the Radcliffes. Establishing a practice that was to prevail, the Conservatives used their majority to choose all the eight Aldermen from their supporters, and elect William Jones of the wealthy coal owning family, as first Mayor.

The Conservatives retained control of the Council until 1854 and chose the next two Mayors, James Collinge and James Lees, both prominent cotton spinners and large employers. A by-election in 1853 created a narrow Liberal majority which was sustained at the municipal election in November of that year, a lively contest with 85 per cent of a larger electorate voting in the contested wards, assisted by plenty of free ale and free carriage to the poll. In the following year when four Tory Aldermen were replaced by Liberals, the latter had full control and John Platt became the first Liberal Mayor; after two terms he was succeeded by Josiah Radcliffe also serving two terms. The Liberals were to control Oldham Council for the next forty years usually with

*Overleaf, above:*
**Joshua Walmsley Radcliffe (1843-1895)**, an august figure in this portrait, was the most distinguished of one of Oldham's new elite families in the nineteenth century. His father Josiah had been three times Mayor, and Joshua Radcliffe was three times Mayor in the 1880s and later became High Sheriff of Lancashire, in those days regarded as a signal honour. His sudden and premature death was a loss to Oldham. The Radcliffes and the Platts, neighbours in Werneth Park and connected by marriage, tried to rule Oldham for close on fifty years.

*Overleaf, below:*
**Samuel Radcliffe Platt (1845-1902)**, Chairman of Platts where he was happy to delegate affairs to trusted and dedicated senior managers. As Sam Platt he was a genial and popular leader of Oldham society, lacking "neither in brass nor common-sense", as the Chronicle said. He was three times Mayor after his cousin, Joshua Radcliffe, and went on to become High Sheriff in 1897. A keen musician, he did much to foster the musical life of Oldham; the same could be said of his participatory patronage of Oldham cricket. He played in local orchestras and batted for Werneth at number ten, rarely scoring. Like his parents, a strong Liberal, he changed his politics over the issue of Irish Home Rule and became a Liberal Unionist, a cause of controversy and disappointment in the town. His big luxury was a yacht and it was on his yacht, "Norseman", that, like his father, he died young. He was the last Platt to play any significant role in Oldham.

huge majorities; in the busy 1870s, for instance, there were barely more than seven or eight Tory Councillors. The Liberals made the Mayors and they elected the Aldermen and managed other forms of patronage within the Corporation. Conservatives began to increase their strength after 1890 but it was not until 1894 that they managed to win control of the Council, first by getting a majority of Councillors and then by appointing their own new Aldermen. The Liberals came back in 1898, but thereafter, until 1914, the political composition of the Council was a more closely balanced affair with Conservatives in control from 1903 until 1909.

The Council apart, there was the local bench of Borough Magistrates, set up in 1857 and superseding the older County Bench. Appointments here, as to the County Bench, were reserved for the natural social leaders. This was a cross-party matter but whatever the processes of consultation only the elite were appointed to the Bench. As the town grew more magistrates were needed, but the Bench remained the province of leading Councillors, property owners and successful business or professional men. Only by the 1890s was its composition broadened to include representatives of the working men: Thomas Ashton, the spinners' leader, for instance, became a JP in 1890, William Mullins of the cardroom operatives ten years later.

However keen the party spirit there was little in class or status to differentiate the representatives of the Liberal and Conservative factions. All were men of property and trade and some, on both sides, among the most wealthy and successful of the town's citizens. During this phase membership of the Council was clearly regarded as being a high calling, work of such importance that the great and the good of the town had to be involved. Most of the town's Mayors in this early period were successful businessmen, and especially cotton spinners. Apart from the positive commitment, and the power and the glory, there was also perhaps what has been called "the fear of the penalty of refusal, to be governed by someone worse than themselves". The involvement of the town's elite was to change; subsequent generations of the large private capitalists, with important exceptions such as Sam Platt or Joshua Walmsley Radcliffe or Alfred Emmott, left the town or eschewed Council work, perhaps disenchanted with the process of popular election or the nature of the task. With the ascendancy of the Limiteds, private capital in cotton spinning became less important, in any event. Membership of the Council for which a Liberal flag was the easiest passport, fell to the smaller capitalists, to professional men, to shopkeepers, to officials of the Limiteds, to sharebrokers and insurance agents, to "common-sense businessmen, shrewd men of high standing in the town", as they described themselves. After 1882 the Council was invariably made up of persons with this kind of background, whether Liberal or Conservative. Eventually people of this standing also lost their interest; by 1907 the local press was complaining of "an apathy to public life".

TABLE XIV: COMPOSITION OF OLDHAM TOWN COUNCIL

| Year | 1862-63 | 1882-83 | 1902-03 |
|---|---|---|---|
| Number of Aldermen & Councillors | 32 | 32 | 48 |
| Cotton Spinners/Manufacturers | 20 | 9 | 3 |
| Engineer/ other Manufacturers | 4 | 8 | 3 |
| Professional: Doctor, Solicitor, Accountant | 3 | 1 | 13 |
| Shopkeepers, Publicans | 4 | 11 | 27 |
| Other (Gentlemen etc.) | 1 | 3 | 2 |

*Note:* There were eight wards on incorporation; in 1887, reflecting a much larger population and the spread of housing, the number increased to twelve. Each ward had three Councillors serving three years, one elected each year, and an Alderman elected by the Council for six years.

**Oldham Council on the Fiftieth Anniversary of Incorporation in 1899**: the earnest serious Councillors, all mainly engaged in manufacturing businesses, trade or the professions, stand against the line of portraits of worthy figures from the past. Jackson Brierley, an accountant and estate agent, is the able but controversial Mayor; he spoke of "the sagacity and high purpose, the single-mindedness and devotion" which had marked the government of the town.

The great majority of Councillors, unpaid at this time, served less than ten years but there were some who assumed a professional role, holding office for twenty years or more, usually becoming Mayor and Aldermen for part of this time. They, from their durability and experience, probably had the greatest influence on the town's affairs. A few individuals may be mentioned to illustrate the Council's composition: Samuel Ogden Ward, tin-plate worker who in his youth sold tinware from a stall in the Market Place and went on to become a Director of thirteen Limiteds, and large scale developer of dozens of streets in Westwood, was on the Council from 1868 to 1892; James Yates, a doctor, was involved, on and off between 1870 and 1908, and was three times Mayor; James Eckersley describing himself as a manufacturing chemist, served between 1868 and 1903 and was Conservative Mayor in 1901; Jackson Brierley, an accountant and a combative controversial Liberal personality, "a leader of courage and resource" according to the *Chronicle*, was a member from 1887 to 1907 and Mayor in 1898-99. In all there were fourteen Councillors who served for more than twenty years in the period to 1914. Over the whole period it is fair to say that there was always on Oldham Council competent, experienced, conscientious men who took their responsibilities very seriously. They were not, as Winston Churchill alleged, "happy-go-lucky amateurs".

A substantially larger electorate, and there were over 25,000 voters by the 1890s, the great majority being working men, made little difference to the Council's composition. Most of the larger electorate voted, with turnout in the municipal elections usually reaching 70 per cent; in the 1891 election, keenly fought as the Conservatives revived and political change became a possibility, it was as high as 82 per cent. But the working men, still generally conservative and deferential in their attitudes, voted for their perceived betters, for those who ran businesses or practised the professions, for those who had the time and ability to run the town. A few working class candidates regularly fought elections from the 1890s, usually with derisory results; in 1909 for instance, on a 75 per cent turnout they received 7 per cent of the votes cast. It was not until 1910 that Samuel Frith, describing himself as Labour but with Liberal support, won a seat. And of course the Council was completely male, a monopoly broken only when the redoubtable 'grande dame' of Oldham, Sarah Lees, widow of Charles Edward Lees and heiress with her daughters of a huge cotton fortune, was elected as a Liberal in 1907; she became the Borough's first Freeman and Mayor in 1910.

With little to differentiate them in terms of class or interest, Conservatives and Liberals have to be seen as rival factions disputing the spoils of office, chairmanships of the Council committees, control of the election of Aldermen, patronage within the Corporation, and above all, perhaps, the mayoralty, the proudest position in the town and the focus of display. Along with high status and visibility, being Mayor had its responsibilities, obligations and costs. As the local paper described these, "A Mayor is fair game for all sorts and conditions of suppliants. He is expected to give to all who ask; the only thing he is not expected to give is a refusal. Having begun his year by keeping an open house, he is thereafter required to keep an open purse". These comments referred to the outgoings, not the time. As to the time "he is called to attend 500 meetings in connection with Corporation

**Sarah Lees**, widowed in 1894 became Oldham's first woman Councillor, first woman Mayor and Freeman of the Borough.

business. He is a member of every Committee and must be in touch with the chief part of its business. He must represent the Corporation on all matters". Thus not everyone wanted to be Mayor. William Richardson, a dominant figure at Platts, turned it down although his colleague Edward Hartley had died in the office in 1870. Samuel Ogden Ward, Councillor for twenty-four years, declined the honour. In contrast, William Wrigley, chief organiser of Oldham Liberals and architect of their electoral success over many years used his credit with them to become Mayor in 1872 after only two years on the Council. An inner group or clique within the ruling party invariably made the choice of Mayor, as for Aldermen, and usually their decision held; occasionally there was a contest as in 1864 when William Knott, the former Radical, challenged no less a Liberal grandee than Josiah Radcliffe. Not every Mayor could afford the grand hospitality; Jackson Brierley gave no banquet, nor mayor-making Sunday in 1898. Sarah Lees, Mayor in 1910-11, spent £490 on expenses, much of this on drinks, mainly alcoholic, and cigars, no doubt for her guests.

If elections were keenly fought, all the sound and fury was rarely about differences in policy. Partisan feeling was stoked up by a vituperative local press, and if there were no real issues the personalities of the rival candidates could be attacked. Thus the *Oldham Chronicle* in the 1890s stigmatised Tories as "dishonest and disreputable vagaries of men, impudent, shallow and domineering"; the Tory *Oldham Standard* was scarcely less restrained in its attacks on Liberals. From time to time, individuals introduced a vitriolic tone to local political rivalry; this was true of Jackson Brierley, leader of the successful Liberal fightback in 1898 and Mayor in the following Jubilee year; of him it was said there was no man more feared by the Tories whom he accused of "bungling, boodling and bailiffing"; with his "complete and crushing manner", he was described in the *Chronicle* as "the best hated man" in Oldham. One of his opponents could say of Brierley, "He may have been appointed to the position of Mayor but he is not and never has been Mayor of Oldham". More generally, once elected, the Councillors were on good terms and usually voted on an individual basis, rather than as members of disciplined parties. The parties it was said "were useful in exciting a spirit of competition and vigilance, of bringing a greater degree of energy into the service of the public". That was indisputably true; if party spirit was running high there was much less danger of public interests being neglected. Oldham had a succession of Town Clerks over the period, chosen no doubt because of their acceptability to the dominant Liberal faction, as well as their abilities. Only one, Hesketh Booth, Town Clerk from 1873 to 1884, appeared to manage the Council, intervening to check what he saw as "wanton or mistaken policies"; his outlook coincided with that of the most influential Councillors of the time, Sam Platt or Joshua Walmsley Radcliffe and that gave him his power. Like others, he resented his low reward, £500 per year, and the public discussion of the matter, resigning to combine more lucrative law practice with the office of Magistrates Clerk. His successor was appointed at a salary of £600. Other officials, except for the Medical Officers, had a low profile.

Throughout the period all, or at least most of the Councillors, shared some common principles. Oldham had to be improved, its nuisances abated,

**Water Supply** was Oldham Corporation's great priority, regarded as crucial to the town's comfort and prosperity. For much of the late nineteenth century demand was growing ahead of supply, and periods of drought brought crisis situations. In developing supply, Oldham competed with other authorities for the nearby gathering grounds and reservoir sites. Opening of a new catchment area and reservoir was a major occasion for Councillors and Officials. This group had met to cut the first sod at Rooden Reservoir in July 1894. The Mayor is Joseph Smith. Jackson Brierley, the combative Liberal politician, sits holding a walking stick in the middle of the front row; in the November elections of that year the Liberals lost control of the Council after forty years and the next Mayor was Robert Whittaker, a Conservative.

communities of Ashton-under-Lyne, Stalybridge and Hyde argued that Oldham had no right to take water that "naturally belonged to them"; the Council responded, "Oldham must have water; it has no water of its own". Successive fierce parliamentary contests, expensive to the ratepayer and not always successful, ensued.

Stage by stage, capacity was enlarged, initially at Besom Hill and Piethorn between 1858 and 1868. There was a critical and alarming water shortage in the dry year of 1868, when stocks in the reservoirs fell to two weeks supply at the end of August, and the higher parts of the town were totally without supplies except from water carts. Once again, supplies were being pumped from old coal workings. There were times when mills had to close for lack of condensing water in their lodges, still depending on surface streams and drains, and fears were raised that the progress of the district would be checked. Not without argument about water that ran to waste, and the cost of alternative schemes, the Council, having failed in Parliament with a scheme for the head of the Tame Valley, got powers for new works at Denshaw in the 1870s. This was followed, as demand continued to escalate and there were other water crises, as in 1884, by Castleshaw (1891) and Rooden and Readycon Dean (1894-1901). By the end of the century the total population being supplied had reached 200,000, every house had piped water, and reservoir storage was eight times what it had been in 1850. By then over £1.2 million had been borrowed and spent on land, works, mains and meters. Servicing and redeeming these loans as well as working expenses were financed by water rentals; Oldham gradually paid off its debt, occasionally made a profit, and claimed to have the cheapest water in Lancashire. This was needless to say, the largest municipal enterprise, and the object of much municipal pride; to be Chairman of the Waterworks Committee was the biggest job on Oldham Council after that of Mayor.

Scarcity again threatened after 1900 as further population growth in the district and the gradual introduction of water closets and baths pushed domestic consumption yet higher to a daily average of eighteen gallons per head; thirty years earlier it had been a mere eight gallons but it was to more than double in the next thirty years. There were no more available gathering grounds on the Lancashire side. Oldham had tried since 1877, but unsuccessfully, to gain access to the Lake District (Thirlmere) supplies eventually harnessed by Manchester City Council in 1895. Instead, in 1903 the Council proposed to cross the watershed and build a reservoir at Deanhead at the head of one of the tributaries of the Calder in West Yorkshire; strenuous opposition in Parliament defeated that proposal. The crisis was eventually, if temporarily, alleviated by taking water from disused coal workings at Butterworth Hall in Crompton from 1912. This source was soon providing over 10 per cent of all supplies.

TABLE XV: OLDHAM CORPORATION: CAPITAL SPENDING TO 1899 (£000)

| | |
|---|---|
| Water Supply | 1,160 |
| Gas | 466 |
| Sewers and Sewage Disposal | 351 |
| Public Streets | 107 |
| Town Hall | 61 |
| Electricity | 57 |
| Cemeteries | 55 |
| Tramways | 48 |
| Libraries | 39 |
| Park | 31 |
| Markets | 31 |
| Baths | 21 |
| Fire Service | 18 |
| [School Board | 214] |

## Police and Firefighting

To quote Hartley Bateson, "The Charter had been precipitated by a policing problem and so the most urgent task awaiting the Council's consideration was the establishment of a Police Force." A new Watch Committee applied itself readily the problem, setting up the Oldham force with a Chief Constable, a sergeant and ten constables. The Chief Constable was paid £100 a year, the constables a pound a week. The first job specification had called for young men above a certain height, "of strong constitution, civil and generally intelligent, able to read, write and keep accounts". Political or religious views were to remain private and the policeman could not vote. The numbers of constables increased throughout the 1850s, reaching twenty-nine in 1861, but were "manifestly insufficient" to police the town properly, both by neighbourhood and time of day. The situation in the townships was even worse; in Royton and Crompton the county provided only one policeman to 7,000 inhabitants, compared with Oldham's one to about 2,500. Pay grievances among the Oldham force were to surface from time to time and given the number of occasions when policemen behaved corruptly or were found under the influence of drink, consorting with prostitutes and the like,

**Oldham's Victorian police force** was underpaid and undermanned as the town grew rapidly, reflecting the parsimony of the Town Council. By the late 1880s both the numbers and calibre of the force were more appropriate to the town's needs; a strength of about 140 constables were then paid between £1-5s and £1-10s weekly. They were making about 1100/1200 arrests yearly of which 700/800 were for drunk and disorderly behaviour.

young men of the high standard the Council demanded proved difficult to engage; in 1860 for instance eighteen constables had to be dismissed for taking bribes and drunkenness. There was also concern that the new men brought in were strangers to Oldham, and that in pursuit of their duties they interfered with the "simple pleasures of the town".

Police numbers remained a lively subject for debate in Council, controversial because of the cost as well as their role. Government grant was available but only if the authority had one policeman for each 1,000 people; Oldham remained for many years well below this standard, partly because interference from Whitehall, a condition of grant, was something to be strongly resisted by a Council fiercely protective of its autonomy. Inevitably, if slowly, the police force grew in size and in pride of calling. In 1865 it was fifty-four strong, assisted on special occasions, by twenty uniformed lamplighters, and could be described as a "smart and apparently well selected body of men". By 1870 the Chief Constable's salary had been raised to £300; it went up again to £400 in 1880. Apart from the main station at the Town Hall, police stations were opened in the new residential districts. The force qualified for Government grant in 1880. By 1899 the numbers had reached 156 including 132 constables on the beat; the force was then costing about £14,000 per year before grant and other income; by 1914 the numbers had risen again to 172.

With over 30,000 houses in the Borough the police had plenty to do. The number of persons arrested gives some indication of the workload, although this varied year by year, not least with police attitudes to offenders. It rose strongly in the 1870s to peak in 1879-80, at 2,484; thereafter numbers arrested fell and by the 1890s were down to about 1100-1200 a year, the main offences being drunkenness and disorderly behaviour, assault and theft. Juvenile crime became a growing problem, with gaming the main offence followed by playing football in the street, throwing stones and disorderly conduct; the police became increasingly worried at what they described as

## Police and Firefighting

"turbulent, insubordinate and unmanageable conduct of the young". They had their own methods of dealing with young criminals; three boys found guilty of stealing twist from a tobacconist's shop in 1867 were locked up in a police cell for a day and given ten strokes of the birch rod; prison or a reformatory was the last resort. The Oldham Bench continued until 1914 to meet three and later four times weekly throughout the year and saw a regular parade of drunks, thieves, and pickpockets, disorderly prostitutes, beggars and vagrants and other petty offenders, their exploits reported in detail in the local press. Persistent offenders were harshly punished with hard labour; theft, even petty theft of a shawl or a watch, was invariably committed to the Quarter Sessions.

Given the importance attached to protecting Oldham's mills, the **Fire Brigade** was at times regarded as more important than the Police. Its normal strength was between forty and fifty trained men, dealing with on average one major fire each week, and many minor household chimney fires and the like.

**Devastating mill fires** were a frequent occurrence in Oldham. This one, at Lyon Mill, Shaw in 1911, was clearly spectacular.

There was a town Fire Brigade before incorporation, working from a Fire Station at Bottom of Moor, the regular firemen being augmented by the uniformed lamplighters and others when an incident arose. The new Council built a second station in Clegg Street, purchased more equipment, built houses for some of the firemen and stables for its horses. A Municipal Fire Brigade was established in 1864 and another fire station built in Werneth. By the end of the century the Fire Brigade was an important establishment with forty-five men, four fire engines and six tenders working from three fire stations, and covering the Borough and the adjacent urban districts. There was always plenty to do, with mill fires, and other incidents, a fairly regular event; thus in 1892 there were seventy-six fires destroying £37,000 of property, in 1907 eighty fires and damage caused over £73,000. Given the risks, to mill buildings especially, the Council did not hesitate to spend money on this service; the estimates were never challenged.

## Other Early Priorities

Gas and water and police and firefighting, on a modest scale, may have been head of the list of Council priorities, but they were not the only early concerns. Finding land for the dead of the town was a pressing and immediate issue, the existing churchyards being "already over-gorged, and the greatest of all nuisances". It was resolved outside the Council by the formation in 1854 of a Burial Board, headed by James Platt, which borrowed money to acquire extensive sites on the edge of the town, paying an average of about £200 an acre, about a quarter of the price of building land, but far above that of farm land. Greenacres and Chadderton Public Cemeteries were opened in 1857 and passed into the control of the Corporation in 1865. A third Cemetery was opened at Hollinwood in 1889.

Not everyone took to a cemetery burial. There were many who wanted to lie within reach of a church or chapel. Separate areas had to be reserved for different denominations and for many years problems arose because of the wish of many families to hold their funerals on Sundays. But over the period most of Oldham's citizens were buried in the cemeteries, including many who had taken their wealth and gone to live away from the town. Victorian funereal pomp was fully displayed, especially in the best situations within each cemetery where the well-to-do, paying more for their graves, could establish their own enclave.

Public Baths became fashionable in the new industrial towns by mid-century. The occasion of the death of Sir Robert Peel in 1850 was used to raise a memorial "of public utility", to make provision in Oldham. Subscriptions to the appeal raised an inadequate sum, £1,066, but pressed by John Platt, the Council decided to assume the responsibility and the first Public Baths on Union Street were completed in 1854 at a cost of £4,000. They proved an enormous success, especially in warm weather, among a population working in hot and dirty mills and foundries and living in crowded homes; by 1861, over 35,000 people used the baths, taking advantage of cheap bathing at an entry charge of 1d. They were overwhelmingly male, since mixed bathing was not permitted and women and girls had restricted access, only on two mornings in the week. By the 1870s, with a larger population, throughout the summer months the Baths

**Greenacres Cemetery**, perhaps the less prestigious of Oldham's two municipal cemeteries, opened in the 1850s. The well-to-do reserved plots in the best situation and their lives were memorialised with impressive Victorian pomp.

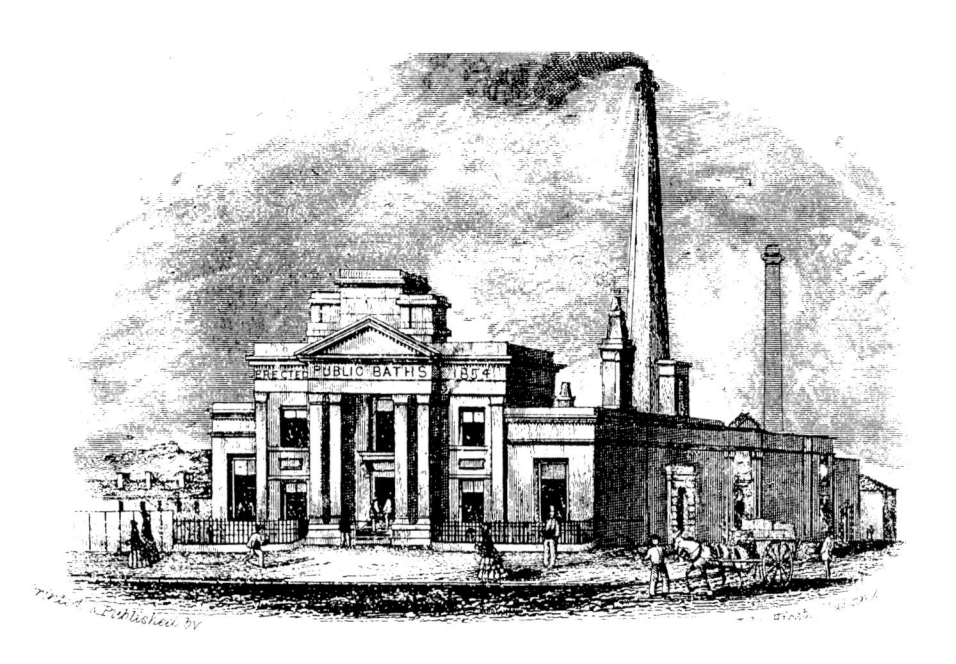

**Oldham Baths** on Union Street, were built in 1854 at a cost of £4,200, part of which was raised by public subscription. They became very popular and quite inadequate as the population grew. Long queues formed at times and keeping the water clean became a problem. Daytime charges were high, but on particular evenings and on Saturday, by when the water was becoming foul, access to the swimming bath was cheaper at $^1/_2$d without towel. The baths were substantially rebuilt and enlarged in 1887 and additional baths opened elsewhere in the district.

became impossibly overcrowded and long queues formed every evening. The Council Committee wrestled with the problems of keeping the water clean and fit to bathe in, removing the thick scum that formed overnight, preventing the use of soap in the main bath, as well as meeting such a popular demand. By 1876 the Committee were describing the Oldham Baths as "of an almost obsolete character, utterly unworthy of an important and rapidly increasing Borough, celebrated for its public spirit and enterprise." Not surprisingly, the Baths were eventually extended in 1880 and again in 1889 and new Baths were built in Hollinwood, Waterhead and elsewhere; in 1899 these, with the Central Baths, attracted over 180,000 visits; in 1914 there were as many as seven separate Public Baths in the town, and others in Chadderton, Royton and Crompton. Swimming towards the end of the century became a highly popular sport in the Oldham district with many competing teams, locally and on a wider stage.

The Baths were an important amenity and, like the cemeteries and the gas and water undertakings, could more or less pay for themselves. That was not true of other important Council responsibilities, roads and street repair, cleansing or scavenging, and public lighting. In 1850 these tasks were given to a new Surveyors Committee and a Borough Surveyor was appointed; as an appropriate gesture of economy, the Council voted to reduce his proposed annual salary from £75 to £70. To make, mend and clean the streets a direct labour force was hired at wages of about two shillings a day; their numbers, seventy-four in 1861, were attacked as excessive for the task. Except in the streets in the town centre, now paved for the first time, and here and there straightened and widened, little was done. Main roads remained the responsibility of the old turnpike trusts, tolls were still collected and repairs farmed out to contractors; the trusts did little about the pavements which remained a problem the Council was reluctant to take on. Although the Improvement Act of 1865 gave it powers, not until the 1880s did the Council take full control of its main highways, the last toll bar being removed in 1883.

Away from main roads where many rows of houses were being built in the 1850s, new streets remained unmade, unpaved, filled with ashes or building refuse, undrained and unlit, as had always been the case, although in the past on a smaller scale. The wretched condition of the residential streets of Oldham, the most apparent result of the Council's concern for economy, attracted harsh comment from Robert Rawlinson, the Government Inspector in charge of public works during the Cotton Famine. "A town," he said "could suffer something worse than moderate and wise taxation. The authorities of Oldham could not begin their improvements an hour too soon." It was only in 1864, with the aid of cheap loan money from Whitehall and as a means of creating employment, that Oldham Council applied itself to making and mending residential streets on any scale. Thereafter it assumed powers, in the Oldham Improvement Act of 1864, to make, drain, flag and pave private streets, the costs of this work to be recovered from the developers/owners of the adjacent houses.

The outspoken William Knott, Mayor in 1865, urging his fellow councillors to make good the town's "cheap and worthless streets", made the point that

> "unfortunately they had gone on for the last fifty years extending the town without attending to these arrangements which were necessary for its good. Oldham was an adult still wearing child's clothes; you cannot govern the town both well and cheaply".

Many regarded his views as "steeped in extravagance", but to a large extent they prevailed. Grudgingly more was spent, especially as the Council became more efficient at recovering the costs of making streets from property owners. Within a few years nearly 200 streets, chiefly in St Mary's, Coldhurst and Mumps, the older parts, had been improved at a cost of approaching £100,000. Thereafter as new streets were built the Council put them in good order and charged the developer. By the end of the century nearly fifty miles of private streets had been made and financed in this way although unmade backstreets, dirty and full of ruts, were to remain the subject of complaint. The cost of private streets, of course, encouraged ribbon development along the public roads wherever possible; it probably also, in the 1860s and 1870s, encouraged building outside the Borough boundary where the same rules did not, at the time, apply.

Apart from scavenging the main streets, for many years the Council did little or nothing to cope with household refuse, the contents of ash pits, middens and privies; these continued to be left to the "caprice or neglect" of individual tenants and landlords. In the early 1860s two open carts were employed to remove nightsoil throughout the town, at a cost of no more than £39 each quarter; this was compared with nearby Rochdale which was spending three times as much. There was no depot to receive the nightsoil and the Council complained that rather than being able to sell it, 10d a load had to be paid for it to be removed. By 1867 a yard had been set up at Rhodes Bank where collected nightsoil was held until it could be cleared to farmers. As a further attempt to reduce the nuisance, two covered vans replaced the open carts, managing to clear about 100 privies each night. The total expenditure of the Surveyors Department with its many other duties including public lighting and fire fighting, came to £20,597 in 1867, a cause of deep concern as total Council spending had risen three fold mainly if not wholly as a result, and the rate, in 1868-69 had to be set as high as 2s 6d. Edward Mayall, Mayor in 1870, was the main "economiser" at this time, engaging in fierce argument with Knott; as he frequently reminded people, he remembered when the town "had been kept in good order for £6,000"; he went on to say "the pockets of some people are quite large but that is not the case with everyone in the Borough." For a time, he won the day.

When the Borough was incorporated an organised market was an urgent requirement. Of course there were plenty of shops along the principal streets and, on market days, scores of stalls crowding and obstructing these streets and the adjacent Tommyfield, paying tolls where these could be collected. Shopping in the open street, on dark wet Saturday evenings in wintertime was a miserable affair. What was lacking was an adequate covered market. The Council seemed reluctant to commit itself, that is to spend money, and an attempt was made to raise capital up to £10,000 to finance a private New Market at the end of Curzon Street and on part of Tommyfield. The covered Victoria Market was opened in 1856 but failed commercially during the Cotton Famine and was sold to the Corporation in 1865 for £10,654. Thereafter with the return of prosperity and a rapidly increasing population, the Markets Committee became an Oldham success story, regularly making a surplus to relieve the rates. A new Market Hall was built in 1904-1906.

**Oldham's first Market Hall**, was built in 1856 and taken over by the Corporation in 1866. This view looks down Curzon Street which was lined with stalls on shopping days.

## Alexandra Park

The Council might be bold where provision could pay for itself or the vigour and prosperity of local industry was at risk, but remained reluctant towards any initiative that would merely impose expenditure. Central government was generally willing to give powers but not impose obligations or responsibilities. The town, growing rapidly, increasingly dirty and smoke polluted, lacked any amenity, especially as the open green fields were disappearing fast, or for many, becoming an increasing distance away. If the well-to-do could escape, argued the *Oldham Chronicle*, working men "were chained to the neighbourhood of their toil".

The town's leading public men, in the 1840s, had been willing to urge that

## Oldham Brave Oldham

**Alexandra Park**, built in the Cotton Famine and opened in 1864. The handsome villas of Queens Road with Park Road behind, to the right, are conspicuous in this aerial view of the Thirties.

Oldham should have a public park but would not pay for it and the new Council took no initiative in this direction although it had ample powers to do so. The Cotton Famine brought a change in attitude. To alleviate distress government was urging useful public works and making cheap loans available for the purpose. Now, given this opportunity, was the time to create a park. A scheme was accepted in June 1863 and seventy-two acres close to the town centre purchased cheaply for £18,000 or £250 an acre; sixty acres were laid out as a park, and twelve acres reserved as building land. The completed park was opened with a few mishaps on a day of torrential rain in August 1865, the whole project having cost £31,000.

Of course there was controversy which reflected the concerns of the time. The level of expenditure was challenged; too much had been spent and the *Chronicle* accused the Council of "playing ducks and drakes with the public's money": £710 for a bandstand, over £2,000 for entrance lodges and £2,500 for a refreshment room, which yielded an annual rent of only £5. There was pressure to sell or lease the land reserved for building and achieve some income; the town it was said "could not afford an idle shilling". In the event plots were leased on terms which ensured large villas were built and in this way Queens Road, one of Oldham's best addresses, was developed. But high controversy surrounded the terms on which the Refreshment Room in the park was contracted out for the provision of food and drink. Oldham Council had the greatest difficulty, in face of massive petitioning and agitation by the Sunday Schools, the Sabbatarians and the Temperance movement, in deciding whether the Room should open on Sunday, or should sell intoxicating drink

# Alexandra Park

at any time. In the event after heated debate and several changes in policy, it was agreed wines, ale and porter could be sold in the park but only on weekdays.

More importantly, the town now had a public park, "an oasis in the dreary desert" said the *Chronicle*, "its pride and boast". Not a grand park perhaps, not an amenity that would attract visitors to the town, but a symbol, a token, to show that money values were not entirely uppermost in Oldham, as many claimed. Robert Rawlinson's rebuke, that "in Oldham they had gone on accumulating wealth and driving trade and had been in too great a hurry to pay attention to such things as health and comfort", had been partially answered, at least.

## Housing Control

It was not enough, as William Knott urged upon his colleagues, to do something about "cheap and worthless streets". Paving, lighting, draining was in hand, at the expense of the property owner. Those concerned with poor public health increasingly put the blame on bad housing, and especially on back-to-back cottages, often one up and one down, homes for families of five to ten people, situated in airless confined courts and yards and narrow back streets, filthy with privies and ashpits and foul smelling drains, "human kennels jumbled together" as they were described. By the mid 1860s, Oldham had about 5,000 back-to-backs, mainly in St Peter's, St Mary's and Mumps wards. There were also about 700 cellar dwellings in Smethurst Street, Hopwood Street, Cheapside and elsewhere, "wretched miserable dens, dank and seething with impurity, plagued by intolerable smells", where the poorest would live at rents as low as 1s 3d for one room.

Clearance of unsatisfactory housing at this time was out of the question. Indeed back-to-backs were still being built to meet the demand for cheapness.

**St. Mary's** was rapidly built in the boom period of the 1850s. As this photograph shows, the houses were small, closely packed together, and many back-to-back. But they were close to the town centre, to Tommyfield and the markets and, for many at the time, to work; they were also cheap to rent and well served with corner-shops and pubs. Rock Street at its junction with Radcliffe Street is in the foreground, adjacent to the corner of the graveyard of the Parish Church; Egerton Street is prominent in the left-centre.

**Glodwick** again, the respectable suburb of superior housing, built in the late 1870s to improved by-law standards, with individual backyards and sculleries and without pubs. The church on Glodwick Road in the foreground is St. Marks, built with Lees money from Greenbank Mills.

Knott and the reformers were concerned that new houses be built to proper standards, that streets should be wider, that there be plenty of air and light around houses and that these should be through and well ventilated accordingly. Standards of this kind would require more land per house, more ground rent and mean higher rent or less profit to the developer, and many, including the numerous building societies that had sprung up, opposed them. The Council had secured powers to regulate standards for new housing in the Improvement Act of 1865 and new tighter bye-laws were introduced in 1867. Street widths for the first time had to be at least twelve yards, only through houses were to be approved, and the yards behind parallel streets of new houses had to be separated by a back passage at least five feet wide. The result, reflecting also the most economical layout, was long parallel rows of uniform terrace houses, all similar in type, two up two down with a small yard at the back. Monotonous bye-law housing, stigmatised in later comment, was nevertheless a vast improvement on the crowded back-to-back courts of the past.

Knott and his supporters urged with some passion that a separate privy should be provided in a yard behind each house so that every family could benefit from "its clean and orderly habits" and a degree of privacy, as it could not do when facilities were shared among a whole street. In a town where the old standard was one privy to six dwellings (thirty or more people), and in a common court or yard, this was going too far. Those who objected argued that rents would be 6d a week higher, and that tight regulation would encourage building outside the Borough. Principle was also involved. The *Chronicle* could ask why the law of supply and demand should not regulate the commodities called houses; why Liberal councillors should interfere with the workings of the market? Knott's argument for a better class of property failed and a standard of one privy to three houses in a common yard was accepted by the Council by fifteen votes to ten.

Better housing, achieved by regulation in this way, and gradually through market forces as growing numbers of people could afford to pay more rent and buy more domestic space and more privacy, was a feature of the 1870s and 1880s. Between 1866 and 1881, 12,322 houses were approved by the Council to be built in the Borough. Except in the middle class neighbourhoods such as Coppice and Queens Road, all relied on the outdoor privy. The contents of thousands of privies and ashpits receiving the night soil and refuse of over 80,000 people from 18,000 houses in 1871, their numbers growing fast, was a problem the Council could no longer ignore. Such a task could not continue to be left to private initiative, or to a couple of carts roaming the streets at night. Oldham, like other towns, searched for a solution. Water closets and sewers were many years away. The immediate answer was the sanitary pail, introduced after 1872 and made mandatory in every new privy in 1877, provided free by the Corporation, and emptied and cleansed street by street between 10 p.m. and 6 a.m. on a regular basis. This was expensive but it removed the nuisance, and the hazard to public health, from streets and homes.

As the sanitary pail was introduced, a new problem arose; what to do with the contents of the pails. Mixed with shoddy, this continued to be collected and stored at Rhodes Bank now a "monstrous nuisance", and then at a new depot beside the gas works at Higginshaw, then the edge of the town, prior to sale as manure to local farmers. There were, needless to say, a constant stream of complaints; a serious outbreak of typhoid fever was blamed on contaminated milk from animals grazing in fields on which crude night soil and butcher's offal had been spread. Business enterprise offered solutions and in 1874 the Carbon Fertiliser Company of Broad Street, London contracted with the Corporation to collect, dry and treat the waste matter, bag it and ship it for sale to farmers in West Lancashire and elsewhere. To the Council's disappointment the Company failed in 1876, despite a subsidy of three shillings per house, leaving a huge dump of 4,000 tons of night soil at Higginshaw. The Corporation itself, for many years, then continued to perform the same task. There were suggestions the nightsoil depot should be moved outside the Borough, to Royton or elsewhere, but these were stridently rejected. So Higginshaw remained the centre of operations. In 1880-81, the Nightsoil Department spent £8,532, chiefly on collection, mixing into shoddy manure, and railway/canal charges; this was offset in part by revenue from the sale of manure leaving a charge to the ratepayer of £5,236. Ten years later the same system was in force, costing close to £10,000 with about 30,000 sanitary pails throughout the town, being emptied each fortnight. With offal from slaughterhouses, butcher's shops and fish shops, about 1,000 tons of manure were then sent out of the town each two weeks.

The contents of the town's privies were seen as a more pressing problem than general household refuse, ashes, waste food, peelings and the like, still commonly thrown onto shared ashpits, often large enough to hold several months accumulation of refuse. Attracting great numbers of flies, with an abominable stench, the ashpits remained a grave nuisance and serious menace to health in the older more crowded parts of the town.

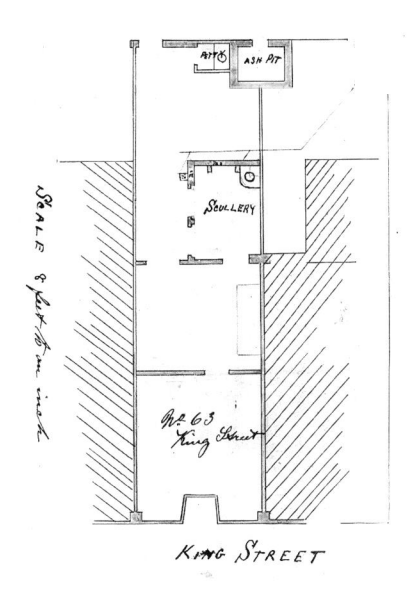

**By-Law house plan, dated 1878**, typical of the two-up two-down terrace houses built in many thousands in the last quarter of the century. The rooms were about fourteen feet square. This house was an improved version with a scullery, individual yard, privy which would have a sanitary pail and shared ashpit. Access to empty the ashpit and sanitary pail was by the narrow passage-way to the rear. A more expensive terrace house had a small third bedroom over the scullery extension.

## Public Health

High infantile mortality, high death rates, the incidence of consumption, contagious diseases like smallpox, typhoid fever and scarlet fever, bronchitis and other respiratory illnesses, and the child killer, diarrhoea, were, at the time, facts of life. Their causes were complex. Improved housing, more domestic space, more light and air around the dwelling, would help the situation as would efficient removal of refuse and waste from the privy or ashpit and similarly the widespread availability of abundant clean water. Concern for public health, for sanitary improvement, was always there in the background as these various initiatives were pursued. From time to time this concern assumed greater urgency and called for more drastic remedies, namely when an epidemic of contagious disease struck the district. Smallpox was always a problem but without ever assuming alarming proportions. The first real panic took place in 1872 with a serious outbreak of scarlet fever. Deaths from this cause rose rapidly to such an extent that Oldham's death rate for a time was the highest in the country. 404 deaths from scarlet fever occurred in four months from August to November. The Corporation and its newly formed Sanitary Committee was ill-equipped to deal either with the causes or the remedy. A government inspector visited the town to make a report. He identified a number of problems and recommended the appointment of a Medical Officer of Health. Oldham's first Medical Officer, Dr. J. Maule Sutton, was appointed in 1873 at a salary of £400.

Thereafter the Council received a regular commentary on public health issues, on nuisances and their remedy. Some, like bad housing, night soil removal and water supply, it was coping with; others it was not. The almost evangelical pleas of the Medical Officer of Health and his successors were often received in stony silence. These were "the nostrums of expensive sanitary doctors, over-zealous officials vain of their authority," argued the *Chronicle*. Accomplishment of some of their ideas would require expenditure, perhaps large expenditure when it came to a proper system of drains and sewers, while other unhealthy nuisances were caused by the principal

**Mill Lodges**, shown blue, adjoined every mill, essential for cooling purposes at the steam engine. Many of them were supplied with polluted water from drains and sewers; they also became a receptacle for rubbish and dead animals. The foul gases rising from the lodges in hot weather were a major health hazard to adjoining houses; "**the** nuisance of Oldham", according to one Medical Officer. This map dates from the 1880s.

industries of the town. To impose expenditure or restriction on the cotton mills, on the councillor's own businesses, in many cases, was not a popular course to follow. The Town Clerk was quite clear where the priority lay; "the manufacturers of Oldham are practically the sole source of support and wealth to the population of the Borough". Associated with almost every mill was a lodge or small dam of water, whose principal purpose was to condense steam from the mill engines. Water to the lodges came from "the natural surface drainage of the town which for many years had been collected into sewers formed out of natural watercourses." These were the words of the Town Clerk in 1880; he acknowledged that the waste water of many thousands of houses, and often the contents of a growing number of water closets in the better homes, was going into these natural sewers, along with slaughterhouse offal and the like. Not surprisingly, and especially in hot weather, the mill lodges were appallingly foul and offensive, "in loathsome and fever breeding condition", "the nuisance of Oldham" as one Medical Officer emphasised. But short of a general system of drains and sewers, and adequate public water supply, little was done.

Smoke pollution was the other notorious result of Oldham's industry, and especially so-called black smoke caused as mill boilers were fired. Scores of mill chimneys polluted the atmosphere every working day, along with the coal fires of practically every house. Blackened stone and brick, dead vegetation and a pallid population, plagued with bronchitis and other respiratory complaints, were the consequence. There were partial remedies; attempts were made to curb black smoke emissions and to impose penalties on the mills but they were weakly applied. Even if the mill-owners of Oldham were to conform, much of Oldham's pollution came from the communities on the western side, Chadderton and Royton in particular. The different local authorities met and debated the problem to show they were doing something but there was little result. Oldham retained its reputation as a town under a

**Black smoke** from a few hundred mill chimneys was a notorious feature of Oldham, as of other cotton towns. Attempts to control it were feeble and difficult to enforce. This photograph of Royton looking towards Oldham Edge and Werneth illustrates the problem. The direction of the smoke reflects Oldham's prevailing westerly wind, bringing a damp climate from the Atlantic.

constant pall of smoke, drab, dull, gloomy and dirty as a result, all "soot and stink", as one visitor complained. The issue remained a lively one throughout the period.

The Medical Officer, his small staff, and with less zeal, the Sanitary Committee had as their objective a steady sustained improvement in Oldham's health. Nuisances of any kind were to be rooted out. Pigsties, offensive private slaughter houses throughout the town attracted particular attention as being "among the worst evils of the Borough". In 1876 there were still as many as seventy-one slaughter houses, scattered all over the town, at which it was estimated over 45,000 animals were slaughtered in the course of the year; a public abattoir was regarded as the only solution but this was not to be provided for many years. Not much could be done beyond inspection to try to see the premises were clean and that blood and offal was properly disposed of. And then there was polluted, badly kept and watered milk, (often 20 to 40 per cent water might be added), a constant problem involving perhaps a fifth of all the milk on sale; on top of this was adulterated food and bad meat. All these matters kept the sanitary inspectors busy.

By the 1890s the worst housing in the town, the older congested streets near the town centre or at Bottom of Moor, again attracted attention for their high death rates and squalor. The Medical Officer contrasted "the especial pride" taken by people in the new streets "to keep their houses clean and bright", with some of the worst neighbourhoods. His language, year after year was repetitive: "dirty and overcrowded back-to-back houses, the walls and floors more or less damp, the rooms small and low-roofed, not a few of them with windows that do not admit of opening, the ventilation very deficient, foul drains and filthy privies and all sorts of rubbish put onto ashpits too near the back doors." Some of the worst houses were in Back Greaves Street, close to the Town Hall, owned by the Corporation as firemen's dwellings.

Many of the worst houses near the town centre were cleared over the years for redevelopment and replacement with shops, offices and workshops. The cellar dwellings were generally closed by the 1890s, and some hundreds of insanitary houses were also left unoccupied or closed on a voluntary or compulsory basis. Finally, a great deal of conversion or "knocking through" took place and the Medical Officer in 1914 was so bold as to estimate that only 300 back-to-backs remained, far too optimistic a statement since a survey in 1919 was to identify 2,640. There were still many slums in Oldham in 1914 but the Council had not the stomach or the powers for large scale compulsory clearance, nor would it have been willing to assume the responsibility of re-housing the population that would be displaced. What house closures or conversions there were aroused strong resistance as local communities were broken up and dispersed, with those forced out left to their own resources; small local tradesmen bitterly resented the loss of trade. Early clearance and rehousing projects on a limited scale were carried out in Manchester in the years before 1914; there was even a modest scheme in

**Cemetery Street**, old housing close to the town centre, still occupied at the end of the nineteenth century. The tin bath hanging outside was the common arrangement.

Saddleworth where fifty-five houses replacing older property were built by the Council to be let at modestly subsidised rents of 4s 6d a week. But Oldham's initiatives in this direction would have to wait for a more pressing situation and substantial government aid after the Great War. Already by 1914 there were indications of what would become all too evident after the war, namely that private enterprise could no longer build houses that were affordable for a great many people.

As the century grew older the greatest sanitary challenge remained, to drain the town, to link every house to a sewer, to build main sewers to convey the sewage to a treatment works before discharging it into the Mersey or its tributaries. As early as 1880 the Town Clerk could write that "the question of purification of the sewage of the town is of such magnitude as to give the Corporation the gravest anxiety." Expenditure of "scores if not hundreds of thousands of pounds" was contemplated. But there was no agreement "within sanitary science" on the best system and hence the Corporation "had been wishful to delay". A comprehensive scheme came only in the 1890s after much wrangling and heart searching in Council, afraid of the expense, but in the end given no alternative, not least because of recrimination and legal threats from other local authorities, both to clean up the town and purify its effluent. Against an initial estimate of £131,000, the completed sewerage scheme eventually ran up costs of over £350,000, a major undertaking at the time. Unlike the other large capital spenders, water and gas, these works could yield no revenue, they merely improved public health and convenience and protected other communities. The rates had to take the burden.

A proper system of drains and sewers and an adequate water supply now permitted the replacement of the sanitary pail with the water closet and water carriage, at the time quite a revolution in domestic convenience. In 1899 there were only 5,000 WCs in Oldham's 30,000 houses. As water carriage spread, the so-called slop, or waste water closet, was generally adopted, using water from the household sink or rainwater from the roof fed into a "Tippler", rather than a separate flush supply. By 1914, following a vigorous Council programme, nearly 30,000 houses had a WC of one kind or another, mainly waste water; the number of sanitary pails had fallen to 4,000. Unsatisfactory, unhygienic, but cheaper in that much less water was used, the waste water closet only gave way to the flush closet after the first World War. Nonetheless in its progress in these matters Oldham was ahead of most large towns; in the adjacent districts, half the houses in Chadderton and Royton still had sanitary pails or tubs in 1913, three quarters in Crompton and a similar proportion in Saddleworth.

Along with the water closet Oldham finally began to insist that a dustbin or ashcan became a feature of every house, and undertook refuse collection on a regular weekly basis, albeit at greatly increased cost. In 1914 there were still over 4,000 ashpits in the town but the Council could claim credit that the most crowded wards, Mumps, St Mary's, St Peter's and Coldhurst were entirely free of this offensive relic of a dirtier unhealthy past. Destructors at Rhodes Bank and Hollinwood were installed to burn and reduce all the household rubbish; mindful of economy the heat so generated was used to produce steam to turn turbines at the nearby electricity works; the clinker was used to make paving flags.

The scarlet fever epidemic of 1872 had led to the appointment of the first

Medical Officer. It also prompted recognition of widespread ignorance about contagious disease and the need to ensure that outbreaks were promptly notified. Isolation had then to follow but there was no means within the town of isolating and treating infectious diseases other than the Union Workhouse. Following a smallpox epidemic in May 1877 involving 163 cases and several deaths, a temporary wooden isolation hospital was built hurriedly at Westhulme close to the Chadderton boundary, on open fields at the time. A permanent building followed, costing £6,000, with wards for scarlet fever and typhoid as well as smallpox. It was made available to the adjacent townships provided they contributed financially. Initially there was much resistance on the part of parents to parting with sick children to the care of a strange hospital, just as there was to compulsory vaccination against smallpox. But Westhulme's reputation for excellent treatment grew, outbreaks of smallpox and scarlet fever remained high, and the hospital was extensively enlarged in 1882 and subsequently.

The spread of housing, especially in adjacent parts of Chadderton, led to objections to using Westhulme for smallpox especially when, in 1888 and again in 1892-93, there were serious outbreaks close to the hospital. In the latter period there were 491 smallpox cases in Oldham, 194 in Chadderton, mostly close to Westhulme; fatalities were as high as 10 per cent. Consequently a new smallpox hospital was proposed well away from buildings, Westhulme to be given over mainly to scarlet fever, typhoid and consumption, or tuberculosis (TB) as it was becoming called. A site at Delph was suggested but roused strenuous and outspoken objections in that district to "an intolerable imposition", and eventually the new facility was built at Strinesdale, isolated but within the Borough. Chadderton meanwhile provided its own small isolation hospital at Cinder Hill. By 1914 when smallpox had practically disappeared (the last serious outbreak was in 1905), Strinesdale, with its lofty bracing situation, became a sanatorium for early cases of TB.

The dogged persistence and professionalism of successive Oldham Medical Officers, the unpopular diligence of Sanitary Inspectors, and the initiatives the Sanitary Committee and the Council took, undoubtedly had its effect. Improvements in public health, along with other influences derived from higher living standards, contributed to the fall in Oldham's' death rate that was evident in the years before the World War, as has been noted. Infantile mortality was still far too high and well above the County's average, but down on what it had been. Taking pride in his Department, the Medical Officer described the first School for Mothers, opened in Hollinwood in 1910, where babies were weighed once a fortnight and mothers given lectures on child-care. Tea, bread and butter and a biscuit was provided for which the charge was 1d. Seventy four mothers attended on average in 1913. A start had been made.

**A Bigger Town Hall**

Certainly by the mid 1870s, the Town Clerk was pressing the need for more accommodation to house the Corporation's growing activities. The old building of 1841 had only seven rooms on the ground floor to house the

# A Bigger Town Hall

**The Town Hall**, the dignified front of the old building, described in 1876 as "utterly inadequate to meet the needs of the Corporation". In making extensions at that time and again in 1912 the Corporation was unwilling to pay for "purely symbolic buildings". It did not follow the example set, for instance, by Bolton, Rochdale or Leeds in creating a grand Town Hall.

police station, magistrates court and Council staff; the first floor had a hall for public meetings and a Council Chamber. The Town Clerk argued, "the situation is highly objectionable, the various departments of the Corporation being squandered about the town, instead of being concentrated in one building."

Here was ground for lively controversy, led by the "economists" and their supporter, the *Oldham Chronicle*. Extension of the existing building was eventually agreed, at a forecast expenditure of £12,000. Work started in 1877. As was often the case with Town Hall projects, many modifications were made to the original scheme, mainly it seems to provide "the first instalment of the grand town hall of the future". When the work was completed the cost was around £30,000. Predictably, led by the *Chronicle*, the public were outraged, for a while, but the issue was soon forgotten. The extended building had a handsome front faced with local sandstone on Greaves Street, while its staircase, public rooms and chandeliers were grand and serious. While providing more accommodation, a fine court room for the Petty and Quarter Sessions, and a police station with several cells, it quickly proved inadequate. There were complaints that it could seat only 130 for dinner and the Chamber of Commerce was driven to holding its annual events in Manchester.

Oldham was still almost alone in not having a Town Hall that would do the town credit. It compared shabbily with its neighbours, Manchester, Rochdale, which had spent £155,000 on its own Gothic splendour, Bolton

**The new Council Chamber of 1879**, described as a "noble room".

**The Grand Staircase**, the main feature of the Town Hall extensions of the late 1870s.

£166,000, Leeds £105,000, Bradford, even Todmorden. Perhaps no-one in the town cared; a place like Oldham, it was said, did not require "the adventitious aid of magnificent buildings". The Town Hall was further extended in 1912, again with rather fine interiors and a pretentious Egyptian room inhabited by clerks; long before then, Council staffs had established themselves in offices throughout the centre of the town; offices that were often "dingy, dismal and depressing, no fireplace, no ventilation, no oilcloth, unbearable" as the Borough Accountant complained in 1892. The Town Hall, massive building that it had become, remained a modest symbol; what dignity it gave to the centre of the town still derived from the fine portico of 1841.

## Oldham Library

When services did not pay, or did not meet a critical need, successive Oldham councils were reluctant to commit capital or incur expenditure. It was especially with regard to proposals for a public library, art gallery and museum that these values surfaced. Here was a service that would bring back little if any revenue. Many of the Councillors themselves, whatever their success in business, made no claim to literary knowledge. It was said of them that "their acquaintance with books is confined to the Bible and the bank book, chiefly the latter". There were those who argued that a library would be of little benefit to most working men, that only a small minority would use it.

Oldham in any event had lending libraries for those who wanted them, provided by the Co-operative Societies, the Lyceum, the Werneth Mechanics Institute, the Henshaw Street Mutual Improvement Society, even the Sunday Schools, and in 1879, on a limited scale in Greaves Street, by the philanthropy of the private mill-owner, Alfred Butterworth; between them these had several thousand books. Thus, whatever the position in other industrial towns, and it has to be said that many of them were equally tardy, whenever a library initiative was proposed in Oldham it met with indifference or hostility. Moreover, it was argued, there was always the possibility that "some liberal minded person" might give such an institution to the town, since wealthy benefactors had founded libraries in other towns; the brewer, Bass in Derby; Coats, the sewing cotton millionaire in Paisley; Palmer, the biscuit king, in Reading, for instance. Such a hope, however, was at variance with all experience of Oldham philanthropy.

The only strong proponent of a free library was James Yates, son of a wealthy cotton spinner but trained and practising as an Oldham doctor, a long serving Liberal Councillor, School Board member and throughout his life a champion, not merely of public but of mental and social health. As Mayor in 1880-81 and the subsequent year he used his position to press the need for a free public library. "Oldham", Yates argued strongly, "is probably the

**Opening of the Library, 1883**; although built reluctantly and after much controversy, the opening was a grand public occasion and Oldham became proud of its fine new building.

largest town in England without its free library. If we are to keep pace with the intellectual progress of other manufacturing towns, we must neglect no means of cultivation and improvement, nor must we complain of the costs of altering them." To Yates, a library was a ladder for the aspiring young. A Council worried about spending money, and looking at the huge overspend on the enlarged Town Hall, was apathetic. Yates eventually found influential support from Samuel Buckley, self-made man and hugely successful in the town, and also to become Mayor on three occasions. The Council was persuaded, albeit reluctantly.

After various attempts to delay the project, a suitable central site on Union Street was leased at eighteen pence per yard (equal to a capital value of about £7500 an acre) from the Emmott's; the rent was well below the market value but a vast increase on what George Emmott would have paid many years earlier, probably at best three pence a yard; thirty years later nearby land was leased at three shillings a yard. To somewhat lavish designs the Reference Library, Art Gallery and Museum was built, unfortunately at a cost of £26,748, substantially above the initial authority which was for a building not to cost more than £8,000; as a gesture of reproach to its main proponent, it was christened "Yates's Folly". The expensive new building was opened with formal ceremony in 1883, a procession through the town was followed by a large banquet; later in the evening the men were joined by their ladies for a ball which went on until 4 in the morning. Going beyond the original concept, and to meet public demand, a Lending Library was opened in 1887. Following the gift of a building a branch Library was also opened at Northmoor in 1883. The main Library was extended in 1894 at a further cost of £8,640 and several "distributing stations", in effect small branches working from shops or schools, were subsequently opened throughout the town.

**The Library Interior**, rather forbidding and with no open access. The newspaper room was a busier place.

Charles E. Lees, the wealthy resident of Werneth Park, became a major donor to the Art Gallery, bequeathing a large collection of valuable water colours; he wanted Oldham to be "a cultivated as well as commercial society". Slowly the art collections developed, both from bequests and purchases from a budget of £500 annually. There were the usual passionate arguments about Sunday opening, that being the day when working men and their families could best visit the Gallery; in the end strong Sabbatarians like Thomas Emmott supported Sunday opening on the grounds that it offered an alternative to the pub. Suspicion of the type of user precluded for many years open access to books in the Reference and later the Lending Library; probably the type of books available was also inhibiting. Generally, for many years, the use of the Library and the Northmoor branch was disappointing in so large a community. Gradually, of course, improved education and greater leisure

# Oldham Library

**The Art Gallery** was opened in 1894. Its large permanent collections which benefited from donations as well as acquisitions, reflected the tastes and aspirations of an increasing prosperous middle-class. It was also able to stage annual exhibitions which attracted a large public. At the opening there was a large exhibition of the work of John Everett Millais. The *Standard* could write "Oldham may not be a lovely town, but it cannot be said that Oldhamers do not appreciate beautiful objects".

changed the situation, but even in 1899 there were only 4,600 registered borrowers at the central Library and 700 at Northmoor, in a town of 30,000 households. By 1910 these two Libraries and the "distributing stations" throughout the town were lending about 180,000 books a year. Attendance at the Art Gallery was stimulated by special exhibitions, some of which were highly successful, attracting as many as 20,000 visitors; in 1910 the Gallery had over 70,000 visitors. The Library also became a popular venue for public lectures. By the end of the century, and perhaps sensitive of Oldham's image as a humdrum place, more preoccupied with creating wealth than with beauty, amenity and culture, the Library and Art Gallery was made an object of municipal pride, along with the Lyceum and the Park. It was the mark of a civilised town. Apart from the multitude of mills, there was not much else to show.

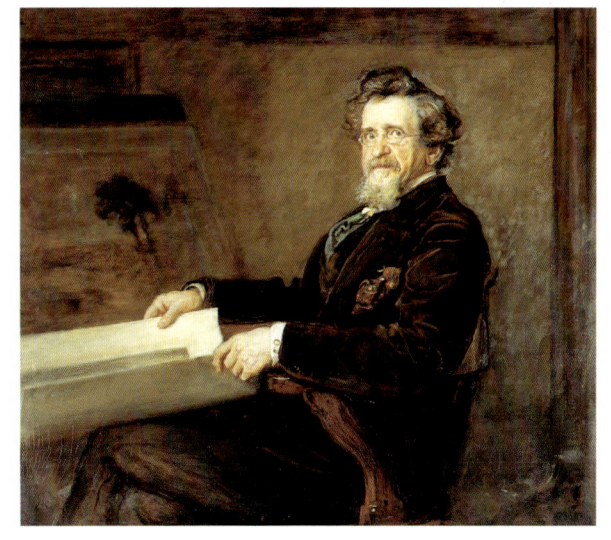

## Tramways and Electricity

Oldham Corporation built the first tramlines in 1880 over five miles of road from Waterhead to Hollinwood, and along Union Street in the town centre but they were then leased to the operator, Manchester Carriage and Tramways Limited, for a period of twenty-one years. By May 1881 the Borough Surveyor could report "a constant service of well appointed and handsome cars". These early trams were horse drawn with a standard fare of threepence; a penny fare for short distance journeys was introduced in 1888. The early tramline network was greatly expanded and other operators took leases, notably, after 1887, the Bury, Rochdale and Oldham Steam Tramways

**The Portrait of Thomas Oldham Barlow** by Millais, was one of the new Gallery's most valuable acquisitions. Barlow, born in Oldham in 1824, had a distinguished career as an engraver and was well regarded in London art circles. He died in London in 1889. The Millais portrait was purchased by a descendant of the Oldham coal-owning Jones family, John Joseph Jones, then living on a Worcestershire country estate; he presented it to the Gallery.

161

## Oldham Brave Oldham

*Right:* **Horse Buses** were the first means of public transport, used from the 1860s. They were infrequent and irregular, slow and uncomfortable, and quickly replaced by the horse tram. Three horses were needed to cope with the up-and-down roads of the district.

*Below:* **Horse Trams**, running on smooth rails, faster and more comfortable than the horse bus, were the first form of popular public transport on Oldham streets, introduced in 1880. This view of the Market Place shows several Hansom Cabs waiting hire.

*Facing above:* **Steam Trams** were run on a few main roads by a private company from 1885. They were noisy, jerky and unreliable, if rather faster than the horse-tram and cheaper because each tram carried more passengers. The drivers earned 5s per day but worked from 6.30 a.m. to 10.30 p.m., received no paid holidays and were penalised for arriving late. The trams carried advertisements, showing how certain soaps and foods were becoming popular brands.

Company. Their tramcars were hauled by a box-like steam locomotive, slow especially on the steeper inclines, but much better than walking.

Most of Lancashire's tramways had been established on this basis. As the initial leases approached expiry, municipal authorities gave notice of their intention to terminate. The view still prevailed that municipalisation was a

## Tramways and Electricity

*Below:* **The Electric Tram**, introduced in 1901, and run by the Corporation, transformed local public transport, quickly replacing horse and steam trams. Laying new tramlines was a major operation as this turn-of-the-century picture, taken at the junction of Greenacres Road and Cross Street conveys; the cost far exceeded estimates and became a minor scandal at the time. With the cheap tram, starting at 4.30 in the morning, people began to live farther from their work. They also came to the centre of Oldham in far greater numbers to do their shopping, and neighbourhood shops began to lose trade. The number of tram passengers rose steeply for many years after 1903, checked only by periods of bad trade. Fares were a sensitive issue, however, and except in the boom years of 1906-07 the tramways were generally run at a loss after financing. Traffic peaked in 1926 and thereafter the more flexible motor bus took over.

sound way to achieve efficiency and economy. In 1901 Oldham Corporation assumed responsibility for all services within its boundaries, replacing and extending much of the tram line network so that it reached over twenty-seven miles, linking communities in the whole district with the town centre, as well as with Manchester, Rochdale and Ashton. Eighty tramcars, electrically

**This Hollinwood Street scene**, shows the Manchester-Oldham tram and a local tram. Traditional horse-drawn vans and wagons were the other main traffic on roads that were still relatively quiet.

powered from overhead wires, were quickly carrying 250,000 passengers a week, the first trams as early as 4.30 am, the last at 10 pm. Over £280,000 was spent on capital works and the fact that the service was not at first a financial success gave fruitful scope for much controversy; the Conservatives were in office at the time and probably lost their majority over the so-called tramlines fiasco. The trams, of course, now immensely popular, went on running, however marginal their economics. The Council continued to wrestle with the cost to the rates on the one hand, and the level of fares and the frequency of services on the other, both sensitive issues; by 1906 a profit was being made, in 1907, £9,327. Those working on the trams, some 300 or so, were quick to realise and use their bargaining power to raise their wages. A speck on the horizon only, two motor buses were introduced, for the town centre services in 1913.

**Greenhill Power Station**, built in 1903, was the first cautious, even reluctant, electric power venture. It quickly proved inadequate as demand for electricity exploded. The boiler house, at the start of the operation, employed plenty of men physically shovelling coal.

The Corporation began making electricity in an unpretentious way at Rhodes Bank in 1890. Many businesses in the town were already using supplies produced on small inefficient plants; they threatened to set up their own company if the Council did not act. No-one anticipated the scale on which demand would develop, from the tram service, businesses and some private homes, The undertaking moved to new works at Greenhill in 1903, but its history remained one of successive increments to capacity quickly being overtaken by rampant demand. Fast as the new works, stark and ugly, were enlarged, supply was restricted and would-be users had to wait. In 1914 there were about 3,000 customers consuming a million units, still a tiny fraction of subsequent demand; in the same year Belgrave Mill was the first to use the new power to drive machinery. Electricity only became a large business after 1918.

**Expenditure and the Rates**

Expenditure inevitably grew in all branches of the Corporation's activities, as population grew and as services were introduced, developed and improved. So of course did the rateable value, especially in the 1870s with the town's extraordinary development. This indeed was the period when the rates could be reduced for a time as they were in 1872 and 1873, to as low as 1s 4d in 1873, an achievement of enormous satisfaction to the ruling Liberal faction.

This fortunate combination of circumstances did not last for long. Oldham's dynamism did not cease but new mills, streets, shops and pubs were going up in the adjacent districts, creating rateable value in Chadderton, Royton, Failsworth and Crompton. Some of Oldham's services were being developed to the benefit of those communities. Collecting the rates was also a problem, keeping track of the changing occupation of thousands of new houses. Given the ups and downs of trade, short time working and strikes, there were many who could not or would not pay their rates; every year in setting the rate an allowance had to be made for so-called "leakage", in bad years as much as 10 per cent. Meanwhile significant new demands had arisen for the ratepayer to meet, particularly those linked to public health, the sewerage and sewage treatment system and rubbish clearance, and, on an even larger scale, popular education. Oldham's School Board, elected in 1871 and independent of the Council, raised income to some extent from fees and government grant but mainly by precept on the town's rates. In 1903 the School Board's work was assumed directly by the Education Committee of the Council and education, although assisted by large government grants, became the principal area of Council spending. The development of popular education in Oldham will be described in a later chapter.

Inevitably the rates had to rise; they went up by 60 per cent between 1891 and 1901 and by a further 22 per cent up to 1914. Not merely had expenditure risen steeply relative to rateable value; the contribution from the town's commercial activities, gas, water, tramways and later electricity remained disappointing. Successive Councils struggled to make these activities pay at all, especially when poor trade or industrial disputes reduced demand. They had a difficult choice; the price of gas, like tramway fares, was a sensitive political issue but losses on these services were also unacceptable.

By the end of the century, each new Mayor, reviewing the town's progress

TABLE XVI: OLDHAM CORPORATION: FINANCIAL POSITION

| Year Ending | Expenditure £000 | of which Education £000 | Income £000 | Rateable Value £000 | Rate per Pound |
|---|---|---|---|---|---|
| 1851 | 7.6 | - | 1.7 | 106.2 | 1/3 |
| 1861 | 10.6 | - | 2.9 | 151.2 | 1/- |
| 1871 | 40.1 | - | 7.0 | 314.8 | 2/- |
| 1881 | 68.3 | 3.7 | 15.1 | 485.3 | 2/3 |
| 1891 | 81.7 | 9.5 | 10.3 | 581.5 | 2/6 |
| 1901 | 129.9 | 27.0 | 16.0 | 461.7 [1] | 6/- |
| 1914 | 188.9 | 49.4 | 11.8 | 546.6 [2] | 7/4 |

Notes 1. In 1897 the rateable value was assessed on the same basis as for the poor rate, that is at two-thirds gross value.
2. The Corporation set its rate on the assumption that a proportion, usually 6 or 7 per cent, but in years of depressed trade up to 10 per cent, would not be collected for one reason or another.

on their election, had ceased to boast about frugality and prudence. Rather they emphasised the enormous scale of the Council's achievements as well as its concern for economy. They had inherited no more than a small Town Hall and a fire engine in 1849. By the Jubilee in 1899 they had borrowed over £2.5 million for capital works, and were spending over £125,000 a year on their various services, including spending on schools, four times what they had been spending thirty years earlier, but at a municipal rate that had only doubled. The Corporation had become a huge undertaking, a large employer of labour, supported by a growing body of professional specialists, providing services crucial to the local economic structure and the quality of life of the people. At the 1899 Jubilee, Jackson Brierley, the Liberal Mayor, spoke of

> "the sagacity of high purpose, the single-mindedness and devotion, of the town's municipal rulers in performing their high obligations; the protection of person and property from molestation and destruction; the providing of accessories for the personal comfort of the inhabitants in the shape of good roads, gas, water and electricity for the home and factory, in tramways for easier locomotion, hospitals for the sick, better houses to live in, food for the mind and instruction for the growing youth; and when this earthly pilgrimage is over, providing a resting place in dignified and pleasant surroundings."

These eloquent words summarise what the Council felt they had accomplished, however grudgingly, and not, at times without "big fights to put the Corporation upon its feet", and conflicts with "the meddlesome bureaucrats of remote imperial government". Even the *Oldham Chronicle*, a consistent critic of Council spending, seemed content; "everything is in as fair apple-pie order as we can look for in this wicked world", a leading article proclaimed, "our manufacturers and tradesmen are not unnecessarily and stupidly interfered with in carrying out their business, the people are prosperous and happy and the rates are not too high". The 1899 Jubilee and the industrial and commercial prosperity that followed in the early years of the new century, saw the Corporation at the peak of its vitality and power.

There had been many ups and downs but this was the high point of Oldham's confidence and pride, not merely in the local economy, but in its municipal achievement.

TABLE XVII:
OLDHAM CORPORATION: NET EXPENDITURE BY DEPARTMENT (£)

|  | 1870/71 | 1890/91 | 1913/1914 |
| --- | --- | --- | --- |
| Town Clerk, Treasurer, Town Hall etc. | 5,814 | 7,097 | 8,643 |
| Lighting | 4,039 | 5,078 | 9,280 |
| Police | 3,378 | 5,885 | 8,354 |
| Fire Brigade | 1,267 | 1,813 | 1,615 |
| Highways & Scavenging | 17,848 | 24,401 | 34,199 |
| Health/Hospital | - | 4,810 | 9,800 |
| Sewerage | - | - | 22,384 |
| Water Carriage and Night Soil | 1,726 | 6,839 | 7,328 |
| Ashes | 1,122 | 4,756 | 13,127 |
| Parks etc. | 3,257 | 2,826 | 4,835 |
| Cemeteries | 1,000 | 2,070 | 2,211 |
| Baths | 336 | 656 | 7,350 |
| Libraries | - | 4,965 | 5,821 |
| Miscellaneous | - | 1,033 | 3,340 |
| Education | 300 | 9,500 | 49,354 |
| Total | 40,087 | 81,729 | 188,904 |

## The Townships

As their population grew, and as the pressure for improvement required stronger forms of local government, the old townships responded by setting

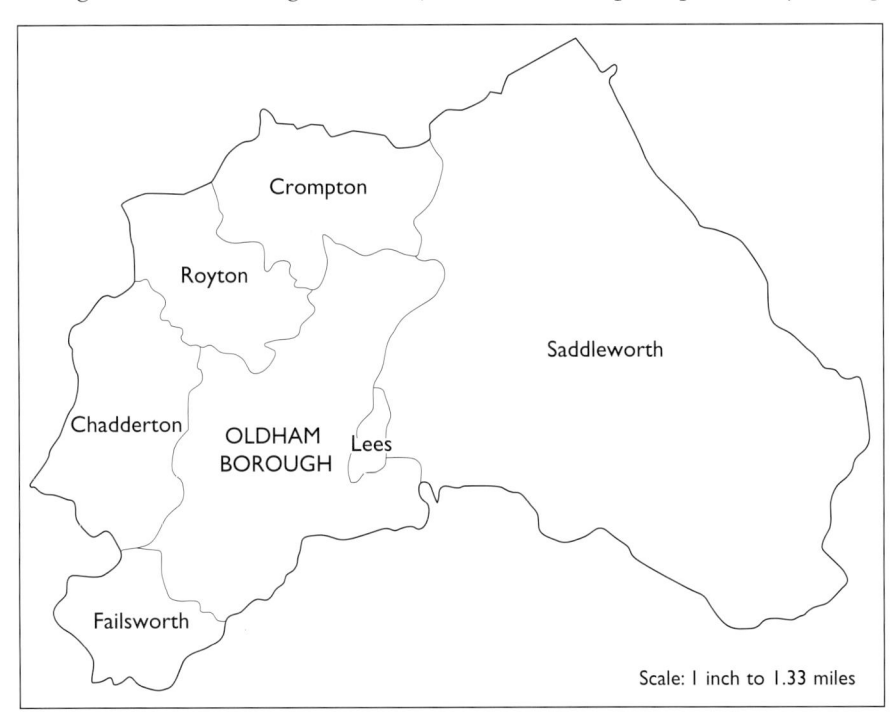

**District Councils**: the old townships reorganised to form Local Boards and then Urban Districts with their own Councils in the late nineteenth century. Oldham became a County Borough.

up elected Local Boards with powers to levy a rate. Royton, Crompton and Failsworth did so without delay in the early 1860s; Chadderton, which already had a rudimentary authority to pave, drain and light its roads, was more reluctant and did not respond until pressed by Whitehall in 1873, following serious smallpox and scarlet fever outbreaks. A visitor at the time spoke of the people of Chadderton "still wading in mud and moving in the midst of disease. A vast township was arising without proper drainage, with no proper closet accommodation, with houses built just as the owners had a mind. Now they found death around them on every hand." Lees, with a much smaller and more slowly growing population, also set up a Local Board in 1876, but remained starved of resources for improvement because of its low rateable value. The Local Boards became Urban District Councils in 1894 and then shared provision of services with Lancashire County Council which had been formed in 1888.

In each Local Board or District the new councillors were mainly cotton spinners and tradesmen, the latter predominating towards the end of the century as in Oldham; their main concern throughout was to keep down the rates. Gas and water and fire fighting were supplied from Oldham, initially at about 10 per cent extra to charges in the Borough; the surcharge was a contentious issue and, on gas, was successfully challenged by Chadderton in 1882 and then removed. Policing was a County responsibility. Locally controlled activity was mainly concerned with paving, draining and lighting the main roads and streets, curbing nuisances and improving sanitary conditions, removal of night soil and eventually providing sewers and sewage dispersal; these were similar problems to the Borough, but apart from small areas the Districts did not have the legacy of crowded old housing. There was a degree of rivalry between the Districts. Chadderton had a public swimming bath in 1894, Crompton followed in 1899 and Royton in 1910. Each by the 1900s had a free public library, assisted by grants from the Carnegie Foundation. Royton and Crompton had their own cemeteries and parks. Each of the Districts built its own Town Hall, and certainly by the end of the century there was a strong sense of local identity, local pride and concern for local autonomy. Because spending on the services and improvement was later and more modest than in Oldham, local rates in the Districts were below those of the Borough. In 1889 for instance, a £10 rental house in Oldham paid £1 5s compared with 16s 8d in Royton, 14s 4d in Chadderton and 13s 4d in Crompton. Chadderton, in 1911, had about one-fifth of Oldham's population, a quarter of its rateable value while its net expenditure was only one-seventh of that of the Borough; Royton and Crompton were in much the same relationship. These were cheaper places to live, a consideration that weighed heavily with local employers and tradesmen as well as householders.

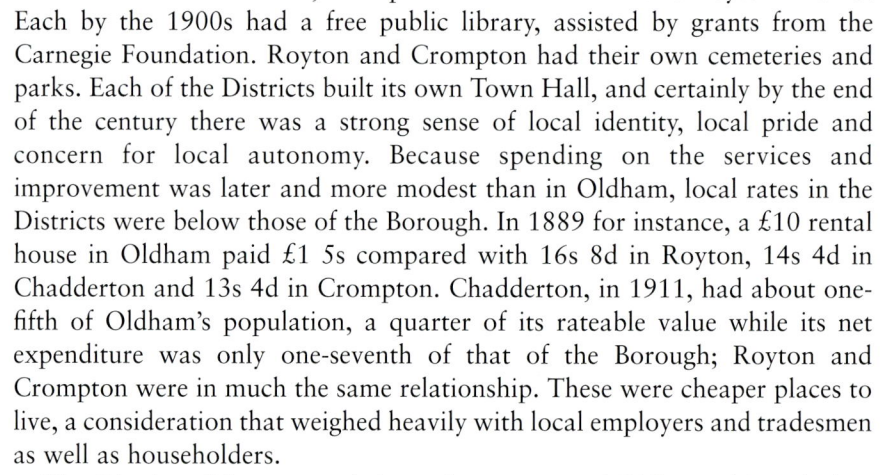

The Districts did not regard themselves as part of Oldham although they were happy to buy Oldham services, use the facilities and public market of its

**Royton Town Hall** was opened in 1880. The adjoining 1907 Public Library, like many others, was built with funds from the Carnegie Foundation. It replaced a much smaller Co-operative Library.

central area, its baths, cemeteries and park, and benefit from the drive of the cotton spinning industry and the prestige and renown that Oldham provided. Oldham, at different times, saw the situation differently. As the Borough filled up, mills and housing had spread to the surrounding districts which became "one large town with Oldham as the centre". In the case of Chadderton the boundary with Oldham was quite artificial; urban development along and off the Middleton Road was continuous; no-one could tell where one place ended and the other began. Joshua Walmsley Radcliffe, Oldham's powerful Mayor in the 1880s, had no hesitation in proclaiming that "Chadderton should be an integral part of the borough of Oldham"; others described it as "an Oldham suburb, part and parcel of the town". Oldham, as its own services became more expensive and the growth of its population and rateable value slowed, coveted the rateable value of the Districts as well as their vacant land. Its Councillors and Municipal Officers also believed, and rightly, that services would be more efficient and more economical if they were provided on a larger scale across the entire district, that is the Borough and its contiguous Urban Districts. This was particularly true of a comprehensive drainage and sewage disposal scheme, a pressing concern at the end of the 1880s. Hesketh Booth, the former Town Clerk of Oldham was outspoken in 1888 when he said, "I believe the interests of the whole district are substantially identical and indissoluble, and that those interests would be promoted and strengthened, not only in Oldham but in all the out-townships if the extension of the Borough were accomplished."

**Chadderton Town Hall**, a fine Renaissance style building, completed in 1913, marked the independence of the District Council which strenuously resisted Oldhamisation.

So the issue of amalgamation or "annexation" surfaced from time to time. Oldham first tried to merge with Chadderton in 1878 but was rebutted. A more serious attempt was made with the Oldham Extension Bill of 1890 when the Borough sought powers to include in its boundaries, Chadderton, Crompton, Royton and Lees. Failsworth was approached but made it clear that amalgamation with Manchester was the preferred course; in the end Manchester was not sufficiently interested to make the required gestures. Failsworth apart, the townships were worried about their representation on the enlarged Borough Council, how far their local interests would be looked after, and above all about their rates. Long and anguished meetings were held throughout the district over the winter of 1889-1890. "We cannot stick in the one groove, remaining passive and making no advances," said Sam Platt, Mayor at the time, to loud applause. "It would not suit the temper of the people of Oldham to remain standing at the one condition of things. They wanted to have one united family." At first Royton and Lees favoured amalgamation. But opinion shifted; the new Lancashire County Council was firmly opposed, fearing a large loss of rateable value. Chadderton and Crompton "declared war to the knife", as the *Oldham Chronicle* put it; "Oldhamisation", as it was described, was particularly opposed by the spinning companies, concerned about higher rates. The matter was put to rest when a poll in Royton showed 1,178 against and only 430 for. Oldham quickly accepted defeat and withdrew its Bill. But the question was to be raised on many occasions in subsequent years before it was finally resolved in 1974.

## Saddleworth

Saddleworth was not regarded as part of Oldham at this period and never figured in the debate over extension of the Borough. Indeed the two districts had no evident relationship, in provision of the main utilities, in police, sewerage, poor law, or any other service, except tramways where Oldham's system reached Springhead. Saddleworth went its own way, revelling in its distinctiveness and different historical connections. While Oldham was red brick, Saddleworth's houses and mills were built in stone; it was Yorkshire rather than Lancashire. With a dispersed population it had not the same problems as Oldham; water supply, drainage, refuse disposal could almost take care of themselves. Springhead had a Local Board in 1864, Uppermill in 1868, but their activities remained modest, while the other large village communities, Delph, Dobcross and Greenfield retained their long cherished independence. In 1894 Saddleworth Rural District Council was formed, to become an Urban District Council in 1900; with Springhead, also by then an Urban District, it was linked to the new West Riding of Yorkshire County Council. There were no striking initiatives during this period beyond limited attempts to improve water supply or better deal with sewage to avoid polluting the Tame. Those governing the district roused themselves

**Dobcross about 1890:** whatever was happening in Oldham, the separate villages of the upper Tame valley went their own way, growing modestly with expanded mills and new housing but retaining their historic character and Pennine charm.

**Delph**, like Dobcross, expanded but retained its traditional character.

passionately and successfully when Oldham proposed to build an isolation hospital for smallpox cases beyond its borders in Delph.

To Oldham, Saddleworth, from which many Oldhamers or their parents had come, was a poor and backward neighbour, that had "let its advantage slip unseized", and was struggling, "a patent drudge, toiling for naught", left behind in the drive for economic success and civic renown. The farmers and workers in the small spinning and weaving mills of the district were seen as "country cousins". Condescension met resentful pride and cold civility. Saddleworth wanted nothing to do with Oldham, although it looked in vain to its famous sons who had made fortunes there for help in rebuilding churches or providing schools. It pursued its own unambitious but sturdy self-reliant course, not uncomfortable to be a slow quiet backwater. Its more enterprising young people could migrate to the metropolis if they wished, just as they could visit its entertainments; otherwise they could earn a modest living and enjoy a slow undemanding traditional but not unpleasant semi-rural life in sometimes harsh but often beautiful surroundings.

Chapter VII

# EDUCATION FOR ALL

At the time of the 1851 Census, the voluntary schools, that is day schools set up by the main religious denominations, Church of England particularly, followed by Methodists and Congregationalists, were well established in Oldham and the out-townships. Built with money supplied by the church members, helped by large contributions from the wealthier ones, often substantial buildings taking hundreds of children, they had made an important start in providing elementary education to the working classes. But they reached only part of the population and they were not free. In a town that was beginning to swarm with children, many, for whatever reason, did not go to school at all or went to school only to the extent that the law required it as a condition of working half-time in factories. In many parts of the town there was no school available. If one includes the private schools, it is reasonable to assume perhaps only forty per cent of the children of school age were receiving some form of elementary education at mid-century. For the remainder they ran about in the streets, did errands or worked in other ways, stayed at home as child-minders while mother went back to the mill, and received a rudimentary instruction at the nearest Sunday School. School attendance in the Borough was greatly behind what had been achieved elsewhere; progress in education was retarded by lack of provision, ignorance and prejudice.

As Oldham's population grew rapidly over the next twenty years, the

**St. Domingo Street Day School**, dating from 1822, was one of the few nonconformist denominational schools. It was also the Sunday school of the nearby Manchester Street Wesleyan Methodist Chapel.

voluntary schools struggled to keep pace. Many new schools were built or older schools enlarged by all the denominations, to cater for growing demand and the needs of newly developed districts. The Roman Catholic Irish built their own church schools. Serving the poorest parts of Oldham at Grosvenor Street and Mount Pleasant where school pence was out of the question, two Ragged Schools, supported financially by the town's leading public men, were started in 1862 providing free instruction to about 400 children during the day and another 400 in the evening. But provision and attendance was still quite inadequate. Of about 18,000 children of school age, the average number attending school at the time of an enquiry made in 1871, was about 6,800. Many children were not enrolled, while others, if enrolled, were, for one reason or another, not at school. Most children it would seem were still playing in the street, at work, or helping at home; the position had scarcely changed in twenty years.

The 1870 Education Act was intended to make elementary education more widely, indeed universally, available. If the working man had been given the vote in the Reform Act of 1867, then he must be able to read and write. Elected School Boards could be set up to meet unfilled need, with powers to borrow money and to raise a rate to cover their expenses. Government grant depending on numbers in each school and the standards achieved, was available to both new board schools and to voluntary schools. Education was not to be free; nor was school attendance made compulsory. Factory legislation in 1874 introduced other relevant changes; the minimum age at which a child could work half-time in a textile factory was raised from eight to ten and the full-time age from thirteen to fourteen; provision was made for exemption from school at thirteen if certain standards of attainment or period of attendance had been reached.

## Oldham's School Board 1871 - 1903

Oldham's ruling elite welcomed all these changes. William Fox, the Borough's Radical member in the 1850s, encouraged by the Platts, had campaigned unsuccessfully for publicly provided and popularly controlled unsectarian or secular education. Many prominent Oldham men including John Platt, Thomas Emmott and Eli Lees had been active in the National Education League which campaigned for the same ends. John Platt, speaking in Higginshaw in 1870 at a church bazaar, was eloquent on the subject; "You cannot any longer have an ignorant population. Mind governs the world and controls its destinies. With an educated race inhabiting these islands, I can see no bounds to our future prosperity". There was no hesitation, accordingly, on the part of the Council in deciding that Oldham should have an elected School Board.

There were those to whom the work of the Board was simply seen as a matter of efficient school provision for all, "a school place for every child, and every child in its place, and that a good place". Not all shared this view. Given the position of the voluntary schools in Oldham and the perceived importance of religion in the education of children, to many the real issues were how far existing and future needs should continue to be met by voluntary schools, motivated by the wish to instruct a child in one or other religious faith as well as numeracy and literacy, rather than godless or secular board schools that would be a burden on the rates. So far as board schools were concerned, the form of religious instruction in those schools was of crucial importance. The formation of a School Board in 1871 was not therefore without controversy and although an election was avoided, the outcome was tense, and to many crucial. In the event the first School Board was split on party lines, achieving a Liberal majority when Rev. R. M. Davies was elected Chairman with the support of the single Roman Catholic, the priest of St Mary's, who became Vice-Chairman; the majority included prominent Liberals like Thomas Emmott, the Quaker millowner, and William Wrigley, a Unitarian and leading Liberal organiser in the town, who were determined to keep any new board schools secular; the minority, mainly Anglican, and including important Tory millowners like Hilton Greaves and T. E. Lees, were voluntary school enthusiasts.

On its formation the School Board estimated that it needed to provide between 2,500 and 3,000 places. It acted quickly to provide schools at Smith Street, a poor district in Greenacres, and in Westwood towards the Chadderton boundary, followed by Hathershaw and Wellington Street. These early schools, often improvised from existing buildings, were spartan rather grim affairs, built with regard to costs rather then amenity. They were cold and damp in winter, heated only by coal fires in a corner and lit by flaring gas jets; their sanitary arrangements were typically trough closets. The rising value of land in a booming town was a problem, and as much as £1,500 an acre, or its equivalent in ground rent, had to be paid. Space per child was at the minimum standard, playgrounds were small if they were provided at all. The Board at first congratulated itself in keeping the capital costs of new schools per pupil below that in other towns. But by 1883, apologising for the poor standards, it could claim

**Wellington Street School**, one of the early board schools, built in 1879 close to the town centre to provide 450 places, very quickly had 592 children on the register although they did not all attend regularly. It was described in 1880 as "crowded with ill-clad often dirty children, noisy with iron-shod clogs, and on rainy days damp wet clothes". The rooms, shared by seven standards, were heated by open fires in the corner, and lit by inadequate gas jets. Many children had to stand during lessons. These conditions were relieved when the nearby Scottfield School opened in 1884.

"experience has taught wisdom as to the erection of schools. Those built in the past three years are so perfect as to leave little room for improvement in like undertakings in the future; the apartments are lofty and cheerful, the light is abundant, ventilation is on the best known scientific principles. Architectural ornament has been sparsely employed, the aim having been to secure adaptation to the purpose and at the same time to illustrate that what is uncostly need not be unsightly".

Twenty years later these schools were to look outdated and inadequate. The early board schools were much like the voluntary schools which they complemented, often no more than a large room or hall with a platform at one end. Infants were taken at age five and at age seven the child moved to the mixed department. In districts where new streets were springing up, the schools quickly became grossly overcrowded and teaching suffered. Emphasis was very much on arithmetic, reading, writing, dictation, spelling, grammar and perhaps composition for the older ones, sewing and knitting for girls. Written work was done on slates to be cleaned off, once they were marked, with a coat sleeve or a skirt. School fees were charged, rising from 2d a week in the lowest classes to 7d in the higher ones. Few children dared to present themselves at school on a Monday morning without their school pence or a good reason for its absence. Teachers were badly paid, £40 or £50 a year for an assistant, women not more than two-thirds the rate for men; generally they were poorly trained; a large part of their time was spent in administration. Many pupil teachers were employed, as well as monitors, little more than older children, but a low cost means of supervision; such training as they received was given by the headmaster before school began each morning. There was no unanimity on teaching methods which were often experimental. Classes were large, often over sixty, and discipline was harsh, using corporal punishment liberally with birch and cane. Government inspectors visited the schools regularly to judge and advise on educational practice and the standards reached, as well as make an assessment for grant; they were not themselves trained experts and their comments and conclusions attracted frequent criticism. In the voluntary schools, the senior teachers were expected to show enthusiasm for the particular religious cause supporting the schools, rather than teaching skills; the time given to religious instruction was large and education standards probably lower as a result. In contrast, in the early Oldham board schools, religious instruction was said to be the bare minimum.

**St. Paul's, Royton**, an Anglican denominational school, an infant class with its teachers.

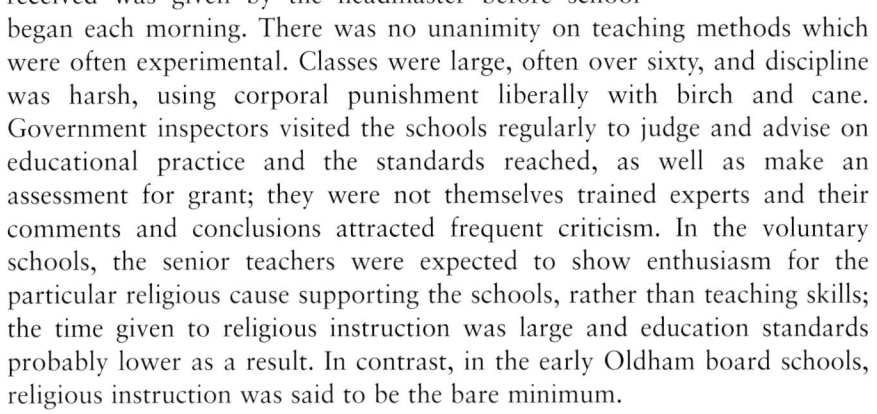

In the twenty years after the 1871 Act, a period of dramatic population growth, the voluntary schools retained their vigour in Oldham while the Board moved comparatively slowly, partly due to concern about the rates. By 1891 the Board was providing only 6,400 places in eleven schools compared with 20,800 places in the voluntary schools. But by then most if not all needs were being met; there was a school place including an infant school place within reach of most working-class households, and the numbers enrolled in both types of school had doubled between 1871 and 1891. Most, if not all, children were on the books of one school or another. Outside the Borough, elsewhere in the district, voluntary schools remained the main or indeed only provider. This was the position in Crompton, for example, and in Saddleworth. No board schools were built in those Districts.

School attendance had remained a problem although far improved from the 1870s; by 1891 average attendance had reached 78 per cent, compared with 56 per cent in 1871. Going to school had been made compulsory in 1880 but many excuses continued to be found, sickness in the family, sickness of the child, the need for the help of young girls in child-minding and the like, while in many cases parents probably made no effort to get their children to school, pleading lack of means, even to buy footwear let alone pay the school pence. The Board could give assistance to poor parents and did so, but on a most sparing basis. Only the Roman Catholic church schools were free and there were four of these by 1891, all well attended. Average attendance was

**Children in the street**, attracted by an unusual incident in Thompson Lane, Chadderton, the result of subsidence. Probably many of them should have been at school; non-attendance or irregular attendance was a major problem at the time.

also reduced by the numbers working half-time between the ages of ten and thirteen at which age they could, if the conditions were met, go full time as many did. Throughout the 1880s the number of half-timers in Oldham, at various ages from ten to thirteen, still approached 4,000, boys and girls; they made up about one-fifth of those attending school, although earlier when the numbers exceeded 5,000, they had been as many as one third. These considerations apart, however, the proportion of children attending school had risen dramatically, thanks to the efforts of the Board through the school "bobbies" to enforce attendance, if necessary by prosecution; in the early School Board period many hundreds of parents were brought before the magistrates and fined, usually 5s.

Irregular attendance and the presence of half-timers in most of the older classes made a well planned and efficient teaching routine and timetable almost impossible. Half-timers were dirty, unruly and insubordinate, often tired and bringing the language of the mill into the schoolroom, but generally more spirited and independent than the rest. Needless to say the educational establishment lobbied hard for an end to the system. Parents and employers clung to it; the former needed the additional family income, and had grown up with the system and survived and progressed themselves despite it; the latter needed cheap assistants in the card and spinning rooms.

In 1891 board school education was made free and parents had a right to demand a free place. There were many districts in Oldham where there were only voluntary schools which had generally no alternative but to charge fees. Inevitably, as a result, there was conflict between those wishing to extend board school provision making it available to all, and those struggling to maintain the voluntary schools, increasingly lacking in resources as they were. Meanwhile, although shifts in population within Oldham were creating additional demands for further school places in some districts, the dramatic fall that was taking place in the town's birth rate was leading to a sharp fall in the number of children of school age. Against that, the minimum age at which a child could work in a factory was raised to eleven in 1893 and twelve in 1900. The numbers of half-timers fell steeply as a result and by 1903 was down to 1,153.

Conflict within the School Board intensified in 1888 when the voluntary faction, associated as it was with the Conservative party, gained a majority. Their particular platform was the increasing burden of extravagant board schools on the rates; the precept had reached £10,000 in 1887-88. Led at first by the formidable Joshua Walmsley Radcliffe, Liberal Mayor but committed Anglican, and by two Anglican parsons, Canon James Rountree of St Thomas' Werneth, joined in 1892 by the Revd. John Gouldie French of Waterhead, they fought a determined action to preserve the church schools and constrain further building of new board schools. To Conservatives at the time, as their mouthpiece, the *Standard*, put it, expensive fancy schools were "an utter mistake" in a town like Oldham, "where the vast majority of school children must necessarily go to the mill or workshop". Given the voluntary schools, they felt "all was well and wisely put". Using their majority they were determined to go further and amend the form of religious instruction practised in the godless board schools. In particular they objected to "the reading of the Bible without note or comment." They now proposed extending the time devoted to religion and introducing a liturgy of responses resembling Anglican prayer, as well as explanations of the Bible readings. A minority of people cared about these issues but they cared passionately. Nonconformists objected to any possibility that the rates they paid should be used to promote denominational religious instruction in board schools, as they did to any question of using rates or taxes to support denominational voluntary schools. So intense was the argument that Joshua Radcliffe withdrew his support for the Anglican view and resigned from the Board. In the end the Liberal party regained control in 1897, and religious instruction reverted to earlier practices.

TABLE XVIII: DEVELOPMENT OF ELEMENTARY EDUCATION: 1871 - 1911

|  | 1871 | 1881 | 1891 | 1911 |
|---|---|---|---|---|
| Population | 82,629 | 111,343 | 131,463 | 147,483 |
| Children aged 3-13 | 18,000 | 26,000 | 29,000 | 26,000 |
| School places provided | 12,700 | 22,000 | 27,200 | 28,041 |
| Board | - | 3,000 | 6,400 | 17,572 |
| Voluntary | - | 19,000 | 20,800 | 10,469 |
| Numbers enrolled | 12,200 | 20,500 | 24,000 | 25,609 |
| Average attending | 6,800 | 14,500 | 18,700 | 20,412 |
|  | (70%) | (78%) | (84%) | (80%) |
| Board | - | 1,800 | 5,600 | 12,897 |
| Voluntary | 6,800 | 12,700 | 13,100 | 7,515 |

The period after 1891 is featured by a marked increase in the number of board school places and a marked decline, indeed collapse, in the voluntary schools. This was a period when church attendance was in decline. Many of the voluntary schools closed, many were taken over by the Board. The remaining voluntary schools, some still charging fees especially where they were Church of England, lost enrolments and were often only half-full, their buildings in poor repair. Roman Catholic schools, free as always, were the exception providing for the large, compact and loyal Irish community with over 2,400 pupils in 1903. Opening a new school at Royton, the Catholic

Bishop of Salford was outspoken on his church's views; "education is inseparable from religion. A Catholic child must have a Catholic education and that can be given only in Catholic schools with Catholic teachers". That was to remain their position.

Many new board schools were built in this later period, larger, better and more ambitiously designed and more costly than the earlier examples. Space standards per child were more generous, large playgrounds were provided, functional layouts became standard providing for boys and girls entrances and cloakrooms, a large well-lit central hall with separate classrooms opening from it. Some of the new buildings included architectural detail that went beyond the functional: Werneth school, opened in 1892, had a campanile that became a minor landmark in Oldham. These later board schools were costing as much as £16 per place to build compared with half or less of that amount for the early schools. In 1903 Oldham had twenty-one board schools

**Higginshaw Board School**, built in 1897 with places for 850 children, to a much higher standard of space and construction than the early Board Schools. Its cost at close to £19 per place compared with £13 for the much earlier Wellington Street School and £6 for the first Board Schools.

*Above:* **Werneth School**, completed in 1897.

averaging 600 pupils each, attending in mixed and infant sections, and eighteen voluntary schools averaging about 500 pupils. To most parents the modern new schools were the obvious choice compared to the crumbling old voluntary schools. Thus they chose to have their children "educated on the rates."

If Derker School, opened in 1898 is taken as an example, it had accommodation for 1,120 pupils and 400 infants but average attendance of about 890 and 270 infants in 1913. There were equal numbers of boys and girls, divided into eighteen classes averaging above forty-five, the desired norm. The day started with twenty minutes religious instruction featuring hymns, bible reading and the Lord's Prayer. The curriculum included the three Rs, but was now extended by music, drawing, history, geography, elementary science, with needlework and cookery for girls, and drill and carpentry for boys. The school had a gymnasium. Both boys and girls were taught to swim and the school had a boys' brass band and a lending library as well as a penny savings bank. In 1903 its costs were £3,740 of which £2,687 was teachers' salaries; average cost per child was £3 6s. The headmaster of the Mixed

School was paid a salary of £260; he had two male assistants paid £120, and eighteen young women teachers earning an average of £70, aided by seven pupil-teachers earning £15 to £20. The Infants School had a headmistress paid £130 and seven assistants and four pupil teachers and monitors. Women predominated in what had become an important profession in Oldham; the 1911 Census showed 786 teachers resident in the Borough of whom 614 were women. Women at the time were paid less than men. Both men and women teachers complained bitterly of low pay comparing Oldham unfavourably with other towns of similar size. In 1901 in successfully claiming higher salaries they argued that many local teachers had to augment their salaries by doing other work, and were unable to maintain the social status their occupation required.

Early in the new century school attendance was approaching acceptable levels, 84 per cent in 1903. The elementary school provision was mature and did not change a great deal for many years thereafter. Within the existing schools, the special needs of handicapped children, the blind and the deaf, were being met. From 1904 free meals were being provided for the poorest children, although only on a limited scale since the service had to be financed by charitable appeal, rather than the rates. A Medical Officer for Schools was appointed in 1907 and children began to be examined with results that showed the extent of malnutrition and neglect. Popular culture and attitudes to school had changed; rather than get their children away to earn some money, the school experience was perceived as a necessary and valuable one; regularity, obedience, the sense of discipline began to be prized. In a more affluent community these attitudes led to the collapse if not demise of half-time working. There was a dramatic fall in illiteracy.

Meanwhile the huge expansion in board school provision, better buildings, better pay for more adequately trained teachers and many other improvements, including the beginnings of secondary education only partially met by government grant, resulted in a huge increase in the School Board precept which fell on the town's rates. By 1903 this had reached £33,600, the fastest growing part of the Corporation's spending, now accounting for close to a quarter of the whole. Understandably there was resistance; the School Board was condemned by the *Chronicle* as a "wilful spendthrift who had a wealthy purse to go to"; money it was said "was absolutely thrown away and wasted". These arguments fell quiet when the School Board was abolished by the Education Act of 1902, its responsibilities passing to a newly formed Education Committee of the Council. The Act provided that voluntary schools were to be maintained from the rates, a matter of intense controversy nationally since they retained the right to appoint their staffs and to continue denominational religious instruction. Nonconformists continued to object to public money going to church schools of a particular sect. But in Oldham, where so many voluntary schools had closed or passed to the Board in the 1890s, the heat had gone out of that controversy.

**Beyond the Elementary School**

The powers of the School Board were strictly limited to elementary education and that is all that most children received. Especially once the age of compulsory attendance was raised to fourteen, many wanted to provide something for those who wished to extend their learning. Oldham, skirting the law, but encouraged by suggestions from Whitehall that elementary education could include whatever subjects could be taught within the limit of fourteen years of age, introduced a more varied and advanced curriculum at Waterloo School from 1887. Built as a mixed school, part of the building became known as the Higher Grade School. Fees of 9d weekly had to be charged, even when fees in the board schools were abolished. Government grants provided by the Department of Science and Arts in South Kensington were also an important source of income, the Board's precept covering the balance.

The School was a great success, the numbers increasing so much that the space occupied had to be extended, displacing the Infants Department for which a new school was built. Many of the scholars at the Higher Grade School, aged up to fifteen, came from outside the Borough, there being no similar facilities available elsewhere in the locality. A government inspector was impressed by the well-to-do appearance of the boys "with turned-down-collars, carefully starched ...... a recognised mark of a boy coming from a comfortable home". On enquiry he found that most of the scholars were "children of professional men, of ministers as well as of tradesmen of the town".

By 1900 there were 231 students, some coming only in the evenings, and as many as nine teaching staff, some with university degrees. Not everyone was happy. Private schools found they were losing their business. Others argued that older children should not be a charge on the rates, that "free education must be elementary and the more elementary the better". When the Whitehall Board of Education objected to higher grade Schools on the grounds that they went beyond legitimate use of the School Board precept, Waterloo School was designated as a School of Science, carrying on much as before. Such was the beginning of popular secondary education in Oldham.

The School Board had taken another important initiative to provide continued education for those leaving school at thirteen or fourteen. From 1885 Evening Continuation Schools were provided, both in buildings belonging to the Board or in voluntary schools where rent was paid. A slow start was made and in 1890 there were only 564 pupils in average attendance. Strenuous promotion followed and by 1900, total enrolments in thirty-eight schools reached 4,848 although average attendance was only 2,902. The Board regarded such attendance figures, spread as they were over several year's attendance, as disappointing given the 5,000 or so leaving the elementary schools each year; it provided various rewards for good attendance, prizes, rebates off fees and the like. Some students attended for several years; some quickly dropped out. Sadly, to some, the night classes never caught on. Many young people working in the mill saw no need for further knowledge. Many still could not write a readable letter; their reading was restricted, it was said, to "spicy divorce cases, murders, suicides, football, sporting and comic news". Not much was to change in the century to follow. Nonetheless, if falling far short of the potential, numbers attending evening school in Oldham compared favourably with the best figures achieved in similar towns.

The range of subjects was much the same as in the elementary school, the

**Evening Classes**, attended by many young Oldhamers seeking to improve their education, after a day's work in the mill.

level being more advanced. The evening schools were said to be filled with young men, mainly in white-collar jobs, well grounded in the day schools and eager to learn more and improve their prospects. Notable at the turn of the century was the growth in demand for instruction in typewriting, shorthand, commercial correspondence and office routine, and bookkeeping. Here there was a serious purpose related to employment possibilities and levels of income. This demand was met at Wellington Street School, near the town centre, and designated as the Commercial Evening School in 1896.

All these secondary provisions, like the elementary school, were intended for the working class, the great mass of Oldham's population. For those few who could afford there were a growing body of so-called public schools and certainly many of Oldham's elite sent their children away to be brought up as gentlemen; a few, like Elliott Lees, son of Thomas Evans Lees, the wealthy heir of Greenbank Mills, went to places like Eton and on to Oxford or Cambridge. But this was the privilege of a tiny group. Higher education had been provided on a very small scale by the old Grammar School in the town centre and that in Hollinwood. These were neglected and obsolete certainly by the 1860s, if not earlier. For the small but growing middle class, their interest in education stimulated by what was happening after the 1870 Act, there were only the private schools, still advertising their services in the town, attractive perhaps to tradesmen and mill managers for their families, but of doubtful quality. Oldham's Bluecoat School, prominently situated on the Edge, was known to everyone but took less than 100 boys, and these from a wide area extending well beyond Oldham.

It was probably due to the energy and commitment of Hesketh Booth, for a time Oldham's Town Clerk and subsequently a prominent solicitor, and Joseph Travis, long serving School Board member, that the Hulme Trust, an old Prestwich charity which was devoting its funds to educational purposes, was persuaded to provide resources for a grammar school in Oldham. The grant of £18,000, and a yearly covenant of £1,200, enabled a site to be purchased and a school to be built; this was the genesis of Oldham Hulme Grammar School, opened in 1895. In 1902 the average number of boys

**Hulme Grammar School**, the architect's drawing of 1894.

attending was 140, of girls 125. Some of these had qualified by scholarships; most were paying fees at £8 8s per annum, beyond the means of the working man, but affordable to the managerial, professional and commercial classes.

Hulme Grammar School apart, the new Education Committee appointed by the Council after the 1902 Act, had a duty "to make provision" for secondary education. It did so to a limited extent by converting an existing school at Greengate Street into the "Oldham Municipal Secondary School". 25 per cent of the places had to be free; the rest paid up to £3 3s yearly. Nothing more was made available in Oldham prior to the First World War. Real provision of secondary education remained a matter for the future, and the many who improved themselves and progressed in Oldham during this period did so through the elementary schools, augmented by the evening schools. What can be described as technical education was another route.

## The Lyceum and Technical Education

The Lyceum, in effect a Mechanics Institute, had been set up in 1839 with the object "the moral and intellectual improvement of the inhabitants". From the start it achieved distinguished patronage, James Platt becoming its President at the age of twenty-four in 1848. As with the abortive public park project he took a high-minded view of the needs of a community like Oldham and the responsibility of its successful men to provide leadership. He could describe as a "self-evident truth", "the duty and expediency of educating the masses of the community." Education, he said was "the surest means of rendering England great, powerful and contented." In particular James Platt took the view that the Lyceum needed a building of its own, and a fine building in a desirable situation. A large well publicised exhibition organised in the rebuilt Working Men's Hall in 1854 raised £3,669 mainly in admission tickets, and, after expenses, £2,155 was available for the new Lyceum. A huge banquet held on the occasion of the stone-laying in June 1855 raised from subscriptions another £1,920. Financed in this way the new building was opened in September 1856 with a grand parade. Sadly James Platt died in a shooting accident in the following year. But if his energy and leadership had created the new Lyceum, it did not lack other important patrons. All the leading figures of Oldham were now associated with the cause. The debt of £2,000 on the new building which had cost £6,500 was quickly cleared after John Platt came forward with an offer of £500 and his workpeople and senior managers with a further £186, to be followed by a long list of donors, led by the Radcliffes and the Emmotts, and many others, mainly Liberal in their sympathies. With larger facilities the Lyceum extended its library and its adult and elementary classes. In particular, and reflecting the commercial interest of the Platts, and the businesses of the town generally, in a steady supply of trained men capable of being overlookers and foremen, it now introduced technical subjects, mathematics, mechanics and various types of geometric and machine drawing, building skills and chemistry.

As technical study increased at the Lyceum a "Science and

**The Lyceum**, completed in 1856 at a cost of £6,500, partly with funds from the Exhibition. The Trust Deed provided that "the building shall be for ever devoted to the moral and intellectual culture of the inhabitants of Oldham." The first building had a library, newsroom, reading room, billiards room and various class rooms.

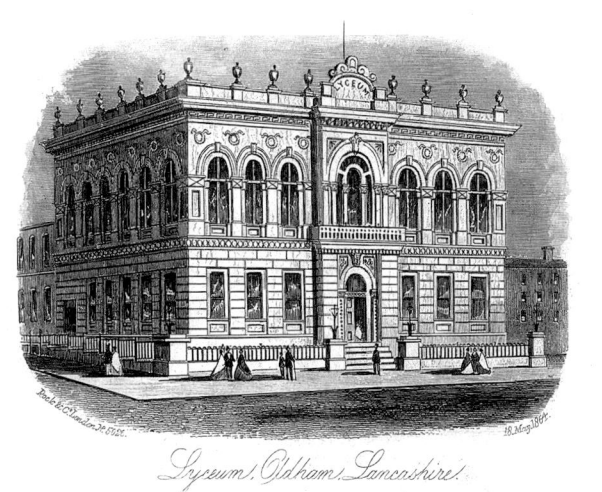

## The Lyceum and Technical Education

Art" school evolved, occupying more and more of the accommodation. The next step was a new one-storey building adjacent, the Science and Art School, completed in the Gothic style in 1865, and presented by the Platt concern, having cost about £2,000. The number of students grew, participation being encouraged by the award of numerous medals and prizes, but was still only 162 in 1873 having doubled in five years. On John Platt's death in 1872, his widow endowed two exhibitions, tenable at Owens College. Other scholarships followed. William Richardson, long serving senior manager and director of Platts, who had come to Oldham as a journeyman apprentice mechanic, now became closely associated as President. He gave financial help by purchasing and donating the site, and also by providing laboratories and demonstration workshops. Richardson was followed by Eli Spencer, his fellow director at Platts; Sam Platt became closely involved in 1878 and for many years was the chief patron. It was his initiative that prompted the rebuilding of the Science and Art School in 1880 and 1881 to provide much needed extra space; the new building, in the classical style in close harmony with the original, cost £9,000, given by Sam Platt and his brothers. At the grand opening Sam Platt, no doubt with the achievements of Platts in minds, spoke of

"Oldham holding the supremacy in science, holding that supremacy as they had hitherto done against all comers. The old system of rule of thumb, although it might be good in the hands of practical men, could not be carried out through all generations. His father thought that future generations ought to have a better knowledge and better education on technical subjects than he and his contemporaries had".

**The School of Science and Art** was built in 1865 to provide additional classrooms and a gymnasium for the Lyceum. John Platt paid for the extension and furnished it. Sadly only a one-storey building could be afforded which quickly became inadequate as Oldham's growth quickened. The spire of Union Street Congregational Chapel, 1855, is prominent in the background.

These important useful and practical objects apart, the enlarged handsome and dignified building was seen as an architectural ornament to the streets of Oldham, evidence of local patriotism and public spirit, and as such regarded as a guarantee of the maintenance of kindly feeling between rich and poor. Ever partisan, the Tory *Oldham Standard* saw the Lyceum differently, as "very much a Liberal meeting place", "a society for adulation of the Platts". It went on to refer to the contrast with people "living in abject and helpless poverty within the shadow of Platt's works".

It is difficult to assess the contribution of the Lyceum and, more importantly, the Science and Art School to Oldham's success and prosperity. The period of the 1870s and 1880s was that of its prime, when Oldham's cotton spinning industry was expanding so dramatically. Aspiring young engineers and managers came to study in the evening, after a hard day's work, and at their own expense, for fees were charged. What they learned must have been worth while; a contemporary wrote, "most of them are in training to fit themselves for their after-career, chiefly young mechanics at Platts and other works in the district". In fact almost all Platts young men went to the School where they made up at least a quarter of the students. Standards were assured by the nationally recognised qualifications such as City and Guilds Institute that students aimed to acquire. Apart from technical classes in science and engineering, instruction in the processes of cotton manufacture had also been introduced. The number of students, 163 in 1873, had reached 383 by 1877. The new building of 1878 was designed to take 680 students; by 1881-82 the number had risen to 676, together with 110 art students, the high point. High as these numbers seemed, they were small in relation to the vast army of school children who year by year were joining the workforce in Oldham at the time, perhaps one in twenty. Meanwhile in the old Lyceum building young people now well grounded in the elementary schools, extended their studies of language and literature. But their numbers were in decline. The town's Central Library had usurped part of the Lyceum's functions. Billiards, chess, music, socialising had become the main activities of the Lyceum by the 1900s among about 600 subscribers paying a fee of one guinea; the institution began to augment its income by letting its rooms.

**Union Street, 1885** the first School of Art had been demolished to be replaced in 1881 by a larger building, designed to be fully compatible with the original Lyceum. The sons of the late John Platt met the costs of the new building. William Richardson, Vice-Chairman of Platts, himself a half-millionaire, bought the land occupied by both Lyceum buildings and presented it to the Trustees, freeing them of ground rent. The Chronicle could write "Union Street is gradually being filled up with buildings of at least more than a respectable appearance. It will be a thoroughfare quite unique in up-and-down Oldham, its best street and a credit to the town". The horse and wagon with empty yarn skips were standard elements in growing street traffic.

Employers were full of praise. Giving evidence to the Royal Commission on Technical Education in 1884, James Taylor, partner in Buckley and Taylor, thought the School "very beneficial; it has caused the men to be more intelligent workmen, they understand the working better. Our foremen draughtsmen are now all taken from the Lyceum. Before we used to get Swiss and Germans; now there is hardly a foreigner in town." William Richardson said much the same about working mechanics. Braddocks Meter Works claimed that it was "a good deal easier for foremen to take charge of men than it was formerly. The men could be more readily trusted with a job".

The Lyceum and School of Art and Science attracted most attention but it was not the only institution in Oldham supplementing the work of public

**Werneth Mechanics Institute**, opened by Gladstone before large crowds in 1867; subsequently he said he had never seen such intelligence on the faces of any multitude as he saw when speaking in Oldham.

elementary schools. In many parts of Britain support for the early Mechanics Institutes had fallen away. This was less true in Oldham. The Mechanics Institute at Werneth, opened by Gladstone in 1867, and as many as nine similar institutions elsewhere in the district and three in Saddleworth, in some cases described as Mutual Improvement Societies, continued to meet local needs. Werneth for instance, open until 10 pm, had a well lit newspaper room, reading room, library and billiards room, as well as a lecture hall available for hire. Its educational provision, however, as at the other institutions, with some day but mostly night classes, remained mainly at the elementary level.

Meanwhile responding to national legislation to encourage technical education, Oldham Corporation acquired the School of Science and Art in 1893. The purchase value, some £8,750, went to the Platt family but was used to endow more Platt scholarships. The technical curriculum was now greatly enlarged with classes covering most branches of practical science, mechanical engineering, building construction, technical drawing, as well as cotton spinning and weaving. Tradesmen's skills such as plumbing and carpentry were included. Finally to meet demand commercial subjects were added, book-keeping, typing and shorthand, foreign languages. By 1896 there were 1,208 students, aged from fourteen to twenty. To cope with growing numbers, new rather grim premises were built in 1897 at Ascroft Street, the first Municipal Technical School proper, but the older buildings on Union Street continued to be used. In 1902 there were 2,010 students, some going on to take University degrees with the help of scholarships. To the enthusiasts this was a disappointing number for a town the size of Oldham. All the study was done in the evening after a day's work. Fees had to paid. Prior to 1914 public opinion was not ready to accept that young people should be trained during the day. For the many, it was still believed that a lad should learn his job on the shop floor roughing it like his father before him; the widespread view was that "workshops were the proper technical schools for a spinning town." Why should people pay rates, it was asked, "for teaching of which they do not approve".

Finally, as a beginning in what eventually came to be called "continuing education", an Oldham branch of the Workers Educational Association was formed in 1908. The Co-operative Societies, the trade unions, as well as prominent churchmen and school teachers all became engaged. Sarah Lees was a particularly strong supporter, providing a meeting place for classes in her own home. The object, it was claimed, "was not to teach people how to make a living, but how to live splendidly." Early lecture subjects to adult classes meeting on Saturday afternoons covered The Greek Temple, Art and Life in Florence, and similar subjects, illustrated by lantern slides. Students had to produce a written essay each fortnight. Modest fees were charged, 3d for a single lecture. Needless to say participation was limited but a start had been made.

**The Education Committee**

Whether through voluntary schools, the School Board, the Lyceum and their successors, much progress had been made in establishing provision of elementary, some secondary, some technical education by 1914. Compared with what was to be provided to the next generation it was rudimentary and, it has to said, most of the young people of Oldham received little beyond a basic elementary education. The same, needless to say, was true of the Districts. To go beyond this basic elementary education in the years before 1914 required great motivation and initiative by the young, although a few did this. Gradually all this was to change. In 1903 the Oldham Education Committee assumed responsibility for all forms of education in the Borough, elementary, secondary, technical. It made a slow start but in the end, much later, it and its successors, would transform provision.

*Chapter VIII*

# LIFE IN VICTORIAN AND EDWARDIAN OLDHAM

For the mass of the working people of Oldham, life continued to revolve around the cotton mill or the engineering workshop, the family home, the pub, and, for some the church or chapel. But as the century grew older, living standards and the quality of life improved significantly, at least for the great majority. As we have seen local government, however slowly and imperfectly, was meeting essential needs for services, for decent streets and improved sanitation. At least elementary education became available for all. New houses offered more space, more comfort, more privacy. Earnings were higher, food was cheaper, and households could buy more and better quality goods and services, provided by the burgeoning co-operative societies and an enterprising competitive retail trade.

People were having smaller families. Shorter working hours and higher real incomes enabled them to take more leisure, filled by new and affordable forms of popular entertainment, organised sport, and the adventure and respite of day excursions and eventually, longer holidays by the sea. When Herbert Asquith, later Liberal Prime Minister, described Oldham as "one of the most dismal of manufacturing towns" after his visit in 1890, he failed to understand the mood of the people. They had a sense of the enormous and wonderful changes that had taken place in their own lifetime, both in Oldham and in Britain and its place in the world. Confident, thrifty, busy, hard-working, persevering, self-reliant, proud of what had been achieved in the town, conscious of their new political power, the popular mood was echoed by the *Oldham Chronicle* when it hailed the 20th Century as "the working man's millennium". Life in Edwardian Oldham, whatever its humdrum monotony, its shortcomings and imperfections, had never been so good. As one contemporary observed, "should anyone desire to know what Victorian progress means let him go and look at Oldham".

Of course there were widening contrasts between the different social groups or classes. At one extreme of the spectrum, were a handful of notables, the capitalist elite of the town who had accumulated great wealth; their lifestyle bore no resemblance to that of their local contemporaries and was increasingly separate and remote. In Oldham they maintained large mansions in extensive private grounds in Werneth Park and its adjacent areas, supported by a retinue of servants. Many had used their money to acquire houses and estates in more congenial locations, in coastal resorts or the hunting shires, or in the fashionable parts of London. More numerous but still small was the comfortable middle class, the lesser capitalists, professional men, successful shopkeepers, wives not working, employing at least one servant; they were concentrated in their own distinct neighbourhoods, Werneth Coppice and the environs of Alexandra Park. Then there was the

**Woodfield**, in large grounds adjoining Werneth Park, built by Thomas Evan Lees about 1870, was the grandest of the homes of Oldham's nineteenth century millocracy.

overwhelming majority who would describe themselves as the respectable working class, well-off by the standards of the time, working hard, paying their way, not in debt, not depending on charity, keeping their children clean, well fed, neatly dressed. Finally there were many who had not shared in the huge progress that had been made and lived in poverty; some, the very poor, lived a hand to mouth existence in chronic want, in some cases in squalor.

If in the early nineteenth century all classes were mixed together in the same streets and close to the centre of the town, by its end they were living apart, in separate districts, socially segregated as later jargon put it. The segregation of the different groups (and the sprawl of the town) was

**Woodfield:** the drawing room in the 1890s.

## Life in Victorian and Edwardian Oldham

encouraged and facilitated by public transport, the horse-tram and its successors, and by the hackney cab, a service that developed in Oldham for the better-off at least, from the 1850s. A visitor to Oldham in the 1880s would be aware of large contrasts in living conditions from one neighbourhood to another.

**Washbrook, Butler Green, Chadderton**, typical of the hundreds of working class streets built in the 1870s and 1880s. There are nice curtains, blinds and plants in the windows; the doorsteps are scoured.

**A court off Eagle Street**, one of the many decaying slum areas close to the town centre.

## The Working Man's Millennium

The very substantial increase in the money earnings of cotton mill operatives, certainly matched in machine-making workshops, foundries and elsewhere,

**Emigration** was a safety valve. Employment and earnings in Oldham were unstable but for the enterprising there was opportunity overseas, in the United States, Canada, Australia and the like. The shipping lines constantly advertised their services and Crossley's Emigration Office, in Henshaw Street could make all arrangements. In 1889 steerage to New York cost £3, saloon class £12 on the White Star Line. At particular times, some of the Australian states offered free or assisted passages; to attract people they always tried to be cheaper than the North American fares.

has been noted. Oldham working men were generally well paid and increasingly well organised to protect that pay. Especially after 1870 there was a fall in prices, particularly of basic foodstuffs such as flour and bread, meats, dairy products, sugar, tea and coffee. Oldham's Liberal MP, John Hibbert, praising Free Trade, could say in 1885, "there was food to be had cheap, nay, far cheaper than had ever been known at any previous time." Others went farther, talking of "the age of cheapness". Mass production and competition were improving the availability and lowering the price of factory-made goods. Rail and horse-tram transport cost 1d a mile. Coal remained cheap, about 1s the cwt. Real wages had surged in the later 1850s; after the temporary setback of the Cotton Famine, living standards rose slowly but steadily between 1870 and 1900; over the period, they improved by perhaps as much as 50 to 60 per cent. After 1900 up to the Great War the increase in money wages was slower and prices rose; there was a surge in trade union militancy in the years before the war, not least in Oldham.

All these statements need to be qualified, however, to take account of the inherent uncertainty of work and wages in Victorian times. The *Oldham Chronicle* in its appreciation of the progress that had been made, spoke of "full work and full wages". In periods of bad trade, wages were often reduced. More importantly, short-time working, sometimes for extended periods, remained a constant hazard, in the engineering workshops as much as the cotton mills, and more than anything else, a cause of loss of income that could not be foreseen. Some occupations such as working for the Corporation, the railways, shop-work were steadier than cotton or engineering but did not pay so well. Some like the building trades were notoriously seasonal and irregular. And then there were the disputes; in the major strikes in the local cotton industry income was sharply reduced if not removed altogether. Distress was widely felt at these times; tradesmen, publicans and many others also suffered.

The ordinary working class family had to cope then, with an unstable income, worse in periods of depression when to widespread short-time there was an increase in unemployment, unrecorded but in bad years like 1894 probably many thousands of men. People adjusted by pulling up the ladder, cutting out discretionary spending, drawing on savings, looking to landlords or shopkeepers for help with rent or basic purchases, pawning their possessions, all traditional sources of relief. 1911 saw the beginnings of the welfare state with compulsory insurance against sickness, and on a more restricted basis, unemployment, but the benefits of Lloyd George, as the scheme was called, were for a later day. During the great strikes especially, many, with no reserves to draw on, went hungry, children going to school half-starved, relying on handouts and gifts of food provided by the political parties, chapels or tradesmen with an eye on future support. In 1892 the Oldham Rugby Football Club gave a good feed to 2,000 poor children; the Salvation Army in one week supplied 1,174 quarts of soup and 314 loaves of bread to 2,348 persons, and so on; week by week the local press printed details of relief given. In that dispute, as in the past, families would leave the district, others would emigrate as many did not merely in the hard times; the shipping lines that offered cheap passages to North America or to Australia ran regular advertisements in the Oldham press.

As earlier in the century, the cycle of family income over a lifetime remained the other principal source of comparative affluence or hardship. The young, newly married with two incomes and small outgoings, were well-off; in many cases they doubled up with parents, saving until they could afford and find their own home. The next phase of family building, numbers of children, increased outgoings and reduced income, inevitably meant hardship if not poverty; married women seldom worked when the second child came along. The situation of Thomas Shaw, described as a club steward, living in Back Grove Street, a poor part of town at Bottom of Moor, in 1891 is illustrative; he and his wife had six children aged between three months and twelve years. As children began to earn, enhancing the household income, there was a high period lasting five to ten years. Again to illustrate, also living cheaply in Back Grove Street in 1891, Benjamin Dunkerley, a fifty-four year old minder, had three sons and two daughters all earning, one of the sons, already a minder; their combined income with full work would be not less than £6 or £7. Young working children would give their earnings to their parents, being given back as a rule, a penny in the shilling. As they got older they would begin contributing board, spending more freely, and perhaps saving prior to marriage.

As children married and left home, household income and outgoings fell, and approaching old age cast its shadow. The numbers of elderly people in the town and district crept higher, both with the total population and as people lived longer. Old women could cope better than old men, fitting into a younger family, helping out with the children, not eating much; they were also more determined to remain independent. There were many older women with no family, unmarried or widows with no income provision; they tried to earn small sums by sewing, washing, minding children, hawking, and eking out a scanty living while keeping their independence. To them the workhouse - or outdoor relief - was repugnant, and rather than seek this final refuge they bore the pinch of hunger, insufficient clothing or lack of warmth. Old men were a different problem, lost without work, more in the way if they had family, and lacking the means and ability to look after themselves, more likely and indeed willing to get out of the way and to finish up in the workhouse. The introduction of old age pensions in 1908, 5s a week at the age of 70, paid at the post office and so escaping the stigma of poor relief, undoubtedly provided great help. Alfred Butterworth, eccentric but successful at Glebe Mills, Chadderton, had already introduced his own arrangements; 5s weekly for everyone over 65 who had worked at the Mills for over twenty years. No-one had followed his example.

By the standards of the time most Oldham working-class families would regard themselves as quite well-off, and much better off then they or their parents had been a generation earlier. Comparative affluence, in Oldham as elsewhere, was reflected in the huge increase in national consumption of basic food, meat, butter, cheese, sugar, tea and other "necessaries of life". Tea consumption, for instance, rose three-fold from the 1850s to the 1880s. A wider range of fresh vegetables, imported fruit like oranges, bananas, nuts and rice became staples rather then luxuries to be enjoyed only at Christmas. Then there were manufactured foods, jam, treacle, canned food, biscuits, sauces, confectionery, cocoa, mineral waters. Finally and of high significance in a working town was the immense convenience of prepared food, bakery bread, cakes, meat and potato pies, and perhaps most of all, fish and chips. Working class families came to depend on these. A vastly broader range of manufactured goods was also contributing to comfort and lifestyle; articles like soap, safety matches, patent medicines, cooking utensils, crockery, cutlery, ready made clothing, footwear, furniture, clocks, mirrors, ornaments, curtains, bed clothes, wall and floor coverings; all these became available and within the reach of working class budgets. Shawls and clogs were supplemented with hats and shoes, fustians and prints gave way to broadcloth and silks, all for Sunday best. In the home flock beds were replaced with sprung mattresses, horsehair with plush upholstery. What may be called discretionary was spending on luxuries and status symbols, on finer fancy fashion clothing, sewing machines, pianos and gramophones, on holidays and entertainment, and on grand funerals. It was said that people preferred to spend on these rather then pay higher rent for better housing.

Oldham claimed there were few towns where "thrift was so persistently taught and so diligently practised". That was manifest in the continued growth of friendly societies providing funeral and sickness benefits, the Oddfellows, the Rechabites and many others. Then there was widespread share ownership, saving though the co-operative societies, or the loan accounts of the Limiteds, penny savings banks in the schools, the going-off clubs, house purchase through the many building clubs and societies.

If it was more comfortable, working class life in Oldham was still a very standardised uniform experience. The discipline of the mill or the workshop was common to most families; being knocked up at 5 am, to start a long day's work, for most monotonous and tedious in far from pleasant conditions. Overwhelmingly people were living in the same kind of house in much the same kind of street, a red brick terrace house, two-up-two-down, front door opening onto the street, back door onto a small yard with privy, ashpit or dust bin, coal hole or its equivalent, giving way onto a narrow unmade passage. At the Census of 1911 about two-thirds of all families in Oldham lived in a four-roomed house, with an average of between four and five people to the household. The same was true of the Districts, except that the proportion living in four rooms was rather higher.

Most occupants rented their homes and rents generally were affordable, 4s to 5s weekly in the 1870s, by the 1900s 5s to 6s, on terrace houses; these rents included the town rates, much higher at the end of the century. For the better-off and larger families there were bigger houses, perhaps with an attic, a scullery at the rear with the addition of a storey over it to provide a third small bedroom, a bow window, even a tiny garden at the front; here the rents would be higher. About 23 per cent of the population in 1911 lived in houses

**The rent-collector**, employed most probably by an estate-agent, would call weekly for the money and mark his own record as well as the tenant's rent book. Top Street was in Greenacres; 5s. 6d. was a typical rent, including rates, for a good quality terrace house at the time.

with five rooms or more and it was beginning to be argued that many more larger three-bedroomed houses were needed. Very few of these terrace houses had a WC before the 1900s, or a bath, but almost all by then would have gas, piped water and be connected to a sewer.

There was an active market in terrace houses, whether for sale as new or for resale. Typically, they changed hands at £100 to £150, depending on age, size, location. They were readily bought by widows, unmarried daughters with a modest inheritance, shopkeepers and publicans. Investment in house property to let was seen as safe and remunerative, an asset that was close to home, easy to grasp and observe, less risky than railway shares let alone cotton spinning businesses. Estate agent businesses could handle the letting for a landlord, collect the rent and earn a commission. The landlord expected to earn a safe 5 per cent on the investment having paid the agent and allowing for ground rent, rates, voids, repairs and maintenance and the like. There were hundreds of small landlords in Oldham before 1914, owning several houses typically worth together £500, in some cases up to £1,000, rarely more than £2,000. There were many others who invested similar sums in ground rents, less trouble and more secure than owning a house with its letting problems, voids and repair bills. Most of these investors received less than £1 a week net, perhaps as little as 10s, but this was a useful supplement to earnings, income from other savings, especially for an unmarried woman, widow or those in old age. In the older parts of the town, many houses were still owned by the private millowners although these businesses, as they changed hands, were losing interest in what was becoming a poor and unnecessary investment. In the years immediately before the Great War there were the first signs that this traditional system was failing to provide enough affordable houses to rent; builders were finding it unprofitable to build, and the traditional investors were losing interest in owning houses to rent. This problem would become acute a few years later.

There was an increasing class of working men who wanted to own their own homes. Their interest was met by the multitude of building clubs and building societies that developed in the town. The former attracted regular savings from members that were pooled to enable individual members in rotation or by drawing lots to withdraw the sum needed to buy a house, repaying this over a period of years. The latter, like the Oldham House and Mill Company, the most prominent, took savings from the public and made mortgage loans to those with adequate means who wished to buy a house; in 1913 Oldham House and Mill had £219,000 on deposit, and had made loans exceeding £1 million since its formation. Apart from the building societies, the Co-operative Societies, in Oldham, Royton and elsewhere were willing to make mortgage loans on house property to their members. Working class owners were likely to be the better paid, skilled machine makers, minders, building craftsmen as well as overlookers. By the 1900s it was estimated that approaching 30 per cent of Oldham's houses were either owner-occupied or in the process of being bought by their occupiers, a very high proportion, reflecting the prosperity of the town and the thrift and independence of many of its people. "This is ours", was the claim of the owner-occupiers; "there is no chap that comes for rent here".

The four-room terrace house, two-up, two-down, holding on average a

**Oldham House and Mill**, the largest of several Oldham building societies financing owner-occupation which developed on a larger scale among the town's prosperous working class than in most parts of the United Kingdom. Originally this was a cooperative believing that "working men best know their wants and are able by organisation to supply them." It did not aim to make its members rich but "more independent and more secure".

**A typical Oldham living-room** with its open fire, boiler on the left, oven on the right, fender and mantelpiece, ornaments and wall clock. Warm, not uncomfortable depending on the furniture, but usually crowded, this room accommodated most of a family's domestic activity.

family of four to five, but in many cases several more, offered a crowded comfort. The kitchen at the back was the family living room; its door might be screened to prevent draughts. The kitchen had a range with open grate, oven on one side, boiler on the other, and since this was the place for cooking, toasting bread, heating flat irons, and the source of hot water, the range would often have a fire kept going all day, all the year round. Chimney sweeps had a regular trade; chimney fires were a regular hazard. A stone sink, or slopstone, with cold water tap was the other basic feature; washtub, metal bath, maybe a mangle would be outside in the yard. Cooking, washing, eating, indeed daily life took place in this room. A scullery at the back, enabling cooking, washing, to be separated from the living room was a valuable additional amenity of the later, larger terrace homes.

Monday washday imposed particular inconvenience; clothes were hand washed in a tub with scrubbing board and posser, mangled and hung to dry in the yard or the street, often attracting plenty of dirt. In the Oldham climate they had to be aired, if not dried on a clothes-horse in front of the fire or hung from the ceiling, usually throughout Tuesday which was also ironing day. Wednesday was the day for darning and mending. The housewives work was never done; baking bread and cakes occupied Thursday; Friday was cleaning day, including sweeping and scrubbing the pavement at the front, the yard at the rear, blackleading the fire range, polishing fenders and the like. Oldham housewives took great pride in a clean and tidy doorstep, diligently scoured with a donkey stone, as well as clean curtains and something pretty, even an aspidistra in their window. Bath night was also on Friday, the metal bath both having to be filled with hot water by hand with a lading tin and then tediously emptied, usually after a succession of baths. Shopping as a rule took place late on Saturday with a visit to the central markets in Curzon Street and Tommyfield. Much of Sunday was spent preparing dinner, the big family meal of the week.

So far as home lighting is concerned, until the 1880s it was mainly supplied by paraffin lamps and candles. Gas did not reach the average working man's home before 1875 but became almost universal in the 1890s, probably earlier than in many towns. Once the gas meter - penny in the slot, many made in Oldham - and the gas mantle, were perfected, they were very quickly adopted. Gas rings and cookers were introduced gradually with the meters; gas boilers and gas fires came later. All were significant conveniences, labour saving and far cleaner than the open fire range. In 1914 about 45 per cent of homes supplied by the Corporation had gas cookers but fewer had gas boilers, partly because of expense. Hot water for washing or baths came from the fireside boiler or kettle and pans on the gas ring; where a house had a scullery there might be a coal-fired copper. Most homes would have some form of floor covering over flagstones or boards, typically from the 1880s linoleum, while cheap wallpaper had replaced the earlier whitewashing.

The front room or parlour was "for best" and not everyday use. Visitors at weekends, special occasions, were accommodated here. Furniture, carpets, ornaments, pictures, brass fenders and fire irons, a fancy fireplace, curtains, increasingly a piano would be features of the better homes, indeed of most respectable homes, as families could afford; the furnishing and style of the front room was a main indicator of status. In many homes, given the infrequency with which the front room was used, the front door was rarely opened. Bedrooms were crowded places; chamber pots were prominent and as a rule there was no heating. Very cold and often damp in winter, comfort in bed came to rely on night shirts, heavy blankets and hot water bottles or the like. This was a coal-fire society but with the fire in one or at most two rooms.

**The Poor**

There were many in Oldham who did not share in this working class progress but lived in poverty. No social surveys were made comparable to those of Charles Booth in East London or Rowntree in York but the circumstances would not be entirely different. Booth found that nearly one-third of the population did not have the means to maintain the most frugal mode of life. Rowntree put this proportion of York's population at about 28 per cent. Certainly in Oldham town, if not throughout the Districts, the proportion in poverty at the end of the 19th century would be close to 25 per cent.

Among the poor would be families where the chief wage earner had died, or deserted his wife and children. There would be others whose situation was reduced by illness, unemployment or irregularity and seasonality of work, especially prevalent in the building trade. More numerous would be those in poverty because of large numbers of children, or because of low and casual wages, labourers on the fringe of the building trades, in transport, often working for the Corporation repairing or making streets. Then there were pedlars and hawkers, rag and bone men, sandwich-men, messengers and other last-resort casual occupations. Finally there were the aged poor, unable to work, and not supported by their families. All these groups of people were in what was termed "primary poverty"; they did not have enough money coming in to provide a decent living for themselves and their children. Their

**Edge Lane Hollow**, miner's homes in an old part of Royton.

**Cannon Street** at its junction with Garlick Street, about 1900, poor parts of Oldham, close to the town centre.

**Tommyfield**, late nineteenth century, with its open stalls offering variety, cheapness and the ability to pick and choose. It was also a lively communal place, at its best packed with people.

social differentiation between different neighbourhoods, the old and the new, the poor and the respectable, grew sharper decade by decade. Such wards as St Mary's, St Peters, Mumps and Coldhurst had the largest concentration of poor people. Many of the houses there had been built in the early part of the century or the 1850s; many were back-to-backs, in narrow streets and courts, sharing inadequate privies and filthy ashpits. Infant mortality and death rates were all higher in these wards than elsewhere in the town. But the houses were low rent, and life in the street and court was convivial and supported by mutual neighbourhood help and kinship ties in stable if poor communities, no longer disturbed by newcomers. The town centre was close at hand, with opportunities for odd jobs as well as cheap food, cheap second-hand clothing, cheap furniture, and other necessaries of life from Tommyfield and the markets. There were plenty of public houses.

Finally in these neighbourhoods poverty was anonymous; there was no sense of shame as in the respectable streets. Plenty of financially inept households would use the thirty-five or so pawnshops, the poor man's parasite, the surest indication of a hand to mouth existence, usually pledging articles for a week or less at extortionate rates of interest. Children could run around in rags or bare-footed, earning casual coppers and avoiding school, with little attention given. They were usually the worst victims of poverty and neglect; if they survived early childhood many went hungry to school and too early to work; under nourishment left its mark in heads alive with vermin, rickets, bow legs, knock knees, hunch-backs, and in death from consumption. Every year in Edwardian Oldham the Mayor made an appeal to fund a free breakfast on Christmas Day to several thousand poor children.

Up to the Great War, over 40,000 people lived in the four crowded wards, roughly 30 per cent of the town's population. As older houses were cleared to make way for street improvements, shops or commercial premises, as the worst houses were condemned as insanitary and as back-to-backs were made through, the poorer inhabitants moved into adjacent streets. In 1908 an enquiry claimed that at least 10,000 were living in a state of overcrowding. This was disputed but there can be no doubt that overcrowding, that is more than two persons per room, persisted in the poorest areas. At the 1911 Census, 10,400 people - over 7 per cent - were overcrowded at this level, a much lower proportion than in other industrial towns; this was not relieved until slum clearance and rehousing in council estates followed after the Great War.

Within the poor as in every large town, were the lowest class, variously described as the "residuum" or the "submerged tenth", living in acute and wretched poverty. Many were failures, drop-outs, outcasts from the respectable streets. In Oldham the poor of this description were living in the worst and most insanitary streets and courts. The notorious neighbourhoods were still off West Street, especially around Smethurst Street and Cheapside, the site of today's Civic Centre. Lords Hill in St Mary's, close to Tommyfield and the Parish Church was almost as bad, as were some of the old back-to-

**An Oldham Lodging House**, about 1900. The men have been hearing the Gospel from a member of the Oldham Mission. At the time there were ten registered lodging houses ranging from fourteen beds to 285, all in the poorer parts of Oldham; the largest were in St. Mary's and off West Street. At the time the police estimated that over 250,000 bed-nights in lodging houses were taken each year, mainly by single men, perhaps one third "wanderers", but the rest incomers looking for settled accommodation or homeless middle-aged and elderly men on the margin of destitution and the workhouse.

back courts in Mumps or nearby Mount Pleasant. Common lodging houses remained located in these areas, still seventeen taking an average of over 800 people nightly in the 1900s, some very filthy. Oldham's Medical Officer, more concerned than most with his responsibilities for public health, could ask in 1890, "Is there necessarily a squalid and degraded class in all big towns, of inferior calibre, whose instincts lead downwards, who are destitute of self-control, who work that they may indulge in excess, to whom it is an impossible labour to create a home?" Alfred Emmott, aspirant Liberal MP in 1899, but also landlord of some of the poorest streets, complained that at the bottom of Oldham society were people who lived in "poverty, degradation and sin, untouched, unreformed, unremedied by all the progress of fifty years." The *Chronicle* spoke of a community apart, "a black and putrid stream of human misery". The churches and chapels, the Oldham Mission founded in 1859 or the Temperance Movement, those who were closest to the poor and concerned about them, saw the problem primarily as one of drink, drink leading to feckless improvident behaviour, filthy habits, neglect of children, starvation, immorality and crime. That would also be the view of the magistrates and the police, coping several days a week with a stream of cases of drunkenness, disorder and assault.

One police court witness in 1870 claimed to have seen more disturbances in Oldham in half-an-hour than in eighteen years in his native Yorkshire town. Street fights, fights in public houses, fights with the police, were commonplace in the poorest areas, as were household brawls. In the 1870s there was concern at the increase in brutal and violent crime, often with fatal consequences. In 1873 there were three incidents where youths died following the "hand and foot" treatment; that is the victim was set upon by a small gang, pummelled with the fist and kicked or "punced" in the head with the clog. The use of knives in fighting was frequently reported. Not surprisingly, most respectable people would avoid the worst streets and neighbourhoods; certainly on Saturday or Sunday nights they were no-go, even at times to the police. Whenever there was riot in Oldham, the mob would usually originate in the poorest streets.

The greatest indignity of the poor was pauperism, to turn to the Poor Law for help. The Oldham Union Guardians had continued to provide outdoor relief, on a huge scale in the Cotton Famine, but more generally on a very limited basis to widows, deserted wives and to the old and the unemployed. Such relief was on a most meagre scale, 2s weekly for each adult and less for a child, perhaps with a bonus at Christmas; the numbers receiving it, usually about a thousand, rose and fell with the state of trade; they were low in Oldham compared with other towns. Those living in the Union Workhouse, built in 1851, included the aged poor, more men than women, unable to support themselves or live with children; "imbeciles and lunatics"; and "orphaned children", badly treated in bare and desolate rooms. Eventually the mentally ill, about 300 in 1900, were segregated in mental wards. By the end of the century some 200 children, orphans or given up by parents, were being fostered in "Scattered Homes". Old age was probably the greatest factor in pauperism; the number of aged paupers grew with the population; there were 400 in 1870, over 1,000 by 1895, and in 1909 about 1,600. Thereafter old age pensions did something to reduce the numbers. Many of

**A Bible Visitor** making her calls and leaving tracts in an Oldham slum. The Oldham Mission, formed in 1859 and financed by private mill owners such as the Emmotts and Alfred Butterworth, sought to "extend knowledge of the Gospel among the poor and criminal classes". Its fourteen visitors made 40,000 house-to-house calls in 1909.

# The Poor

the aged poor finished up in the hospital wards that the Workhouse eventually provided; typically they went there to die.

The Workhouse would also take as many as 250-300 vagrants each night, many of them tramps but others men on the move looking for work, and often abandoned destitute women with small children who had lost their homes. Pauperism was regarded with shame, "a curse to our population, a tax upon every honest man", as R. M. Davies said to loud applause on one public occasion. Vagrants were given a bite to eat and then locked up in a cell; the next day they were given work chopping wood, breaking stones or scrubbing floors; after another night's lodging they were sent on their way. These were the harsh disciplines of Victorian England; vagrants apart, for a town the size of Oldham, the numbers in the Workhouse were low, reflecting the strong impulse of self-reliance and independence among the town's population.

*Above:* **Miss Suthers**, for most of her life a stalwart of the Oldham Mission and a formidable do-gooder.

*Left:* **Old Men in the Workhouse** about 1900. Men were more likely to finish up in the workhouse than women who could better look after themselves or mix-up with families. But men's lives were shorter and the Oldham Workhouse had more old women than old men.

## The Irish

For most of the mid and late Victorian period the Irish were regarded as part of the poor, perhaps the worst part. The numbers of Oldham people born in Ireland peaked at around 6,000 in 1861. The numbers and proportion were fewer than in other Lancashire towns, certainly than in Manchester or Liverpool. As elsewhere the recent Irish immigrants were living in the most crowded and squalid circumstances in the worst streets in the town. In the aftermath of the Great Famine they were usually destitute when they arrived and until they got some kind of work they had little choice but to double up with friends or relatives. When they got work it was usually as poorly paid labourers, pedlars, hawkers. They were viewed with deep hostility because of their Roman Catholicism and because, in their poverty, they were a threat to the livelihood of other working poor. Oldham, like other Lancashire towns, had at least one lodge of Orangemen, whose traditional animosity persisted.

# THE ENGLISH VERSUS THE IRISH.

## SERIOUS RIOTS IN OLDHAM.

## DESTRUCTION OF PROPERTY.
### ATTACK ON THE ROMAN CATHOLIC CHAPEL.

**The War of the Races**, the Chronicle's headline on 8 June 1861.

Given this hostility the desperately poor Irish found ethnic support and solidarity in the small Oldham Catholic church, St Mary's on Shaw Street. Enlarged in the 1850s, St Mary's set up a mission at Bank Top which became St Patrick's in 1858. The neighbourhoods round these churches were where the Irish community concentrated, and the priests of these churches became the recognised leaders of the harassed Irish community, at first virtually the only Catholics with any education or experience of local conditions.

Popular resentment towards the Irish at the time, less in Oldham than elsewhere, surfaced on the occasion of the Whit Walks in 1861. A procession of children from St Patrick's Catholic church clashed with a similar Anglican procession in the Market Place. The incident led to violent anti-Catholic riots the same evening and the following day when gangs of youths stoned and smashed the two Catholic churches. Heavy rain on Whit Sunday seems to have quietened the mob, but incidents, more or less serious, continued over the next week involving as many as 15,000 people. The "Liberal" *Chronicle* condemned "lawless and outrageous" behaviour, but spoke of "ignorant and turbulent" Irish, "a dangerous element in our society", "alien in blood, language and religion, opposed in their feelings and interests to the people of England". The *Chronicle*'s concern was that the Irish, with their "wild habits", would be "mere serfs", increasingly antagonistic to their employers and the wider community.

There were fears of similar incidents a few years later when the inflammatory demagogue William Murphy came to Oldham on his tour of the north, denouncing Romanism in lectures on Popery, the Sacrifice of the Mass, the Glories of Mary and similar subjects; his real object, the *Chronicle* claimed, was "to rouse the rabble against the Irish". His visit was shortly after the Fenian outrages in 1868, and, in the Mayor's words, calculated to "excite angry feeling". When he came, Irish women came out to abuse him and Irish men in large numbers to defend St Mary's against a roused mob of young men and "lads of the rougher sort", singing "Rule Britannia". The police intervened belatedly and attacks on the church were renewed on the days following; the damage was such as to prompt subsequent rebuilding of what was by then a dilapidated St Mary's. In Ashton, in Rochdale, in Manchester and elsewhere, Murphy caused far more serious incidents.

The Irish continued to have a difficult time although prejudice no longer resulted in violence. Half the drunks arrested each year were Irish; in 1871, thirty-eight of the town's fifty-eight known common prostitutes were said by the Chief Constable to be Irish. In 1879 the *Chronicle* described Irish homes that were "a sink of misery, squalor and filth", full of children without food. Many businesses would not employ the Irish; if they found regular work, they were condemned to the least congenial occupations, unskilled labourers on the roads or building sites, night soil men, at the gasworks shovelling coal, in the scutching room in the spinning mills. J. R. Clynes' Irish born father was a gravedigger at Greenacres cemetery, earning 24s a week, at least a steady wage. Young women had less difficulty in finding work in the carding rooms.

Many Irish families, crowded as they were, willingly took lodgers, usually young Irish men, providing income from rent and from laundering services.

As the century grew older the number of Irish born dwindled, while Oldham's Roman Catholic population, largely of Irish descent increased. The term "Irish" became less frequently used; instead by the end of the century the Roman Catholic population was recognised; it had grown to about 14,000, about 10 per cent of the town's total, still in the same districts around St Patrick's and St Mary's except that new clusters had formed in Greenacres, in Hollinwood and in Royton, each with their own churches. If Roman Catholics, whether Irish or not, were regarded with distrust in Victorian England, politicians now sought their vote, partly because of their numbers, partly because Irish issues at times were dominating Westminster politics. A branch of the Irish National League was started in Oldham; local Liberals sat on the platform at its meetings. Those of Irish descent in the 1874 election and subsequently used their votes to further the interests of "their country", generally, by voting for Gladstone and Home Rule, but there were exceptions in 1885 when, on the advice of Parnell, they voted Tory. In later years much of the support for the Labour party came from Oldham's Catholics.

Meanwhile the families of Irish descent were improving themselves, climbing from the ranks of unskilled and casual labourers. Their comparative poverty would often be the result of large families as well as low earnings. The number of children at the Catholic Church Schools who received free meals in 1904 and subsequently, as well as the numbers described as undernourished at those schools when medical inspections began in 1910, all suggest that this was still a poor struggling part of the community. But it had established itself, and those of Irish descent were to become prominent if not ascendant in the Oldham of later years.

## Co-ops and Shops

From its beginning with the Rochdale Pioneers in 1844, the idea of retail co-operative organisations, started and managed by working men, was to spread dramatically throughout the new towns of the Midlands and North, and nowhere so than in Lancashire. Oldham was quick to follow the Rochdale model once that had proved its durability and vitality.

As elsewhere the first moves were humble and fragile; a number of working men met in a cottage, argued the concept through, put together what small capital they could muster, purchased at wholesale prices a stock of provisions and distributed these according to the capital each had subscribed. By co-operative purchase they were saving a few extra shillings week by week. The next stage was to rent suitable premises for a small shop and widen the number of participants. Oldham Equitable started in this way in the east end of the town with a house/shop in Derker Street, opened early in 1851. The origins of the Oldham Industrial Co-operative Society followed the same pattern. Much of the initiative here derived from William Marcroft, the energetic but crusty abrasive idealist, who was to go on to help start the Sun Mill and some of the early Limiteds, and to become a leading temperance reformer and prominent Unitarian. Marcroft was a passionate advocate of co-operation among working men, not merely to improve and cheapen the cost of provisions and secure the retailer's profit, but also to organise

**William Marcroft**, illegitimately born in the most humble workhouse circumstances, entirely self-educated, made his mark as a co-operative idealist in the third quarter of the century. He was involved in the formation of the Oldham Industrial Co-operative Society, the Sun Mill and a number of other Limiteds.

**Oldham's first co-operative store**, in Derker.

manufacturing or any commercial enterprise. It was in Marcroft's house in November 1850 that the Industrial was formed, starting business with capital of "£56 odd", and renting a shop in Manchester Street for £30 a year.

From the early years certain basic rules governed the way the Societies traded. Members had to purchase shares contributing modest capital. All transactions were for cash, no credit being given, and to that extent the Co-ops may not have done much business with the very poor who relied on credit. Prices were set competitively but not below those of other shopkeepers. The emphasis was on pure, wholesome, unadulterated food. The margin between purchasing at wholesale prices and selling at retail prices met rent and operating expenses and yielded a surplus. This surplus was the dividend, the "Divi" which those who shopped at the Co-op received quarterly in proportion to their purchases.

Of course, Oldham did not need two co-operative organisations and it was the pride and independence of the personalities involved that kept things that way. Generally the two worked in harmony. In other towns there were many more separate societies than the two in Oldham. What was happening in Oldham was followed a few years later in the townships of Royton, Crompton, Lees and Failsworth; Saddleworth had at least three Co-ops. Chadderton did not start its own society; as population grew around the new mills on the fringe of the Borough, branches of the Oldham Industrial could meet its needs.

Progress of the new societies at first was slow; they were feeling their way and established traders, the competition, did their best to rubbish the new shops. Over the years they were frowned on by many churchgoers, not least because many of the enthusiastic co-operators were free thinkers or atheists, willing to work in the shop or open their newsrooms or even hold classes on Sundays. The movement grew massively in the great Oldham boom of the 1870s and in the next two decades, as population continued to grow throughout the district and as the Co-ops proved themselves as efficient retailers. By the end of the century there were over 26,000 members of the two Oldham societies; it is reasonable to conclude that about 70 per cent of all households did at least some of their shopping at the Co-op. Penetration was about the same in Crompton, Lees and Failsworth, but rather lower in Royton.

Such a huge increase in the numbers using the Co-ops reflected the vast increase in their operations. This was achieved by opening new branch stores at convenient locations, by enlarging these stores and the range of goods they offered. Thus most of the stores by late century were offering a comprehensive range of groceries, with the emphasis on food. Fresh bread, baked centrally, was a convenient replacement for bread that had traditionally been baked at home; butchery was another essential area. As individual societies merged their purchasing operations in the Co-operative Wholesale Society, set up in 1863, their volume enabled them to achieve much better buying prices than the independent stores. For staple items such as jam or biscuits the movement could itself become a manufacturer and make its own brand, offering better value than the other brands available. Flour was a principal item of sale; every other town seemed to have a corn mill so why not Oldham. Thus in 1868 the Societies invested in the Star Corn Mill, in Glodwick.

## Co-ops and Shops

As Oldham grew in the late nineteenth century its two Co-operative Societies boomed. **New Central Premises for the Equitable Society** in Huddersfield Road were completed in 1900 to celebrate its jubilee. The architect's drawing catches the confidence and pride of the time. The building became known as Hill Stores; its large hall, capable of seating 1,000 people, later became Oldham's principal dance venue.

In these ways the co-operative stores were able to offer good wholesome quality foodstuffs at competitive prices to other retailers. That was the strength of their proposition; they did not succeed for reasons of idealism but because they gave better consumer value, in efficiently run convenient stores. They extended their operations into other types of merchandise; bagged coals, clogs and shoes, drapery and with much less success into tailoring, furnishing, mantles and millinery. It was said that all a family's household wants could be had at the Co-op. That may have been true and the huge central stores of the two Oldham societies, in King Street and in Huddersfield Road, were in their ways vast emporiums. But that having been said the greater part of Co-op business, as much as 75 per cent, was done in groceries. The societies increased their business by attracting new members and not by increased sales per member; in fact as the members grew, average sales per member fell, with too many of the new members interested only in "milk and water', that is immediate necessities.

For working class households the Co-op retained one big advantage, the "Divi". In most cases the woman of the household took the shopping decision, she hoarded the tin checks received from each purchase and presented them for the quarterly dividend which went straight into her purse; so far as she was concerned this was a way of saving that provided a regular invaluable lump sum. The several local societies for years paid a dividend of 3s in the pound, an average sum of £1 for each member paid four times a year. To Co-op members the regular Divi was a vital feature.

Other retailers successfully fought back against the co-operative tide. Side by side with the branches of the Co-ops were hundreds of small independent family run shops at the corner of every street, offering convenience, and also, when the need arose, credit, and open all day and late into the evening. Many of these bought their supplies from large provision dealers in the town centre; only by the end of the century were they served by specialist wholesalers, or the salesmen of the emerging manufacturers of branded packaged groceries,

**Specialist food shops**, butchers, bakers and greengrocers flourished. Brierleys in Royton was famous for its pork pies.

Horniman's tea, Huntley and Palmer's biscuits, Fry's cocoa, Sunlight soap and so on, the well-known names of the time. This period, in fact, was the heyday of the corner shop, a convenient and social place to those who used it, a passport to modest independence and status to those who owned and ran it.

On a neighbourhood basis there were specialist fresh food retailers, over 200 butchers, many still killing and dressing their own meat until late in the century, nearly fifty tripe-dressers, a multitude of bakers, greengrocers and fishmongers. Then there were the hawkers, travelling the streets, selling bread and muffins, fish, greengroceries, crockery, haberdashery, almost anything that could be carried about. Other travelling tradesmen provided services, sharpened knives and scissors, and repaired furniture. Most people still got milk delivered, in many cases twice a day, from the farm by horse and milk float, not with perfect hygiene, but fresh from the cow; the town centre also

Important as the Co-ops were, there were a multitude of **independents**, like this one in Westwood.

had its milk shops. And then there were the first multiple grocers, as they succeeded opening dozens of branches, using their volume to support an aggressive low price, high turnover policy; generally they were cheaper than the Co-ops. Such a prominent chain in the Oldham and Rochdale district was James Duckworth and Sons, Meadow Dairy was another. There were many small multiples each with half a dozen or so shops around Oldham who in the end went out of business. All of them offered competition and choice.

Finally, of course, there were the markets and specialist shops of the town centre. Tommyfield with its scores of stalls, and the covered Victoria market provided intense competition and the ability to "look and pick" across a wide range of provisions, cheap clothing and household goods. Tommyfield provided not merely variety and cheapness, but colour, vitality, crowds of people, humour and diversion. There was the indescribable rush on Saturday evenings, dealers competing to shout their wares, the army of quacks selling remedies of various kinds, crowds of people, many of them young roughs, anxious to see "what was stirring". There were beggars too and street singers who, it was reported in 1881, could take as much as 15s on a Saturday night, especially if they sang psalms rather than popular ballads.

There were dozens of specialist shops selling clothing, footwear, furniture, ironmongery and almost any type of merchandise, in the Market Place, High Street, and along the main roads leading from the centre. Some household name multiples had established a foothold in Oldham before the Great War. Yorkshire Street was lined with shops and public houses along its length; Mumps remained a secondary sector. Here was Oldham's department store, Buckley and Proctor, emporium for fashionable clothing, millinery, dress fabrics, drapery, carpets, household linen. Many of these shops advertised

**Corner Shops**, like this one in Washbrook, Butler Green, were a feature of most working class streets.

**Tommyfield** again, where the poor of Oldham bought the cheapest fruit and vegetables.

Oldham Brave Oldham

vigorously with extravagant but rarely unique claims as to cheapness and quality. For the well-to-do, of course, there were visits to the even more fashionable Manchester where Kendal Milne was an established specialist for furniture and carpets and even furs in the 1860s. Towards the end of the century when cheap public transport developed and especially the electric tram, more and more people came to Oldham to shop from the Districts; what specialist shops there were in Royton, Crompton and other places, declined accordingly. "Going up town", a regular visit to the centre of Oldham, became a feature of life in the entire district.

At the end of the nineteenth century, in a town where so large a proportion of the population worked long hours in the factory, shops were open until late in the evening. This was especially true on Fridays and Saturdays when the stalls on Tommyfield and the Market Hall did not pack up until 10 or 11 pm. Any voluntary move to close shops early or to have a half-day closing proved impossible to enforce in an intensely competitive situation. Nor, if they worked long hours, were those working in the shops well paid; in 1899 the Co-ops were paying branch managers 32s a week and adult employees 24s. Even so a shop assistant's job was preferred to one in the mill; in 1911 the Census recorded over 1,700 men and youths and 2,700 females working in retail trade of one kind or another. Many small shops were in effect family businesses, whether for the wife of a working man, a widow or unmarried woman or for a whole family, and as such they made their own trading rules. If opening hours could not be regulated, at least Sunday was observed; the Sabbatarians retained a powerful influence in Oldham and even if fewer and fewer people went to church or chapel, shops did not open on Sunday.

Retailing before the Great War, as subsequently, was a dynamic sector, endlessly adapting to consumer needs in a highly competitive situation. The Co-operative Societies of Oldham, as elsewhere, established their ascendancy in the years before 1914. Even then it was a far from complete ascendancy

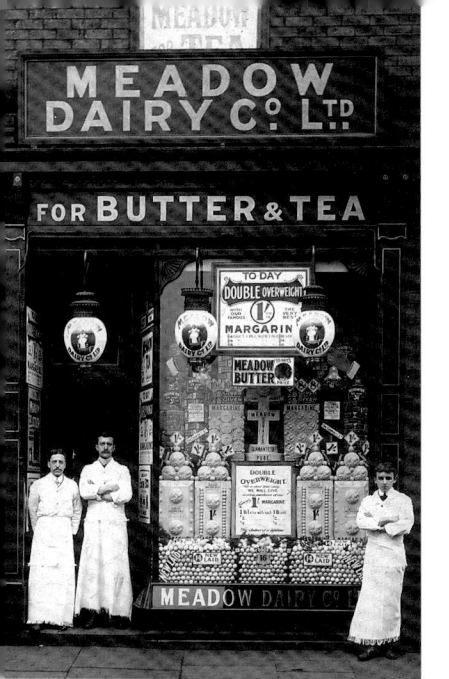

**Retail grocery chains** began to develop, exploiting the advantages of larger scale buying and a successful management style. Meadow Dairy was one of several that had many branches in Oldham.

**Bamford's Hosiery** in Yorkshire Street, next to Bradbury's selling Oldham-made sewing machines.

and it was to shrink in subsequent years. If the Co-operative Societies played their major role as the largest grocery retailers of the period, this was not their only role; they provided a range of services used by their more enthusiastic members. They attracted savings on a large scale and paid competitive interest. Apart from financing their own fixed and working assets, they used their surplus capital to make large mortgage loans for house purchase by members, and to build house property for letting while retaining possession. To the end of the century the two Oldham Societies had loaned over £350,000 in this way, financing purchase of over 2,500 houses. Royton was more modest but in 1907 owned twenty-two houses, had built and sold forty-five and made loans on another forty-seven. Certainly in the 1870s the Societies also were willing to buy shares or make loans to the new Limiteds, Sun Mill in particular and others where active co-operators were involved in the flotation; subsequently, after much argument among members, they backed away as the Limiteds changed their co-operative style, seemed to take the side of the capitalists and, in any event lost their appeal as an investment. The two Oldham Co-ops had lending libraries and reading rooms where newspapers were available; they organised lectures and excursions; their large Co-operative Halls were principal venues for public meetings, parties and dances. In their prime, the two Oldham societies were as central to the life of the town as church and chapel; everyone was aware of them, most people used them; the spirit of co-operation and self help which they embodied were part of the culture of the time.

**Buckley and Proctor**, the Mumps Bazaar, almost a department store, for all kinds of clothing, furnishings, carpets and the like.

**Fast Food**

A working town, and one where many women worked, had a need for fast food, for a meal that could be purchased ready to eat or needed a minimum of preparation. That was true of the mid-day meal in the mill but also of the evening meal to be available to a family returning home tired between 6 and 7 pm or later.

Weekend and especially Sunday was the occasion for formal meals, for roast beef and Yorkshire or, increasingly, joints of mutton and lamb accompanied by vegetables and not complete without a pudding of some kind. And Sunday tea was the occasion for something good or fancy, cold meats, canned salmon, salads, trifle, cake, canned fruit. But during the week speed and convenience were the requirements as well as cheapness and wholesomeness.

Fish and chips met this market opportunity admirably, although it was not until the last decade of the nineteenth century that the fish and chip shop became universal in Lancashire mill towns. Fried chipped potatoes became popular in the 1860s, fried fish in the next decade and the two in combination developed rapidly in the Eighties. Oldham's versatile and enterprising engineers, two firms in particular, John Rouse and Faulkners, became the earliest specialist suppliers of gas-fired frying ranges, potato peelers and potato chippers. Fast reliable railway services brought fresh fish, packed in wooden boxes, from fishing ports such as Fleetwood, Hull or Grimsby. Fleetwood in particular supplied Lancashire with silver hake caught in the Irish Sea; the other ports with cod and haddock. Potatoes were near at hand and the fat could be beef dripping if more modern alternatives were not available. Above all this was fast food, warm, good, nutritious, easy to eat "animal style" with the fingers, and cheap, costing as little as 2d. Before the Great War there were over 500 fish and chip shops in the district, one to every 400 people, conveniently located near the mills and among the terraces of working class houses, open for dinner, for tea and into the evening, catering for late night cravings for an extra snack.

If fish and chips took the market by storm, other quick alternatives were bought pies, potato pies, or meat pies, and baked savouries such as onion cakes. The local baker's shop would supply all these, but enterprising bakers developed their business to supplying a widening clientele of small shops with fresh bread, pies and cakes on a daily basis. Deliveries were made by horse-drawn carts and, when motor vehicles became available, daily distribution over a wide area became possible. So the large central private baking concerns such as Holland's evolved. Other convenience foods of the working class town tasty, wholesome and good value, were tripe in its various forms, alternatives to cold meat, needing no preparation, and black puddings, heat and serve.

**Tripe** was almost a universal food, cheap, filling if not a delicacy. Dunkerley's were Oldham's leading tripe dressers supplying dozens of small local outlets.

## Health Care

Late 19th century Oldham was an unhealthy place, although no more so than other northern industrial towns. The Council had struggled over the years to put things right, at least so far as water supply, sanitation, removal of nuisances were concerned. Slowly the death rate and the infantile mortality rate came down.

The epidemics of contagious disease, smallpox and scarlet fever in particular, that had not infrequently taken a heavy toll and caused great concern if not panic, became almost a thing of the past. The last serious smallpox outbreak had forty-nine victims in 1903-1904 and measles at times, as in 1906, was more often fatal than a much milder scarlet fever. Many of

# Health Care

**Funerals** could be major events. That of Colonel William Clark, a well-known local showman, in March 1909, was the largest seen in Oldham for some time.

the principal causes of illness and premature death remained, however, especially for the poor in the crowded older streets. The overheated dusty cotton mills remained unhealthy places, Oldham's air remained polluted, its weather could be rude as well as bracing. Bronchitis and pneumonia still caused hundreds of deaths each year, a fifth of the total, TB was still a killer. Infant deaths remained very high, not so much because mothers went back to the mill too soon, as from ignorance of proper care and feeding and poor household circumstances. Children were born at home, except for the well-to-do, with assistance from neighbours or midwives, mostly unqualified.

There were, by the end of the century, many more doctors in the district, making their calls with pony and trap, or on horseback, carrying coloured lanterns at night, tethering the horse to the nearest lamp post; they became among the first users of motor cars. Such a man was Thomas Fawsitt, Oldham's "beloved physician", who pursued his career as a "general practitioner" for over fifty years from 1869; he was made a Freeman of the Borough in 1922. The doctor's services were not free, however, and there must have been many who would not incur a bill of 2s 6d except in the gravest circumstances. Typically a collector would visit the homes of those who had incurred bills, for a few pence paid on a weekly basis. Illness took its own course, for many, or was treated with pills, patent medicines or traditional herbal remedies. Alfred Butterworth, the wealthy millowner, helped to fill the need in neighbourhoods such as St Mary's with his Medical Mission, dispensing free medicines as well as spiritual guidance to poor applicants.

Oldham, "alone among towns of its size", complained the *Chronicle* in 1868, had no hospital. If hospital services were needed, following a mill-accident for instance, the injured would be taken to Manchester, probably in a horse cab. There could be no question that a rapidly growing district, with a population approaching 100,000 required a local hospital. There was no

**Dr. Fawsitt**, one of Oldham's most familiar figures, family doctor and a practical and sympathetic friend to rich and poor alike.

government responsibility; neither the Council or the Poor Law Guardians had any powers to spend rate money on such a purpose. As elsewhere, it would have to depend on philanthropy or charitable giving. For years it was talked about but nothing was done; there were fears an infirmary would be a burden on the rates, suggested projects were dismissed as too extravagant, no-one would take a lead. The *Chronicle* was outspoken:

> "few towns require to learn more thoroughly the very elementary basis of genuine sacrifice for the good of the poor, the maimed, the unfortunate. There seemed no better illustration of the ungenerous character of Oldham's many self-made men; they had become wealthy from humble beginnings but their habits of caution and frugality had not changed."

In the end, John Blackburne, a well-to-do coal agent, respected by the leading families, took the lead. £1,100 left over in the Relief Fund at the end of the Cotton Famine gave a start towards £10,000, the probable sum needed for a site, building and equipment for a proper Infirmary. About £1,200 a year would be needed for running expenses. The leading families were all persuaded to subscribe as well as many groups of working men.

The stone-laying ceremony took place in 1870, the Infirmary opened in 1872; it had thirty-seven beds and in 1873 it treated 113 in-patients and 328 out-patients, a beginning but little more than that given the population of the district. The running costs of the Infirmary had to be raised by appeals and collections. Extensions to the first buildings and wards depended on gifts. All the great and the good were persuaded to join the Board of Governors; many of them eventually left valuable legacies, notably Asa Lees (£10,000), William Richardson of Platts (£5,000), Charles Edward Lees (£3,000), and Sam Platt (£2,000). By 1887 the annual budget had reached £4,000, met by subscriptions, collections from the annual fund raising event, Hospital Saturday, which yielded £1,136, and interest from various endowments. The number of beds had been increased to eighty, there were 663 patients and

**Oldham Infirmary**, opened in 1872; in its first year it treated 113 in-patients and 328 out-patients.

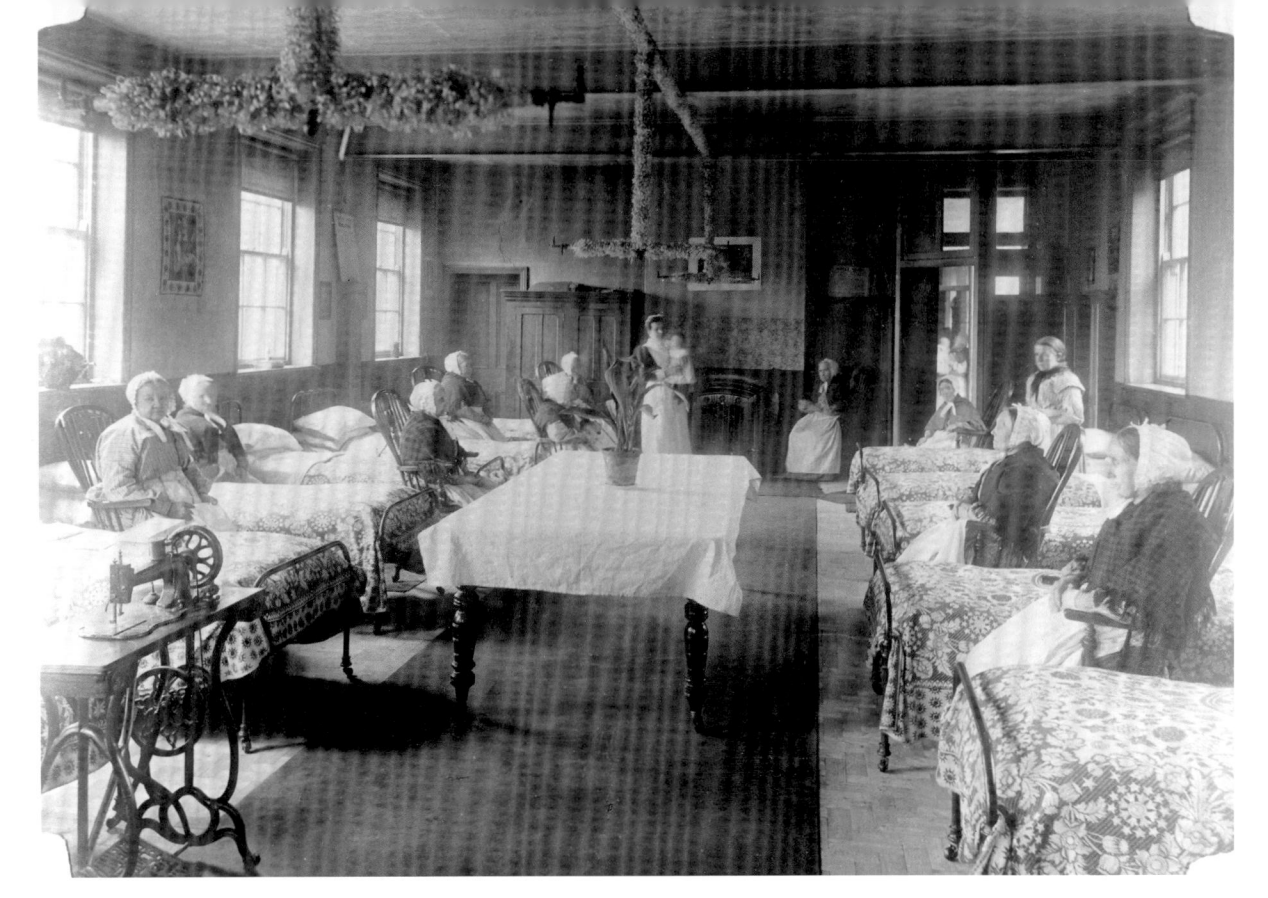

2,860 outpatients, a great many being treated for accidental injury, others being referred by doctors. The average stay in the Infirmary was forty days. Typically for Oldham, the matron took pride in the fact that average costs per patient were lower than in twenty other infirmaries with which Oldham could be compared. Slowly, year by year, the Infirmary enlarged its services, raising more money, providing more beds and treating more patients. Its status was enhanced when it was given the designation "Royal" in 1911. Nonetheless it remained quite inadequate for a community the size of Oldham. The only alternative were the sick wards in the Workhouse.

Such was the position of health care in Victorian and Edwardian times. The progress that had been made can be measured by the Census numbers of those engaged in medicine: there were only 37 in 1861, but 342 in 1911 including 202 women. A great deal was eventually to change but not for several decades. The beginnings of free access to doctors, on the panel if only for those in employment, was beginning to make itself felt by 1913 following the Liberal reforms of 1908. But for the most part people still had to fend for themselves; organised health care was a small scale affair.

**The Workhouse at Boundary Park** had its own hospital for its inmates, chiefly the elderly infirm but also with a small maternity ward.

## Beautiful Oldham

Women emerged as the reformers of Oldham, and none more than Sarah Lees, widow of Charles Edward Lees, who had inherited a large cotton fortune from his father Eli Lees. Sarah and her daughter Marjory, remaining in Oldham all their lives, used their energy and means to support all kinds of good causes. They became pioneers in women's work in public service, concerned with the right of women to vote, but especially with disadvantaged children, education, and the health and amenity of their town. They were joined by their contemporary Mary Higgs, the Girton educated wife of T. K. Higgs, the Congregationalist Minister of Greenacres Chapel, who had come to Oldham in 1891. She achieved national prominence by her investigations of vagrancy and the needs of unmarried mothers, and of conditions in casual wards and common lodging houses. She complained of a "great mass of vice" in Oldham and sought with great energy to improve the way of life of those at the bottom of the social scale.

Perhaps above all, Mary Higgs and Sarah Lees wanted to mitigate the ugliness of Oldham. They could do little about the shabby buildings or the all-pervading smoke. But they could make people more aware of their surroundings, less willing to accept "the ordinary condition of the town", and determined to do something about improving things, to break the Oldham rule that "everything is for use, nothing for ornament", and to make the town less dreary. Mary Higgs launched the idea of making Oldham beautiful as soon as she arrived in 1891. With Sarah Lees and other idealists she campaigned the idea for many years, starting the "Beautiful Oldham" movement in 1902, and eventually involving thousands of school children in planting bulbs and growing flowers, culminating in an annual flower show. Beautiful Oldham embarked on a programme of tree and shrub planting in the town, campaigning to abate the smoke nuisance and do something about the many patches of waste and neglected ground, often the sites of old mills, which disfigured the central areas particularly. In part this was a yearning for a vanished past when Oldham was still a land of grass and trees and wild flowers, where birds sang. Mary Higgs worried about the innumerable "hen runs" which were a feature of the town, "railed in by the most nondescript fences", unsightly but useful hobbies for the working man; her pleadings in this direction fell on deaf ears. Her ideas caught on elsewhere, a Beautiful Chadderton Society was formed in 1910.

A related initiative, inspired by Ebenezer Howard and Letchworth, as by

**The Beautiful Oldham Society**: Mary Higgs, whose vision it was, and Sarah Lees, its chief patron, are seated either side of the Chairman in the centre of the front row. Mary Higgs wrote that Oldham people "love having things about them nice, a clean and tidy doorstep, clean curtains and something pretty in the window." She urged more greenery, plants and trees throughout the town. Her ambition would eventually be realised.

Bournville and Port Sunlight, was the Oldham Garden Suburb. A company was formed in 1907 to buy land, build larger and better houses to an improved layout and lower density, incorporating gardens and public open space; the houses were to be let to yield a modest return on capital. The venture got a promising start when Sarah Lees sold land cheaply at Hollins Green, off the Ashton Road, a penny tram fare from Union Street. Perhaps the initial proposals were over-ambitious, envisaging 700 houses, and not to be realised, but by 1914 the Suburb had completed and let 183 houses and was paying a modest dividend. A contemporary spoke of "semi-detached houses, well built and of artistic appearance, having each a kitchen with a good range, a back kitchen with a bath with hot and cold water laid on, a pantry and three good bedrooms." This was creditable progress indeed. Oldham Corporation, with its housing estates, was subsequently to take on the challenge of creating a new urban environment.

In these ways something was done to relieve the grim drab town. But many Oldhamers who accumulated wealth, whether on a large or a modest scale, sought to escape in their later years. Oldham, said the *Chronicle*, was "a place where people make money to spend it elsewhere; there is nothing in Oldham's air and scenery to attract and much to repel". The Platts and Radcliffes led the way to North Wales. Many of the Oldham middle class sought retirement there, forming a particular colony in Colwyn Bay, especially after 1880. John Hibbert, the local MP, had established a family home in North Lancashire and this perhaps encouraged another Oldham colony to form at Grange-over-Sands. Like Colwyn Bay, Grange gave the well-to-do social safety at distances beyond the reach of the working class. But for many the Lancashire coast was still the obvious choice, Southport and Lytham St. Anne's, refined, discreet and less vulgar than Blackpool. All these places were an easy railway journey from Oldham for those who retained connections there, as many did. Many

In the days before council estates the **Garden Suburb** was perhaps the most determined initiative to improve living conditions and amenities in the town. With the first houses completed and occupied, Mary Higgs is planting a tree. The houses were too expensive for most Oldhamers.

of those who retired elsewhere still wanted to be buried in the town where they had made their wealth. For those who stayed in Oldham, comfortably off or not, there was scorn for those who had turned their back on their origins, for softer healthier places elsewhere.

## Church and Chapel

As the number of people grew and houses spread throughout the Borough and the townships, churches and chapels struggled to keep abreast. Older buildings continued to be rebuilt or enlarged. New places of worship and church schools were built in the newer districts, usually following the success of a simple mission or branch set up by an established parent institution. The Church of England and the main Nonconformist denominations, competed vigorously and replicated each others initiatives; each was determined to be represented in all the new neighbourhoods. The Roman Catholics set up their own new chapels wherever their adherents were living in appropriate numbers, maintaining a strong cohesion and sense of sectarian identity. The number of places of worship in the district rose from seventy-one in 1861 to one-hundred-and-eighty in 1911. They saw themselves as providing for spiritual needs, but also increasingly recreational ones, and for education through their schools. They were important social institutions; whether worshippers or not, everyone was touched by their influence in some way or another.

Voluntary effort paid for the extended range of buildings, both initially and then over the years as debt was repaid through fund-raising sales of work and other events. In the wealthier chapels, pew rents were an important source of income. As the years went by further expenditures were needed for refurbishment, new organs, heating, electric light and so on. However austere and smoke blackened the exterior, great effort was made to achieve an impressive and serene place for worship. The town's notables, MPs like John Hibbert, John Platt, later Alfred Emmott would willingly patronise stone-laying, opening events, bazaars and the like, drawing good attendances by their presence, using them to make speeches on important subjects of the day. In some cases Oldham's rich elite were willing to make a major contribution: thus the Platts provided land and financial support for St Thomas's, Coppice, the church they used; the Mellodews funded St Thomas's at Moorside; Thomas Evans Lees, heir of the Greenbank cotton fortune, gave £20,000 to finance St Mark's, Glodwick, in the neighbourhood where many of his company's workpeople lived; Alfred Butterworth, the large private cotton spinner at Glebe Mill, gave generously to finance the building of Christ Church at Butler Green in Chadderton; John Bunting, hugely rich from his involvement with the Limiteds, was a prominent supporter of Henshaw Street Primitive Methodists; Sarah Lees continued to help Hope Chapel. There were many other prominent donors among the well-to-do, but Oldham did not benefit from competing philanthropy in church building as was the case in some other towns; in Halifax, for instance, the Crossleys and

**Henshaw Street Primitive Methodist Chapel**, opened in 1871 to replace a smaller earlier building, had one of Oldham's largest congregations.

## Church and Chapel

the Akroyds tried to outdo each other in the splendour of their churches, as with their model houses.

Despite all this vigour, church attendance fell as the century progressed. The poor, deterred among other considerations by their lack of suitable attire, had never been churchgoers in nineteenth century Oldham. Attempts to reach them through the Oldham Mission, visiting houses, lodging houses, the workhouse, distributing tracts, holding services in the Mission Rooms or in the street, probably ineffectually, were willingly if modestly supported by the Emmotts, the Platts, Alfred Butterworth and others. But the problem now became the more respectable working class. They sent their children to Sunday Schools and these continued to flourish. Many hundreds from each church and chapel continued to walk in the Whit Friday processions, still the big event in the year. But after Sunday School, religious observance declined. Married women, zealous in requiring their children to go to Sunday School, tended to restrict their own church going involvement to Sunday School anniversaries, the big event of the year for attendance and for fund raising, and to sales of work, concerts and socials. Many men gave up attendance altogether, although no doubt, they thought they had accepted the basic tenets of Christianity. Various causes of the decline were identified and analysed. One historian observed that "the advance in material comforts made men much less concerned with pie in the sky". Another factor was boredom, at a time when not going to church was no longer regarded as a matter for shame. Limited free time, many felt, was for the pursuit of pleasure, not for the tedium of religious life, augmented as worship was by music, song and the sense of community these generated.

**Henshaw Street Chapel Sunday School**, typically Spartan, would take hundreds of scholars in separate classes.

**Greenacres Congregational** was the oldest and one of the most enduring of Oldham's non-conformist churches; this group posing outside the buildings used for the first meetings is a good example of chapel-going folk at the end of the nineteenth-century.

**Union Street Congregational chapel interior**, dating from 1871, with its prominent pulpit, choir seating and organ facing the congregation, a very typical chapel arrangement.

Attempts to retain the interest of young men through the Pleasant Sunday Afternoon Society had limited success. Churches and chapels began to provide enjoyable and vigorous social and leisure activities for their members; cricket and football teams, excursions, picnics, concerts, drama, even dancing, something for almost everyone. Nevertheless, regular church going in Oldham by the 1880s had fallen to less than 20 per cent of families, least among the poor, less among the working class, more among the respectable and well-to-do. The churches in the town centre, "down town" as they were called, had the greatest problem since the wealthy part of their congregations had moved away; not everyone would walk or use a cab or had a private carriage although dwindling numbers did. Many of the "down town" chapels became extinct. Generally the church was becoming out of sympathy and out of touch with the masses. One committed Oldham churchgoer, Miss Elizabeth Suthers, bound up all her life with the Mission and Hope Chapel, could protest in 1915 that

"young men and women, now rush about for pleasure, visit music halls, and indulge in dancing to the great danger to their health and detriment to their morals. Life is so much faster now than it was; fifty years ago girls came home from their work and after tea sat and did crocheting. Now they spend too much time on the streets, overdo their pleasures on Saturdays and cannot take any serious interest in school on Sundays, as they ought to do".

Given this situation, there was great chagrin, jealousy perhaps, when the Salvation Army came to Oldham in 1882 and, under the charismatic leadership of a young woman officer, Captain Jackson, graceful, dignified, urgent and earnest as she was, seemed to take it by storm. It was described at the time as "a mighty movement". Oldham, the Army claimed, had been "captured in the name of the King". If thousands were attending its meetings and rallies, they were from the poorer parts of the working population, outside the pale of the established churches and chapels. The vicar of St

**The Salvation Army** sent a highly successful mission from Manchester to Oldham in 1882 led by the youthful Jackson sisters. Much to the chagrin of the older churches and chapels their flamboyant noisy open-air meetings, inspirational music and fervent singing and preaching attracted a large and enthusiastic following, especially among the poor.

## Church and Chapel

Mary's boldly decided to engage these new converts and invited them to service in the Parish Church; never before had it been so crowded and the huge congregation sang with enormous enthusiasm the Old Hundred and heard an appropriate sermon punctuated by cries of "Alleluia". The hymn that closed a service described as "majestic" was the stirring "Stand up, stand up for Jesus", sung with waving arms and a volume of sound that shook the roof.

In the next few years noisy, vigorous, Salvationist marches on Sunday mornings, songs in music hall style, accompanied by tambourines, were such as to disturb sedate worship and prayer in the chapels of central Oldham. In 1885 Army meetings in the Market Place were described as "an intolerable nuisance" and the police were instructed to constrain them; the rough lads of Oldham tried, on more than one occasion, to break them up. There were about 3,000 regular adherents at this time, sufficient to warrant a visit by General Booth in 1886, a great occasion with thousands of people and four bands processing through the town. Booth proclaimed that "the open air is our cathedral", but the Army were able to raise funds to build its Citadel on Union Street. Salvationist fervour on this scale did not last the initial novelty, although the Army, persistent as it was, established its presence at various places within the district. The gradual decline of organised religion continued, not peculiar to Oldham, but frustrating to the dedicated nonetheless.

With the decline in church going went relaxation of keeping the Sabbath. Argument about refreshment in Alexandra Park on Sundays had wracked Oldham in the 1860s. There were similar, if less intense, arguments about Sunday opening of the Library and the Art Gallery in the 1880s. Slowly, inexorably, Sunday observance weakened, although only to a limited extent at the time compared with subsequently. If pubs opened on Sundays, as they always had, shops did not follow. Sunday, however, became a big day for excursions, to Belle Vue, Hollingworth Lake, even to the seaside. There was no uneasy guilty conscience, and church attendance ceased to be considered for the many.

There was a well defined "pecking order" among the Nonconformist chapels of Oldham with the Congregationalists like Hope or Queen Street, ahead of Wesleyans and below them, if not at the bottom, the Primitive Methodists. If anything Nonconformism was seen as the religion of "the bosses" rather than the working class, not least as it became associated with the Temperance movement. Anglicans throughout the district, perhaps especially in places like Crompton, continued to attract the support of the working class, partly because of the predominance of church day schools. From one place of worship to another, much depended on the energy and personality of the individual parson. Of the many hundreds who served in Oldham, there were those whose charisma, preaching skills and kindliness attracted and held large congregations. That was true, for instance, of John Hodgson, a saintly figure at Queen Street in the heart of Oldham, loved by the poor, from 1848 until his death in 1883; or of George Grundy, the towering Anglican influence as Vicar of Hey from 1838 to 1901. Others combined the pastor's role with a wider influence in the town and became among its most prominent and influential citizens. They could bestow prestige and assurance on any cause or venture. No major public occasion in

*Below:* **James Hodgson**, pious, devoted, much-loved minister of Queen Street, later Union Street Congregational Chapel. Coming to Oldham in 1848 he retired in 1883. His ministry saw a huge increase in the Chapel's membership and Sunday School attendance; he retired saddened at falling numbers, "when parents and children prefer self-indulgence on the Lord's Day to Christian instruction and worship."

*Bottom:* **George Grundy**, aged but revered after over sixty years at St. John's, Hey. When he died in 1901 the reports suggested many thousands walked miles to attend his funeral.

nineteenth century Oldham was complete without endorsement from a clergyman.

Notable among all the many Oldham parsons was Richard Meredith Davies (1815-1903) who was appointed pastor of the then struggling Hope Chapel in 1843. He remained there for over fifty years until his retirement in 1895. His capacity for work, broad sympathies and gifts as a preacher raised Hope to one of the most important chapels in the North. Such was his appeal that in the 1870s there was a waiting list for pews at Hope, although by then it was surrounded by poor streets and mills; pew rents were then bringing in £550 a year. During his ministry Davies preached over 3,800 prepared sermons to his congregation; annual collections at ordinary services rose from £38 in 1843 to £87 in 1863 at the height of the Famine and £228 in 1883; additionally collections at packed anniversaries would raise up to £150. Although a humble man who gave much of his income to charity, Davies was paid a stipend of over £500 a year, for a time more than Oldham's Town Clerk, and his manse in Waterloo Road was one of the finer houses in that neighbourhood. Beyond his role at Hope, R. M. Davies was described as the Nonconformist Bishop of Oldham, "writing his name boldly across the social, political, educational, moral and religious life of the town". His manner and views were completely acceptable to the ascendant Liberal faction without arousing the hostility of other persuasions; he could add wisdom, grace and wit, and often inspiration, to any public meeting or convivial dinner. Not surprisingly he was elected first Chairman of the School Board in 1871; for many years he was "the life and soul of the Lyceum"; he was a long-serving Chairman of the Infirmary Governors. In his last years he left Oldham to join his son in Southport but was buried in the town on his death.

Among prominent Anglicans was J. P. Rountree, incumbent of the fashionable St Thomas' in Werneth Coppice from 1879 until 1904. Described

**R.M. Davies**, Nonconformist Bishop of Oldham, approaching the end of his fifty years ministry at Hope Chapel.

**Noblesse Oblige**: Sarah Lees and her daughter Marjory arrive for some event at Hope Chapel. Originally built in 1824 by her husband's grandfather, in what became one of Oldham's poorer districts, it was surrounded by mills and foundries at Bottom of Moor; at the date of this photograph most of the congregation lived elsewhere.

as an old fashioned High Churchman, his congregation included Sam Platt and Josiah Walmsley Radcliffe and many of the most notable families in the town; he was a vigorous but controversial chairman of the School Board from 1888 to 1894, and a staunch and very public Conservative. In the later phase, and succeeding R. M. Davies, there were substantial figures like A. J. Viner (1864-1922), also of Hope Chapel. He may not have had so large a congregation, although he was a "a daring and brilliant preacher", but the wisdom and authority of his opinions gave him great influence and standing in the town. Especially was this so on educational matters where he was seen as an enthusiastic, far seeing and persistent idealist; few educational initiatives succeeded without his endorsement. It was said of him, approvingly, that "he carried into the pulpit something of the air of the businessman. Whilst he did not conform to the cloth, he religiously conformed to the custom of the tall hat." As an incomer he probably never understood Oldham folk with their "ready brusqueness, lack of refinement or even politeness, and rollicking humour", but he strove to become a good Oldhamer and was widely respected accordingly. He was probably the last of the towering religious personalities in the life of the town.

**Canon J. D Rountree**, the Anglican vicar of St. Thomas's, Werneth Coppice, the church of the Radcliffes and the Platts. Canon Rountree was a controversial chairman of the School Board, determined to strengthen religious instruction in all Oldham schools.

## Chapter IX

# LEISURE AND SPORT

During and after the 1850s a new habit developed among Oldham people as their spending power grew; they took advantage of the railway to get away from their working environment. Holidays from work were brief but the opportunity they presented was eagerly seized. Easter Saturday when the mills began to close on that day as they were doing by 1869, was the first annual occasion; Good Friday was traditionally a day for spring cleaning and white-washing. For many years May Day featured a grand parade of horses and carts, all done-up, witnessed by many thousands. Whit Friday remained the occasion for walks with huge numbers of Sunday School children parading the streets throughout the morning, usually in new clothes, accompanied by teachers, banners and bands, grouped under their respective schools. The walk may have been followed by games in a convenient field, coffee and buns, but the rest of the weekend was a major time for rail excursions and from the 1860s many thousands of Sunday School children would take cheap trips to destinations that were growing in popularity, Blackpool, Southport, Liverpool, and further afield. For the multitude of children Whitsuntide was the happiest time of the year.

Within shorter range, the alternatives, not merely at recognised holidays but at weekends, were the train to Manchester where Belle Vue with its zoo, huge gardens and boating lakes, and constantly changing entertainments, including fireworks, was a regular place of affordable excitement for the masses from the 1840s onwards; in 1875 the return fare and admission cost

**Whit-Friday** morning in Yorkshire Street, 1907.

## Leisure and Sport

1s 2d. The train to Hollingworth Lake, also developing as a place to promenade, take a boat or picnic, was another possibility at 1s return fare. The trip to Greenfield by train and rambles to Saddleworth Church or, for the scene of a macabre murder in 1832, Bill's-o-Jacks or the Moorcock Inn high on the moor, were frequently mentioned. Nearer at hand there was the new Alexandra Park or, provided by private enterprise, Strawberry Gardens at Glodwick; Daisy Nook on the edge of the Borough was another popular beauty spot. When the tram came people could readily be conveyed, not merely to Manchester or neighbouring towns like Rochdale, but to the open fields and moorland fringe at the edge of the district. Walking, through the remaining meadowlands or on the moor, remained an active Sunday pastime.

The Wakes at the end of August remained partly traditional and still locally based; places like Lees, Saddleworth, Crompton and Royton had their own Wakes at a different time to Oldham. In Oldham the fair with its swing-boats, merry-go-rounds, rifle galleries, travelling theatres, curios and freaks on Tommyfield, attracted huge crowds, including many visitors from the surrounding factory communities. In Oldham town at least, if not in Saddleworth, Failsworth and elsewhere, ancient customs were in decay in a rapidly changing community. It had become "no easy matter to get up a rushcart" and in 1871 there was only one; the people of Oldham, it was said, were "too busy building mills to bother with rushcarts". The Wakes

**Daisy Nook** was a popular and accessible place for Oldhamers to visit at weekends.

**Shaw Wakes** had the more traditional attractions.

**Rushbearing** survived in many of the communities in the Oldham district, if not in the town itself. This picture shows the Uppermill rush cart in 1880; the young men, if not the boys, would drink plenty of ale and there would be much horse-play before the day ended.

**Railway Excursions**: quick cheap railway journeys brought the Lancashire coast within affordable and convenient reach of the working population of mill-towns such as Oldham. Resorts like Blackpool and Southport boomed as they provided amenities, attractions and accommodation for the multitude seeking a break from their humdrum working environment.

## LEES BRASS BAND.

The Members of the above Band respectfully announce to their friends and the public generally that they have made arrangements with the London and North Western Railway Company for a

### CHEAP EXCURSION TRAIN TO LIVERPOOL

### ON WHIT-SATURDAY, JUNE 11TH, 1870.

The Train will Leave GLODWICK ROAD STATION at 5 30 a.m., Calling at LEES at 5 35 a.m., Returning from LIVERPOOL at 7 30 p.m.

FARES THERE & BACK
COVERED **2s. 8d.** CARRIAGES

A few First Class Tickets, at 3s. 8d. each, may be had of the Members.
An EARLY APPLICATION is Indispensible, the number of TICKETS being Limited.

Passengers by this Excursion will be allowed admittance into St. GEORGE'S HALL (free), from 10 a.m. to 4 p.m., the DERBY MUSEUM and FREE PUBLIC LIBRARY, from 10 a.m. to 6 p.m., and the TOWN HALL, from 11 a.m. to 3 p.m.

Arrangements have been made with Mr. MILLS, GREAT EASTERN HOTEL and PIC-NIC GROUNDS, NEW FERRY, to accommodate all Passengers with Hot Water, for Tea, in the New Ballroom, at a moderate charge. Various old English sports and unequalled amusements on these grounds; also, a first class Quadrille Band in daily attendance. The Lees Brass Band will also play a Selection of Dance Music at intervals. No charge made to Excursionists for admittance. The "DONEGAL," the "ACKBAR," the "CONWAY," and all the Public Training Ships are now lying at the foot of these Gardens.

TICKETS may be had at the following places, viz:—In LEES: Messrs. James Lord, Printer; R. Travis, Pork Butcher; P. Ormrod, Boot and Shoe Maker; J. Pemberton, Grocer; J. Wrigley, Grocer, New Road; J. R. Walsh, Atherton Buildings, Woodend; J. Dean, Co-operative Street; E. Hall, Woodbrook Newsroom. SPRINGHEAD:—Mr. W. Buckley, Grocer. MILLBOTTOM:—Mr. J. Tweedle, Eastwood Street. OLDHAM:— Messrs. T. Emmott, New Earth; W. Edwards, Lees Brook; B. Wild, Pork Butcher, Side o' th' Moor; J. Halkyard, Greengrocer, Side o' th' Moor; J. Bottomley, Roscoe Street; J. Healey, Confectioner, Curzon Street; Heywood Brothers, General Dealers, Union Terrace; H. Daltry, Temperance Hotel, Yorkshire Street; and any of the Schools can be supplied with Tickets from the Band and Committee.

James Lord, General Printer, Stationer, and News Agent, Lees.

was still, however, an occasion for hearty jostling, brawling and heavy drinking and the Oldham Temperance Society were usually bold enough to parade at the same time.

This was now becoming the main occasion for the majority of people to take day trips out of the town. As, gradually and informally, more time was taken off work at the Wakes, the practice of "running-off", so longer trips, staying for a few days, became increasingly common. By 1871 the mills were reopening on Thursday morning; it was estimated that 30,000 people had left the town on excursions during that year's holiday, many to visit London. By 1879 the Wakes had become so important that to escape the regular wetness of the end of August, a controversial attempt was made to take the holiday a month earlier. The change was not popular and the traditional time soon reasserted itself.

By the 1880s employers throughout the district began to close for a whole week. The holiday was unpaid so people saved the better to enjoy it. "Going-off clubs" seem to have evolved in Oldham as soon as a longer seasonal holiday became established; following the example of Platts there were many in the town by 1877; by 1884 there were scores raising over £60,000 organised by places of employment, by churches, and especially by public houses. In 1886, after the strike, the total saved fell to £36,000 but then rose steadily; in 1900, over £140,000 was raised, a new high; in 1907, a boom year, the figure was set at £200,000. The principles were straightforward;

## Leisure and Sport

**Blackpool** was the most popular destination for Oldhamers "going-off" to spend part of a year's hard saving on their Wakes holiday at the end of August. There was plenty of cheap accommodation at a shilling nightly per person; most families took their own food which would be cooked and served by the landlady. Oldham families would stick together, staying in the same boarding-house year after year.

members paid in modest sums week by week, these attracted interest and a worthwhile accumulation could be taken out as Wakes week approached. Some of the money saved might be spent on clothing and furniture, and retailers of these goods were busiest before the Wakes. But most, almost certainly, went on having a good time; "nowhere else" said the *Chronicle*, "are holidays greeted with greater glee or taken with greater gusto. The vigour people throw into work they now fling into play". If Oldham people had the "facility of working when they professed to work", so they had of "playing when they professed to play". Many Oldham weddings also took place at the Wakes. So people saved to spend; a household with two people working might have saved £20 in a year, a not inconsiderable sum at the time; £10 for an individual was typical.

By the 1890s, Wakes had become a major exodus from the town. Dozens of crowded special trains to the most popular resorts were leaving on Friday evening and Saturday, bringing back the multitude a week later. This was, of course, a Lancashire phenomenon, of which Oldham was a part. Resorts on the Lancashire coast developed to provide the necessary facilities to meet popular demand. None, of course, more than Blackpool, with its huge accommodation to suit every budget and its proliferating range of popular attractions, the sea close to the promenade, and an ample supply of public houses. Blackpool was a pleasure factory, its charges varied but could be as low as 1s per night, shared bed. For one week each year this was Oldham by the sea. Other resorts followed, but were more sedate; none compared with Blackpool's "easy going homeliness". All offered a complete change, sea air, the opportunity to release energy, to let rip and find adventure and romance.

When they could afford, people wanted to try something different, go beyond Blackpool, Southport, New Brighton, Cleethorpes, the North Wales coast. More adventurous trips featured the Isle of Man or the South Coast. Years of prosperity encouraged adventure; in 1907 Oldham people went as a

### Hotels and Boarding Houses.
#### BLACKPOOL.

**BLACKPOOL.**—Mrs. RAYNER, 98, Albert Rd.; public or private apartments, with or without board; terms mod.; near all places of amusement and Central Sta.

**BLACKPOOL.**—Mrs. G. H. MILLER, Knottfield House, 137, Albert Road; apartments, with or without board; piano.

**BLACKPOOL.**—Mrs. RIDING, 57, Albert Road (late of Yorkshire-street); apartments, public or private, with or without board; near station; piano.

**BLACKPOOL.**—Mrs. WHITTAKER, 63, Albert Road; apartments, public or private, with or without board; terms moderate; near station; piano.

**BLACKPOOL.**—Mrs. ROBERTS, Ramsbottom House, 104, Albert Road; apartments, with or without board; terms moderate; piano.

**BLACKPOOL.**—Mrs. JAGGAR 8d, Albert Road; summer and winter apartments; public or private, with or without board; piano.

**BLACKPOOL.**—Mrs. E. SIMPSON, 88, Albert Road; public or private apartments, with or without board; near Central Station and sea.

**BLACKPOOL.**—Messrs. BRIDGE & HOLMES, 25, Albert Road; public or private apartments, with or without board; one minute from Central Station and sea.

**BLACKPOOL.**—Mrs. F. PICKLES, 28, Albert Road; home from home apartments, public or private; near Central Station and sea.

**BLACKPOOL.**—Mrs. BRIGGS, 22, Albert Road; public or private apartments, with or without board; one minute from Central Station and sea.

**BLACKPOOL.**—Misses CARTER, 114, Albert Road; pleasant apartments, near sea and all places of amusement; terms moderate; piano.

---

### OLDHAM HOLIDAYS.
TO ENJOY A HOLIDAY TRAVEL BY
#### COOK'S EXCURSIONS
### MIDLAND RAILWAY
TO
EDINBURGH, BRISTOL,
GLASGOW, etc. LONDON, etc.
BATH, CHELTENHAM,
AND THE **WEST OF ENGLAND.**
NOTTINGHAM, LOUGHBORO', LEICESTER,
and
**MIDLAND COUNTIES.**

**THROUGH EXPRESS TRAINS WILL LEAVE OLDHAM ON** (MUMPS) **FRIDAY NIGHT, AUGUST 26th,**

At 3 35 p.m. TO EXETER, TORQUAY, PLYMOUTH, etc.

At 11 25 p.m. TO CARLISLE, EDINBURGH, GLASGOW, etc.

At 11 15 p.m. TO LONDON (St. Pancras), BIRMINGHAM, WORCESTER, CHELTENHAM, GLOUCESTER, BRISTOL, BATH, & BOURNEMOUTH.

THESE TRAINS WILL CALL AT CENTRAL, WERNETH, and HOLLINWOOD.

**Helen Bradley** was born and grew up in Lees. She took up painting in her later years to record the scenes of her early life. Here she paints a family group in Spring Lane, clearly dressed-up, apparently before setting off for Blackpool next morning.

For those who stayed at home during Wakes, the fairground was the big attraction. No doubt a sensation at the time, would be **the first moving pictures**.

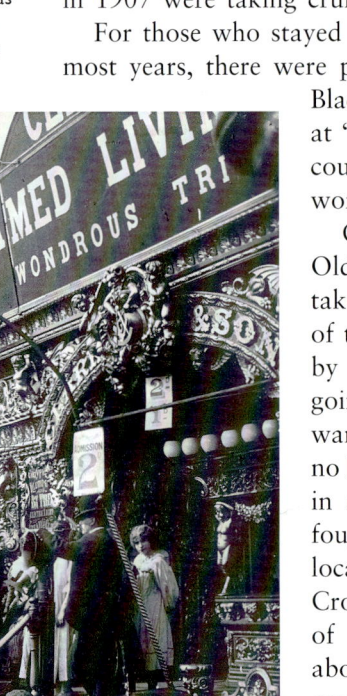

body to Torquay where it was claimed they spent £10,000, and in some cases slept five to a bedroom. Some in that year went in organised parties to visit places as far afield as Jersey, Switzerland, even Rome; Thomas Cook, Dean and Dawson and other organisations, were quick to offer these different possibilities to those with the enterprise and the means. A seven day package to Paris was being offered at £5 9s; 200 people took it. Oldham's well-to-do in 1907 were taking cruises to Madeira and the Canaries for £15 to £18.

For those who stayed at home, and they were probably the majority in most years, there were plenty of day excursions, 2s 6d for a day trip to Blackpool, as well as the traditional Wakes attractions at "dear old Tommyfield". There were also those who could not afford the loss of earnings and sought to find work and wages elsewhere during Wakes week.

Chadderton took Oldham Wakes. Ever resisting Oldhamisation, Royton and Crompton continued to take theirs earlier in August. In Royton the high feature of the holiday was the Royton Sports, often attended by as many as 20,000 people; many postponed their going-off until after the Sports. While both Districts wanted to distance themselves from Oldham, there was no love lost between them. They were rivals not merely in mill building but more widely; their young men fought each other; their sporting teams competed in local "Derbys." The superior thrift and acumen of Crompton or Shaw people was revealed in the results of the going-off clubs; each year, Crompton, with about the same spindles but a smaller population, could raise more money then Royton; in 1912 "rich and prosperous" Crompton's £25,000 compared with a mere £15,000 in Royton.

Christmas was the other great seasonal occasion when the mills closed for one or two days. Christmas Eve became the main shopping time, with the streets crowded until midnight, a lively and busy market, and the pubs doing a tremendous trade, not least with young people, in their drink rude and impertinent, the boys jostling and chaffing the girls. In 1881 the *Chronicle* reported beggars lining the streets. At midnight the Church bells were rung, and brass bands and carol singers began their walks and the streets became alive with music throughout the night and the morning of Christmas Day. Practically every church and chapel held tea parties, frequently on Christmas Day. Some private employers gave "treats" to their workpeople, dinners of roast beef, plum pudding and plenty of ale, followed by singers of popular glees and dancing. Platt's and Asa Lees' skilled workmen regularly had their own dinners each New Year, on much the same lines. This was the time too of charitable giving, of breakfasts and dinners to the aged, and especially to poor children. It was also an occasion for great co-operative parties when hundreds of members would enjoy "a good baggin" in three sittings, followed by "gradely good old fashioned songs", and, on many occasions, humorous readings by Ben Brierley, the celebrated dialect writer of Failsworth, famed for his interpretations of Lancashire life and character.

To the regular seasonal breaks, may be added the one-offs, the grand occasions for celebrations, processions, bands, festivity. On a local basis they might be the occasion of a notable wedding or coming of age. The Clarksfield Lees, with their coal and land wealth, had such a huge extravagant party when Edward Brown Lees, son of John Lees of Higher Clarksfield, came of age in 1863; thousands of the local poor, tenants and colliery workers were entertained on a scale that "topped anything of the kind yet attempted in this district"; the procession of 2,000 miners to their dinner, "could only make the butchers smile", reported the *Chronicle*. The private millowners in Crompton did much the same, more modestly; following his neighbours, the Milnes and the Cheethams, Joseph Clegg of Sandy Lane, High Crompton gave a huge party in March 1873 to 600 workpeople and tenants, as well as Sunday

**Royton Sports** was the big occasion held on the first Saturday of the annual Wakes. It attracted athletes from all over Lancashire.

The huge bonfire on Oldham Edge would conclude the day's events at **Queen Victoria's Diamond Jubilee in 1897**.

**Occasional royal visits** were the memorable events of a lifetime for many. In 1913 the new King and Queen visited Oldham on a tour of Lancashire. This was their reception at the Town Hall.

School children and old people, to celebrate the marriage of his son; the object clearly was to foster good feeling.

Affecting everyone were the national occasions: the Prince of Wales marriage in 1863 was a public holiday, with a huge procession of notables, local organisations and bands, that paraded the streets for about three miles. Years later the two Jubilees of the Queen and the Borough's half-centenary in 1899 were big events in Oldham as were the Coronations in 1901 and 1911. At the 1887 Jubilee the *Chronicle* reported a parade of 30,000 Sunday School children with over twenty bands, over two miles long and taking one hour to pass, witnessed in gaily decorated streets by 70,000 spectators followed by tea parties for the poor, a banquet for the elite, and in the evening a big bonfire and fireworks. In 1913 there was a royal visit, part of the new King's Lancashire tour, and this eclipsed all, with a great crush of people at the main places along the route and in front of the Town Hall, and a pageant of 14,000 school children in Werneth Park, still the home of Sarah Lees and her daughter. More modest than these national occasions but still an event that drew the crowds was the annual Mayor-making, when councillors and magistrates, officials, police and firemen, in uniform and regalia, marched through the town accompanied by bands, Volunteers, Sunday School-children and many voluntary organisations. The pomp on this occasion seemed justified; this was an event that brought "before the people in visible form the personality of its government".

These were the main breaks from the monotonous drudgery of the workshop or mill. But for working men, the public house, usually at the

corner of the street, remained the chief ongoing means of socialising and escape. It was still open from early in the morning until late at night but the weekend, after pay-day, and especially Saturday night and Sunday were the busiest times. In many households a quarter, even a third, or more of income was spent on beer and tobacco. The latter was a market that expanded dramatically with the shift from pipe smoking to cigarettes at the end of the century; in 1888 Woodbines were launched and nationally advertised at five for one penny.

Beer consumption and drunkenness appeared to diminish after 1880; the number of Oldham pubs had ceased to grow with the population. There were still 362 pubs in the town in 1913, one for every 380 people, as well as off-licences, and licensed clubs, but that number of pubs was less than it had been in 1870 when with 420 licences, the ratio was one to 200 people, much as it had been in 1850. Various licensing laws clearly had some effect on the number of outlets and the hours they could open; closing time was fixed at 11pm and Sunday opening hours restricted to eight; it also became an offence to serve anyone who appeared to be younger than sixteen. In 1913 an average of eighteen people weekly still came before the magistrates for drunkenness; the *Chronicle* put the number arrested and charged at about 5 per cent of the real incidence. The position was not different elsewhere in the district; Shaw, for instance, on Saturday night, was described by one of its councillors in 1907 as a "drunken hole" with more drunks "than anywhere else in Lancashire"; depravity among young women was described as "something dreadful". Middle class Oldhamers would rarely if ever be seen in a pub; they consumed their wines and spirits in clubs or in their homes.

In 1893 there were seventy-four clubs in Oldham, forty-one being political, at the time not subject to control or inspection. Many of the non-political clubs opened when the pubs closed and stayed open until 3 or 4 in the

**Public houses** remained the chief leisure outlet for working men: the old Pack Horse. dating at least from 1751, was beside the Oldham road at Failsworth. When this picture was taken in the early 1870s, the landlord still brewed his own beer.

## Oldham Brave Oldham

Fighting drink was the **Temperance Movement** which had a staunch following in Oldham included many prominent men. Most of those who signed the pledge joined the Band of Hope which had branches at most chapels.

**Dancing**, became an increasingly popular and regular rather then occasional activity among young people. The Dancing Academy in Henshaw Street met the demand to develop this necessary social skill.

morning, and all day Sunday, said to be "drinking and gambling dens". The political clubs were better run with more emphasis on games like billiards, cards and dominoes; it was said "if you want to get away from politics in Oldham, go to a political club". There were also many working men's and sporting clubs, described as "well conducted and appreciated", that by the end of the century combined drinking with entertainment in an atmosphere congenial to the factory worker. In a vain attempt to compete with the pubs and clubs, determined teetotallers like Alfred Butterworth and Thomas Emmott, both wealthy millowners, started coffee taverns at Rhodes Bank and Bankside, but neither survived for long. The Temperance Movement with all its single-minded zeal continued to remind Oldhamers of the perils and immorality of drink but its adherents did not grow and it probably had only a modest influence. Having said that, perhaps one in eight households were teetotal in late nineteenth century Oldham, including many prominent people. There were fifty-nine Band of Hope societies in the district in the 1890s claiming 9,000 members who had taken the pledge.

A growing number of public houses offered more than food and refreshment; live entertainment, music, singing and dancing became increasingly popular. Some of these places became the notorious "singing saloons" where hundreds of young people of both sexes mingled noisily on Saturday nights, much to the disapproval of the church-going middle classes. There were other diversions offering escape and pleasure. Various circuses, the largest being those of Sangers and Barnum, would visit Oldham as they toured the northern industrial towns, bringing performing horses, camels and elephants within their retinue, "instructive and amusing entertainment to which a refined Christian mother can take her children with satisfaction", as Sangers claimed on their visit in 1875.

## Leisure and Sport

From the 1860s the "Peoples Hall of Varieties" in Rock Street, the Adelphi Music Hall in Union Street, and later the Gaiety, became immensely popular among working class families; the Adelphi was rebuilt in 1875 to provide room for 3,000 people. Oldham's Colosseum Theatre was built as a circus in 1885 but was to survive as a music hall and then a theatre. Soon the town had a nightly variety of affordable entertainment, increasingly professional, much of which drew its humour and sentimentality from the everyday lives and romantic hopes of working class people. In 1875, Christy (Black and White) Minstrels were a huge attraction, as for many years subsequently. For the carriage-keeping class, a popular evening venue for both sexes was the Alexandra Skating Rink off Union Street opened in 1875, where couples could skate on rollers to a brass band accompaniment; on the club night, Wednesday, it was common to see twenty or thirty carriages outside the Rink and many Oldham marriages were apparently hatched there. Also for the better-off there was the Theatre Royal in Horsedge Street offering pantomime at Christmas, and various drama productions round the year with seats at 3d and 6d and 1s 6d for boxes.

For the middle classes there were a growing number of societies, learned, musical, choral, and social. Lectures, illustrated by magic lantern, were always popular, especially where they described countries overseas. Sam Platt, in particular did a great deal to encourage music, both at the Lyceum and by his own participation as an instrument player and a vocalist, organising Platt orchestras and choirs. For many years the Hallé Orchestra gave concerts at Oldham's Theatre Royal, although by the 1880s the well-to-do were going to their Thursday concerts in Manchester. Within the town there were people like Robert Jackson, organist at St Peter's, who devoted their lives to organising music, conducting orchestras and choirs. Charles Walton, father of William, came to Oldham to be employed by Platts as an office worker; well known as a bass baritone he became organist at St John's, Werneth and music teacher at Hulme School. In 1911 there were nearly 500 people whose

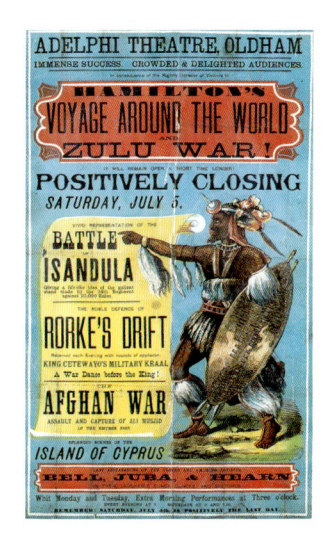

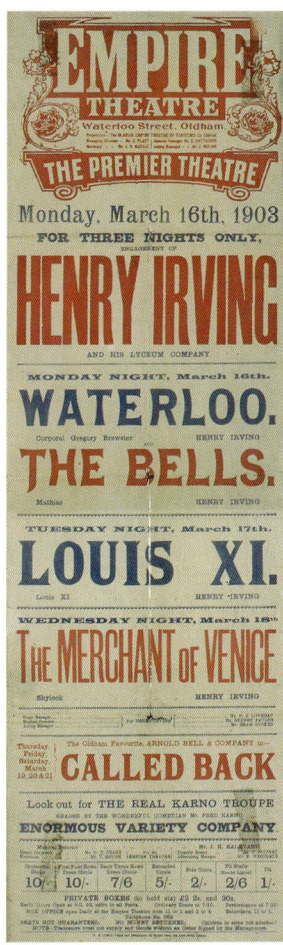

**Oldham Orchestral Society**, formed in 1893, " to save local ladies and gentlemen the inconvenience of travelling to Manchester." A number of its players were filched from the Halle. Finding a suitable hall was a problem until after 1901 when its concerts were given in the Hill Stores of the Equitable Co-operative Society.

occupation was described as "art, music, drama", compared with 120 in 1851. But music was more than a middle class interest. Every church and chapel had some sort of choir, and there were several vocal societies; many Messiahs and Elijahs as well as other oratorios were performed in Oldham every year. The Oldham Musical Society formed in 1886 and the Lyceum School of Music started in 1892 encouraged all forms of musical endeavour. In 1907 there were over 300 entries to an Oldham Choir Competition, mostly local; the winners were the East Oldham Vocal Society. The Oldham Orchestral Society was founded in 1892 under the presidency of Charles E. Lees, soon to die young when he was succeeded by Sam Platt. With forty musicians the Society gave three subscription concerts each winter over the period to the Great War, attracting as many as 170 subscribers paying £1 1s for two seats at each concert. The objective was "to save local ladies and gentlemen the inconvenience of travelling to Manchester"; several players, all Oldhamers, were filched from the Hallé. Venues were a problem and the concerts were held in a number of halls, none of them ideal.

Membership of a band was another agreeable outlet, affording a uniform and a prominent place on special occasions as well as the pleasure of music-making. There were a multitude of brass bands throughout the district, many relying upon and receiving financial support from the wealthy. Most of them competed locally every year at Saddleworth, and the best, at the annual competition at Belle Vue; several won national prizes, such as Shaw Prize Band, Champions at Crystal Palace in 1909; or Dobcross Band, founded in 1875, feted as heroes when they won first prize at a contest in Wales; they went on to become "Champion of Champions" at Belle Vue many years later.

Oldham, at every social level when account is taken of the singing pubs and the music hall, as well as the brass bands, was an intensely musical place; there was a huge appetite for music. The same, needless to say, was true of the Districts, and not least of Saddleworth; here the lack of alternative commercial provision in the form of music halls, and local pride, encouraged a climate where bands and choirs could flourish. Music, in Oldham and elsewhere, brought all classes together.

**Sport**

What of sport? The traditional rough, brutal and illegal sports, that is dog fights, clog fights, pitch and toss, all occupied young and not so young men on Sundays in the 1850s and 1860s, as at an earlier time. But alternatives were developing. Interest in horse racing was growing; many visited Manchester races on Kersal Moor, while betting in the pubs and elsewhere was increasingly popular. An attempt was made in 1864 to start horse racing in Oldham in a field on Greenacres Moor. The course, one mile, involved three circuits round a flimsy fence; reported crowds of 10,000 or more would attend. The crowd proved difficult to control; horses fell as dogs ran in their way, and one jockey was killed; the venture petered out in 1868. Gambling habits were already well established in Oldham, in shares of the Limiteds and in the traditional sports, but when horse-racing developed a national reach and the telegraph and cheap newspapers publicised the events and starting prices, a flutter on the horses became a popular working class pastime, offering release and excitement, pursued in the mill, in the pub, through plenty of street bookmakers and their runners.

Leisure pursuits were enormously stimulated by reduced working hours, especially the "short Saturday", after 1874. Organised competitive sport now developed rapidly. Oldham Cricket Club had been started in 1852, playing initially at Watersheddings, but elsewhere cricket clubs were established at Werneth in 1864, at Royton in 1868, at Delph and Dobcross in 1873, and at Crompton rather later in 1884, to name but a few examples. Most social classes participated. Certainly Werneth Cricket Club, where Sam Platt was President, and Honorary Captain, showing great enthusiasm but little prowess for the game, would at the time be a middle class affair, very much for Platts people; the other clubs were much more open. Interest in the game was stimulated by the achievements of W. G. Grace and other prominent cricketing personalities. The Australians came to play at Werneth in 1878 and again in 1880, the Indians in 1886. The principal teams of the district were competing home and away with teams from other localities, playing twenty or so matches in a season, employing professionals at a modest retainer. Thus George Rhodes, born in Saddleworth, was Oldham's professional in the 1880s, and also for several years professional at Crompton, all the time working in a cotton mill. There were also many well-remembered amateurs, men like Zadok Chester of Royton; of him it was said, "he breaks the ball from either side, and on his day is almost unplayable".

The Central Lancashire League was formed in 1892, when four Oldham teams became members; Werneth joined some years later, influenced by the excitement and interest league competition generated. Apart from the larger clubs many workplaces, churches and chapels formed their teams, as did neighbourhoods. By the 1890s, from late April until September many hundreds would play cricket and many thousands watch. Apart from big league cricket, in a typical week in 1900, there were eighty-four local teams competing in four local leagues, one of which had five divisions; in the Saddleworth and District League there were ten clubs, each with two teams. All the clubs, large and small, had difficulty finding a suitable ground, not least because flat land was at a premium and often, if close to where people lived, expensive. The larger clubs needed not merely a large suitable area of land and a prepared wicket but changing rooms and the like. All - even Werneth with its Platt patronage - had their shaky moments but, thanks to vigorous fund-raising and in some cases generous benefactions, survived to become significant institutions in the life of the district offering memorable occasions to most of its menfolk, as players or as spectators.

Two other main sports developed for the colder part of the year, football and rugby. Several local teams were playing rugby in the 1870s; the Oldham Rugby Club was probably formed in 1876. For several years they used a ground at Clarksfield and then, in 1889, took a lease of land at Watersheddings and shared a pavilion with Oldham Cricket Club. Oldham was one of the first clubs to leave the Rugby Union and helped to form the

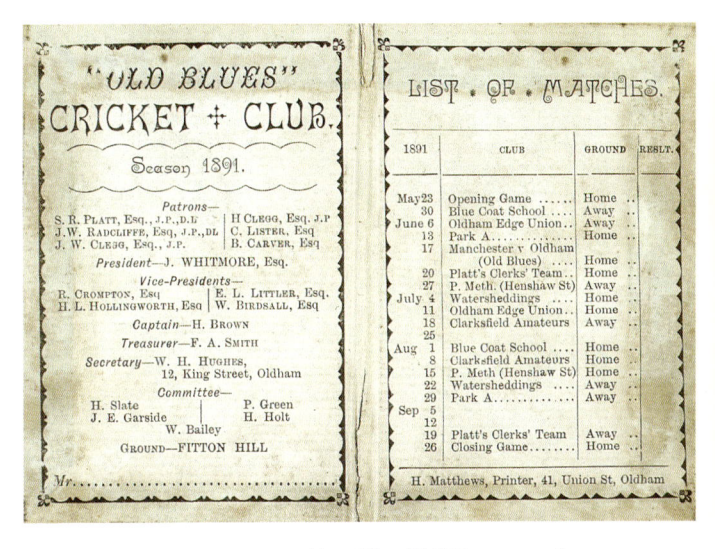

*Above:* **The Old Blues** were the old boys of Bluecoat School

**St. Paul's Royton football team** competed in the Fourth Division of the Oldham Sunday School League.

### SECOND DIVISION.
Northmoor ......... 4  Cowlah ............... 0
Deaf and Dumb .... 4  Hollinwood ......... 2

## OLDHAM AND DISTRICT SUNDAY SCHOOL LEAGUE.

### First Division.
St. Thomas's Church  2   Boarshurst S.S. ....... 0
Doborons United ..... 1   Hey St. John's ........ 0
Lessfield Church ..... 3   Salem Moravians ..... 2

### Second Division.
Christ Church ........ 3   King-street ........... 2
St. Ambrose Mission  2   Edge-lane Wesleyans  1
Excelsior Temp. ..... 5   Hollins-road Prim. ... 1
Hollinwood Bible M.  1   Hollinwood Adults ... 1

### Third Division.
Busk Mission ......... 3   Nile-street Mission .. 0
Copster Hill B'hood  2   Greenacres Cong. .... 1
Macedonia S.S. ...... 9   Glodwick Wesleyans  0
Springhead Cong. ... 2   Waterhead Cong. .... 0
St. Paul's Church .... 4   St. Chad's Mission .. 2

### Fourth Division.
Union-street U.M.C.  0   Christ Church Juniors 0
St. Paul's Church .... 3   Good Templars ....... 0
Werneth U.M.C. ..... 1   Henshaw-street P. ... 0
Old Boys' Institute .. 4   Zion Sunday School  0
Roundthorn Rec. .... 4   Spiritualists .......... 2
St. Michael's Church 2   Watersheddings Wes. 0

## OLDHAM DISTRICT CENTRAL JUNIOR LEAGUE.
Barton Lads .......... 3   Shamrock ............. 3
Heyside Lads ........ 5   Park Albion .......... 0
Edge-lane United ... 3   Robin Hill Lads ...... 1
Falcon United ....... 2   Heyside United ...... 0
Bardsley Juniors .... 8   Celtic Albion ......... 0
Hawthorn Lads ...... 2   Alexandra Lads ...... 1

Pre-match excitement at **Boundary Park** as Manchester United take the field. The date is 1913.

Northern Rugby Football Union, which permitted payments to players and evolved different rules eventually becoming the Rugby League in the 1920s. To its followers and opponents the Club became known as "The Spindles". Its games were attracting crowds averaging 15,000 in the 1890s, and many more at exceptionally interesting matches; in 1912 a record 28,000 watched Oldham play Huddersfield. Most spectators, it seems, entered by what was called "the Penny Rush".

The Football Association had been formed in 1863, the Football League much later in 1888. This was the period when football, played by professionals for the most part, became the main spectator sport of the working man. Looking for a good time in leisure that was scarce, here was a game, as with rugby, that could combine "great drama, with cunning skill and brutal effort". Such was the game's following that many would claim that "the football habit has made Saturday a soberer day"; the public house suffered accordingly. Although there were many amateur football teams competing in local leagues, the professional game came late in Oldham. Oldham County, the first professional team, with a ground at Sheepfoot Lane, where they were attracting gates of about 4,000, failed financially. A local

# Sport

club named Pine Villa (after Pine Mill in Chadderton) which had been successful in the Oldham Junior League, took over the ground at Sheepfoot and changed its name to Oldham Athletic; the ground became Boundary Park. Playing successively in the Manchester Alliance and the Lancashire Combination, the new club joined the Second Division of the Football League in 1907-8 and were promoted to the First two seasons later.

Prior to the Great War the "Latics" were runners up in the League and losing semi-finalists in the Cup. From 1907 they played before crowds regularly as large as 14,000, and exceptionally as large as 34,000 for a game against Newcastle United in 1910, and 35,473 for a cup-tie against Everton in 1912. Notwithstanding these numbers the Club's finances were precarious, just about breaking even most seasons; the wealthy businessmen of the town were not willing to give strong financial backing. The *Oldham Chronicle* had welcomed its formation, claiming "the town demands good soccer and there is plenty of room for both Clubs", but those managing the competing sports, although their fixtures were carefully arranged not to clash, may not have agreed.

Other sports became popular. Bowling was practised on greens associated with cricket clubs, public houses or in the Park. It was well established as a sport in Oldham by the 1880s, attracting many spectators as well as participation. Tennis was more exclusive but Copster Park, opened in 1911, had two bowling greens and six tennis courts as well as a playing field and recreation ground. Pigeon homing was encouraged and facilitated by the railway companies; live pigeon shooting also had plenty of followers with crack-shots competing for cash prizes. Whenever there was a deep freeze, plenty of people skated on the mill lodges. Billiards, whist and chess became popular in the Improvement Societies and in the working men's clubs and political clubs when these were set up in the 1870s. Oldham youth took eagerly to swimming as a competitive sport as more facilities were provided. Henry Taylor of Chadderton won an Olympic Gold at Athens in 1906 and went on to win many trophies. By the 1890s cycling for pleasure was becoming popular, especially when new or second-hand machines became affordable and pneumatic tyres were introduced; in 1900 there were sixteen organised cycling groups in Oldham. Golf, hockey and lacrosse began to be played locally, out of reach, however, of the working classes. Oldham Harriers - athletics - were going strong in the 1890s.

*Above:* **Pigeon keeping** had a small but devoted following. This Failsworth enthusiast kept his birds at the rear of his terrace-house.

*Below:* The success of the Hollinwood born **Henry Taylor** in winning Olympic gold medals in the years before 1914 did much to make swimming popular. As a youth working in a Hollinwood cotton mill he trained in the local canal at dinner time and in the Alexandra Park boating lake in the evening. He could not afford the local baths, except on "dirty water" days. He won his first gold in Athens in 1906, winning the one mile freestyle in a record 28 minutes.

*Left:* **Cycling** became a popular minority sport; this group outside the Royal George, Greenfield, were either locals or had ridden out from Oldham.

## Oldham Brave Oldham

**The Oldham Volunteers**, formed in 1859, officered by young men from Oldham's elite families, attracted several hundred participants, keen to parade at the Drill Hall in Lord Street on weekdays and enjoy the comradeship of an annual camp.

**Oldham Rifle Band**, formed by members of the Volunteers, one of dozens of brass bands throughout Oldham district. Some, like Shaw Prize Band won national trophies. The bands were in regular demand throughout the year; the commitment of most of their members, the time they gave to practice, was remarkable.

Another diversion for many young men, probably clerks rather than mill workers, was membership of the Oldham Volunteers. Founded in 1859 with many similar companies elsewhere, (Saddleworth Volunteers started the following year) at a time of imagined threat of invasion by the French, it had a shaky start since its hundred or so members had to give their time free and pay for their uniform and equipment. There were those who opposed the movement on the grounds of "no vote, no rifle". But the Volunteers caught on; weekly drill in a purpose-built drill hall, shooting, the annual camp, were congenial manly activities, "an end to lounging and idling about". There was a patriotic motive, they were "England's Guard", and the local Volunteers had pride of place in any Oldham procession. The movement also enjoyed the patronage of notable Tory and Anglican families in the town. By the 1880s the Oldham Volunteers were 500 strong, regarded as an efficient reserve army, accepting "military values" and the authority of their "social superiors", but above all enjoying congenial recreation with plenty of sport, plenty of drinking. At the time of the Boer War the strength numbered 720. "The volunteer movement is no toy", said the *Oldham Chronicle*; many wanted to be involved in the war but in the end only forty-three men went to South Africa, although a crowd of 40,000 was reported to have gathered in the streets to watch them parade down to Mumps station accompanied by the Oldham Rifle Band playing "Soldiers of the Queen". Alfred Butterworth gave each man a gold sovereign. By 1914 the Volunteers had become the 10th (Oldham) Territorial Battalion, Manchester Regiment; the Saddleworth company was part of the Duke of Wellington's (West Riding) Regiment. What had been a pastime now had a serious purpose and both units were quickly mobilised and engaged, not least at Gallipoli and in Flanders.

To the multitude of Oldham children, the street remained the main playground and street games were played, as for generations before. The Park was remote to the many and there were no recreation grounds until one was donated at Northmoor in the 1880s by James Bowker, a small property owner, and, a second, about an acre in size, at Beresford Street, Huddersfield Road by the Dronsfield Brothers on the occasion of the Jubilee in 1899. Others were to follow provided by philanthropy (Sarah Lees created two) or eventually in 1911, as at Copster Park and Derker, by the Corporation; for many years Councillors had been reluctant to spend ratepayers' money for this purpose. Although not without furious controversy, both Royton and Crompton moved ahead of the Borough to provide this necessary amenity.

Another striking change took place after the mid-century. People began to read, the more so as the Board Schools developed and improved literacy. Access to books, if restricted to Sunday Schools, the Lyceums and Co-operative main branches, became universal when the free libraries were opened, disappointing as their use was for many years. But above all what people began to read was a newspaper. The reduction in the paper duties made a cheap local press feasible. The *Oldham Chronicle* was established in 1854 as a weekly paper; the Hirst and Rennie families began their long association shortly afterwards. Priced at 1½d, its circulation grew rapidly with the growth in population in the district. By 1870 it was selling close to 11,000 copies; it had grown to eight pages by then, and in the next decade added a supplement, as well as a week-day evening edition priced at ½d.

The *Chronicle* carried a digest of national and world news and full local reports, not least of the Magistrates Courts, the Council meetings, local political activity and doings at churches and chapels. Liberal in politics, its editorials and columnists, while partisan and often vituperative, were eloquent and learned. It knew the interests of its readers; violent crime, the last hours of condemned murderers, riots, explosion or disaster and violent death were reported in full detail; it also knew how to "name and shame". The *Chronicle*'s rival, the Tory *Oldham Standard*, started in 1865, had not the same success, although its circulation reached 7,000 by 1870. Attempts to launch other newspapers failed. Along with the local press was a great deal of "printed rubbish", not specific to Oldham but sold nationally in magazine form. As people read, and education took its hold, speech also changed; the

*If there were few playing fields, children played in the street, as in this picture of Bower Street with the distinctive Hope chapel in the background.*

broad Lancashire dialect became a thing of the past, with fewer and fewer people able to understand it. What remained was badly pronounced English rather than the dialect of Waugh or Brierley, the renowned dialect writers of the 19th Century. Likewise Oldhamers became less uncouth; still plain and blunt, perhaps, but education, newspapers, travel, greatly softened their manner; they were becoming citizens of the world.

Of course many leisure activities continued much the same as they had been earlier in the century. The streets were not merely the playground of children; every evening, at least in Spring and Summer, after mill and tea time, many of those people who did not frequent the pub, came onto the street, to laugh and gossip from door to door. At weekends visiting, tea in the front room, a walk round the neighbourhood before or after, was standard. For teenagers and young adults gathering in groups at street corners and promenading, especially on Union Street, on weekend evenings, looking for a partner, was the regular practice. Card playing, other parlour games, singing round the piano were other winter diversions. Pets were popular: in 1903 the Oldham police caught and put down 855 stray dogs; the annual Oldham dog show attracted over 500 entries. If the music hall was the working man's theatre, towards the end of the century it began to be rivalled by the cinema which was to prove immensely popular in subsequent decades; in 1913 there were already twenty-two picture houses in Oldham alone, most of them in converted buildings, showing dozens of silent films every week, and children were begging for pennies to go to the pictures, school or no school. In the end it was to be the cinema rather than the library that became the real enemy of the public house.

So, much had changed over fifty or sixty years. If there was poverty and hardship in Oldham, there was also a lot of fun and happiness, and except in brief periods, widespread lack of interest in political or trade union activity. Recreation, holidays, sport, music all played a part in creating that degree of contentment.

*Chapter X*

# OLDHAM POLITICS TO 1914

Radical Oldham; the reputation was established in 1832 and sustained thereafter by the small electorate of shopkeepers and property owners. It was confused in 1847 by the split in the Radical ranks over John Fielden's insistence on John Morgan Cobbett's candidacy. In William Fox, successful in 1847, Oldham's elite found an elderly but still inspirational Radical candidate but subsequent elections, occasions of drama, excitement, disturbance and riot, brought ups and downs in his fortunes. Cobbett, his key adversary, by the 1850s perceived as a Tory, retained a strong following in the constituency, beating Fox in 1852 and retaining an Oldham seat until 1865. Fox, for most of the period until his retirement in 1862, held the other local seat. Perhaps he was Oldham's last radical.

Significant then was the candidacy as a Liberal of John Hibbert, unsuccessfully in 1859, but unopposed to succeed Fox in 1862. Hibbert was the son of Elijah Hibbert, the prematurely deceased founder of Hibbert and Platt. With a comfortable inheritance, and a private education, he had turned his back on trade for the profession of law as a passport to politics. If in Oldham he with his family connection found a comparatively safe seat, he was indefatigable in cultivating it. In 1865 he was joined by John Platt, then pre-eminent in the town, and the two, both committed to laissez-faire, free trade and prudent finance, strong followers of Gladstone, won a comfortable Liberal victory over Cobbett and Spinks, a London barrister, running as Tories.

It was not until the election of 1868, when the electorate was massively widened, that the real political sentiments of the district were properly tested. The Reform Act of 1867, the outcome of prolonged national debate, gave the vote effectively to the working man; not, of course, to women, nor to sons or to lodgers, but any houseowner or tenant could now vote. Oldham's electorate increased about five-fold; more than one in two adult males could now vote compared with about one in eight before. An electorate of 3,000 had become one of over 12,000 in 1868. Elections, politics, became a new challenge. With the beginnings of a mass electorate the main parties had to organise themselves in a different way. They needed to identify and harness political loyalties and set up the means to get their supporters on the register and out to vote. Both the main parties in Oldham responded to this challenge in subsequent years but in 1868 this was barely perceived. A hard fought election produced the narrowest margin of victory for Hibbert and Platt, the latter being a mere six votes above Cobbett. With all the claims of intimidation, bribery, personation and the like, the result was challenged in the Courts, although unsuccessfully. Working class Oldham and the extended franchise, had returned familiar respected local Liberal candidates but with

**John Hibbert**, fought eleven elections and was Oldham's Liberal representative for twenty-four years, much respected in the House of Commons.

the narrowest of margins.

The marginal nature of this massively working class constituency continued for the next fifty years. There may have been a Liberal ascendancy at the Town Hall but that hardly mattered; it was in the Parliamentary elections that the wider Oldham district showed its true colours. Cobbett replaced John Platt at the by-election following the latter's death in 1872 and Cobbett and Spinks won in 1874 although by a narrow margin. There were comfortable Liberal margins in 1880 but the Conservatives were back in 1885 and 1887 and again in 1895. In the period between the 1868 Reform Act and 1914, Tories or Conservatives represented Oldham almost for as many years as Liberals.

The marginal character of the seat gave politics great excitement. It sharpened the need for political organisation to deliver the vote. That was the rationale of the political clubs, variously called Reform, Liberal, Union, Conservative, that proliferated throughout the district in the 1870s and 1880s. They may have had a strong social bias for much of the time but at elections, local and national, they were the base for sharp political activity, aggressive canvassing, and getting the support out on the day. Hugely attended political meetings were the rule, everywhere in the constituency during elections, reported almost verbatim in the press. Sitting members, aspiring candidates, had to work and work hard. Quite remarkable is the extent to which John Hibbert came to Oldham over the years when he represented or sought to represent the town, from 1859 to 1895. He continued to speak at endless meetings, political, religious, secular, wherever support might be mustered; he was member for twenty-four years of the thirty-six, fighting eleven elections. Nor did John Platt spare himself when he was the member. Cobbett, although he contested nine elections, was less assiduous; but nevertheless represented Oldham for eighteen years between 1852 and his death in 1877.

The political speeches these and others made, if not so long as those of Gladstone, were rarely less than forty-five or even sixty minutes, and usually a detailed exposition of the party view on the issues of the day. The issues themselves, at most Victorian elections, were not those that might be expected to be close to the concerns of a working class constituency; not, for instance addressed to the condition of the people, but rather to the lofty concerns of an Imperial Parliament. The Irish Church and the relations of church and state; Irish Land and later Irish Home Rule; Turkey and the Balkans; Egypt and South Africa took many columns in the Oldham press. The working man could vote, but he could not at the time vote on questions that most concerned him; the political agenda was still dictated by a different class and was to remain so at least until the twentieth century. But that did not result in apathy; however remote from day-to-day concerns the political issues, the electorate was anxious to vote and turnout, as in local elections, was consistently high, above 80 per cent.

If one asks why Oldham was so marginal, it is necessary to explain why so many of a predominantly working class electorate were willing to vote Conservative. Where did that vote come from? Perhaps that is not difficult to answer. Many of Oldham's large private employers, the Greaves, Lees and Wrigley, Collinges, Alfred Butterworth were staunchly Conservative and they

*Top:* **John Morgan Cobbett**, Radical and then Tory, always in the running to represent Oldham for over forty years, MP for eighteen years.

*Above:* **Frederick Spinks**, a London barrister, fought Oldham four times as a Tory and won once.

would influence their employees to vote in that direction, especially perhaps, before the secret ballot although their influence remained strong subsequently. Prominent families at the time, the Clarksfield Lees, the Cromptons, Cleggs, Cheethams of Crompton were also fiercely Conservative; the same was true of the town's principal professional men, people like John Blackburne the coal agent, Robert Ascroft the prominent solicitor, or the widely known and respected doctor, Thomas Fawsitt. All these people occupied conspicuous places on Conservative platforms at election times, just as they patronised the Primrose League which had a huge Oldham membership. The Tories claimed to be the true friends of the working man drawing credit from factory reform and the extension of the franchise. They could point to leading trade unionists like James Mawdsley, or to the local miners who were solid Tory voters at the time. The drink trade, and that meant publicans, did not hide their Tory allegiance, especially after the 1872 Licensing Act passed by a Liberal government. The heavy drinkers, that is generally the poor, probably followed the publicans, influenced, it was alleged, by the election breakfast or the election glass freely available in the pubs on the day, and became "Conservative working-class cannon fodder", as one historian described them. The poorest ward in Oldham, St Mary's, was the most marginal, although here many probably voted Tory because of hostility to the Irish. Finally there was the firm support of the Church of England clergy and Anglicans generally, hostile to Liberals on the issue of church schools particularly; in the out-townships like Lees and Crompton where the Tory vote was high the passionately Liberal *Chronicle*, in its disgust, spoke of "the ignorance, superstition and bigotry of working men, under the thumb of the church parson". So, with beer and the church and many leading families, Conservatives had a lot going for them in Oldham. Always in the background was the Queen and the Flag, stirring issues for much of the time, appealing to the masses first as Britons, full of patriotic pride in their country's greatness.

Against them was the Liberal allegiance, ably organised by William Wrigley; if he worked behind the scenes to identify, register and deliver the Liberal vote, those who succeeded as a result were profusely grateful. John Platt could describe Wrigley as his "political godfather". The Liberal vote came from shopkeepers, from Nonconformists, from co-operators and teetotallers, from respectable working men, and from deferential employees of those private manufacturing concerns that had a declared Liberal allegiance, the Platts, the Emmotts, Eli Lees, Buckley and Taylor, Bodden and many others. Some of the Oldham elite, notably Sam Platt, were to part from the Liberals on the issue of Irish Home Rule; on the other hand Gladstone's commitment to Home Rule attracted the Irish vote especially in 1892 and subsequently. Most of the party's support among the business community remained staunch, not least because throughout the period the great Liberal issue remained Free Trade. Oldham, for obvious reasons at the time, was a town of free traders, just as it was preoccupied with low rates and taxes, that is cheap government, the main issue for shopkeepers and small business men. Only in the years before 1914 was the free trade issue becoming confused within the local business community.

The voting at the 1868 election, and again in 1872, following the huge

*Below:* **Alfred Emmott**, third generation Oldhamer and large employer, Liberal, formidably upright, won five elections with comfortable majorities, before being made a peer.

*Bottom:* **Elliott Lees**, heir to one of Oldham's largest fortunes, had impeccable local roots and a strong Tory connection, which helped him to win election in 1886.

widening of the franchise, reveals an interesting pattern of political loyalties that was to persist for decades. There were large Liberal majorities in St Peter's, Westwood, Mumps, Werneth and Chadderton, the newer respectable working class areas under the influence of the large Liberal employers. St Mary's, probably the poorest ward, was evenly split, as was St James. Tories led in Waterhead and enjoyed large majorities in the semi-rural fringe, still less industrialised, that is Clarksfield, Lees (63 per cent), Royton (56 per cent) and especially Crompton (79 per cent). Some of these districts had been seen as true centres of Radicalism at the time of Peterloo; it was here that the name of Cobbett, by now an open Tory, still had some romance, and the influence of Tory parsons, venerable figures like Grundy of Hey, was most powerful.

Success partly depended on good candidates. Hibbert and Platt committed as they were to the Liberal cause, were seen as well known and highly respected local men, as was Alfred Emmott when he first stood in 1899. Emmott was third generation of a successful Oldham dynasty, large employers, well known for their philanthropy and religious involvement; he himself had been a young Mayor at the age of thirty-three, upright and sincere in manner and behaviour, proud of the town, fair minded, wise, and highly regarded; once elected he held the seat without difficulty. Apart from such prominent local men the Liberals ran national figures such as Lyulph Stanley between 1872 and 1885 when he lost on the Irish issue, antagonising the Irish vote by his opposition to Home Rule; Walter Runciman, a rising Liberal personality, also won in Oldham in 1899 losing to Churchill in the Khaki election the following year. All these candidates had the stature to give a lead to local opinion and to create the right sort of image for the town in the country as a whole. Hibbert, became highly respected across Lancashire and in Westminster as an agreeable man, helpful, moderate and conciliatory; he held office as a Treasury Minister and in 1888 was first Chairman of the Lancashire County Council. Emmott became Deputy Speaker of the Commons and, in 1911, a Peer.

Many among the Tory elite disliked Cobbett, possibly because he was a country gentleman of modest means, no more than an ageing populist waffler with a famous father. The Tory families were reluctant to entertain him in their homes on his visits to Oldham; he was quaint, appearing on platforms in "kneebreeches and a green shooting jacket". But Cobbett could exploit his name; he was a plague to the Liberals, a "red herring" as John Platt described him, agitated by his capacity to win elections. And the Tories generally lacked local candidates to match Hibbert, Platt or at a later time, Emmott. Thomas Evans Lees and his son, the Eton and Oxford educated and gentrified Elliott Lees, large Oldham employers though they were, had limited success. Robert Ascroft, local solicitor following his father, and respected adviser of the cotton trade unions during the turbulent 1880s and 1890s, was a popular and successful Tory candidate in 1895, running on a ticket of "Something for Oldham".

Following his sudden premature death, the Tories hastily formed what seemed an attractive partnership in 1899: the youthful Winston Churchill, "a child in swaddling clothes" according to the *Chronicle*, but nephew of the Duke of Marlborough, who could bring the Duke to Oldham, as he did to enhance his appeal as an energetic, eloquent, ambitious but immature young man; and James Mawdsley, General Secretary of the cotton spinners union, honest, intelligent, sound, the epitome of the Tory working man. The duo failed but Churchill, then a national hero following his escapades with the Boers, returned as a candidate in 1900 and, after a campaign of immense energy when he was making as many as eight different speeches a day, touring mills, attending rugby matches, won narrowly. Oldham clearly felt they had found someone special; the Liberal *Manchester Guardian* spoke of "a courageous, engaging and remarkably able young man". The *Chronicle* summed up the Borough's bumptious but immensely popular new member; "not troubled with excessive modesty" but "if you could take away one half of his qualities, you might make a useful public servant of the rest". Churchill, of course, crossed the floor in 1904 and became a Liberal. Ambition rather than principle probably guided him. The Oldham Tories did not press him to resign, but pleaded with him to reconsider; he replied, "I cannot afford to wait. My life is too short. I must anticipate, for I cannot afford to lose." So he left Oldham for another seat; his ambitious political judgement was right and at the next election in 1906 Oldham went Liberal by a large margin, as it was to remain until the Great War.

The closing years of the century, the 1880s and 1890s, were the period of the Tory working-man, evident in the Parliamentary elections but also in local elections when the Liberal ascendancy was eventually broken. The Liberals by the end of the century were divided in their attitudes. The old Liberals, typified by Alfred Emmott, wanted Oldham to be an efficient economic unit; they were still committed to free trade and laissez-faire rather than social reform, as the issues in national politics. There were others in the Liberal party more willing to collaborate with the small but growing labour movement and take up social issues such as old age pensions, insurance

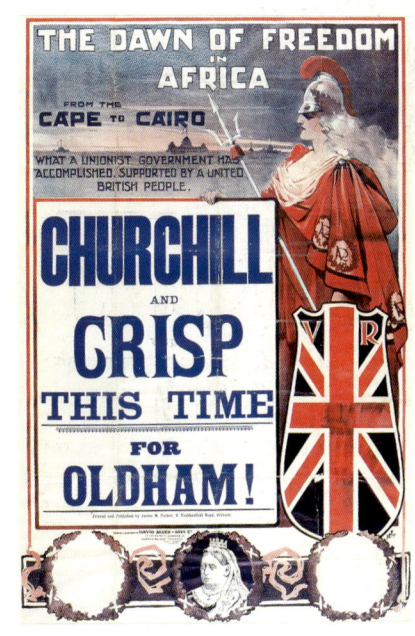

*Top:* **Young Winston**, elected to represent Oldham as a Tory on his second attempt in 1900.

*Above:* **Churchill and Crisp**, Tory election poster from the lively campaign of 1900 when Churchill was elected for one of Oldham's two seats.

*Left:* **Emmott and Runciman**, the Liberal candidates in 1900; Emmott was top-of-the-poll in the two-member constituency, but Runciman failed.

**Robert Ascroft Tory MP 1895-99**, who had fought hard for Oldham, memorialised in Alexandra Park, 1903. Thomas Ashton, the spinner's leader, unveiled the statue. Winston Churchill, still Conservative MP, is speaking.

against sickness, unemployment and slum housing.

The first stirrings of a separate movement to represent working men had become apparent by the 1890s. There had been Socialist speakers on Tommyfield for many years, generally ridiculed as "impractical and foolish" by the press; they belonged to the Social Democratic Federation which gave way to a local branch of the Independent Labour Party, formed in 1892. Meanwhile, the Oldham Trades Council was set up in an endeavour to bring together all working class organisations and represent issues of common concern. J. R. Clynes, second generation Irish, self-educated and rising from humble origins as a gravedigger's son and little piecer at the age of nine, became its active secretary. But Clynes and the council had only limited success. The cotton unions were reluctant to be drawn in; they believed in organising to negotiate from strength with their own particular employers rather than pursuing political action and gave only token support. Nonetheless the two main political parties, Liberal and Conservative, became concerned to retain their working class following. A Conservative Working Man's Association became active in Oldham; Mawdsley's candidacy in 1899 was clearly intended to engage working men, although he probably lost support because he was seen to be "running in harness with the aristocracy", that is Churchill.

As Labour began to move to political action the Liberals were quite willing to accept Thomas Ashton, the popular spinners' leader, as a Lib/Lab candidate in 1906, but responding to his members' wishes he withdrew. In local elections Labour began running candidates in a few wards from 1890 but progress was slow, much slower than in other towns. Two Labour candidates were elected to the School Board in 1898, but there was a big disappointment in 1897 and again in 1900 when J. R. Clynes, failed in Waterhead and then Clarksfield Ward. He had run with Liberal support but clearly many Liberals were not at the time prepared to support a working class candidate; equally many working men still distrusted the Labour movement.

Clynes was elected as Labour MP for North East Manchester in 1906. Attracting widespread publicity, Victor Grayson, standing as Labour and Socialist candidate, secured a dramatic victory in a Parliamentary by-election in the Colne Valley constituency in 1907; Saddleworth was part of the constituency, although generally, Delph apart, regarded as a Tory part. A branch of the Labour party was formed in Oldham in 1907, mainly to secure the election of representatives of working men, and in 1910 a Labour candidate, Samuel Frith, again running with Liberal support, was elected to Oldham Council. At the Parliamentary by-election in 1911, Labour for the first time ran its own independent candidate, William Robinson, a trade union official but not a local man; he was a poor third with 7,400 votes but split the anti-Tory vote. This decision, for Labour to become a separate party, was a portent of sweeping political change in the Borough in subsequent years. The old politics of paternalism, deference, ethnicity, pub, church and chapel, was to be replaced by a more class-based politics in which the working man found his own cause and representatives.

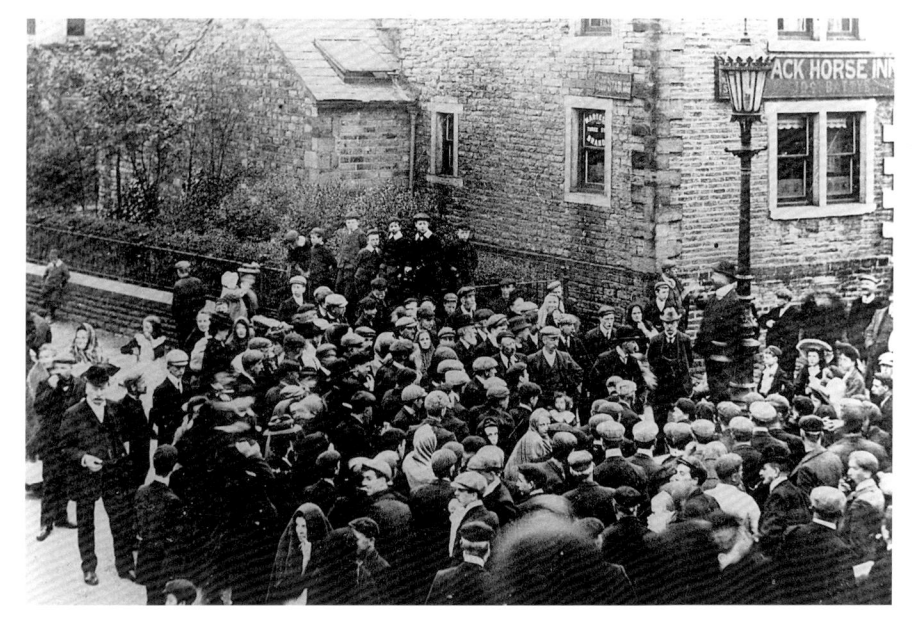

Another portent for the future was agitation for votes for women. Oldham was not in the forefront of the militant campaign of the Pankhurst Suffragettes, although the Waterhead mill-girl, Annie Kenney, became a prominent activist. But led by Sarah and Marjory Lees, the respectable ladies of Oldham joined the Suffragists, non-militant, but effective in drawing attention to their cause by a variety of activities, lectures and processions, not least in marching to London in 1913. Women in Oldham, as elsewhere, got the vote in 1918.

*Above:* **Samuel Frith**, a brass-founder, the first Labour councillor in Oldham and later the first Labour Mayor.

*Left:* The Upper Tame valley was in the West Yorkshire Colne Valley constituency, and participated in the famous by-election of 1907 when the flamboyant Victor Grayson, not hiding his socialist convictions, was the first Labour candidate to secure election against both Conservative and Liberal opposition. The photograph records an **election meeting in Delph** during that campaign.

*Facing, below:* **J. R. Clynes** born locally in 1869, a gravediggers son, became prominent in Oldham working class politics from 1891. He was elected Labour MP for Manchester North East in 1906, and subsequently was a leading member of the inter-war Labour Cabinets.

*Chapter XI*

# FORTUNES MADE IN 19TH CENTURY OLDHAM

Oldham, it was said many times, was a place preoccupied with making money. Certainly its extraordinary 19th Century growth created great wealth, wealth that to a great extent was shared by a large and prosperous working class and small middle class but also accrued to a few successful individuals, capitalists, entrepreneurs, successful men of business or whatever description fits them. Almost without exception at the first or second generation fortunes were self made; individuals rose to riches from humble even impoverished origins. Some of the rich, at the second or third generation acquired their wealth by inheritance. In all cases accumulation of wealth was facilitated by very low taxes on income and by negligible or token taxes on inheritance; at least until the end of the century wealth was passed from one generation to another more or less intact.

Any fortune above £50,000 was considerable, in current value not less than £3 million. Fortunes above £100,000 were regarded as huge by contemporaries; above £500,000 quite enormous. In the period to 1914 thirty-four Oldham men left over £100,000, twelve of them leaving more than £500,000. The total for Oldham half-millionaires was quite exceptional; no other town in Lancashire saw such an incidence of huge wealth, nor indeed did anywhere else in the country. Such large Oldham wealth came from capitalist ownership of successful businesses in the main activities of the town: coal and land; engineering and machine making, and of course from cotton spinning and weaving. In cotton the big money was made in the private firms. No large fortunes were made in the Limiteds apart from such exceptions as John Bunting; share ownership was diffused and for much of the period dividends were disappointing.

The rich of the town were not noted for their philanthropy, rather the reverse. The reputation Oldham had acquired by mid-century when it was seen as a town of small struggling masters, reluctant to part with their money, was maintained when huge fortunes emerged. Giving to churches, to public buildings, to hospitals, to model housing, was token compared with other northern towns. The Platts or the various Lees families or the Greaves, did nothing that could be compared with their contemporaries elsewhere; with Titus Salt, the Crossleys and Akroyds in Halifax, the Fieldens in Todmorden or, closer to home, the Ashtons of Hyde or Hugh Mason in Ashton. Oldham at the time was a mean and selfish place for whatever reason. If the rich did not give much of their money away, what did they do with it; how did their lifestyles evolve? And here there is another conclusion that people reached at the time: that Oldham was a place where people made money that was then spent elsewhere; that the wealthy of Oldham left the town, left it for the Lancashire or North Wales coast, or in some cases the hunting shires, for a place closer to the real aristocracy. It is appropriate to look at the facts.

Those who owned land in nineteenth century Oldham saw its value appreciate enormously, to the greatest extent near the centre of the town, but hugely wherever land was in demand for mills and housing. Equally, enterprise in securing coal working rights and running coal mining operations, although it had its ups and downs, was richly rewarded. Two families in particular had benefited from land ownership and coal, the Jones and the Lees of Clarksfield. On the Jones side, the third generation were prominent in the mid nineteenth century. William Jones (1802-1859) was the first Mayor of the newly incorporated Borough in 1849; he shared with his brother Joseph a rich inheritance which yielded a steady stream of ground rents, royalties as well as profits from colliery operations. William died young in 1859; Joseph left the town to live at Severn Stoke in Worcestershire when he was elbowed off the new Council in 1852. His wealth passed to his son, also Joseph, who lived in a grand style as a country gentleman leaving £500,000 when he died in 1880.

The Clarksfield Lees, with their extensive parkland property on the south side of Oldham, had married into the Jones and were similarly involved in coal operations and land ownership; a high proportion of Oldham's miners worked for the Lees, a fact that may account for their Tory leanings, for the Lees were perhaps the most stalwart of Oldham's Tory families. The three sons of James Lees (1759-1828) did not seek prominence in Oldham; they exercised their influence by stealth, by careful patronage, by involvement through their sons in the Volunteers, by maintaining good feeling and proper deference among their tenants and their employees. When Clarksfield was engulfed by the spread of Oldham, the third generation left the town for more congenial places. The family wealth, much of it in real property, was divided many times but in aggregate exceeded £500,000 and probably matched that of the Jones. The only one of the third generation to remain in the district, James Henry Lees-Milne, married into the leading Crompton family,

**Higher Clarksfield at mid-century**: the Clarksfield estate had been purchased by John Lees in 1625 and remained in the occupation of his descendants until the later nineteenth century. By then they had acquired great wealth through land ownership, active enterprise in Oldham's coal industry, and involvement in cotton spinning. The estate had dramatic views of the Tame and Medlock Valleys: in the 1850s its two mansions, Higher and Lower Clarksfield, were occupied by John and Joseph Lees respectively. The Clarksfield Lees resisted any encroachment on their estate for many years but were eventually defeated by the strong surge of urban development. They sold their land at good prices and went to live elsewhere.

*Bottom:* **John Platt, King of Oldham**, a portrait made when he joined his associate John Hibbert as one of the town's two Liberal MPs in 1865. The *Chronicle*, normally his strongest supporter, described him as "the mighty potentate of our own day ........ the cold iron image with its face of gold and carefully covered feet of clay".

*Below:* **John Platt's tomb** in Chadderton Cemetery.

managed their mills, adding to his inherited Lees wealth to leave £126,563 in 1908. To the *Chronicle* the staunchly Tory Clarksfield Lees were a baleful selfish influence, resisting progress in the town, opposing Oldham's waterworks schemes which encroached on their shooting estates in the Tame valley, "lest their birds and hares should be interfered with", contributing nothing in public work or in aid to schools, churches, or "any schemes for benevolent services". That was the judgement of the time.

Platts engineering enterprise, from the 1840s, dominated all else in Oldham. Here was one of the great businesses of nineteenth century England and recognised as such. The founders Henry Platt and Elijah Hibbert died young; their wealth is not recorded. John Hibbert (1824-1908) the son of Elijah, educated at Shrewsbury School and Cambridge, never joined the business, pursuing a career in law and politics, Oldham's MP, on and off, for many years and a junior minister in Liberal governments. His inherited wealth enabled him to maintain a comfortable lifestyle from a country home near Grange over Sands.

Henry Platt's sons, John and James, stayed in Oldham. By mid-century they were both living in grand style close to their Werneth operations. They found an escape by building the hideous Ashway Gap, a shooting lodge on Saddleworth Moor, and it was while shooting from there that James, already an Oldham MP, was accidentally killed in 1857. He left £140,000. John Platt went on to become Oldham's most renowned citizen, "the foremost man among us" as the *Chronicle* said. Apart from his leadership of a huge and growing business he committed himself heavily to the town's affairs as Councillor and Mayor, and as its representative in Parliament, right up to his premature death in 1872. His death was the occasion for a huge Oldham funeral, organised as a public event by the Council; with over fifty carriages and 3,000 people in procession, some 20,000 lined the streets with shops closed and blinds drawn throughout the town. Understandably, after John Platt's death, the town chose to honour his memory with a statue.

Whatever his achievements, his energy and public spirit and his sagacity, his ascendancy in Oldham was not unchallenged. The Tory faction was offended by the patronage he could bestow and his alleged influence over large numbers of voters, his employees and others. There was delight at his discomfiture when he won the first election after the widening of the franchise in 1868 by the most slender of margins, and one that could be challenged. Others were offended by the alleged assumption that he ruled Oldham, that the town was his, that he could do as he liked. Thus the Liberal *Chronicle* attacked John Platt vociferously in 1861 when Corporation staff turned a blind eye to defective drains at his Werneth Park mansion. "He stands distinct from the herd; he makes laws for others to obey but claims something of an immunity from strict observance of them" wrote the editor, describing him as "the mighty potentate of our own day who binds an iron girdle across the heart of the town." This was strong language indeed which John Platt would not enjoy reading, nor to be described as "the cold iron image with its face of gold and its carefully covered feet of clay." Whatever happened subsequently the *Chronicle* returned to its normal posture of deference to Liberal grandees and reserved its vituperation for the Tory families and their parliamentary candidates.

Insensitively, at the end of the Cotton Famine, John Platt challenged a rate assessment on the grounds that smoke from cotton factories at Hollinwood and elsewhere was reducing the amenities and value of his property at Werneth Park. In 1861 he and his wife, with seven children at home, had an indoor staff of fourteen including a butler and footman and three nurses; living in the grounds were two gardeners and a coachman, and their families, and two grooms. Although he and his family were head of the list of the subscribers to any Oldham charitable appeal, and the Lyceum was seen as a Platt building, his meagre philanthropy was not unnoticed and influenced many others with lesser wealth. Eventually John Platt was to leave £800,000. Most of this was represented by shares in the business; his property was not taken into account. He had used part of his wealth to acquire and develop a landed estate and its village at Llanfair Fechan in North Wales. Perhaps he was influenced by the dictum propounded by *The Economist* that the millionaire who sunk his fortune in land "would be a greater person in the eyes of more people". No doubt he and his family wanted to escape from the ugliness and grime of Oldham; no doubt also he enjoyed managing a country estate, although he was not given over to hunting, shooting and fishing; almost certainly he enjoyed recognition as High Sheriff of Caernarvonshire in 1863.

John Platt, who had married into the Radcliffes, at the time perhaps the leading family in cotton, had seven sons and six daughters. When he died in 1872, aged only fifty-four, his wealth went many ways, mostly out of Oldham. His place at the head of the business went to his second son, Sam, born in 1845, educated at Cheltenham College and in Germany, the only son who showed any close interest either in the business or the town. Four of the other sons became country squires far away from their birthplace. Sam and

**Oldham's capitalist elite** enjoyed marking the coming-of-age of the eldest son by public entertainment. The Clarksfield Lees had staged a large event in 1863; John Platt was determined to celebrate on an even grander scale when his son Henry became twenty-one on the 4th January 1864. In several sittings from 5 p.m. onwards, 8,000 workmen and their wives were entertained to tea, music and dancing at the New Hartford Works. The *Standard* said "scarcely anything has created so much excitement within the last twenty-five years". There were complaints about the catering which featured tea, bread and butter, currant bread and Eccles Cakes; cider, ginger ale or beer had to be paid for.

his family continued to live at Werneth Park in much the style of his father; in 1891 he and his wife, with two small children, were looked after by twelve indoor and six outdoor servants. Outgoing and gregarious, Sam was active and popular in the town; "popular not because of his wealth but in spite of it", as the *Chronicle* described him; "everybody's friend, wanting neither in brass nor common-sense". The natural leader of "all works of progress in the town", he was "the acknowledged head of Oldham society", dedicated especially to music and to sport, both of which he encouraged actively and generously. His lifestyle was reflected in his several yachts and he died, prematurely, on one of these, the "Norseman", in 1902. Leaving £648,642, he was the last of the Platts to live in Oldham.

The Platt business, of course, generated wealth for many others, particularly the senior managers who had been made Partners and then became large shareholders. Most notable was William Richardson. His life was given over to Platts; apart from his involvement with the Lyceum and the Infirmary, he played little part in the life of the town. But he stayed there all his life and died at his home at Werneth in 1892, leaving £580,429. Many other Platt worthies had a similar story, notably John Dodd who succeeded Sam as Chairman, and all left comfortable fortunes if not on the same scale, Dodd leaving £228,616 in 1912. There were other engineers in Oldham, but none made money like the Platts. Asa Lees, contemporary and rival, left £239,000 when he died in 1882, still living in Oldham. Samuel Buckley and William Bodden were other prominent citizens and Mayors, and heads of successful businesses; they left £94,616 and £86,124 respectively. Likewise the Dronsfield brothers of Atlas Mills, the carding machine specialists, all made comfortable fortunes which they took to North Wales.

Turning to cotton manufacturing, those heading the large established private concerns in the pre-Limited period, profiting no doubt from the boom of the 1850s and possibly, by speculation in the Cotton Famine, all left huge

**The Dronsfield family** built a successful engineering business, making large if not huge fortunes, living on Alexandra Road rather than in Werneth Park. The three brothers in the second generation became prominent in Oldham at the end of the century. Here is one of several family weddings, probably that of Samuel Dronsfield's daughter Clara in 1904.

fortunes; in several cases they created Oldham dynasties with notable personalities over several generations. There were the Greaves of Derker Mills. Hilton Greaves - "Owd Darby" as he was known - second generation, staunch Anglican and Tory, quite an eccentric character, who was often seen working as a labourer on building jobs, or in overalls in the mill, divided his time between his Oldham house and a country place in Cheshire; he left £666,311 in 1895, all to his family, none of whom then lived in Oldham. Then there were the Collinges of Commercial Mills and their relation, Edward Abbott Wright, who had control of the business in the high period. James Collinge, Mayor of the town in 1850-51, had left the town for pastoral Cheshire where he died in 1895 leaving £197,000; his son, although involved in the business never lived in Oldham. Wright made the money, leaving £676,238 in 1891; he chose to live at Frodsham in Cheshire but visited Oldham every week, looked in on the business and served on the magistrates bench.

Oldham's half-millionaires included two other Lees dynasties. The Greenbank Lees descended from John Lees of Mount Pleasant, a small cotton spinner at the start of the century. His son James developed the business at Greenbank on Glodwick Lane, and profited greatly from the Cotton Famine, leaving £500,000 when he died in 1871. Most of it went to his son Thomas Evans Lees who seems to have played little part in the firm, although active and respected in the town, as a Magistrate, in the Volunteers, in the Tory party where he ran unsuccessfully for Parliament in 1877, and in the Anglican community. He had moved to Woodfield, a large house in extensive grounds off Manchester Road where he died prematurely of a painful cancer in 1879. He had held onto his father's wealth leaving £600,000 to his son, Elliott Lees, educated at Eton and Christ Church and inculcated with different values to those prevalent in Oldham, which must have seemed to him a drab, dull place, lacking in society, deadening to the spirits. Elliot Lees was willing to trade on the family's standing in the town to meet his political aspirations, running successfully as a Tory in 1886. He lost the seat in 1892 and disappeared from the scene, became a Baronet, and lived as a country squire in Dorset, eventually leaving £516,107. Edward Wrigley who became the dominant partner in Lees and Wrigley when James Lees died in 1871 lived in Oldham until his death in 1900, leaving £139,717; clearly the Lees fortune was made in the Famine if not earlier.

Of the other families making great wealth in Oldham, that of Eli Lees was the only one to remain with the town. Eli, brother of Asa, became a highly successful cotton manufacturer at Hope Mills at Bottom of Moor. He could afford to become one of the first residents of Werneth Park where he maintained a large domestic establishment, cook, maids, coachmen, gardeners, twelve of them in 1861. He also had a house at Lancaster Gate in London. When he died in 1882 he left £856,982, mostly to his surviving son, Charles Edward Lees, who had been educated privately in Paris and Hanover. Charles Lees seemed rather refined for Oldham or the rough and tumble of a struggling strike-torn cotton industry. He is principally remembered for his fine and valuable gifts of water colours to the town's Art Gallery, and secondly, for his wife Sarah. He died within a few years of his father, leaving his widow, and two daughters, the eldest Marjory; in a complex will each

**Colonel Thomas Evans Lees**, heir of the Greenbank fortune and, after John Platt, perhaps Oldham's premier capitalist; he was leader of the Tory party in the 1860s and 1870s.

**Charles Edward Lees**.

*Right:* **Charles Lees, Sarah** and their children.

*Below:* The scroll presented to **Sarah Lees** when she was made a Freeman of the Borough in 1910.

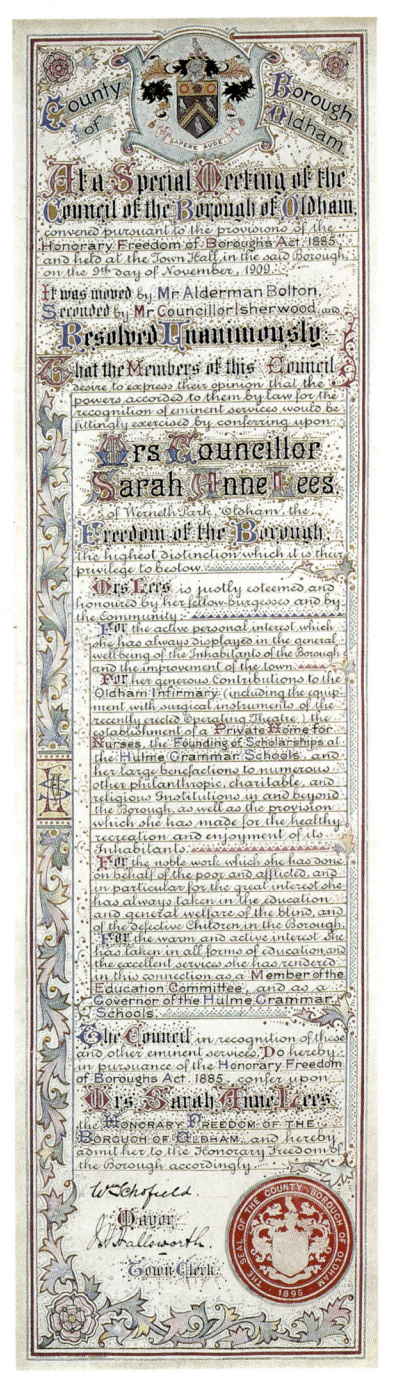

received the income on trust of a third of his huge fortune, £913,974. Of all the elite of Oldham, Sarah and Marjory Lees, not as rich as they seemed, were to be the most dedicated to the service of the town and most consistent and generous in their giving to good causes of all kinds. Sarah achieved distinction as the first woman Councillor, Mayor and Freeman in 1910; that distinction extended to her daughter who also became a Freeman. Sadly and controversially, although long to be remembered, Sarah appeared to take the side of one of two youths who murdered a shopkeeper in 1913; that youth was reprieved, the other, a Roman Catholic, executed. An outraged mob, half-drunken youths, ne'er-do-wells, wild young women, as the press reported, booed Sarah at the Town Hall and tried to assault her home at Werneth Park. Although there were few similar incidents, wealth, and its apparent power, was by then beginning to be resented in Oldham. The same was happening in other Lancashire towns.

There were many other lesser cotton fortunes, almost all associated with the more successful private businesses. At mid-century the Radcliffes, with Lowerhouse Mill and other businesses in Rochdale, seemed ascendant. Two of the brothers, Samuel (1814-1876) and Josiah (1816-1884) built houses in Werneth Park, close to John Platt, their sister having become his wife in 1842. They both left fortunes of about £200,000. Josiah, three times Oldham mayor, married Jane Walmsley, daughter of the wealthy Henry Walmsley of Firs Mill, Failsworth; in later life he went to live near Conway in North Wales. His son, Joshua Walmsley Radcliffe was a distinguished Oldham Mayor, also on three occasions, and High Sheriff of Lancashire in 1894; he died suddenly aged only fifty-two in 1895 leaving £197,537. His family then all left the town. Mention may be made of the Mellodews, ascendant at Moorside, where £51,720 passed to the next generation in 1883, and also the Emmotts. George Emmott came to Oldham to manage the Gas Works in the 1820s, acquired land very shrewdly, and went into cotton spinning successfully buying up several moribund concerns and reviving them. He left £161,757 to his son Thomas, prominent not only as a millowner but as a Quaker and earnest do-gooder in the town, supporting Temperance, the Oldham Mission, sectarian education and many other causes. In the third generation Alfred Emmott, Councillor and Mayor in 1891, developed huge Oldham loyalty as Liberal MP winning five elections between 1899 to 1911, before becoming Lord Emmott of Oldham. Thomas chose to live in comparative modesty on Park Road; Alfred, at least when he became MP, moved to the grandeur of Woodfield adjoining Werneth Park and a good address in Kensington.

Other well known private mill owners in late nineteenth century Oldham included James Stott of Queen's Road who left £254,489, and Thomas Hague who died in Southport leaving £142,920. Outside the Borough there was Alfred Butterworth, eccentric, deeply religious, independent and successful owner of Glebe Mills, Chadderton, pursuing local philanthropy on the one hand with generous aid to churches, medical missions, coffee shops and libraries for the poor, and pensions to his loyal long-serving employers, and on the other living the life of a country gentleman and Lord of the Manor at Hatherden in Hampshire. His will was for £281,000 when he died in 1913. Among the Crompton mill-owning families there were several comfortable fortunes. The Clegg family, noted for their paternal relationship with their workpeople, did well: Joseph Clegg (1817-1885) left a considerable £249,535 when he died. The prominent Joshua Milne Cheetham, Liberal MP from 1892 to 1895, head of the family business at Clough Mills, Shaw, and linked with the Cromptons at Park and Woodend Mills, left £84,441 in 1902; he was then living in his picturesque escape at Eyford Park, Bourton on the Water in the Gloucestershire Cotswolds.

In contrast to these lords of creation, Thomas Ashton, the trade unionist, living in unpretentious circumstances in Coldhurst, could leave £13,047, and William Marcroft, the co-operator £14,000. If these sums seem modest by comparison with the capitalist fortunes, they were surprisingly large amounts for the people concerned, of the order of £800,000 in today's money, and suggest successful share speculation. Ashton was not ashamed of that: "why shouldn't I put money where it'll find work for our own folks", he said in defending his purchase of shares. Jackson Brierley, the controversial Liberal Mayor who could not afford the usual hospitality in his term of office, left £1,937. Needless to say most Oldham people left little or nothing beyond their belongings; a few hundred pounds would be riches indeed, accumulated only by exceptional hard work and thrift, or good fortune in investment. Those who made large fortunes were a race apart.

The huge inequalities in the distribution of wealth in late Victorian Oldham were not seriously challenged at the time. The rich and successful, who were generally perceived to have risen by their own efforts, were an example to others, models to be admired and followed. The less well-off were too busy striving to get on themselves to have much time for envy. To the extent that the well-to-do left the town, the trappings of great wealth were not conspicuous to the mass of Oldham's working population. There is little evidence of envy or class feeling; acceptance of the values of a robust capitalist society were questioned only by the few Socialists who spoke to the

*Top:* **Thomas Emmott**, successful and large private employer, Quaker, Sabbatarian, Temperance reformer, strong supporter of the Oldham Mission and good causes generally.

*Above:* **Alfred Butterworth**, an eccentric but successful millowner, to some a tyrant but committed to good causes in Oldham. He supported the Oldham Mission and set up his own Medical Mission dispensing medicines to the poor. He failed in his attempts to establish "Coffee Palaces" in place of public houses.

small gatherings on Tommyfield. It was not until the Liberal government of 1906 that taxation began to make serious inroads in large incomes or inherited wealth; not until the 1920s that socialism became a threat. In the years between the wars the rich capitalists, so prominent in the nineteenth century, virtually disappeared from Oldham. Their sources of wealth dried up, their accumulated wealth was eroded by the fall in asset values, inflation and high taxation. The grand houses of the Werneth Park district were either demolished or became institutions, museums, study centres, nursing homes and the like. Society had changed permanently and the trappings of wealth, if they were to remain, assumed a different form and a lower profile.

## ANNEX TO CHAPTER XI:
## LEADING OLDHAM DYNASTIES AND THEIR WEALTH

|  | Estate (£) | Residence | History |
|---|---|---|---|
| **The Greenbank Lees** | | | |
| John Lees (1759-1828) | 20,000 | Mount Pleasant | Cotton spinner. |
| James Lees (1794-1871) | 500,000 | Greenbank, Oldham 11 Hyde Park Sq. London | Founder of Greenbank Mills Successful speculator in cotton & railway shares; Mayor 1852-54. |
| Thomas Evans Lees (1829-1879) | 600,000 | Woodfield, Oldham 11, Hyde Park Sq. London | Partner with cousin in Lees & Wrigley, Greenbank Mills. Staunch Anglican, Lt. Col. Oldham Volunteers, Tory candidate 1877. |
| Elliott Lees (1860-1908) | 516,107 | Queen Anne's Gate, London Country Estate in Dorset | Educated at Eton & Christ Church; staunch Anglican; Tory MP for Oldham 1886-92; First Baronet. |
| Edward Wright Wrigley (1823-1900) | 139,717 | Wellington Road, Oldham | Mother a Lees. Became partner & then sole owner, Lees & Wrigley. |
| **The Soho Lees** | | | |
| Samuel Lees (1773-1845) | N/A | Soho House, Oldham | Machine maker, Built Hope Chapel 1824. |
| Asa Lees (1816-1882) | 239,783 | Albert House, Ashton | Founded Asa Lees, machine makers. |
| Eli Lees (1815-1892) | 856,982 | Werneth Park 10, Lancaster Gate, London | Founded Eli Lees & Co, Bedford & Hope Mills, cotton manufacturer. |
| Charles Edward Lees (1839-1894) | 913,974 | Werneth Park 10, Lancaster Gate, London | Educated Paris & Hanover Chairman Eli Lees & Co. Art collector and patron; philanthropist. |
| Sarah Lees (1842-1935) | 24,492 | Werneth Park | Widow of C. E. Lees. Mayor 1910. Freeman of Oldham, philanthropist, pioneer in woman's work in public service; active with her daughter in woman's suffrage movement. Inherited the income of one-third her husband's estate. |
| Marjory Lees (1878-1970) | | Werneth Park, later Frederick Street | Inherited on trust one third her father's estate. Followed her mother as a philanthropist and public servant. |

## The Clarksfield Lees

| Name | | Location | Notes |
|---|---|---|---|
| James Lees (1759-1828) | N/A | Higher Clarksfield | Married daughter of Joseph Jones coal proprietor; coal proprietor and landowner. |
| John Lees (1814-1886) | 26,935 | Higher Clarksfield | Coal proprietor and landowner. |
| James Lees (1817-1871) | 30,000 | North Lancashire | Left Oldham for Alkrington, North Lancs. Children went to Eton and Oxford. |
| Joseph Lees (1819-1890) | 9,792 | Lower Clarksfield | Coal proprietor and landowner. |
| Edward Brown Lees (1843-1896) | 128,918 | Higher Clarksfield North Lancashire | Son of John Lees. Educated Eton & Exeter College, Oxford. Lt. Col. Oldham Volunteers. Left Oldham for Carnforth, North Lancs. |
| Joseph Crompton Lees (1844-1907) | 46,515 | Lower Clarksfield Leitrim, Ireland | Son of Joseph Lees. Lt. Col. Oldham Volunteers. Left Oldham for Ireland. |
| James Henry Lees-Milne (1847-1908) | 126,563 | Crompton | Second son of Joseph Lees. Eton and New College, Oxford. Married into a leading Crompton family. |
| John Edward Lees (1850-1916) | 73,021 | Alderley Edge | Also son of Joseph Lees. Left Oldham. |
| Frederick Lees (1856-1929) | 113,323 | Bakewell | Also son of Joseph Lees Left Oldham. |

## The Platts

| Name | | Location | Notes |
|---|---|---|---|
| Henry Platt (1793-1842) | N/A | Ferry Bank, Huddersfield Rd | Machine maker, Dobcross and Bottom of Moor. |
| James Platt (1824-1857) | 140,000 | Hartford House, Oldham Ashway Gap, Saddleworth | Partner, Platt Brothers, Liberal MP for Oldham 1857. |
| John Platt (1817-1872) | 800,000 | Werneth Park Llanfair Fechan, Carnarvonshire | Chairman, Platt Brothers Ltd, Mayor 1854-56, 1862, Liberal MP for Oldham 1865-72. |
| Samuel Radcliffe Platt (1845-1902) | 648,642 | Werneth Park Steam yacht "Norseman" | Chairman, Platt Brothers Ltd. Mayor 1887-89. High Sheriff of Lancashire 1897. |

## The Radcliffes

| Name | | Location | Notes |
|---|---|---|---|
| Samuel Radcliffe (1814-1870) | 200,000 | Werneth Park | Cotton manufacturer, Lower House Mills. |
| Josiah Radcliffe 1816-1884) | 195,976 | Werneth Park, Conway, North Wales | Cotton manufacturer, Mayor 1857-59, 1864. |
| Joshua Walmsley Radcliffe (1843-1895) | 197,537 | Werneth Park | Cotton manufacturer; married daughter of John Platt; Mayor 1885-87; High Sheriff of Lancashire 1894. |

## The Emmotts

| Name | | Location | Notes |
|---|---|---|---|
| George Emmott (1797-1890) | 161,751 | Queens Road, Oldham Disley, Cheshire | Born Keighley; Gas and Waterworks Manager until 1862 (salary £450). Successful speculator in Oldham land; cotton manufacturer. |
| Thomas Emmott (1823-1892) | 139,370 | Park Road, Oldham Poulton le Fylde | Prominent Quaker, Sabbatarian, cotton manufacturer. |
| Alfred Emmott (1858-1926) | 91,756 | Woodfield, Oldham Kensington, London | Educated at Quaker Schools, became Anglican, cotton manufacturer, Mayor 1892, Liberal MP 1899-1911, Lord Emmott, 1911. |

*Chapter XII*

# EPILOGUE: THE GREAT WAR

The pattern of life in Oldham, humdrum but prosperous and contented for many, bleak and impoverished for some, largely untouched by central government, was to change abruptly in the summer of 1914. The town, it may be supposed, was anticipating the annual Wakes when the events in Central Europe plunged the Continent into war at the beginning of August. Most took their planned holidays despite the new situation.

The Volunteers, now the Territorials, had to respond to the call to arms immediately: the 10th (Oldham) Battalion, Manchester Regiment marched from the town on the 5th August and were shipped to Egypt a month later; in Saddleworth, the 7th Duke of Wellington's spent more time in camp before moving to France in April 1915. For others, the mood of the time was one of optimism; a short war, an opportunity for escape from the confines of the age, for patriotic excitement. As everywhere, large numbers of young men volunteered in August and September; in Oldham they formed a second unit of the 10th Manchester's and then, as in many northern towns, a new army battalion, the 24th Manchester's or Oldham Pals; many also joined other regiments. The flow of volunteers continued for many months but it began to flag by the summer of 1915, despite many attempts by the Mayor, Lord Derby and others to sustain it. Hopes of a quick victory had evaporated; 1915 revealed the emerging horrors of the stalemate in France and, so far as Oldham was concerned, appalling casualties to the 10th Manchester's at the battle of Krithia in Gallipoli, on June 4th. As the army needed more men

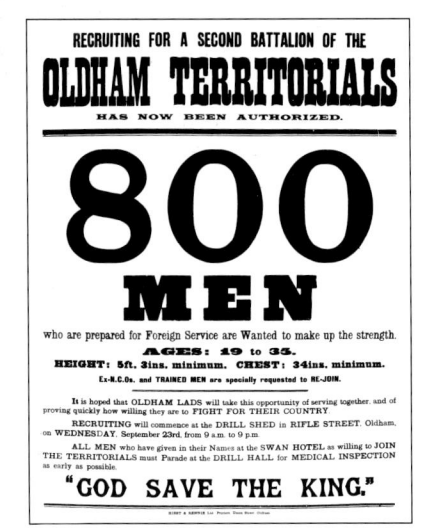

*Above:* **Recruitment**: the first recruits in August 1914 filled up the Territorials, now named the 10th Manchester's, to strength; by September a second battalion was being formed. Subsequent recruits joined the Oldham Pals, the 24th Manchesters, a service rather than fighting battalion. The height and weight requirements in 1914 were not too demanding; would-be volunteers were told that defective teeth were not a disqualification. The recruit received 1s a day plus food and lodging; his wife got 1s 1d a day and 2d for each child.

*Right:* **A platoon of the 10th Manchesters**, shortly to leave for Egypt and Gallipoli; they fought in the battle of Krithia in June 1915 with very heavy casualties.

which voluntary enlistment was not supplying, conscription was proposed, and after anxious debate was introduced in March 1916; up to that time 15,000 Oldham men had volunteered. Thereafter compulsion brought a reluctant response; week by week there were many who pleaded their case for exemption before the local Tribunal, as many as 1,600 through the end of the war. Family dependants, an aged farmer's son, a skilled occupation, conscientious objection: these were all the types of cases, fully reported in the press, that the local Tribunal had to weigh. Each year, of course, there were more eighteen year olds. Young men practically disappeared from the streets of Oldham.

If the men went to war, women had to replace them. With some reluctance the Corporation began to employ women as tram conductors in 1915. Women postmen were an early innovation. Oldham's engineering concerns found busy employment, making shells if nothing else, with large numbers of women on the shop floor. Female shorthand typists replaced the male clerk, a permanent change, with many more women in all kinds of office jobs in banks, local government and the like. The cotton mills had their periods of uncertainty and lost some markets, while raw cotton supplies were controlled; by 1916, however, the reduced mill capacity that was being worked enjoyed very busy conditions, profits increased and share prices rose strongly. In Saddleworth mills making flannel shirtings for the army enjoyed a phenomenal prosperity. In the mills youths and women took the place of the men who were in the forces.

**Platts at war**: older men and young women, making shells.

These changes were decisive for women's emancipation. Women became more independent and more enterprising; they had much more money of their own; dress and hair styles changed; they began to smoke and buy a round in the pub. In December 1917 a bill passed the House of Commons giving women the vote, although at a higher age than men; the bill which also extended the franchise to all men aged twenty-one, became law in June 1918. The Labour movement also became more respectable during the war; some of its leaders and emerging figures, men like Oldham's J. R. Clynes, served in Lloyd George's government in 1917 and 1918. The Liberal party, at least at the national level, split apart on the fall of Asquith and formation of Lloyd George's coalition

For most of 1915 the war had little effect on supplies of food or other goods. Life became harder in 1916, although Oldham Wakes were taken normally that year with going-off clubs yielding over £100,000. But prices were beginning to rise and, as scarcity and shortage developed, to rise steeply. By the end of 1916 some prices had doubled from pre-war levels; milk rose to 6d a quart from the 3d it had been as long as people could recall; canned food, bacon, cheese, staples in every household, had gone up sharply. In the end many prices were controlled for the duration of the war; bread prices were subsidised. Rents were controlled in 1915. Old age pensioners and others on fixed or fairly inflexible incomes, schoolteachers, or staff of the corporation, for example, felt the squeeze severely. At least until 1917 wages in engineering and cotton lagged behind the rise in prices. Youths of both sexes on the other hand saw a large increase in their earnings as they moved to jobs normally held by older young men or adults. The young people of Oldham now became a problem, especially at weekends, with strong complaints of rowdiness, violence, foul language and obscene songs.

War had other effects. Public house opening hours were substantially curtailed; the afternoon closure was introduced and evening closing time set at 10 pm, 9 pm on Sunday; alcohol consumption and drunkenness fell sharply. Oldham's Co-operative Societies, reluctant to pass on all the increases in prices of basic foods, tried to reduce their dividend from 3s to 2s; huge protest meetings cause them to retreat from that course. In the course of 1917, as submarine warfare took its toll, food was not merely more costly despite price control but scarce. Towards the end of the year there were food panics; disorderly riotous queuing followed and eventually a rudimentary rationing scheme was introduced. To ease the food situation, three soup kitchens were opened in Oldham in the spring of 1918. Meanwhile wages began to increase sharply; there were two increases totalling 25 per cent in cotton in 1917 and a further 25 per cent in June 1918. People began to save heavily before the war ended; the various War Loans raised over £3 million in the town.

The public mood in Oldham changed completely as the war progressed. Initial optimism and excitement in the autumn of 1914 gave way to

**Local Heroes**: the sad faces of Oldham youth killed in action became a feature of the local press from 1915 onwards.

Supplement to the OLDHAM CHRONICLE, February 19th, 1916.

**PRIVATE ABRAHAM BUCKLEY**, 1/7 West Riding Regiment, killed in action in France on December 20th, aged 24 years. Home address: 4, Ann-street, Waterhead.

**LANCE-CORPORAL HAROLD CONNOR**, 3/7 West Riding Regiment, killed in action in France about December 20th, aged 17 years. Home address: 28, Clegg-street, Springhead.

**PRIVATE GEORGE BURKE**, 1/7 West Riding Regiment, killed in action by a shell on December 20th, aged 29 years. Home address: Moorgate, Uppermill.

**PRIVATE JOSEPH MILTON WALTON**, C Company, 9th Battalion Duke of Wellington's (West Riding) Regiment, killed in action in Belgium on December 19th, aged 23 years. Home address: Oak View, Greenfield.

**PRIVATE EDWIN ROBINSON**, East Lancashire Regiment, died from wounds on Nov. 12 received whilst on service with the Mediterranean Force in the Near East, aged 22 years. Home address: 551, Lees-rd., Leesbrook, Oldham.

**PTE. JOHN WALTER WOOD**, 8th East Lancashire Regiment, killed by a shell in France on Jan. 14th, aged 34 years. Home address: 4 House, 7 Court, Mount Pleasant-street, Oldham.

**RIFLEMAN FRANK ROBINSON**, 1st Rifle Brigade, of 27, Cairns-street, Oldham, killed in action in France on November 23rd, aged 20 years.

## Epilogue: The Great War

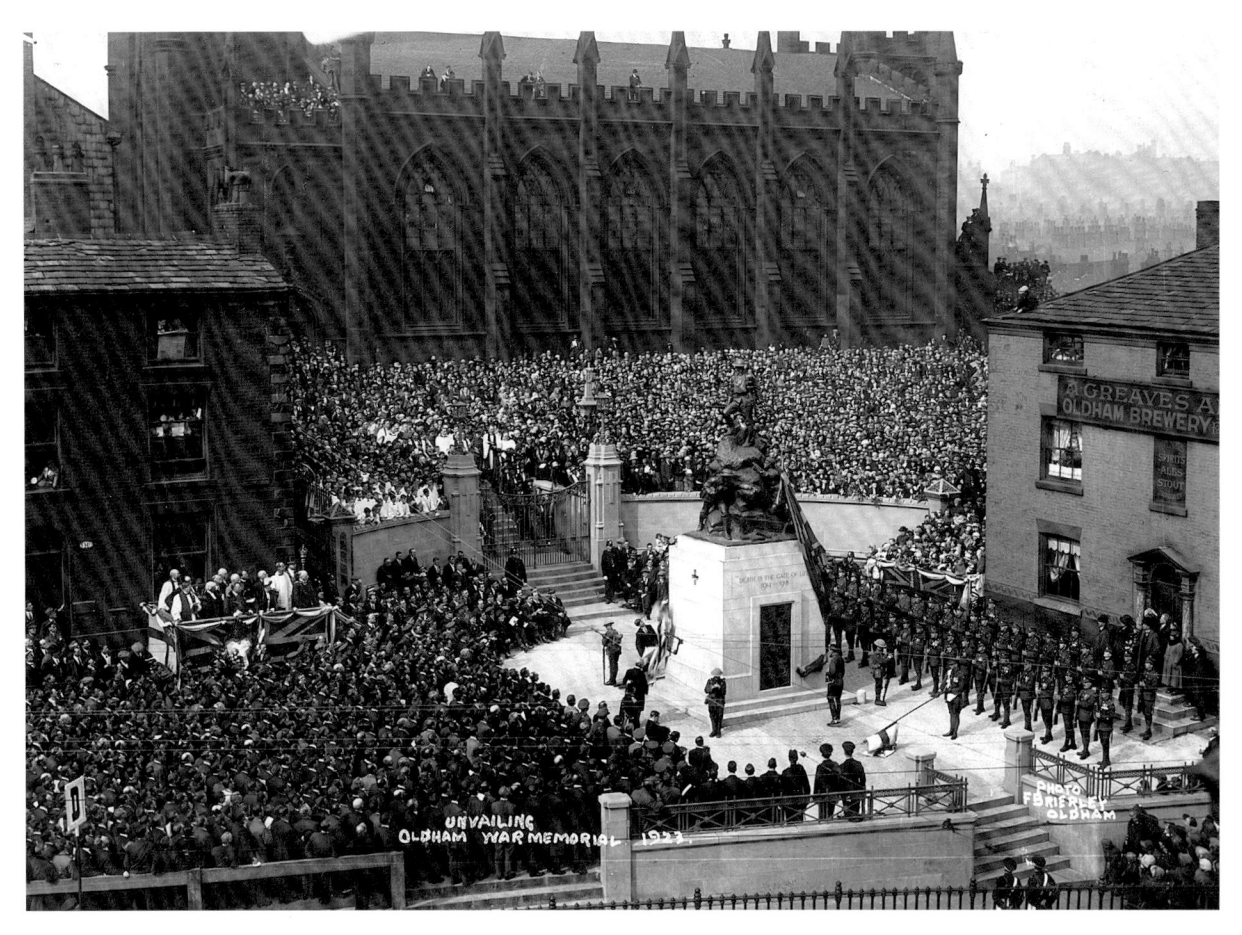

*The solemn, dignified and sad unveiling of **Oldham's War Memorial** in 1923. Oldham and district lost 5,000 men during the war, about 16 per cent of those who served.*

deepening apprehension throughout 1915. Heavy casualties in Gallipoli were followed by the slaughter of the Somme in 1916. The number of Oldham families who had lost one or more sons, or young wives and mothers who had lost a husband, multiplied. Grief, sorrow, distress and anxiety remained. 1917 and the first half of 1918 were the most difficult and depressing period of the war, in Oldham as elsewhere. Heavy casualties continued, life became shabbier and harder, there seemed no end in sight. In the end victory came swiftly, although it coincided with an alarming influenza epidemic. The feeling at the end of 1918 was one of enormous relief, "a triumph of life over death". When the war ended, of approximately 30,000 men throughout the district who had served, over 5,000 never returned; many more were injured and disabled; in Saddleworth and Crompton the fatalities approached 20 per cent. Nevertheless, despite the many empty chairs and the widowed homes, normality could resume. Whatever the mood of returning servicemen, Oldham's millowners, managers and shareholders looked forward to the opportunities to make money in markets that had been starved of goods and from which formidable competition had been removed. Shopkeepers, small business men generally, anticipated the return of business as usual. Trade unionists probably also saw advantage in the post-war situation. It was scarcely perceived that conditions had changed fundamentally; that late Victorian and Edwardian Oldham would never return; and that life in Oldham and Oldham politics would never be the same.

# Decline: 1919 - 1945

*Chapter XIII*

# OLDHAM BETWEEN THE WARS

The rejoicing of November 1918 did not last very long; the winter was severe and the influenza epidemic alarming. Pressures and concerns that had been suppressed or unresolved during wartime now surfaced.

**Post War Problems**

One was money. Prices had risen, wages to a lesser extent. Workers remained scarce, especially in a cotton industry anxious to restore capacity and production once controls were lifted, as they were immediately. The profit opportunity seemed enormous; profits per company had almost tripled in 1918 and the workforce was determined to secure its share in the form of higher wages and shorter hours. A nine-day strike in December 1918, settled by the intervention of Lloyd George, no less, resulted in a 30 per cent increase in wage rates lifting them to double what they had been before the war; prices had gone up by about 80 per cent.

As prices continued to rise and as activity strengthened throughout 1919 a further large wage increase followed in July, again after a three week strike. A new high level of militancy had taken hold among the cotton spinners; officials of the unions, it seemed, had lost control to local shop stewards, less responsible, far more aggressive. Oldham labour unrest mirrored that in the country as a whole, on the railways and in the mines, if not in industry generally as organised labour exploited its new-found power.

Others who had bargaining power were not going to be left behind. Farmers demanded 9d per quart for milk, three times the long-standing price; when the price control authority demurred, they ceased to deliver milk and increases were quickly allowed. In the course of 1919 the milk price went up to 11d in the winter months. Corporation staff were equally and successfully militant. Teachers in Oldham schools had been restrained and neglected accordingly; most had seen only modest increases since 1914. Many were still only being paid £2 per week. The result was an acute shortage of teachers and class sizes of sixty or more, even in one case eighty-eight. Profound discontent and anger and the threat of a strike finally moved the Council to offer very substantial increases. Old age pensioners barely held their own; the pension was doubled to 10s weekly in 1919.

Another issue was housing. There was long-standing overcrowding in the poorer districts aggravated by the clearance of high density streets and courts in the central area. Already before the war private investment in building houses at affordable rents for working people had virtually ceased. Rent control introduced during the war remained in force, and a steep rise in costs of repairs and new building costs brought the market to a standstill. Vacant older terrace houses were now selling at double pre-war values; in contrast,

**W. J. Tout**, Oldham's first Labour MP.

occupied houses were unsaleable. The chronic housing shortage throughout the district in 1919 saw long lists of unsatisfied would-be-tenants on every agent's books; houses to let, it was said, were "a vanished legend". Doubling up, living with parents, delaying marriage, was commonplace.

A third issue was the returning soldier. He needed work, but until cotton and engineering raised their level of activity this was not readily available. Young women doing men's jobs in the mills, as cop packers for instance, or piecers, were reluctant to return to the card room; youths as piecers, and in some cases minders, were even more difficult. In May 1919 the new Labour Exchange reported over 11,000 unemployed in the Oldham district, including 3,000 women. It was only in the summer that these numbers fell as cotton spinning and Oldham's engineering businesses lifted their activity sharply. By November many mills were advertising for labour, especially for the card room and for little piecers, but the union complained there were 600 minders back from the war who could not find places.

Then there was politics. Lloyd George seized on the war victory to call the "Coupon" election in December 1918; he talked of making "a fit country for heroes to live in". With women voting for the first time and a greatly enlarged electorate, Oldham, like many other places, dutifully voted the coupon returning a Conservative and a Coalition Liberal. The old Liberals, now following Asquith, were defeated together with William Robinson, again the Labour candidate, who ran with them. But the Labour vote in Oldham rose sharply. Early in 1919 Labour candidates began to be elected to the District Councils of Crompton and Royton. Labour had come to stay, and was resolved to replace Liberals as the alternative party of government; in July 1919 the local party advised the Liberals of its intention to field two Labour candidates at the next election. When that election came in 1922 Oldham was to gain its first Labour MP, W. J. Tout, helped by the split in the Liberal vote.

**Reflotation Boom**

Huge pay awards, a restless and militant workforce, and the problems of reinstating returning servicemen notwithstanding, the local cotton industry was full of optimism, raring to go. After all, the principal markets of the world had been starved of goods for years. And competition, at least from Continental Europe, had been removed. Another consideration which confirmed this confidence was the demand by the cotton trade unions for a shorter working week, for 48 hours in place of 55½, with a late start at 7.45 am replacing the unsociable 6 am, a vast improvement to the millworker's life. When this was introduced in July 1919, effective capacity was reduced by over 13 per cent.

These were the circumstances of the boom of 1919 and 1920. The strength of demand and world-wide inflation masked the huge increase in labour, fuel and other costs that was taking place. Mills could not fail to make huge profits. The *Chronicle* in January 1920 was apt; "no sooner did a man in this neighbourhood get his hands on a bale of cotton than he had his feet in a motor car". The workforce, in the circumstances, demanded a further increase in wages; they received bonuses early in 1920 and in May an advance of about 30 per cent, taking rates to three times what they had been before the war, well ahead of the increase in prices. Forgetting the tragedies of the war, life in Oldham seemed very good; the going-off clubs in the summer paid out £253,080, well above pre-war totals. Charabanc trips to the coast, uncomfortable as they must have been, were a regular event in 1920. Hope Chapel had a record anniversary with collections raising over £230.

High profits meant hugely inflated share prices, hugely increased values for existing mills. And such an increase in value seemed warranted by the huge increase in the cost of creating new mill capacity, building costs, land values, machinery costs, higher costs across the board; mills that before the war had cost £1 a spindle to build, would now cost at least £4. The stage was set for a huge reflotation and recapitalisation boom to realise for existing shareholders the enormously enhanced value of the cotton spinning mills they owned.

**The Oldham artist James Purdy** conveys the late afternoon townscape with hundreds of brightly lit mills among the darker houses, streets and hillsides.

Thus ensued perhaps the most sordid and tragic episode in the history of the Oldham Limiteds. Once the opportunity was perceived, throughout late 1919 and into 1920, in an intoxicated and euphoric atmosphere, enterprising, plausible and unscrupulous businessmen, assisted by loans from profit-seeking banks, began to bid for the shares of the many Limiteds, offering values far in excess of what the market had ever provided. An auction developed and prices were driven even higher, with bids as high as £5 per spindle. Not all the Limited companies succumbed but well over two-thirds in Oldham district sold out; many of the old private companies including Greaves of Derker, Collinges, Eli Lees at Hope Mill and Butterworths at Glebe were also sold at this time.

Once acquired, at an inflated value, a company was reflicted with new shares being offered at an even more inflated value, in most cases the nominal price being only partly paid. A gullible public, not merely local, fed with the promise of large dividends and aware of the continuing surge in share prices, scrambled to buy the new shares, usually at premiums, at least while the gambling fever lasted. Huge profits could be made by the promoters involved, not least from the difference in value between the shares acquired and the new shares offered in the refloated company. There were all kinds of sharp practices yielding many other pickings for the insiders along the way. So active was dealing in shares that a second share market developed, the Oldham and District Stock Exchange with eighty members. It met daily in a basement at the Lyceum while the older Lancashire Sharebrokers met in a main room. Many of those involved, warned the *Chronicle*, were "not of the highest probity".

This was the time when London papers printed the myth about the millionaires of Shaw. Certainly there were a lot of mill shareholders in Shaw, tradesmen, mill managers and clerks, better paid minders and overlookers, and they were now a great deal richer. But some of the leading promoters in the reflotation boom were well known, colourful and popular Shaw men, notably Harry Dixon and William (Billy) Hopwood, self-made, bluff, outspoken, shrewd, a typical Lancashire business man, who had worked his way up from little piecer to join several Limited boards. Of Hopwood, who had been Chairman of Crompton District Council and conspicuously generous in his local philanthropy, it was said "he loved every stone in Shaw". Both these men, successful, well known and respected, commanded a large following. On paper they were both millionaires; Hopwood was involved with at least thirty Limiteds, Dixon with over twenty. The *Chronicle* was uncomfortable about such men who had "succumbed to the temptation their power and position afforded them". But many in Shaw and throughout the district, followed their example, selling their old shares, buying new shares which were usually only partly paid, and all too frequently borrowing money, even mortgaging their homes, so as not to miss out on the new Eldorado. Wiser men in the industry, John Bunting or J. B. Tattersall, who warned the public of the huge risks they were assuming, were dismissed as "old fogies". The emerging threat of Japan was described by Hopwood as "mere piffle".

The reflotation boom ended in tears. The supposed market conditions that would benefit Oldham were short lived. Immediate post-war shortages were quickly met. In the course of 1920 markets became more difficult, demand slackened, profits shrank, share prices began to fall. Trade collapsed in 1921. Slowly it began to be realised that this was not merely a return to the ups and downs that Oldham had always known but a new situation. The world market had changed; Lancashire, with its huge inflation, had become high cost. Large traditional markets like India and China, many of their mills fitted with Platt's machinery, were beginning to supply themselves; Japan, enjoying cheap labour and also the benefits of Lancashire made machinery and mill practice, was emerging as a formidable low cost competitor, having doubled its capacity since before the war.

So began Lancashire's agony. There were to be huge consequences for those who owned the industry, the mills or the Limiteds; for those who worked in them and depended on them for their livelihood; and for those who serviced the industry with its capital equipment or supplied its requirements. For Lancashire read Oldham; the decline of cotton, meant the decline of Oldham. People in the town were bewildered after all they had been told. Speaking for many, the long-serving Alderman Simister could say:

> "We speak of cotton spinning, we live by it, we live with it, we support it with our money and yet we know nothing of it. Seeing the mills is all we get."

Oldham did not mind seeing the mills when ablaze with light morning and evening, their chimneys belching black smoke; what the town did not like were silent mills.

**Cotton in Decline**

The extent of Lancashire's - and Oldham's - decline can be measured by raw cotton consumption. In the five years up to and including 1914 this had averaged close to 2,000 million lbs. In 1920, after the wartime decline, there was a recovery to 1,726 million lbs; in 1921 consumption fell to 1,066 million lbs; for the rest of the 1920s it averaged less than 1,500 million lbs.

1921 saw unemployment rise, and extensive short time working. The employer's main response was to force down wages, massively in July 1921 (following a lock-out) and with three further reductions to November 1922; rates were then at 90 per cent above pre-war levels. Prices were also falling, but allowing for the incidence of short time, cotton mill workers were significantly poorer than during their short-lived prosperity. On-and-off throughout the Twenties this remained the situation, with earnings savagely depleted by short time; in 1922 and 1923, for instance most Oldham mills worked no more than three or four days a week. Where mills closed, permanently or temporarily, their operatives became unemployed. There was one difference in the post-war situation; whether on short time or unemployed, the insured worker could sign on and draw a modest dole. But conditions were so bad in late 1922 that the Mayor made an appeal for the relief of acute distress, raising £2,667 and promises of sixty-five tons of coal; there were similar distress funds in Crompton and Lees. Attempts were made in 1922 to carry out public works to provide employment, building new sewers and improving the park, but these ceased when government funds were exhausted. A new road through the meadowlands of Chadderton, Broadway, was started in 1922, partly at least to provide work for some 600 unemployed men.

The strongly individualist Oldham spinning industry, with large numbers of competing firms, each with separate managements, all producing much the same kind of yarn, was slow to understand the changed situation, its causes or its permanence. It was divided in its response. Price cutting, weak selling from too much capacity, plagued the industry. Attempts to agree minimum prices or co-ordinate short time working had limited and short-lived success. Mill profits disappeared, and many companies traded at a loss financed by bank borrowings; share prices collapsed accordingly. Here and there, individual enterprises withstood the trend, notably Shiloh Mills in Royton, the group led by Tommy Gartside, which had avoided loan or bank debt and concealed its reserves. He had the confidence in 1926 to finance and build the large Elk Mill, 105,000 spindles, in a prominent roadside situation; his comparative success throughout the recession was partly the result of moving away from the oversupplied coarse yarn market and specialising in soft yarns, mainly for the hosiery trade.

There were short-lived rallies and brief periods of optimism in the industry, in late 1924 and 1925 for instance. But the situation of over-capacity had its inexorable results. Especially the refloted companies, with large bank debt and huge fixed charges, exhausted their paid share capital to meet trading losses, pay interest on their loans or to their bankers. Inevitably they had to make calls on their unpaid share capital. New calls on shareholders reached £1 million in 1923, £2 million in 1924, nearly £5 million in 1926; in the whole decade of the Twenties in the Oldham district it was estimated that close to £25 million was eventually called up to meet losses; how much was paid is not known, but probably more than three-quarters.

So the bitter desperate agony began of those who had purchased, inherited or held on to shares in the failing refloted companies. Their shares were worthless and unsaleable; they were faced with inescapable calls for money to provide unpaid capital; where shares could be sold it was often at a negative price, that is the buyer had to be paid to take them and assume the risk of

**As refloted cotton spinning companies**, burdened with bank debt, fell into financial difficulties calls were made on the partly paid shares that in 1920 had sold at a handsome premium. The shares became worthless and their unfortunate owners struggled to meet their calls; many, who could not do so, pleaded bankruptcy.

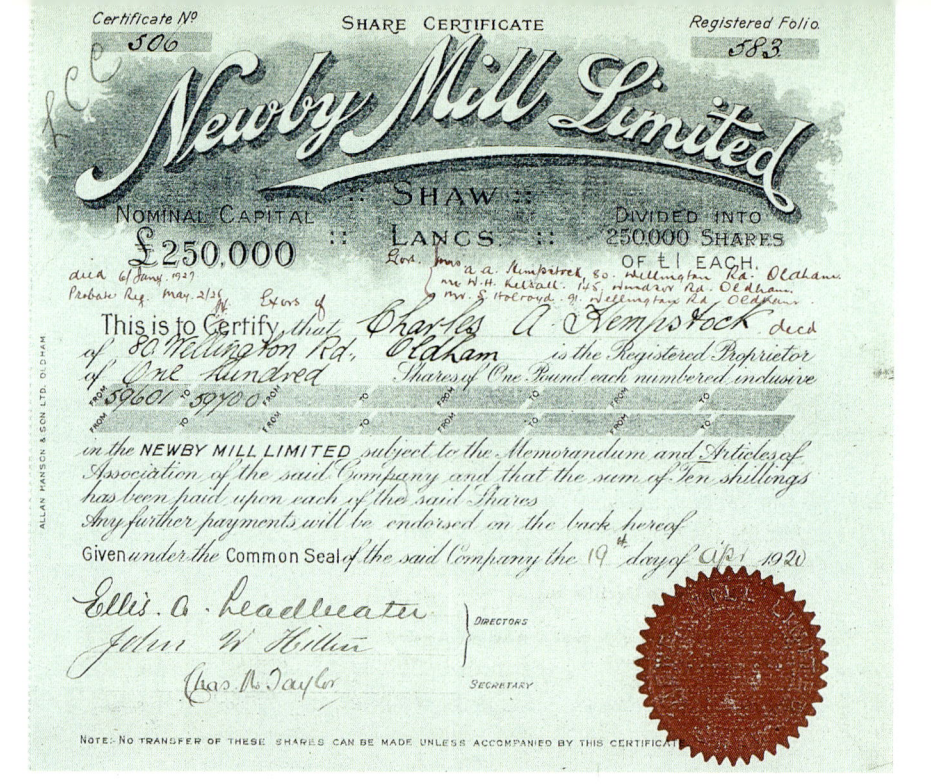

further calls. Mortgaging the mills, where it was possible, was the only alternative source of funds to struggling mill managements. Then there was the status of all the loan capital; after 1926 much of it ceased to receive interest nor could it be withdrawn; effectively, it was lost. This was the travail of Oldham, with many ruined and thousands in hardship as they lost their savings, struggled to meet new demands and adjust to new circumstances.

Some of those erstwhile heroes, who had made their fortunes and misled thousands in the post-war boom, were caught in the trap of their own misjudgement, their "greed and swollen heads". The outspoken Billy Hopwood, knighted in 1921 by Lloyd George, was ruined by the collapse in value of his shares and his inability to meet the guarantees which he had given to support the bank debt of some of the companies he had refloted; Shaw gave him no honours at his funeral in 1936. Other "millionaires" reduced to bankruptcy or comparative poverty included Harry Dixon and Samuel Firth Mellor. Mellor, an Oldham stockbroker, had been involved in twenty-four refloted companies; apart from his wealth on paper, in the reflotation period he enjoyed an income of £4,000 a year; in 1938 when he died at Prestatyn it was claimed that as an undischarged bankrupt he still owed, mainly in unpaid calls and bank debt, £400,000. Dixon lived until 1947; he had been vigorous in remonstrating against the market as it brought down the value of refloted company shares; when bankrupt in 1931 his debts arising from unpaid share calls were £284,000. John Bunting's son, who died in 1929, seems to have lost his father's fortune. There were a fortunate few who had sold out in the boom and taken their money out of the industry and out of Oldham, but for most, boom wealth had melted like snow. Elisha Bardsley, Mayor in 1932, himself a big loser in the cotton collapse, was to say that Oldham was "financially smashed and pulverised".

So far as the problems of the industry were concerned, short time working was only a temporary expedient to cope with unwanted capacity. Some took the view that the only answer was to reduce costs materially, by lowering wages and working longer hours, the better to compete with Japan and others and win back markets. This was entirely unacceptable, and not merely to the trade unions. But if loss of markets was to be regarded as permanent, then Lancashire and Oldham needed fewer mills, and fewer mill workers. Although mills were closing and more and more Limiteds and private companies were going into liquidation, market processes were a slow and painful means to achieve such a contraction.

The Bank of England now became involved because Lancashire's banks were deeply committed to loss-making mills with virtually worthless assets. Maynard Keynes, close to the Bank and the Treasury, began to offer his opinion on the way forward, outspokenly critical of the suicidal behaviour of the many competing enterprises and calling for co-ordinated mill closures; he attracted savage attacks as an academic outsider. After much debate and many reports, plans evolved for a large scale merger of mills, eliminating separate independent managements, and reducing capacity by closing older mills and concentrating production on the most efficient. This led to the formation in 1929 of the Lancashire Cotton Corporation, amalgamating many hitherto independent companies, and some years later in the Thirties to the Cotton Spindles Board, using the proceeds of a levy to buy up and scrap idle capacity.

**The Great Depression**

Meanwhile, in 1930 and 1931, world-wide depression compounded Lancashire's competitive decline. Cotton consumption in the latter year fell to 985 million lbs, half its pre-war total. It recovered subsequently but averaged only 1,100 million lbs in the Thirties. Company failures and mill closures rose sharply and the numbers unemployed now soared. In June 1929 there were about 14 per cent of the insured population wholly or temporarily unemployed in the Oldham district, defined as the Borough, Failsworth, Chadderton, Crompton, Royton and Lees. A year later the total had risen to over 34 per cent of the insured, about 34,000 people; it reached the worst point in the winter of 1931-1932 when for brief periods as many as 50,000 or about 50 per cent of those insured in Oldham district were out of work. A high proportion of those unemployed at any one time, between half and two-thirds, were "temporarily stopped", that is their mill was on short time or shut down but not closed permanently; there was a little more hope in this situation although the immediate effects were the same. The plight of the long term unemployed was far more severe, especially that of older men, and minders who refused to accept work as piecers.

As 1932 dragged on there was slight improvement; by June 1933 the unemployed percentage was down to 27 per cent, continuing to fall slowly as the cotton trade picked up modestly, to 12 per cent in 1937. 1938 was a bad year with a sharp increase but thereafter the approach of war changed the situation dramatically. Saddleworth did not escape the slump if, in a less industrialised community, its impact may have been less severe; local unemployment rates seem to have been less than half those in Oldham, nonetheless affecting 1,500 people in the worst period of 1932.

For those in work, the acute position in the cotton industry brought further sharp wage reductions in September 1929 and again in November 1932; at the latter date wage rates (but not earnings) were about 60 per cent higher then they had been in 1913-14. Lower prices were a partial compensation; the inflation of the immediate post-war period was out of the system, prices were falling although the cost of living was still 25 per cent higher then it had been in 1913-1914. When the clouds began to lift in 1936 wage rates were raised modestly; they rose again in 1939 and 1940.

By 1939 about 40 per cent of Oldham's Limiteds had gone into liquidation. When mills closed, they usually closed for good; removal of their machinery and demolition followed. That happened to about eighty mills. Other mills, about fifty, ceased cotton manufacturing but found other uses, making handbags, bedding and clothing, for example, or as warehouses. Of the district's 320 or so mills before the Great War, fewer than 200 remained in cotton in 1939, many not in production. The number of spindles in the district had peaked in 1927 with the opening of Elk Mill. From close to eighteen million spindles in 1928, the district was reduced to below ten million spindles by 1939, a decline of 45 per cent. Even when cotton spinning began to revive in 1936 and subsequently, it became clear that confidence was lost. Whether because of working conditions, the drudgery of much of the work, its limited prospects or distrust of recovery, young people were reluctant to join the industry. They wanted something better.

Oldham's other staple industries shared cotton's experience. Coal mining continued at the Oak Colliery in Hollinwood, but elsewhere in the district had virtually ceased. Textile engineering enjoyed a brief boom in 1920 and the next two years, supplying machines to Japan, India and elsewhere, if not to Lancashire, and making huge inflated profits, especially at Asa Lees. Overseas demand declined in 1924 while, with the problems of the Lancashire industry, home demand was fragmentary. Profits fell away sharply in the late Twenties but the real collapse took place in 1930 and subsequently. Platts retrenched and economised; abandoning their policy of self-sufficiency, they ceased to mine coal and closed their huge forge and began to buy their

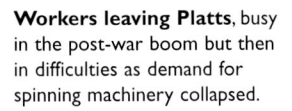

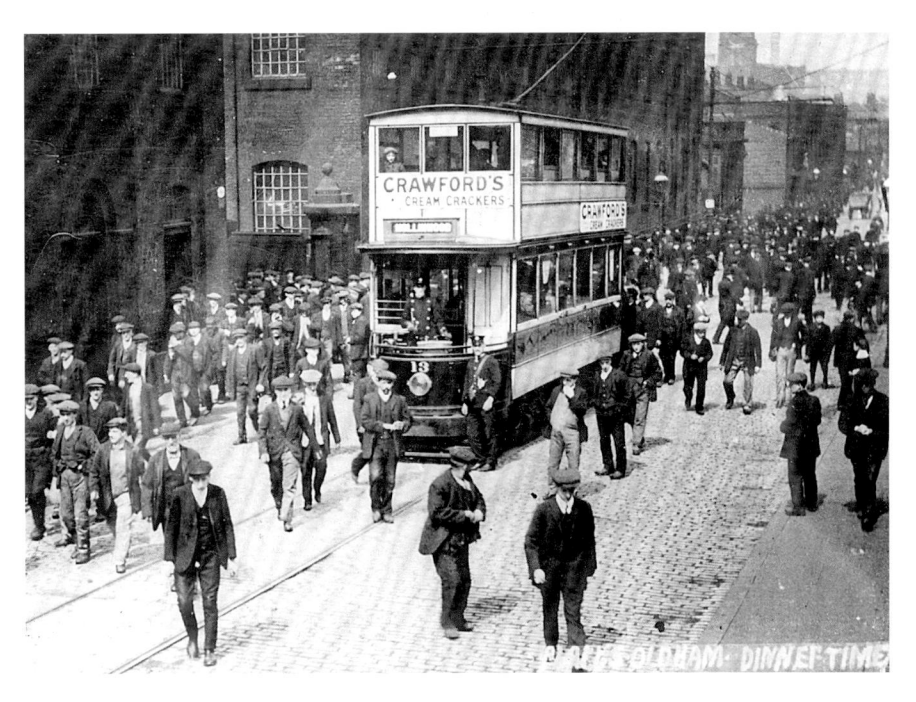

**Workers leaving Platts**, busy in the post-war boom but then in difficulties as demand for spinning machinery collapsed.

**Ferranti**, in Hollinwood, supplied a rapidly growing market in the years between the wars, making equipment for electricity generation and its use in factories, offices and the home.

steel. Many in the industry felt that the firm had lost its edge in quality and innovation. To overcome intense loss-making competition and rationalise the industry's capacity, they joined with other independent Lancashire firms including Asa Lees, to form Textile Machinery Makers Ltd. in 1931. By 1935 modest profits were restored; after 1938 the demands for munitions in face of approaching war changed the situation again. If Platts and Asa Lees survived the depression, the same could not be said of the multitude of Oldham engineers and metal working businesses, many of whom disappeared; others, like Dronsfields and Boddens, less reliant on capital spending, limped through the 1930s.

The decline in cotton spinning and textile engineering showed itself in a large absolute decline in the numbers employed in those industries, by as many as 20,000 in cotton, 5,000 in engineering in the period to 1939. To some extent the decline in Oldham's traditional engineering activities was offset by the rapid growth in the Ferranti business. The firm was already employing some hundreds of people before the World War when it went over to shells and other munitions. Thereafter it quickly developed its reputation around heavy transformers and electric meters but led by innovation, broadened its product range considerably, not always successfully, into various types of instrumentation, domestic appliances and radio. When Sebastian de Ferranti died in 1930 the Hollinwood works was reported as employing about 4,000, a total which it maintained in the Thirties. Another sizeable expansion in employment in the inter war period was in retailing, local and public administration and other services. More people travelled out of the district to work. Attracting new industry was difficult; there were few sites in the town and most of the empty mills did not lend themselves to conversion.

TABLE: XIX: OLDHAM DISTRICT POPULATION: 1911-1939

|            | 1911    | 1921    | 1931    | 1939    |
|------------|---------|---------|---------|---------|
| Oldham     | 147,483 | 144,983 | 140,314 | 124,400 |
| Chadderton | 28,299  | 28,721  | 27,450  | 30,830  |
| Royton     | 17,069  | 17,194  | 16,689  | 15,380  |
| Crompton   | 14,750  | 14,917  | 14,764  | 13,140  |
| Failsworth | 15,998  | 16,973  | 15,726  | 17,720  |
| Lees       | 4,918   | 4,789   | 4,738   | 4,290   |
| Total      | 228,517 | 227,577 | 219,681 | 205,760 |
| Saddleworth| 17,654  | 17,525  | 17,408  | 16,900  |

*Note:* Boundary change raised the population of Lees from 3,650 to 4,918 in 1911.

Meanwhile, throughout the district, an ageing population was barely replacing itself, while as local opportunity shrank many moved away permanently to seek work elsewhere. The trends of population of over one hundred years were now sharply reversed. Oldham Borough, Crompton, Royton and Lees lost over 10 per cent of their population by outwards migration in the Thirties. Chadderton and Failsworth alone showed a new trend; with plenty of building land, made accessible by the new Broadway, private housing development was attracting commuters from nearby Manchester and from Oldham itself.

**Fit Homes for Heroes**

The war aggravated a growing housing shortage. Private enterprise was no longer willing to build houses to let. Meanwhile with longer life spans and smaller families there were many more households looking for accommodation. Expectations of fit homes for heroes had to be fulfilled. The total requirement for new homes was conservatively estimated in 1919 at 2,000 houses in the Borough, including provision for conversion of the 2,600 old back-to-backs; some hundreds of houses were also needed in the Districts. Subsidy to the private builder or subsidised local government provision seemed the only solution.

The problem was a national one, not peculiar to Oldham. Lloyd George's Coalition government moved quickly; the 1919 Housing Act required local authorities to assess their housing needs and themselves provide houses where the existing stock was inadequate. Local rates could be used to augment generous government subsidies; this was to be a crusade for more houses, an insurance, some said against revolution. Oldham Council was quick to prepare its own schemes, initially for 500 houses and then for a further 1,000, acquiring sites, expensively, at Hollins and Greenacres. What was accomplished fell far short of these ambitious plans, partly because of the soaring costs of subsidy. The first Council estate of 300 houses was completed at Hollins in 1922, with a further fifty houses at Greenacres in 1925. The houses on the Hollins estate were built by private contractors to the so-called Tudor-Walter's standard, a density of twelve to the acre, having front room, kitchen and scullery with gas boiler and gas cooker, electric light, indoor WC and bathroom, and three good bedrooms. The estate had "lots of green, trees and grass verges" as well as private gardens front and rear. These houses were

## Fit Homes for Heroes

much sought after, giving rise to acute controversy over the allocation of tenancies, with priority being given to ex-soldiers, and to Council employees amidst allegations that "to get a house it helped to know a councillor". Nonetheless the rents - 15s weekly - were far too high for most people; the houses had cost on average over £1,000 each.

Further Council estates were built under the provisions of subsequent legislation, notably the Labour Government's Act of 1924, which again provided for subsidies from the Exchequer and the rates. The largest was the Limeside estate with 500 houses completed in 1930, albeit to a lower standard, with an average cost about £400 and rents about 10s weekly. Another initiative was clearance of some of Oldham's most squalid area around West Street, the so-called Smethurst Street scheme, the site of to-day's Civic Centre; most of the 1,400 or so persons displaced were re-housed with a further 100 houses at Greenacres and 202 houses at Barrowshaw in the period 1927-1931. These again were cheaper smaller houses, with outdoor

**The centre of Oldham, as it was in the 1880s.** Little had changed by the 1920s; crowded courts at Lords Hill and around Grosvenor Street are conspicuous. Oldham's first slum clearance scheme demolished the decayed Smethurst Street area adjacent to West Street. The area had been regarded for years as the place to build a new town hall.

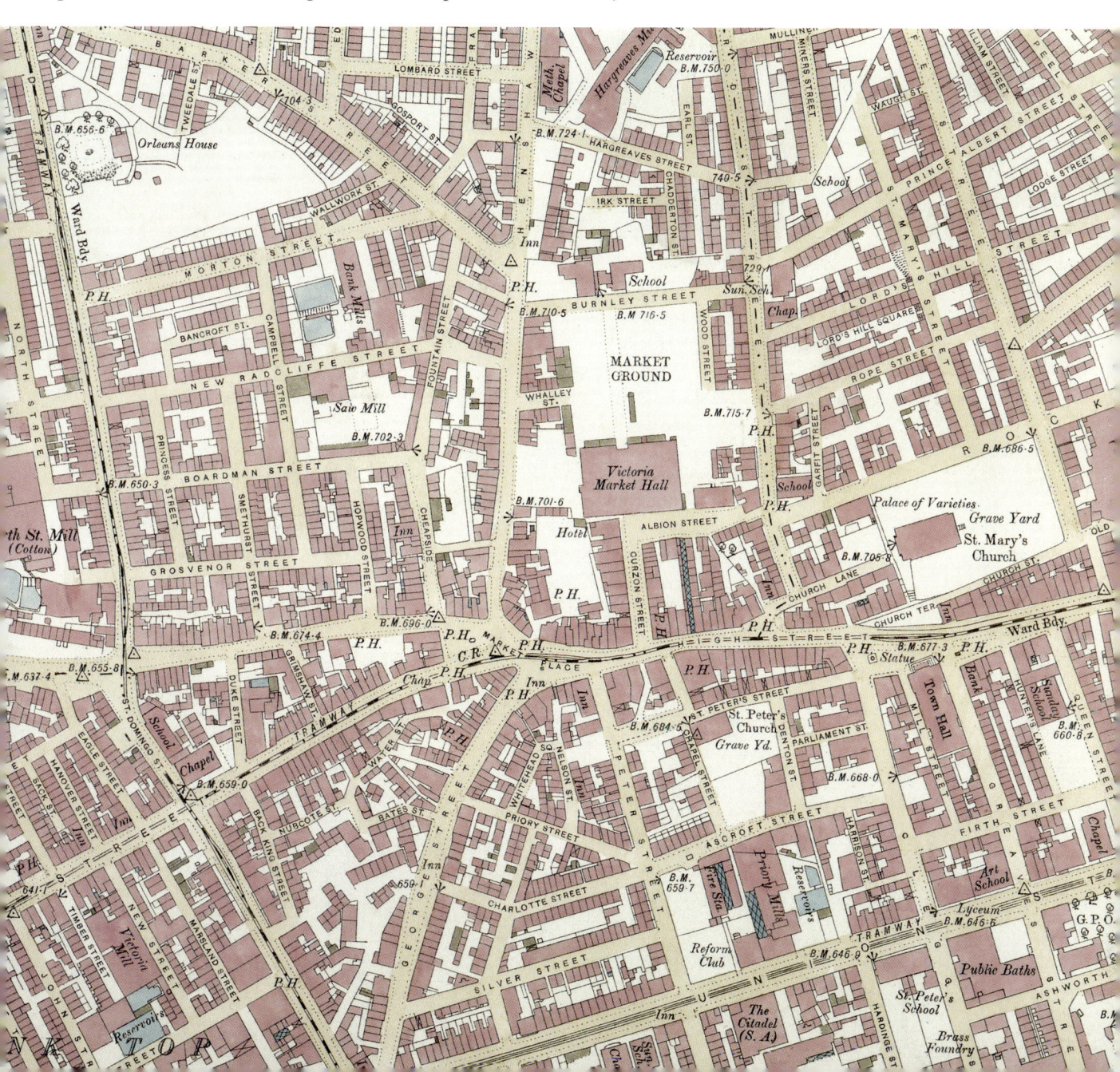

**Abbeyhills**, built by the Council in the 1930s. The houses and neatly planted gardens appear a vast improvement on the old streets they were replacing, although these houses were built to a lower standard with smaller rooms than the first council estates such as Hollins. By the 1970s, Scabbeyhills as it became known, was one of Oldham's major problem areas.

lavatories, on the outskirts of the town, not at all popular, lacking amenities and good transport. The Oldham programme continued with larger estates at Abbeyhills and Derker; the houses were smaller again, with costs as low as £350 at the bottom of the slump; rents at 8s were cheaper accordingly.

Government policy changed in 1933 placing the emphasis on slum clearance; Oldham prepared plans involving the demolition of about 900 very old houses, mainly back-to-backs huddled together in various parts of the town, very dilapidated. Finding cheap building land became a problem. Further estates at Roundthorn, Strinesdale and Stoneleigh followed in 1936 and the following years. The Council by then had acute problems in managing its new domain; collecting rents, keeping the houses in good order, getting tenants to take pride in their gardens and in the appearance of the estates generally. It issued detailed rules for tenant behaviour, probably to little result. Whether people liked living on the estates is doubtful; they had better houses but did not feel at home; there was an uncomfortable prison-like atmosphere. Nonetheless, the Council pressed on. When the second Derker estate was completed in 1942, they had built a total of 2,573 houses, significant but still only a low proportion of the total housing stock. Small Council estates were also built in Chadderton, Royton and Crompton in the Thirties, mainly to replace older unfit houses that were cleared; Royton District Council, for instance, owned 445 houses in 1939.

Private house building revived, especially in the Thirties, but almost entirely for middle class owner-occupation; some 2,600 private houses were built in Oldham, nearly 2,000 in Chadderton and a significant number in Failsworth. In 1939 Oldham still had substantial unmet need, a situation that would be worsened by the Second World War. Although the population had fallen, the number of separate households, especially among the elderly, continued to increase. Equally important, the greater part of the town's population was still badly housed, in the two-up-two-down terrace houses built in the 1870s and 1880s, or, in large numbers, in the crowded old back-to-back streets of St Mary's and Bottom of Moor.

## Council Affairs

Housing apart, and the inadequate initiatives there could only be regarded as a disappointment, Oldham Corporation struggled between the wars to maintain public services. The huge inflation in spending in the post-war period was met by a sharp increase in rates which reached 16s 8d in the pound in 1921, more than double the pre-war level. Revaluation of property in 1923, and lower expenditure as prices fell then brought lower rates which settled at 12s 2d for five years from 1927.

The financial problem became acute in the depression. Closed mills and empty shops meant that rateable values were static throughout the period. Difficulty in collecting rates, delayed payment and default led to falling income. The problem was compounded by reduced surpluses from the gas undertaking and by significant trading losses from trams and buses. Servicing much larger borrowings, mainly the result of Council house building, was another burden. Raising the rate was not an acceptable solution in a depressed community. Following re-rating of industrial property in 1929, which reduced the Borough's rateable value by about 20 per cent, government grants became a crucial element in finance. In 1931-32 and subsequently they provided about 35 per cent of the Council's income. Council spending in total declined in the early Thirties, the worst years; with the growing burden of public assistance, which partly fell on the rates when the council took over the responsibilities of the Poor Law Guardians in 1929, all other services were squeezed. After 1935, the Council's task got slightly easier; the rates were increased, the municipal undertakings, gas, electricity, public transport again generated surpluses, and total spending could rise by about 10 per cent. The Districts had similar problems, Chadderton apart; here, with many new houses, rateable value rose by a third in the Thirties and the rates could fall to 11s in 1938, well below Oldham's 15s.

In the worst years Oldham Council had to scratch and save, reducing the pay of its staff, replacing married women teachers with cheaper newly-qualified recruits from the training colleges, postponing replacement of staff uniforms, deferring open access in the library and similar "economies". What was possible was redevelopment of gas production, with enlargement of the Higginshaw works and closing of the old obsolete plant at Rhodes Bank and elsewhere. Major development of electricity supply, self-financed, was imperative with a new generating plant at Slacks Valley in Chadderton completed in 1929. As industrial demand fell after 1930 it was replaced by dramatic growth in domestic usage; by 1939 there were 55,000 electricity customers. Motor buses were introduced on a growing scale to provide a better and more flexible service than loss-making tramways; in fact there had been quite a revolution in the use of public transport with the number of journeys by bus and tram rising from about thirty million in 1920 to over fifty million in 1940; it had been only about two million when the Corporation took over the trams in 1901. Growing demand for water, not least as flush water closets gradually replaced the more primitive waste water variety, necessitated new reservoir capacity, achieved from Blackstone Edge when Oldham and Rochdale Corporations jointly acquired the old reservoirs of the Rochdale Canal Company. Oldham also successfully established its right to take water from Manchester Corporation's Lake District supplies.

**Armistice Sunday** remained a solemn occasion when the town's rulers appeared before the public. Here, in 1932, the Mayor is Elisha Bardsley. A top hat was still mandatory for an all-male council.

Further attempts were made to amalgamate with Chadderton. In 1926 the Chadderton electors were coaxed with a discount of 2s on the Oldham rate for ten years but this proposition could not be sustained in Parliament; less generous terms were then rejected by Chadderton ratepayers. A further attempt in 1930, driven by Oldham's need for building land, industrial sites and additional rate income, was firmly resisted.

Sadly in the Thirties, housing apart, the Council was unable to afford any significant public works, a new fire station, library extensions, larger swimming baths, street improvements, town centre redevelopment, and the

**Chadderton Council in the 1930s**, proud and independent.

like, that would have provided work for the unemployed; many schemes were discussed but they remained blueprints for the future. The cleared central area site at Smethurst Street remained unused, indeed unlevelled, strewn with rubble and rubbish. The *Chronicle* described the town centre as "mean and squalid, utterly inadequate and discreditable, a collection of afterthoughts". At least in 1934 the old graveyard of St Mary's became an open space in the town centre. Two years later, following the death of Sarah Lees, her daughter, Marjory, gave Werneth Park to the town. Stoneleigh Hall, where another of Oldham's elite families had lived, the Greaves of Derker Mills, also became the property of the Corporation. These had been the last of the large mansions built by the previous century's elite to survive as private homes; the rest had then gone or become nursing homes or similar institutions. Slowly over the years the community had added to its public open space. In Royton, Tandle Hill, 118 acres, was given as a park by Norton Bradbury, a local businessman who had made a fortune in the post-war cotton boom.

This was not a period of educational progress. The school leaving age had been raised to fourteen in 1918 when the half-time system was abolished; year after year proposals to raise it to fifteen were deferred because of the expense. Thirty-five old board or voluntary schools remained in out-moded buildings, in many cases under-used as school populations fell, but three new council schools were built to provide for the new housing estates as at Limeside. Over 50 per cent of children were in classes larger than forty. If the conventional view had been that working class children needed no more than an elementary education, there was now increasing demand for secondary education. Indeed there was strong objection to the word "elementary"; the Hadow Report in 1936 introduced the distinction between "primary" up to eleven, and "secondary" beyond that age, with secondary education to be provided by either modern or grammar schools. Implementation of these ideas had to wait until after the war.

In Oldham provision for secondary education remained inadequate, taking less than 5 per cent of the age group. The Municipal High School on Greengate Street did not have enough places; selection was by entrance examination and in the Thirties fees were charged except for the poorest children; uniforms, the cost of getting there, were other deterrents. Compared with nearly 13,000 in the elementary schools, below 450 were going to the High School. In Chadderton the situation was much better when a new County Secondary School was built by Lancashire County Council off Broadway. Meanwhile Hulme Grammar flourished as an independent fee paying school for girls and boys. Oldham's old Technical College remained cramped and unsatisfactory but the range of courses, in textiles, engineering and building was extended and, very gradually, employers became converted to the idea of day release rather than evening classes alone. Although many still saw technical education as a wasteful and unnecessary luxury, about 1,200 students enrolled in 1939. To meet a different demand a School of Commerce opened in 1932, attracting about 1,000 students in 1939. Oldham continued to pioneer provision for special educational needs; in 1936 it was able to afford an Open Air School at Strinesdale. And for those who wanted to add to their elementary education, Evening Schools were maintained across the Borough, probably being attended by about 2,000 young people.

## Life between the Wars

For most of the people of the Oldham district the years of depression were a shabby and bleak period. Not a few had the bitter experience of losing both savings and income with the collapse of share prices, default on loans, and passing of dividends; many were cruelly reduced in circumstances if not ruined by the incidence of calls on their shares. But these harsh experiences were generally the plight of the better-off who had trusted the Limiteds, with savings or with borrowed money. Far more numerous were those whose income was savagely reduced by wage cuts, short time and prolonged unemployment, as mill after mill closed down or went on three days a week.

Unemployed insured men received the dole, approximately 17s weekly for a man, 8s for his wife and 2s for a child. If they did not qualify for dole they

**Depressed Oldham**, Bow Street, one of Oldham's oldest streets, had pockets of poor house property mixed up with a slaughter house, cattle lairage and a hides and skins yard. The picture catches the gloom and grime of a wet day in the early 1930s.

got the more meagre poor relief, administered by the Council's Public Assistance Committee when it took over the role of the old Poor Law Guardians in 1929. If this was barely enough to live on, at the worst point of the slump, in September 1931, the unemployment benefit was cut by 10 per cent and limited to twenty-six weeks; thereafter application had to be made for "transitional benefit", subject to a test of means. A searching and public scrutiny of circumstances, savings, assets and chattels such as pianos, additional sources of household income such as war pensions and children's earnings, was carried out before assistance could be given.

The Means Test was the most hated feature of that bleak period. It was unfair, humiliating and encouraged dishonesty. It had to be administered by the local authority, namely the Public Assistance Committee, chaired by Marjory Lees. In 1932 Oldham's Labour councillors, finding the task completely repugnant, refused to take any part; standing as "friends of the poor", they had sweeping success in the local elections in November. The Conservative councillors then followed suit and Oldham took the position they would not apply the Means Test. Whitehall responded by threatening to withdraw "transitional benefit", when the unemployed would only have poor relief to fall back upon and would become a charge on the rates. The Council then climbed down. The harsh Means Test continued until 1935 when central government took over the responsibility through the Unemployment Assistance Board. The unemployed then signed on at the Labour Exchange and received a modestly improved dole, not subject to the same vigorous scrutiny of their circumstances.

What can be said of Oldham's many unemployed? There was boredom, disillusion and bitter despair, the feeling of wasted lives. More immediately, there was not enough to live on, the struggle to make ends meet. Families had to rely on the cheapest food, broken eggs, bruised fruit, poor cuts of meat, frequently bought on Tommyfield late on Saturdays. Many went hungry, physical stamina fell, malnutrition took its toll. Children, perhaps, suffered especially, going hungry to school, wearing patched cut-down clothes, living on a diet of bread, margarine, jam, chips and little else in many cases. As the *Chronicle* wrote "it is a desperate struggle to feed and clothe a child, week in, week out on 2s". Among the unemployed, clothing got shabbier; holidays, luxuries were foregone; credit and debt became commonplace, with the collectors call a weekly event on Friday evening; the pawnshops did a lively trade, not least on Monday mornings. There was no riot or disturbance, rather dull misery, crowds of men hanging around in idleness. Keeping warm in winter was a problem; fuel was saved by staying in bed, and frequenting the newspaper rooms at the public library. The *Chronicle* reported long queues of unemployed waiting for cheap admission to local cinemas in the afternoon, seeking warmth, comfort and escape from the monotony of workless days. Not surprisingly, the more mobile and enterprising left the district to seek work where it was available, in the Midlands and South.

In a town which had lost much of its wealth, charity was not as forthcoming. The Mayor continued to make his annual appeal to provide poor children with a Christmas breakfast; in 1931 only £107 was raised, still enough with help from chapels and the Oldham Mission to feed over 3,700 children across the town, provide special trams to get them to the Co-operative Halls, and give each child an orange, an apple and a new penny.

While Mayor in 1932, Elisha Bardsley organised a **soup kitchen**; children came with jugs and ladling tins to collect their household's share.

day and half-day excursions by train or motor-coach for those unable to afford the full week. In 1933 and each year thereafter, up to 3,000 Oldham children saved the 10 shillings needed to join a schools rail trip to London; five special trains were involved, to be met at Euston by a large number of buses, each following a carefully planned itinerary around the sights and attractions of the capital. The London trip, a feat of organisation and co-ordination, was a memorable experience opening the eyes of a multitude of Oldham children to another world.

Organised sport retained its vigour, uniting all classes, with the King at Wembley or at Test Matches. Admission prices at local clubs were kept down

*Above:* **The cheap railway excursion**, day or half-day, remained the stand-by for those who could not afford a boarding-house.

*Right:* **Motor transport**, and the open charabanc before the more comfortable coach, enabled people to get away.

or even subsidised. There were still huge crowds at important games although the clubs struggled financially; Oldham Athletic attracted 47,671 to Boundary Park for a game against Sheffield Wednesday in January 1930 but still had a loss of over £3,000 on the season. Central Lancashire League cricket had the appeal of overseas players, West Indians and Australians as professionals. 4,000 watched the semi-local boy Jock McAvoy box in Oldham Drill Hall in 1937. Big sporting names, Larwood, Hobbs, Dixie Dean, Alex James, Steve Donoghue, Gordon Richards, Tommy Farr became national celebrities, their status enhanced by the popular press and their images on cigarette cards, eagerly collected by the young. Gambling flourished on horses and dogs, and with the rise of the football pools.

The cinema boomed, especially in the Thirties, with a vast flow of talking films and a pantheon of stars and idols, even technicolour. Oldham's many cinemas offered up to three hours of affordable entertainment in a warm and comfortable situation. Some, like the Odeon and others in the town centre provided luxurious surroundings, the theatre organ and special sound and lighting; others, in the neighbourhoods, remained cheap flea-pits. At least half the town's population went to the cinema once a week, many more frequently. More than three-quarters of the seats cost 6d, or less. Multitudes of children went to Saturday matinees, in some cases gaining admission with empty jam jars instead of cash. Oldham parents complained of the harm films of violence and horror might do to the minds of their children. Gracie Fields, nearly local, became a national celebrity; her films provided pluck and

*Facing, above:* Depression or not, the **annual Wakes** remained the occasion when all who could afford escaped whether to the Lancashire coast or to more exotic places further afield. Here, a crowd awaits its train at Mumps Station in August, 1939.

**Central Lancashire League Cricket** had its golden age in the 1930s and the immediate post-war period with four clubs in the Oldham district competing. The excitement of keenly contested afternoon games was enhanced by professionals imported from the County game, from the West Indies and later Australia and India. Here the Royton crowd watches the home team playing Werneth in a local 1939 Wood Cup Derby.

optimism, a ringing voice and broad comedy; she was a symbolic figure, the "template for the strong Northern Woman", and she gave "a smile you can keep all the while". George Formby was another Lancashire icon whom the film makers of the time popularised. The cinema to many became a "substitute for real life", a means of forgetting drab surroundings and harsh circumstances.

In contrast, music halls disappeared and live theatre had faltered, its venues converted to picture houses. But there was an important revival in 1937 when a new Oldham Repertory Theatre emerged, using the old Temperance Hall for its productions; it opened with Shaw's *Arms and the Man*. In 1939 Oldham Rep, by then attracting a large membership, and strongly supported with full houses nightly, could move to the old Colosseum, renamed the Coliseum. Meanwhile music remained a distinctive feature of Oldham, although there were fewer brass bands and choirs. If the Oldham Orchestral Society struggled, the Oldham Musical Society now maintained a high reputation with many voices competing to secure a place in an elite ensemble. Locally performed operetta was immensely popular in the Twenties; nearly everyone knew the tunes from the *Desert Song, The Student Prince* and *Rose-Marie*, as well as many others. Perhaps reflecting this background, from an ordinary if not poor home, William Walton was establishing a distinguished reputation as a composer. His viola concerto, performed by the Hallé in January 1932, was praised by the eminent critic Neville Cardus: "the work settles Mr Walton's position amongst the most interesting, the most truly musical, minds of our day". Eva Turner, born in Oldham, was another gifted and spirited artist, making an international reputation as an opera diva. Several other prominent musicians came out of Oldham at this time, Frederick Dawson, the concert pianist and Sara Buckley

**The Coliseum** in the 1930s, formerly the Colosseum, became the home of Oldham Repertory Theatre Club in 1939. It re-opened in January 1938 with a performance of Shaw's *Arms and the Man*. By then, the Club had 2,000 members, performances had queues and a new play was presented each week.

and Marjorie Thomas, both fine female voices.

For the young of both sexes, the proliferating dance halls now became the preferred meeting ground, especially the Hill Stores in Greenacres and many others in the town centre and the Districts; they were supported by schools of dancing, such was the importance attached to proficiency in this social skill. The "monkey parades" on Sunday evenings were another important feature of life for the young, walking up and down Union Street or other less popular venues, "dressed to kill", all part of the mating process. Apart from these meeting-places, there were other well-known courting places and a well established courting process and etiquette, often extending several years, and involving parents at the appropriate time.

In another direction, borrowings from the Public Library rose dramatically, closed access notwithstanding; the total in 1930 at 619,000 was well over three times what it had been in 1910. Most homes would take a daily or at least a Sunday newspaper; the *News of the World* was the most popular read. Radio, or the "wireless", became fairly universal in the Thirties, with more popular programmes, dance music and variety, and new favourites, Henry Hall, Arthur Askey, Tommy Handley. There were many fewer public houses than there had been but more clubs. Not surprisingly, the numbers summonsed for drunkenness fell throughout the period. In 1931 there were 148 cases, in 1938 only seventy-two; there had been 900 in 1913. It was now rare to see a drunk in the streets.

Notwithstanding hardship, and poor housing conditions for many, the health of the community continued to improve. The death rate had fallen steadily; it was now down to about fifteen against nineteen to the thousand at the turn of the century. The birth rate had fallen even more dramatically, and was well below the national average. Oldham between the wars had many more deaths than births. Child mortality, falling to 60 per 1000 live births in 1939, was massively lower than it had been before the Great War, but still had a long way to fall; most babies were still born at home but now with more qualified assistance. There had been a large decline in deaths from TB and from the old contagious diseases, but diphtheria remained serious. Malnutrition continued to take its toll with the incidence of bow-legs and rickets.

Oldham's Royal Infirmary, still relying on appeals and donations, was able to raise the wherewithal to double the number of beds to 400, adding two new operating theatres and an X-ray facility. Westhulme remained as a fever hospital, and in 1930 the Union Workhouse passed into the control of Oldham Council and, while remaining an institution for the aged poor, was able to build additional wards and become Boundary Park Hospital. Its new wards, when opened in 1937, were described as "an oasis, amongst the finest hospital wards in the whole of Lancashire".

There were many other new forms of health provision in the town, for school children, expectant mothers, the elderly and the disabled. Free school

**Eva Turner**, born in Oldham in 1892, went on to become a world famous Opera diva. Here she returns to Oldham to be welcomed by Elisha Bardsley, the Mayor in 1932, and Dame Sarah Lees.

*Facing, below:* **The cinema** brought a new dimension to leisure. Here an excited crowd of Hollinwood children awaits admission to the La Scala on New Years Eve 1937.

milk, one-third of a pint daily, was introduced in 1935 as an attempt to combat child malnutrition. Dental health improved modestly; more people "kept their own teeth", partly the result of school dental inspections and more emphasis on dental hygiene. Nevertheless, apart from meagre medical provision for working men, paid for by national insurance contributions, fear of doctor's bills remained a nightmare for most families. In many households, the doctor's man, along with the insurance man, was a weekly caller on Friday night, collecting perhaps 6d, perhaps only a penny. A universal free health care system, much talked about, remained a remote promise in the inter-war period.

The new transport was taking over. There were buses, motor lorries and growing numbers of motor cars; 8,000 in the district by 1939 compared with 800 in 1920. Cycling became very popular, for travel to work and as a leisure pursuit at weekends. The cotton mills were swift to replace slow and

**Buses** were replacing trams by the 1920s; lorries were quick to replace the horse and cart and finally broke the resented monopoly of the railway in carrying raw cotton from Liverpool or yarn to the weaving towns, Blackburn and Burnley.

expensive rail transport with flexible and cheaper road vehicles to deliver skips and boxes of weft or beams of warp to customers in Blackburn and Burnley; scores of haulage contractors developed. The horse drawn cart and wagon, and landau, did not, needless to say, disappear from Oldham streets. Until 1934 there were no driving tests, no speed limits. Road safety only became an issue as the numbers of accidents grew, 285 in 1936. Congestion in the town centre, and to a lesser extent parking was becoming a matter of concern.

Apart from the Catholics, the trend against church and chapel continued with attendances falling, influence and authority diminished, and income depleted. Special occasions, anniversaries, retained a modest hold. Chapels began to close, especially in the central area where fewer and fewer people lived; a few new chapels were built to replace them. Children now went more reluctantly to Sunday School, often forced by their parents. The different branches of Methodism merged in the Thirties to reduce their overhead costs. Religious institutions were seen by many as dull, inefficient, old fashioned; faith and belief no longer had a hold for the majority. Nonetheless, Boy Scouts, Girl Guides, Boys Brigade companies flourished, with well over seventy units in Oldham alone, apart from thirty or so church Youth Clubs. The Whit Walks continued but lost their sparkle, not least because the processions were usually now unaccompanied by bands; whether families could afford or not, young girls were found the traditional white dress. Sunday observance still remained staunch; shops were shut, pub hours restricted and, after a referendum of all voters, cinemas refused permission to open; controversially, Oldham Council agreed to allow band concerts in the Park on Sunday evenings but only after the end of church services.

**Coronation 1937**, celebrated in St. Mary's.

**Shaw Road, Royton,** a royal visit by the Duke of Kent in the early 1930s; Winston Churchill later recalled "the warm hearts and bright eyes of Oldham people".

War memorials had been built throughout the district, all unveiled in moving ceremonies. Armistice Day became a sad reminder of the ghastly experience of the trenches and of dead relatives and friends. On the following Sunday, year after year, thousands witnessed or joined mournful processions and services, not least that at the Memorial in front of the Parish Church in the middle of Oldham. More joyfully, the Coronation of a new King in 1937 was a major and memorable occasion, a public holiday with huge processions, street parties and gifts to school children; a royal visit in 1938 brought an enthusiastic loyal response.

### Politics between the Wars

Labour had become respectable in the early Twenties, winning one of the parliamentary seats in 1922 and again in 1923. As Frank Tweedale, one of its leading Oldham personalities, put it at the time, "our aim is to improve working and living conditions, to guarantee that our children will not have to struggle and scrape". The appeal was a very relevant one in a working class town. What was lacking was trust and credibility, while there was still widespread fear of socialism. The first minority Labour government was a disappointment, not least to its supporters. Prime Minister McDonald resigned in October 1924 and, amid allegations of Bolshevik association, Labour was defeated in the subsequent General Election. Nationally the Labour vote rose but a collapsing Liberal vote moved to the Conservatives. In Oldham the struggling and divided Liberal party had formed an alliance with their historic opponents to keep Labour out, attributing its support to "the scum of the town"; Labour increased its vote but lost to the

## Politics between the Wars

Conservatives by large majorities.

In 1929, when all women over twenty-one got the vote, Labour, now standing for modest change, better financed by the trade unions, better organised, increased its national vote substantially. In Oldham the party won both seats comfortably. But the second Labour government, again in a minority, and divided at a time of crisis, completely lost the country's confidence in the slump of 1931. Ramsey MacDonald and some of his colleagues joined the Conservatives and some Liberals to form a National Government which swept the country at the October election. Oldham followed the national trend; Conservatives won both seats with nearly two-thirds of the vote. They retained them in 1935 but with the most slender majority. Conservative members, upper-class and remote from local experience, then represented the Borough through until 1945.

Whether fighting the occasional Parliamentary contests or the annual Council elections, Labour was handicapped by factionalism within its ranks. It was helped by the fact that Oldham was a town of working men, and the younger men especially, unlike their fathers who remained distrustful, were taking the view that Labour was best for the working man. The Catholic vote had also become fairly solid for Labour. The Party had a moderate cautious group of members, mainly trade unionists who predominated, but a noisy band of left-wing zealots, mainly white-collar and members of the Independent Labour Party (ILP), pressing for more socialism; they frightened much potential support. But none of this prevented a steady increase of Labour representation on Oldham Council where it approached but did not quite become the party of government.

From only two councillors in 1920, Labour had climbed to seventeen by 1929. They had firmly replaced the Liberals as the alternative to the ascendant Conservatives, although the Council, for most of the period, had no overall control. Samuel Frith (1926-27) and Isaac Crabtree (1929-30) were Labour Mayors, elected under a new understanding whereby length of service rather than party majorities determined the Mayoralty. With a Labour government there were hopes by 1930 the party could gain control but that was not to be. In 1931 the party crashed, falling back to ten members facing a large Conservative majority. But Labour opposition to the Means Test, their stand as "friends of the poor", brought large gains in 1932 and again in 1933; they were then the largest party, but not in decisive control.

Labour faltered when in control, attracted criticism for various initiatives and shortcomings, and continued to be discredited by factionalism among its members. Its position in the Spanish Civil War when its activists supported the Republicans, upset much Catholic support among the rank and file who supported Franco. James Shannon, born in County Clare, working his way up from being a labourer in a railway goods yard to a leading provisions merchant, had become the first Catholic Mayor in 1933-34; James Bannon followed him a few years later. By 1936 the Conservative party were firmly back in control and that remained the position until after the war. No visitor to Oldham in the mid or late Thirties would have judged this to be Conservative territory; on the whole, this had become a town of "have nots" but the conservative and deferential tradition among Lancashire working men persisted. If the difference between the parties can be summarised, the

---

Oldham Municipal Elections,
*Monday, November 1st, 1937.*

CLARKSFIELD WARD.

*With the Compliments of*
**Mr. A. Tweedale,**
*THE LABOUR CANDIDATE.*
*Soliciting your SUPPORT & VOTE.*

**Arnold Tweedale**, running for Council in 1937, was the long-time unpaid Labour agent, helped by his property owning wife. Following his uncle, Frank Tweedale, he was a power in Oldham politics and Council affairs over fifty or more years, often behind the scenes.

Conservatives looked after the ratepayer and the propertied business class; Labour put the needy first. The Liberals were squeezed out. Labour's problems remained competence and trust; to many working men they offered "summat for nowt", not a credible proposition.

The trends in Oldham were mirrored in the District Councils, all of which remained in Conservative or Liberal control. The new Royton constituency, taking in Crompton, formed when the electorate was enlarged in 1919, stayed Conservative throughout the inter-war period, as did Middleton which included Chadderton. Saddleworth, still within the Colne Valley constituency, was seen as a Conservative redoubt.

## World War II

As elsewhere, the approach and outbreak of war transformed the situation in Oldham. Young men went to serve. For the majority who remained, plenty of work became available, not perhaps in cotton, where the number fell by almost half, but in munitions at Platts and elsewhere, in the much enlarged Ferranti and especially at Avro in Chadderton, where as many as 18,000 were employed building Lancaster bombers. For women there were many opportunities to replace men, on the buses, in Council offices, shops and elsewhere. Wages, generally, were higher.

Hardship, as it had existed, was reduced by the war. Austerity became the word. Food and clothing rationing figured prominently in people's lives. Casualties there were but not anything like the scale of 1914-18. As victory approached there was a feeling that the new peace would be different, not squandered as it had been in 1919. The wasted years of the Thirties, it was felt, were over. All could look forward to security, fuller employment, enhanced education, an improved environment, a better life, a better Oldham. That was the promise of 1945.

**Winston Churchill** returned to Oldham in June 1945. Crowds lined his route through Failsworth and Hollinwood and then through the town towards Huddersfield. Here he speaks on the "spare land", off West Street. He prefaced his remarks "My dear friends" but Oldham returned two Labour MPs in the election.

# Renewal and Modernisation:
# Oldham since 1945

*Chapter XIV*

# OLDHAM: 1945-1974

### Oldham since the War: an Overview

Whatever the high hopes of 1945 there were many formidable challenges facing post-war Oldham. The traditional economic base, cotton spinning and textile engineering, had been shattered by the inter-war experience; there could be no real confidence that it offered a sustainable future. A huge legacy of decayed old housing, much of it in slum condition, remained. Practically everywhere the close proximity of houses to mills and businesses, once a virtue, now met condemnation. Most public buildings lacked any dignity and were old, worn out and inadequate; the Town Hall was far too small to administer the town properly. Obsolete mills, old housing, derelict sites, were visible and intrusive; the place was grim and ugly as it had been for decades. The road system and the town centre were increasingly outdated and unable to cope with growing motorised traffic. Schools and health services did not

**Obsolete, grim and ugly,** Oldham looking along Yorkshire Street towards Bottom of Moor, the post-war challenge for renewal and modernisation.

match the standards and expectations of post-war society. Public utilities, gas, electricity and water, the high achievement of the old Corporation, were now perceived by government as uneconomic local units.

Thus, after the wasted inter-war years, the need for urban and residential renewal and modernisation was as great in Oldham as anywhere in the country. The history of the next fifty years was to concern itself with meeting this need; with creating a strong new local economy from the ashes of the old; and providing not merely work but a more secure standard of living, better homes, better healthcare, better education, an improved environment, for all of the district's 220,000 people.

The transformation of Oldham was to take place during a period of profound social and economic change, part peculiar to the local community, part common to most if not all of the United Kingdom. Traditional manufacturing employment declined, to be replaced by a huge expansion in service occupations, health care, government in its various forms, education, retailing, media, financial services. The role of women in the workforce, full-time and especially part-time, was transformed. If Oldham became a district of comparatively low incomes, it was still a great deal more affluent than ever before; between the end of the 1939-1945 war and the end of the century living standards almost tripled. People worked fewer hours and had longer holidays. Drudgery in the home gradually disappeared with central heating, proper bathrooms, washing machines, refrigerators, convenience foods, and eating-out. Everyone belonged to the National Health Service and could call on the services of a doctor, round the clock, without even thinking of the cost. The health of the community improved dramatically, not merely because of better health care but also better housing, better diet and better lifestyle.

**Tommyfield**, still the heart of Oldham's central area, perhaps had its busiest period as living standards improved after the war.

Leisure activities were transformed, new forms of recreation and leisure facilities emerged. Spending patterns changed in a multitude of ways. Dress became informal but far more important. Home entertainment saw the virtual collapse of the cinema and to a large extent local spectator sport. For the young, the disappearance of the dance hall was matched by a new culture of pubs, pop concerts and especially night clubs.

The massive growth of car ownership and the number of car journeys revealed the obsolescence of the old maze of roads and streets and gave imperative to a new traffic infrastructure. It led to the sprawl of the residential area and a greater physical separation of workplace and home. It contributed to the transformation of shopping patterns, the collapse of hundreds of small neighbourhood shops, the rise of the superstore, often out-of-town, and redeveloped town centres that tried to combine the traditional with the contemporary and to accommodate personalised as well as public transport.

Oldham's population ceased to grow but its composition and distribution changed. Residential suburbs developed, especially in the Districts, to house commuting locals and incomers. Immigrants from the New Commonwealth created significant ethnic minorities concentrated in the older parts of the Borough. The community grew older and rising numbers of aged people created new demands on the housing market and for health care. The traditional family unit declined; divorce, co-habitation, different sexual mores resulted in more one person households and many more one-parent families. Social behaviour changed in other ways: less deference, the decline of religious observance, less respect for parents and for authority, greater permissiveness, the influence of TV and tabloid media had many negative results in terms of vandalism, crime, drug use, indiscipline in schools. Comparative poverty and deprivation remained while dependence on benefits from the state expanded on a scale inconceivable to earlier generations.

All these social and economic changes influenced and shaped the experience of the later decades of the century. But whilst accommodating these changes, responsibility for planning Oldham's renewal and modernisation, and attracting the support and resources to turn vision into reality, lay with local government. Central government was never a consistent support; with the shifts and turns of public policy and a stop-go national economy plagued at times by high inflation, funding for local initiatives, housing, education, roads or health, was generally unstable, inadequate and unpredictable. These problems notwithstanding, the leaders and managers of Oldham have largely met the enormous challenges they faced, but not without traumas, controversies, mistakes, delays and set-backs. Oldham today is a vastly different place to the Oldham of 1945; it is also a far far better place to live and work than ever before.

In the immediate post-war period Oldham Borough and the several District Councils remained independent authorities. All this was to change in Local Government reorganisation in the early 1970s. Within the major conurbations this favoured large strong all-purpose or unitary authorities, responsible for all local government services within their area, which desirably covered about 250,000 people. Oldham was recognised as such a unitary authority and after so many failed efforts at voluntary amalgamation the separate authorities in the district came together in 1974. Not that the process was uncontentious; generally, to many in the Districts, joining Oldham and losing independence was accepted reluctantly, and various alternatives were vigorously canvassed. The authority that emerged in the end, Oldham Metropolitan Borough, brought together Oldham, Crompton, Royton, Chadderton, Failsworth and Lees, and added Saddleworth with its different culture and traditional allegiance.

In recording the history of Oldham since 1945 it is convenient to recognise two phases: the post-war period of urban renewal prior to the formation of the Metropolitan Borough in 1974, and the subsequent period of modernisation that has been the feature of the last two decades of the century. This chapter is concerned with the priorities and accomplishments of the renewal period up to the late Seventies; an account of modern Oldham follows.

Table XX: OLDHAM: POPULATION 1939-1991

|  | 1939 | 1951 | 1971 | 1991 |
|---|---|---|---|---|
| Oldham Borough | 124,400 | 121,266 | 105,913 | (100,500) |
| Lees | 4,290 | 4,160 | 4,335 |  |
| Chadderton | 30,830 | 31,124 | 32,320 | 32,300 |
| Crompton | 13,140 | 12,589 | 16,915 | 21,200 |
| Royton | 15,380 | 14,781 | 20,290 | 21,000 |
| Failsworth | 17,720 | 18,032 | 23,220 | 21,300 |
| Saddleworth | 16,900 | 16,761 | 20,570 | 23,300 |
| Total | 222,660 | 218,713 | 223,563 | 219,600 |

*Note:* Total population of the Metropolitan Borough in 1991 is estimated for the former Borough and Districts.

## Change in the Local Economy

Just as the General Election of 1945 swept a Labour government into power, so in Oldham Labour made large gains in the local elections, and secured firm control of the Council. Labour were idealistic and determined but their priorities were not controversial. Immediate housing needs were at the top of the list, along with education and the implementation of the Butler Act of 1944. Low fares on the town's cream and maroon buses, still in the Council's hands, were also important; the last trams had run in 1946. Gas and electricity had been quickly nationalised after the war, the undisputed logic being to create larger production units, coordinated in a common distribution system, benefiting the user in lower charges and improved service. The North West Gas and Electricity Boards took over the Borough's old facilities which in course of time were all to be closed down. The Council retained for the time being its responsibility for water and sewage.

The state of the local economy was not at the time a Council worry. On this fundamental matter, the post-war scene seemed favourable. At the centenary of the Borough in 1949, the Mayor could describe Oldham as "highly prosperous, vigorous and optimistic", with "unemployment at its lowest level ever". The pain of the Thirties, it would seem, had been forgotten, at least for the time being, and certainly after the sharp contraction during the war, cotton was busy in the immediate post-war period. "England's bread hangs by Lancashire's thread" was the cry. Markets around the world were starved of goods as they had been in 1919; competitors like Japan had disappeared for the time being. The remaining spinning concerns, and the Oldham district still had well over one hundred active companies and over eight million spindles, could not get enough workers. Great emphasis was placed on raising productivity, on new machinery and shift working. To attract workers the employers were willing to provide cloakrooms, canteens, crèches, amenities that were never dreamt of in previous times. But if some responded, especially women and older men, the young were not attracted. Only one quarter of Oldham school leavers were now going to work in cotton mills; fifty years earlier that figure had approached three-quarters. Instead the industry recruited displaced persons from Central and Eastern Europe who brought a new element to Oldham's population, over 2,000 by 1951; many, quiet and law abiding as they were, settled in the Glodwick area. The cotton industry's workforce throughout the district, about 31,000 in 1947, had recovered to over 40,000 by 1951. Similarly, the woollen mills of Saddleworth, busy during the war, had a prosperous post-war period, replacing old equipment and struggling to hold on to workers while making good profits.

The post-war cotton boom was faltering by 1952, and collapsed in the next decade. If imports of raw cotton were close to one million lbs in the early Fifties they were below 700,000 lbs ten years later. Pre-war trends reasserted themselves with a vengeance. Lancashire was not competitive in supplying export markets when capacity in Japan, Hong-Kong and elsewhere had been restored. Overseas sales evaporated, while even in the home market cheap imports became predominant. By the late Fifties all firms were working below capacity, few were making profits. Some of Oldham's most famous firms had sold out before or during the collapse; Stotts who employed 1,400 people in their prime at Coldhurst, Werneth, Hartford and Pine Mills, were sold in 1955; Lees and Wrigley, once with 300,000 spindles in Glodwick Road, but now a sadly reduced concern, was sold for closure in 1956. A huge proud industry now entered its death throes. Mill closures again were depressing events, the process of removing capacity being assisted and accelerated by government with the Cotton Industry Reorganisation Act of 1959. By the early 1960s the Oldham district was down to about 2.5 million spindles, now more rings than mules. The workforce collapsed accordingly with many older men taking retirement and many women withdrawing from active employment. Down to 20,000 in the mid Sixties, it had fallen to about 10,000 by 1980. What someone had predicted earlier was now true: "the men are spent, the machine is broken, the glory is forever departed". The spinning capital of the world was reduced to a shadow of its former self.

A handful of textile mills continued to operate, many now part of the Courtaulds empire and involved in man-made fibres and specialist cotton yarns. Such was the loss of confidence among the traditional local workforce with its higher expectations, the mills found themselves short of workers, especially at relatively low wages for shift and weekend working. They began to attract Asian immigrants, as did the worsted industry in Bradford. The new Asian community, mainly at first young men from Pakistan and India, if

*As cotton spinning declined, the traditional workforce began to be replaced by **Asian immigrants**. Their youth and loneliness is caught in this photograph.*

finding low-skilled factory employment throughout the district, established itself in Oldham Borough. In 1971 there were about 4,500 residents from the New Commonwealth, almost all of them at work in textiles, living in poor crowded conditions and meeting many human indignities.

Oldham's engineering companies enjoyed a brief post-war boom, but demand for Lancashire-made textile machines collapsed in the Fifties even if "out-workers" from Platts and Asa Lees still travelled the world, if not "setting up" so much as "servicing" Oldham-made machines. The merger of textile engineers formed before the war, TMM, continued to rationalise its capacity; Asa Lees works was closed in 1951, and Platts old works the following year. But retrenchment was an insufficient response and attempts to diversify, into air-conditioning or refrigeration equipment, for example, did not succeed. By the late Sixties, Platts, on the one Werneth site, were employing only 1,700 people; ten years later they were to close completely and sell their works to the Corporation. Another smaller but long standing Oldham activity ended with the closure of the last coal mine in 1954.

If Oldham's traditional economic base collapsed in the Fifties and Sixties, the district did not become depressed. Unemployment, which had been virtually nil in the early Fifties, did not rise above 5 per cent. Ferranti remained a large employer, making power transformers and electricity meters at Hollinwood and expanding and diversifying its operations in converted cotton mills. Avro continued at Chadderton, to become part of newly formed aero-space businesses such as Hawker Siddeley; its activities were not on the huge scale of wartime but it continued to design and make bodies and parts for a large number of aircraft. Within the Borough a variety of new manufacturing industries was slowly taking the place of the old, while there was a continuing increase in employment in construction and the service industries, the latter including local government, the health service, retailing, financial and professional services. By the Seventies about 50 per cent of the occupied population still worked in manufacturing, compared with close to 70 per cent twenty years earlier. Meanwhile, many people migrated from Oldham to live and work elsewhere and the population continued to fall.

**Ferranti**, a different kind of work for women.

**Avro's vast design office** in Chadderton, 1956.

Others commuted from the district daily to employment in adjacent areas; to that extent Oldham like Chadderton, Crompton, and Royton, was becoming a dormitory.

All these changes must not understate the profound consequences for a time of the decline and collapse of the traditional industries. Massive job redundancy, the redundancy of skills native to the district, the number of residual disadvantaged Oldhamers who did not find other work and in many cases withdrew from the labour market, were all traumatic circumstances. To many older people their life's purpose had been to work in a mill. Coinciding with the massive clearance of old neighbourhoods in the Sixties, the collapse of cotton spinning and textile engineering engendered a loss of pride, a mood that Oldham was "dying on its feet." That mood did not persist; in time it gave way to new confidence and optimism but the Sixties were a difficult period.

The district had advantages and disadvantages in seeking to attract new industry. It was close to Manchester; there were over ten million people living within a thirty mile radius. It had its workforce, cheerful, willing, adaptable, but increasingly without particular skills if with a long tradition of factory employment. Against this, whatever progress was being made in urban renewal, the image, especially in the Borough, remained grim; old terrace houses, empty mills, many patches of derelict cleared land, congested roads and poor rail access. It could not offer incentives to incoming industry like more depressed areas in the north-west. Except in parts of Chadderton, it had no large vacant sites to accommodate firms seeking to build modern single-storey plants, away from residential areas and with good access for cars and lorries. And the empty multi-storey mills, if in reasonable condition and cheaply available, were not suitable or readily adaptable to many industrial purposes. For many small manufacturing ventures the prospect of sharing mill space with incompatible neighbours was a deterrent.

Nonetheless, by the mid 1960s, a wide variety of light industries were established in the district, several from before the war. Clothing, hats at Failsworth, bedding and furniture, electrical goods, surgical dressings, wallpaper, cake manufacture were all prominent. There were still many small engineering concerns. Seddon had established a significant vehicle building business on the Royton side of the Borough. Two industrial estates had been established on cleared factory areas close to Bottom of Moor where Platts old works and Asa Lees had stood, offering small modern buildings to Oldham firms displaced by clearance or to new enterprises. Of 115 cotton mills remaining in the Borough in 1965, forty-five were still connected with cotton either for active spinning, or waste processing, and twenty-six were empty, their ownership often confused. More importantly, forty-four had found other uses, twenty-seven for manufacturing purposes, thirteen as warehouses and three for mail order, the latter employing 1,600 people, mainly women. Mail order was to become important elsewhere in the district as well as in the Borough, not least in Shaw. Significantly many of the new industries had been attracted by cheap premises and available workers, mostly at low wages. Oldham was acquiring a clear profile as a district of low pay, offering, as the *Chronicle* complained, "second-rate, shoddy, skill-less jobs". What it lacked was commercial and office employment and, Ferranti and Avro apart, high technology.

Whitehall at the time did not regard Oldham as an area with severe employment problems, despite the decline of its traditional industries, its poor physical environment and ageing population. Thus it was never a Development Area and did not benefit from the stick and carrot attempts of government policy to direct industry to particular localities. It did not, for instance, receive the priority given to North East Lancashire. Eventually in 1972 it was designated an Intermediate Area which gave some grant assistance but that status was lost in 1979. In the recession of the early 1980s the employment situation deteriorated sharply showing how precarious the economic base had become; at the beginning of 1982 unemployment was as high as 15 per cent in the Metropolitan Borough, a figure compared with below 5 per cent three years earlier. At the time, with many further mill closures, the district was again cluttered with obsolete mill floor-space, itself a discouragement to new enterprises. Confronted with that situation the new Borough had to prioritise its efforts to strengthen the local economy, attract new employment and stimulate higher local earnings. That was to be the economic development challenge of the Eighties and Nineties.

**New Homes for Old: Overview**

Housing was the particular post-war priority: immediately to provide affordable houses for every household in need; subsequently, once the pressing general need had been met, to provide everyone with a decent quality of house, replacing the slums of the past. No longer could these requirements be left for the market; more clearly than before they were seen as an obligation on the community, a matter of social policy. Housing issues were at the forefront of politics, nationally and locally. That had been true in 1945 when Labour promised "Five million houses in quick time". For whatever reason the Labour government did not meet the expectations it had created.

The post-war marriage boom and the bulge in the birth rate kept the issue alive. The Conservatives won the 1951 general election partly on a more modest but still challenging commitment to build 300,000 houses a year, a target that was met in 1953.

So far as Oldham was concerned, apart from the immediate post-war shortage of homes, there was the enormous scale of the problem of defective old housing. Of 39,000 houses in 1951 in the Borough, no less than 9,000 were regarded as unfit to live in, whether because of overcrowding, layout, damp, structural defects; they included the remaining 2,400 back-to-backs that had been identified as unsuitable housing sixty years earlier. Over 60 per cent of all houses had no bath or piped hot water; a high proportion were still sharing an outdoor water-closet. As the years passed the legacy of obsolete housing would continue to grow in a town which had seen such explosive growth in the period before 1890. As old houses were cleared, the next generation of houses came to be regarded as unfit to live in, or in need of improvement. Standards of unfitness were also raised progressively. Thus, despite all that was accomplished, there were more unfit houses in the Oldham of the Nineties than were so described in 1951. There were similar problems of bad unfit housing, if on a smaller scale, in the Districts.

**St. Mary's** soon to be cleared. Many of its families moved to Fitton Hill.

To the replacement of unfit houses had to be added the effects of growing numbers of households, a lower total population notwithstanding. By 1951 the average number of persons per household had fallen below three compared with four between the wars and five when most of Oldham's houses were built. Over the next forty years it was to fall further to below two and a half; that meant that virtually the same population needed 25 per cent more houses. There were many causes of this crucially important social trend; earlier marriage, smaller families, the tendency of young single people to set up on their own, divorce, single parenthood and, of course, longevity, more old people, many living alone. Smaller households needed different types of dwellings; in particular the elderly needed smaller and specialised forms of accommodation.

So great a problem could only be handled by a programme extending over many years. The physical task of demolition, clearance, new building necessitated that. Clearance of slums and old streets rested on compulsory purchase and many years could elapse between designating property, hearing representations, arranging compensation, and starting the task. There was the formidable logistical problem of having new houses of the right size available to accommodate people displaced as slums were cleared. Then the resources required were huge. Private enterprise would not deal with the situation; this was a task that only the Corporation could handle. How was it to be financed? How could the huge costs of compensation, clearance, new building be shared between government, ratepayers and the tenants of the new homes? The capital costs of the programmes were met by heavy borrowing; large debt charges were partly covered by rents, but partly by generous government subsidies as well as assistance from the local rates. It was government subsidy in particular that gave the necessary fillip to the massive Council housing programmes. But as always with government, the level of subsidy changed from year to year with the state of public finances and the policy leanings of the party in power. Subsidy meant a degree of control, not merely on the volume of activity but on the type of housing provision and the changing emphasis on meeting general need relative to slum clearance. Housing policy and programmes pursued a far from steady course.

Where were the new houses to be built within the Borough? Oldham's lack of land for housing as for industry had again prompted proposals in 1946 to extend the Borough and incorporate the contiguous Districts; yet again these were strenuously and successfully challenged. Large housing estates on open ground at the edges of the town seemed the only solution, given the densely built area around the centre. If remoteness, a more exposed climate, the cost of travel to work and the amenities and services of the town centre, were objections to the peripheral estates, redevelopment within the older districts was not for many years a feasible alternative. It became possible only when substantial areas of old housing had been cleared. And the new estates were seen at the time as clean, quiet, healthy with a pleasant open outlook compared with the crowded decayed old neighbourhoods.

At first in post war Oldham the emphasis was on meeting general need - that is the shortage of homes. Massive clearance of older unfit houses only got under way in the Sixties. The town then had to face the social implications of clearing streets that for up to a century had housed generations of Oldham people, with life-long family, kinship and neighbourhood ties and a traditional social life partly based on the small corner-shop and the nearby pub, a type of social life vividly depicted in *Coronation Street*. Compulsion could rouse passionate opposition; compensation to people who owned their homes was another immensely controversial issue, especially until a value was attached to the dwelling itself, as distinct from the site. Many people did not want to be uprooted and moved, least of all from close to the town centre to a remote, bare housing estate away from friends and relatives and where rents and living costs seemed significantly higher. In the end their objections, and the availability of cleared land in the central areas, led to new provision in the form of high rise or multi-storey accommodation at high density. For all who had to move, there was the stress of living for a time in a condemned or threatened property, waiting and not knowing when it would happen or where they would finish up, this to be followed by the upheaval of moving and settling down in a new different alien neighbourhood,

Oldham was to replace old problems - the squalor of the slums and obsolete housing - with new problems, the obscenity of badly built houses and flats on run-down estates where people became reluctant or ashamed to live. But this was a problem that only emerged as the rehousing programme was accomplished. The stage was to be reached when the challenge became not that of meeting housing needs or replacement of obsolete housing, but rather upgrading the new housing, making life on post-war estates tolerable and acceptable. But that was for the 1980s; first to look at the brave new post-war world again.

## The Council House Boom

350 temporary houses, the so-called "pre-fabs", had been built at the end of the war. To meet urgent general need, a programme of 3,000 houses in three years was proposed in 1946. Shortages of labour and materials made that

The beginnings of the huge **council housing programme** at Strinesdale, 1948.

impossible. Initially, there was rounding-off to complete the pre-war estates, notably the extension of Limeside in the late Forties with another 1,085 dwellings. The first entirely new post-war estate was at Fitton Hill, built from 1952 to 1955, initially 950 houses. Here, as at Limeside, the Council spoke with pride of the range of amenities, shops, places of worship, community buildings, schools that would be provided, the whole "planned in accordance with the most modern thought with open development and close attention to amenity". Dwellings were of various types and sizes, ranging from one bed bungalows to five bed houses, all incorporating "up-to-date labour saving devices and many improvements due to recent technical advances". These statements, made in 1949, were to ring hollow in later years, as defects in construction emerged. Speed and low cost were the priorities at the time. Nonetheless Fitton Hill, with its wide roads and many trees could only seem a vast improvement on Oldham's old streets. To the end of 1954 Oldham had built 2,070 new Council homes as well as the temporaries. There had been similar progress in the Districts especially in Chadderton and Failsworth, with a further 1,645 new homes. In Crompton and Royton by 1954 local programmes were changing from council estates to provision of bungalows for the elderly; Royton was proud to open the first two-storey blocks of flats at Luzley Brook, a cautious innovation for the district.

By the mid-Fifties, both nationally and locally, general needs had been substantially met; waiting lists were down and could partly be met by vacancies. Whitehall decided the time had come to tackle replacement of decayed old housing. Subsidy to general needs housing was withdrawn, to be replaced with subsidy for houses built to replace cleared slums. Oldham, where the Council building programme had fallen to 300-400 houses a year, responded, if only slowly for several years. In this respect the appointment of Thomas Cartlidge as Architect and Chief Planning Officer in 1961 brought new vigour to the situation. Gradually the clearance and rehousing programme moved into high gear, eventually averaging a clearance rate of 1,000 houses yearly. The peak year was 1968 with 1,200 dwellings cleared. Between the end of the war and 1974, 13,578 old houses were demolished in the Borough.

Up to 30 per cent of the families displaced re-housed themselves either by renting or using their compensation to buy other older houses close to where they had lived within the town; the larger proportion in the early stages were offered houses on more huge new estates on the fringe of the Borough. What

**Fitton Hill extension**, on the edge of town, neat geometry, spacious layout, library, shops, parks, churches, schools and playing fields. The first estate had been built between 1952 and 1955; the extension, with 929 dwellings, followed in the Sixties.

had been destroyed had to be recreated. The new building rate was averaging 700 houses a year by the late Sixties; a Council target of 1,000 houses a year was never met, the peak being 919 completions in 1970. These were the years which saw Fitton Hill extended by another 1,001 dwellings including twelve-storey flats, and the Holts estate providing a further 1,003; both these estates were tenanted by many third and fourth generation families of Irish and Catholic descent, moving from clearance areas in St Mary's and Coldhurst. The smaller Alt estate, an extension of the pre-war Abbeyhills, followed. More central was Littlemoor on Greenacres Hill, the first major clearance area involving 445 families, living in cramped small streets. After demolition they were re-housed before the new Littlemoor estate was built; it featured a prominent twelve storey block of flats among 527 new dwellings. Eight years elapsed in this case, between conception and completion. Generally the houses built in this busy period were smaller and of poorer quality than those built earlier.

Of all the new peripheral estates, that at Sholver, built in the late Sixties on an exposed hillside, high above the town and three miles from the centre, was most controversial. Many opposed the scheme at the time; what drove the Council was the lack of alternative building sites. Nonetheless, at first the Sholver estate was popular, not least among many young professionals, attracted by the low rents, contemporary architecture and long moorland views. But quickly the estate became unpopular, and especially its extension, Sholver II, whether because of lack of adequate shops, pubs and other community facilities, the cost of fares into town or to work, and a cold damp

**Sholver estate** with its notorious multi-deck access flats.

situation aggravated by defective construction resulting in pronounced discomfort and excessive heating costs. The two Sholver estates provided 1,780 dwellings, many in two blocks of low rise flats, Pearly Bank and Wilkes Street in Sholver II, that were subsequently to acquire some notoriety. Not surprisingly, many of the flats were hard or impossible to let; people would not live there, whatever the Council said.

As extensive cleared areas become available close to the town centre the emphasis shifted to replacement housing there. This was in line with national policy which was turning away from peripheral estates, with their endless rows of monotonous more-or-less identical houses and their geometric layouts, apart from their other problems. Government subsidies were changed to encourage high-density development, including high-rise flats, "lifting the streets into the sky". Oldham now became a guinea-pig for what was described as "social building". Progressive and idealistic planners in central government were to focus on its needs and opportunities. The model, hopefully for other towns and cities to follow, was the redevelopment of St Mary's, the heart of the town, with its dense network of decayed housing close to the Parish Church. After clearance in the mid-Sixties, the new St Mary's, an estate of 530 dwellings of various sizes and types, in four and five storey deck access flats and terrace houses, was built in 1966-67. It was meticulously planned to provide an ideal living environment, constructed in the interests of lower costs by a Scandinavian system of industrialised building, incorporating a large district heating scheme, and designed by leading architects of the day.

Richard Crossman, the arrogant and forceful Housing Minister in the Labour Government of 1964, charged with a new target of 500,000 houses a year, was enthusiastically involved in the idea of low cost system-built housing. Excited by the "Oldham experiment" which his Ministry were conducting, studying the sociological aspects of slum clearance, and planning a new environment, as well as building it, he visited Oldham to give the project a push. Crossman found the councillors "an attractive group" but the cautious officers, who were unconvinced of the merits of system building, "dim to the nth degree" and "drearily incompetent". The councillors were mainly worried about their financial situation, the rising cost of new houses, the mounting burden of housing debt and pressures on rents and on the Borough rate. They were attracted by a low cost scheme accordingly, especially one with such powerful blessing. Apart from the features of the individual dwellings, each with bathroom, indoor toilet and central heating, first tenant reactions found the new estate pleasing with its white cladding, open layout and grassy surrounds. People appreciated being near the town centre; initial concerns, given the open balconies which were a feature of the scheme, centred on lack of privacy and noise. One visitor spoke of "one of the most attractive gatherings of factory built houses in Britain; in every sense a town within a town". The Chairman of Oldham's Planning Committee could hail the St Mary's redevelopment as "one of the finest schemes of its kind in the world, a new design for living, combining community with beauty. In planning and architecture, Oldham is now within the first division". That proud boast was not to be realised. The *Oldham Chronicle*'s judgement was to prove a wiser one; "bad, sad and mad", was its comment on St Mary's.

**Oldham's "new design for living"** has the multi-deck access flats of St. Mary's contrasting with other more traditional types of social housing in the Egerton Street, Barker Street and Coldhurst Hollow estates. The Parish Church has been cleaned; the new leisure centre is in construction; Bluecoat School has been extended to become a comprehensive; elsewhere extensive cleared areas await redevelopment.

Following the model of St Mary's, 544 multi-storey deck access factory built flats with low-cost district heating were the central feature of the large Shaw Road estate, built on a cleared area of 1870s terrace housing on the eastern slopes of Oldham Edge. This large estate was completed with hundreds of flat roofed terrace houses, again an innovation. Another high density estate in the inner area followed at Crete Street, off the Ashton Road; as at St Mary's, this estate was carefully planned and designed by prominent architects. When things began to go wrong with these controversial schemes, with the district heating, for example, or through defects in construction, Oldham Council was criticised for doing things on the cheap. In their defence Councillors argued they had taken the best advice available, the new estates had attracted widespread attention and acclaim at the time. Oldham's mistakes in this period were the mistakes of most large urban areas with similar problems.

TABLE XXI: OLDHAM METROPOLITAN DISTRICT: HOUSING STOCK

|      | Population | Dwellings | People per Dwelling | Council | Private Rented | Owner Occupied |
|------|-----------|-----------|---------------------|---------|----------------|----------------|
| 1951 | 218,713   | 70,600    | 3.10                | (5,000) | (43,600)       | (22,000)       |
| 1961 | 215,669   | 76,000    | 2.84                | 11,700  | 24,800         | 39,500         |
| 1971 | 223,563   | 80,600    | 2.77                | 21,300  | 11,800         | 47,500         |
| 1981 | 219,461   | 87,300    | 2.52                | 27,200  | 6,000          | 54,100         |
| 1991 | 216,531   | 89,000    | 2.43                | 21,400  | 7,600          | 60,000         |
| 1998 | 220,000   | 91,500    | 2.40                | 20,500  | 8,500          | 62,500         |

*Note:* Composition of the housing stock for Oldham and the Districts is estimated for 1951.

Up to the formation of the Metropolitan Borough in 1974, over 13,000 new dwellings had been provided since the war by the old Borough Council. The Districts had also remained active in clearing old streets and developing new estates. Together they brought 6,000 dwellings to the new Borough, half of these having been built after 1954. In 1974 the stock of Council housing was over 22,000 dwellings of all kinds. Clearance programmes and new smaller housing schemes close to the town centre - the West Street and Werneth estate incorporating three high-rise blocks of flats was a good example, or the Barker Street or Egerton Street schemes, others - continued in the mid and late Seventies. Many of these were better designed than their predecessors, more attractive in appearance, avoiding through traffic by use of cul-de-sacs, and providing open space and greenery. By 1981 the new Council owned over 27,000 dwellings. Nearly one Oldhamer in every three was then a Council tenant, a far higher proportion in the old Borough.

The Council had thus become a huge public landlord, taking the place of the multitude of small private landlords that were characteristic of the old Oldham. In managing its vast domain of properties there were formidable problems: setting rents, collecting them and controlling rent arrears; minimising voids or vacant unlet properties; prioritising the waiting list and allocating vacancies; giving people a choice of homes; achieving the right mix of dwellings; minimising overcrowding here and under-occupation there; maintaining properties and estates in good condition. The staff of the Housing Department and the Chairman of the Housing Committee, had plenty to occupy them. Their difficult task attracted constant criticism.

At periods housing finance came to dominate the affairs of the Council. Borrowing to invest in the huge housing stock resulted in a large burden of debt which had to be serviced; compared with £4 million in 1954, by 1973-4 housing debt exceeded £40 million, nearly 72 per cent of the new Borough's total debt. Interest charges on that debt were variable and escalated dramatically when interest rates rose in the early Seventies. The high inflation of that period caused a steep increase in costs of repairs and maintenance as well as management. Over the years government subsidies, if to a variable extent, contributed significantly to housing costs. As these costs rose in the Sixties, the proportion met by subsidy also increased. Thus the council house tenant, irrespective of means, paid much below an economic rent; in 1974 rents were less than half of the costs of housing provision, the balance mainly

**Rent strike 1973**, the result of reduced Whitehall subsidy.

being met from Whitehall or from local rates. But Government policy changed in the early Seventies, partly for political reasons, partly because of Treasury concerns. Subsidies from Whitehall were reduced and rents began to rise steeply, progressing towards what were described as "fair rents". Means-tested rent rebates were introduced to protect those who could not afford. Reluctantly, and with many protests, Oldham Council had to manage these changes. Controversially it increased the subsidy to council rents from the general rate fund, over £1.2 million in 1974-5, about 10 per cent of the Borough rate; without that subsidy from the rate payer, rents would have been a quarter higher. All this was the stuff of vigorous local political debate.

Meanwhile there had been dramatic changes in the private sector. In total, up to 1981, the number of private houses fell only modestly. But the private rented sector, that is private landlords renting to tenants, which had hitherto been the most widespread form of occupancy, had collapsed. This was partly because of clearance of unfit rented houses by the thousand, partly because many of the "less unfit" old rented houses had been bought by their occupiers or by families displaced by clearance. Oldham's better old terrace houses were cheap and affordable in a more affluent society; they could be improved with aid of a grant to provide a bath, hot water, even an indoor toilet. They offered independence to those who did not want to live on a council estate, and there was always the likelihood they would appreciate in value. To buy an improved terrace house for £4,000 or so in the Seventies was not unattractive compared with paying rent of £6 a week for a council house on a windy estate.

In this way much of the old private rented housing stock changed hands to owner occupiers. But this development apart, from the Fifties onwards, new private housing saw massive growth. It was stimulated by growing affluence and the ability to afford a new and better home, by the mobility conferred by car ownership, as well as by subsidy in the form of mortgage interest relief. Thus the housing landscape changed, as many of the older semi-rural communities became dormitories with extensive privately built estates encroaching on the green hillsides and meadowlands surrounding Oldham. While Oldham's population fell sharply between 1951 and 1971, there had been significant gains, especially in the 1960s, in Crompton, Failsworth, Royton and Saddleworth, nearly all resulting from new private housing, normally developed in estates. These trends continued in the Seventies although mainly restricted to Crompton and Saddleworth where suitable land remained available. Many of the incomers moved into the district from elsewhere in Greater Manchester; on the western side of the Borough the M62, completed in 1968, and its Chadderton spur in 1972, gave significantly improved access to the Manchester conurbation. In some parts of the district, incomers were willing to restore and refurbish with the aid of grants older stone-built detached cottages and farm houses, creating a quite different social character in the old communities, in Delph, Dobcross and parts of Crompton again. Thus new and different contrasts between pleasant hillside traditional housing, or modern owner-occupied estates attractive to an affluent social group, on the one hand, and deprived occupants of Council estates or the residual old housing of the inner areas, on the other, became a strong feature of Oldham.

## Changed Housing Priorities

By the late Seventies, it seemed to many that Oldham's main housing challenge had been met. There were enough houses although not necessarily in the right place or the right quality. There was still an unmet housing need especially for small units suitable for elderly persons and one parent families. The fluctuating waiting list was the best measure of this. Significant re-letting possibilities within the public housing stock could meet much of the demand. Government policy meanwhile had shifted from encouraging Councils to build more houses. Constraint, cuts, economies, became the watchwords.

Several thousands of unfit houses still remained, however, and year by year several hundred more were becoming obsolescent. For the most part they were in scattered small pockets, rather then large concentrations. Local clearance and re-development in small schemes rather than large new estates, could gradually meet part of this problem. Many of the small new building schemes were now being carried out by Housing Associations rather than the Council. The other important policy thrust towards the remaining old housing stock was "Improvement", cheaper than demolition and new building and more acceptable to the residents. Encouraged by significant government assistance under various schemes within so-called Housing Improvement Areas, the Council offered grants up to 50 per cent of the cost of approved improvement. Over 6,000 houses had attracted such grants by 1974.

The unfit houses remained in the older parts of the town, in neighbourhoods scarred by residual obsolescence and derelict sites and buildings. Many of Oldham's problems were concentrated in these "inner areas". Glodwick, Westwood, and elsewhere were becoming areas of multiple social deprivation in which the poor and especially the growing immigrant population concentrated. This deprived inner area was to be a major problem for the future. Equally serious at the time were the other emerging problem areas, the large existing Council estates, especially those that dated from the 1930s. Abbeyhills and Barrowshaw had originally been built to rehouse people from Oldham's worst slums at the heart of the town. Probably they had presented problems before the war, the result of what the Council described in 1971 as "hard use by indifferent tenants". Certainly by the Seventies they were featured by neglected gardens, litter strewn public space, a rundown appearance now increasingly aggravated by vandalism and crime. But the problems of physical and social deterioration were not confined to these old estates. Sholver was unpopular from the start. Fitton Hill and Holts were developing similar problems of housing stress, manifest in properties that could not be let, and rent arrears. St. Mary's and Shaw Road, briefly Oldham's pride, now showed formidable shortcomings; defective construction, cold damp dwellings, and an estate-wide district heating system which was constantly failing and had to be replaced at great expense in 1972. By then, St. Mary's was being described as a disaster; one third of its tenants said they wanted to move.

Thus while housing need had broadly been satisfied, the leaders of the new Metropolitan Borough had many challenges in the housing field to meet, in part the consequence of earlier mistakes, in part of social change, in part a residual legacy of the past. Housing would remain at the forefront of their concerns to modernise Oldham.

## The New Education

Educational provision, especially beyond the elementary stage, had been one of Oldham's deficiencies before the war. The Education Act of 1944 called for major changes, in Oldham as elsewhere. It introduced the distinction, long recognised by reformers, between primary and secondary education. At the secondary stage, beyond the age of eleven, various forms of education were envisaged, reflecting the aptitudes of each child, academic or grammar, modern and technical. The Act did not specify in detail what each education authority should do. The long standing problem of the voluntary or denominational Schools - still numerous in the Oldham district - was resolved by giving them access to local government finance either as "aided" or "controlled" schools.

The school leaving age was raised to fifteen in 1946, substantially increasing the numbers to receive secondary education. School populations were to rise anyway as the post-war baby boom moved into primary and subsequently secondary schools. These challenges to provision apart, many of Oldham's old schools fell far short of modern standards of space, layout and facilities; 80 per cent had been built before 1914. Many were badly situated. As new peripheral housing estates were built in the Fifties entirely new schools were required. And when congested older neighbourhoods began to be cleared, many old schools became obsolete and redundant. Finally, after the war, there was a sharp increase in demand for technical and commercial education, vocational day release as well as evening, no longer perceived as a costly luxury. In this area of provision the existing facilities at Ascroft Street, close to the town centre, were grossly inadequate and unsatisfactory.

Clearly Oldham's education establishment had much to do. It was quick off the mark in 1946 in reorganising its existing facilities into distinct primary and secondary schools. For the future a bold Development Programme was the blueprint. It aimed to reduce substantially the number of primary schools, whether council schools or denominational schools, retaining separate provision for infants and for juniors. Many new buildings were envisaged and much larger playgrounds and playing fields. Seven nursery schools for children between two and five were proposed in various parts of the town. Finally, grasping the nettle firmly, seven new large comprehensive schools, fully equipped with laboratories, dining halls, gymnasiums and swimming pools were proposed, each admitting six class streams with total accommodation for about 1,000 children. This intention to go comprehensive and abandon selection showed Oldham to be quite radical in its approach; it was to be twenty years later before Whitehall was pressing all education authorities to adopt the comprehensive route. Outlining the proposals, Oldham's Director of Education wrote in 1949:

> "the authority hopes to avoid many of the mistakes and dangers which beset the older system of distinct types of school, some of which sprang from the attempt to divide children up at the early age of eleven by setting an examination, the results of which were often imperfect, and the approach of which could seriously perturb the minds of children and parents and disturb the work of the junior school. It is felt that the comprehensive school, offering facilities for all new methods of

approach, will give the greatest freedom to new developments, and will offer to all children, both gifted and less gifted, the opportunity of testing themselves in the workshops, laboratories and libraries of the new secondary schools of the post-war age."

Not less ambitious was the Development Scheme for Further Education. A new college was proposed on a large central site, encompassing technical instruction and also a School of Commerce and a School of Arts and Crafts. There were other enlightened proposals for new schools for physically and mentally handicapped children, and Community Colleges to provide continuing and adult education.

The Development Programme was a brave vision, the vision in particular of Maurice Harrison who had come to Oldham as Director in 1938 and remained until 1966; his socialist idealism attracted strong support on the Council, not least from J. T. Hilton, elected in 1945, who went on to chair the Education Committee. Many recognised at the time that lack of resources would delay if not prevent its implementation. Introduction of the comprehensive ideal certainly had to be postponed. In the immediate post-war period the old Greenhill High School became a grammar school in 1951. Counthill, opened in 1947 also became a grammar school. A new technical school was opened at Hathershaw in the Fifties. Selection at the age of eleven, to Oldhamers "the scholarship", survived. The remaining eight schools designated as secondary, became in effect modern schools, free to develop their own approach to the four years of secondary education up to the age of fifteen for those not qualifying for grammar entry, but generally perceived as second best, a dead end, "preparing working class children for working class jobs", as one comment put it. But even at the grammar schools, in working class Oldham most children were leaving as soon as they could. In 1951 only one child in five stayed at school having reached fifteen and one in nine stayed on beyond sixteen; very few continued into higher education, perhaps one in forty.

**Maurice Harrison**, Oldham's long-serving and much respected Director of Education who planned Oldham's new schools after the war, and reflecting his firm personal conviction, the speedy introduction of comprehensive secondary education.

Until new schools could be built the old primary schools had to cope with the large increase in the school population. By 1950 there were 15,500 children in schools compared with 13,000 before the war while an increase to 20,000 was confidently projected. The school roll reached 18,000 in 1955. Many new teachers were engaged and for the time being makeshift accommodation provided. Class sizes remained over-large with as many as eleven with more than forty-five children in 1950. The new estates were, however, well provided for, with modern primary schools at Limeside, Fitton Hill and Holts in the early Fifties.

Compared with before the war ancillary services were well established in the schools. Virtually every child had free milk; as many as two-thirds took school meals, a proportion that had increased rapidly as school canteens were built. Medical and dental inspection and treatment, provision of clothing, maintenance and transport allowances were available to help children of poor parents. Whatever the home circumstances, the aim in Oldham was to give every child education suitable to its age, aptitude and ability. As the Director said in 1950, "the future for the children passing through our hands will be brighter than at any time in the history of education in this town."

Step by step as resources became available Oldham's schools were renewed. More than half of all Council revenue spending was going on education by 1973-74; capital expenditure had reached £9 million, substantial but small compared with housing. By the mid-Sixties, half the sixty-one schools in use dated back to before 1914. But these were all in the old inner parts of the town. Of a school population that now exceeded 20,000 - many from the adjacent districts - nearly two-thirds were in schools completed since 1955; nearly 90 per cent of those receiving secondary education were in post 1955 schools. All the new schools - state of art buildings by the standards of the time - had generous space for playing fields and recreation, gymnasiums, dining halls, workshops, libraries, even in one case a swimming pool, facilities and equipment that were rightly regarded as a huge achievement and advance on anything that had existed before. The new primary schools were open plan and the Council could claim with pride that it was leading the way in facilitating the introduction of new informal progressive child-centred methods in place of the old fashioned disciplined whole-class "chalk and talk" approach. The Education Department could note in 1974 a small but growing proportion of children of ethnic minorities in the primary schools, 4·6 per cent of all enrolments but as high as 20 per cent in some of the old inner area primaries. Of concern was the fact that many of the Asian children had no English language when they started school.

When the Labour Government put its influence behind comprehensive secondary schools in 1965, Oldham was quick to move, abolishing the eleven-plus in 1966. The blue-print of 1946 could now be implemented. Needless to say there were serious building problems to meet the needs of individual school populations of 1,000 pupils, a large figure but at Oldham's insistence well below the national norm which was 2,000. Oldham began to build again, modifying its various schools - grammar, technical and secondary modern - to form six comprehensives. For the time being some of these schools had intensely unpopular and inefficient split-site arrangements, involving travel by teachers and pupils. Inadequate buildings remained in use for several years. Parental choice of school was restricted as was the range of subjects that could be offered in potentially small sixth forms, school by school. To cope with needs in the inner areas, Grange, an entirely new school, was built in 1967. The Henshaw Bluecoat Church of England school now ended its long tradition of free residential education and became part of the Borough's system to form a seventh comprehensive after extensive alterations and additions. Two Roman Catholic schools, now comprehensive, were also part of the scheme. None of these changes went down well in the town; they hurt the Labour council politically and contributed, along with various housing scandals and the feeling among Oldhamers of depression and decay at the time, to Labour's resounding defeat by the Conservatives in the 1968 municipal elections.

By 1970 Oldham had three nursery schools and three special schools for the disabled, not as many as had been envisaged but still regarded as an achievement. Of the blueprint of 1946 one major element had been progressed. This was Oldham's Technical College where the first new building on a large central site on Rochdale Road was opened in 1954. A further fourteen years elapsed before the development was completed and all forms

# The New Education

**Oldham's College of Technology**, a source of pride when completed in 1968.

of further education, brought together in 1968. An impressive range of courses were then offered, mainly technical, but including business studies, with a teaching staff approaching 400 and over 5,000 students from all parts of the district. Oldham College of Further Education as it became known, was a municipal status symbol at the time.

Post-war educational development in the Districts followed a similar pattern of development to that in the Borough. There were important differences in two respects. School populations grew more rapidly with the significant housing developments of the Fifties and Sixties. There were more new schools, both primary and secondary, all setting high standards in accommodation, light airy classrooms and generous playground space. Secondly there was less enthusiasm for comprehensive education. In Chadderton, Royton and Crompton, Lancashire County Council had established a strong grammar school provision and this continued, the Whitehall directive of 1965 notwithstanding. The incompatibility of the secondary school systems of the different authorities was an immediate problem of the Metropolitan Borough on its formation in 1974. Saddleworth had another variant; it had a secondary school, in effect a modern school, with 900 pupils in 1973, and those of its young people who qualified for sixth form education were sent to the Hulme Grammar School in Oldham at the ratepayers' expense, a happy arrangement for those who benefited.

Oldham's two Hulme Grammar Schools for girls and boys continued to flourish in the post-war period, attracting over 1,100 pupils apart from those attending the preparatory schools, and enjoying a high reputation for their facilities and amenities as well as their scholastic attainments. As many as 50 per cent of the places were filled on an assisted basis, paid for by local authorities, or under the direct grant scheme. Thus many of the brightest of Oldham's youth were going to Hulme, irrespective of parental ability to pay fees. Many also won scholarships to schools outside Oldham, to the prestigious Manchester Grammar School and elsewhere. Roman Catholics who passed the eleven-plus went to Catholic schools in Manchester, making daily train journeys. By the Seventies it is safe to assume that many of the brightest of Oldham's young, and the children of the most enterprising parents, were not being educated in the Borough's comprehensive schools. Not surprisingly, the attainment of pupils in these schools, a closely guarded secret, was probably disappointing as was the staying-on rate beyond fifteen, or after 1972 when the school leaving age was raised, to sixteen. But that was to be a challenge for the new Metropolitan Borough.

**Vision Unfulfilled: The Central Area**

After the war the town centre of Oldham was much as it had been at the beginning of the century, "mean and squalid" as the *Chronicle* had described it. The layout of the streets had not changed and the principal routes of the district converged on the High Street and Market Place. Buses parked on the streets, the few but growing numbers of cars where they could. The old undistinguished and generally inadequate public buildings remained. Apart from the churchyard there was no public open space. Where the slums of West Street had been cleared in the early Thirties a large rubble strewn scar awaited commercial or civic use. The streets were lined with traditional shops, still for the most part independent retailers, and the Market Hall and Tommyfield remained a busy shopping venue for the whole community. Large numbers of people still lived in the crowded old terrace houses of St Mary's and the other neighbourhoods that immediately surrounded the central area.

This would not do. It was shabby and unworthy, inadequate and inefficient. The Oldham of the future needed something radically different and a Master Plan was commissioned and presented to a sceptical public. The Plan clearly recognised the needs of the situation. It proposed for instance a ring road and major roundabouts where this converged with the roads to Manchester, to Yorkshire and elsewhere. It provided several car parks and a

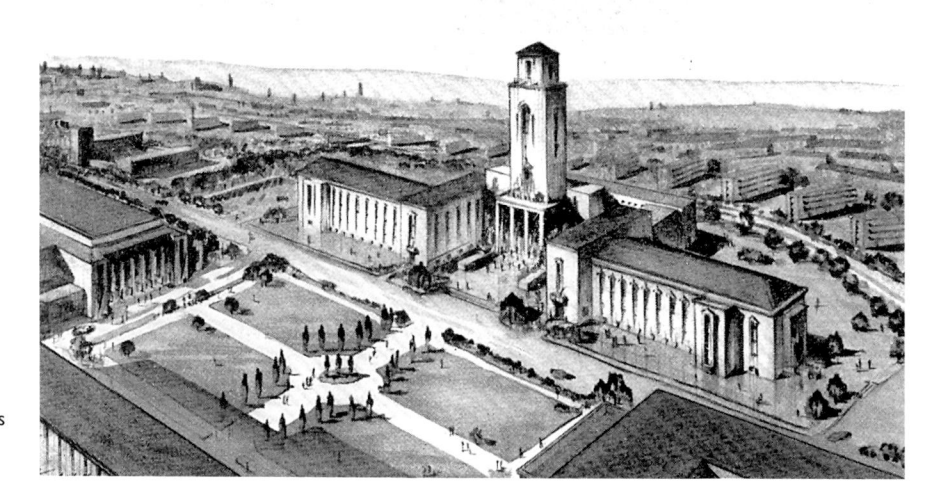

**A Town Planner's vision** of Oldham civic centre, merely a post-war dream. The new buildings and gardens were proposed on the site of Tommyfield.

# Vision Unfulfilled: The Central Area

*Another part of the unfulfilled vision; this square and gardens, incorporating new swimming baths, library and art gallery, faced the Lycium in the background.*

central bus station although the latter assumed an optimistic willingness to walk to shops and facilities. Its great vision was a new and dignified civic centre that replaced Tommyfield with a large piazza surrounded by fine new public buildings, offices, courts, halls. Controversially to make this possible Tommyfield market was to be relocated close to Rhodes Bank. A large Technical College was proposed for the empty West Street site; a new Swimming Baths, Library and Art Gallery and a greatly enlarged Infirmary all featured in the grand design. Appearance in the town centre, the image of the place, was seen as a prime consideration, perhaps in Oldham's case for the first time.

Probably no-one took the Plan seriously; pre-occupied with keeping down the rates and living cheaply there was neither the aspiration nor the resources for fancy schemes. Oldham at the time, it was later said, looked down rather than up. Nevertheless the needs the Plan had identified would eventually be met. Fifty years later Oldham would have a modern town centre. Until that could be realised it would have to live with inadequate compromise between new initiatives and a bad inheritance.

A start was made with the first building of the new Technical College in 1954; the College, on Rochdale Road rather than the West Street site, was to be completed in 1968. That apart, for twenty years after the war virtually nothing was done in the middle of Oldham. Plans in 1955 for a new Central Swimming Bath to replace the hideous old black and uninviting building on Union Street opened in 1854 were abortive; at least the entrance marked "Females" had been boarded up and both sexes could use the same door. When dry rot seized the old Town Hall in the same year, the Council recognised that it could not afford the grandiose post-war Plan. A new Town Hall was then proposed for the empty West Street site, which it "hoped to complete within a few years". That was not to be.

The imperative for change came from the rapid increase in traffic. Street parking had to be controlled; as more vacant sites became available with house clearance around the centre plenty of free parking could be provided there. In 1968 a multi-storey car park was provided at Hobson Street, inconveniently sited as it was and stark and ugly as it appeared. Experimental

**Oldham's much needed by-pass**, in construction in 1969.

one-way systems were introduced and here and there the main streets were widened; a large roundabout was built where main roads converged at the junction of Manchester Street and High Street. None of this was sufficient and Oldham traffic congestion became notorious, not least because a rapidly increasing local traffic competed with a growing road traffic passing through the town, as it had always done, between Lancashire and Yorkshire.

Traffic had to be diverted round the town; a by-pass was the only answer as the Master Plan had envisaged. A scheme emerged in 1967, the Southern By-Pass, using the extensive now redundant, decayed and desolate railway land that divided central Oldham from Glodwick and Coppice. The new mile-long by-pass, Oldham Way as it became called, not completed until 1970, at a cost, huge for the time, of £3.5 million, transformed the traffic situation in the town centre. Equally the construction of the M62 at this time as the principal route between the Lancashire conurbations and West Yorkshire reduced traffic through Oldham. It encouraged the development of new commuter suburbs on the western side of Oldham and potentially it made Oldham far more accessible than it had ever been. The essential link between Oldham Way and the M62, mooted in 1968, had still to wait many years until 1980.

By the late Sixties new initiatives came forward to do something in the town centre, its traffic problems diminished. There was again talk of a new Town Hall, or Civic Centre and plans were brought forward in 1968, using the West Street site that had remained bare and empty since the Thirties. Most significant was the attempt to develop a modern shopping facility in the town centre. A plan emerged between the Borough Council and Oldham Estates, a major property developer that had grown from the shell of an old Oldham land company. After extensive demolition in the town centre including the old St Peter's Church, the St Peter's Precinct followed, completed in 1968. This was not a covered shopping mall but an incredibly ugly open multi-storey shopping and office complex with the shops fronted by windy walkways giving access to the High Street. It proved a commercial disaster, unpopular with both shoppers and retailers, "a hopeless and complete mess", as the *Chronicle* put it. Rents were high and many of the shops could not be let. The place was frequently almost deserted. This was not a basis on which Oldham could compete as a shopping centre with adjacent towns.

**St. Peter's Precinct**, an ill-conceived shopping centre that failed.

The Districts had similar problems, to manage traffic in their centres and to upgrade and maintain their shopping facilities. A by-pass around the old centre of Shaw was authorised in 1968. Not without resistance from shopkeepers all the Districts planned to develop compact local shopping centres, desirably with a supermarket, as well as traditional open stalls, served by adequate parking. If this was the objective, progress towards it remained controversial, not least among local shopkeepers who felt threatened by change, Nonetheless over the years, the small local shopping centres in the Oldham district proved viable and successful.

## Changing Lifestyles

The Fifties as has been noted seemed a prosperous time in Oldham, a much better version of life as it was remembered from before the war, close-knit and self-contained. Cinemas boomed with fourteen in the Borough, more in the Districts, with Abbott and Costello, Humphrey Bogart, Gregory Peck, Marilyn Monroe, Tyrone Power popular stars. Recalling pre-war controversy opening cinemas on Sundays or Good Friday remained a lively issue, Catholics and Nonconformists on the Council voting to block it. Religious issues remained divisive; in 1956 Catholic representatives of wards such as Coldhurst and St Mary's, were able to prevent Council properties being used for birth control clinics. In another dispute the Watch Committee refused a licence for the film *Martin Luther*, which was then shown privately in Protestant churches and chapels.

**The Palladium**, one of Oldham's grander cinemas on Union Street, could seat up to 1900 and for many years "offered the best in cinematographic entertainment". In 1958 it became the ABC but was to close as a cinema in 1977. For some years the building was a Bingo hall before demolition in 1990.

Traditional sport flourished with large crowds: local league cricket probably enjoyed its high period as international professionals provided drama and entertainment in keenly contested matches. This was the golden age of British football with players of the calibre of Stanley Matthews in their prime, and Busby's Manchester United setting new records for team performance; in their winning periods, Oldhamers supported the Athletic to a man. The Wakes remained a standard feature of Oldham, now two weeks in the second half of June with a further long weekend in September; in 1955 £750,000 was raised by the several Wakes clubs including £68,000 at Ferrantis, comfortably double that saved at Platts. Blackpool and other coastal resorts were still the standard venues with Butlins a popular destination for many. For those who stayed at home a day trip to Blackpool now cost 7 shillings by train, 5 shillings by coach.

The young, if they dressed differently and had far more independence, still mixed at dance-halls or promenaded in Union Street at weekends. Older people did not know what to make of Elvis Presley; the Council anxiously debated, in September 1956, a proposal to ban the film *Rock around the Clock*, the cause of rowdy wild behaviour. A teacher's salary in 1955 ranged from £480 to £750; a school cook could earn £6 per week. A good terrace house with private yard could be rented for 10 to 15 shillings weekly or bought for £400, while new three-bed semi-detached houses in Chadderton were offered at £1,850. Council rents averaged £1 10s weekly, only modestly subsidised at the time. A second-hand two year old Ford Popular with 17,000 miles on the clock traded for £400.

Ownership of a car was still beyond most people's means, and so to a lesser extent was television, but both were to grow rapidly; by 1970 more than three-quarters of homes had TV which then offered three channels. Both personalised transport and home entertainment as they became more universal were to have a profound effect on leisure habits, in the Sixties and thereafter. The cinema and spectator sport declined sharply as did brass bands and choirs, other forms of social activity. There were only three cinemas in 1974 and the survivor of these, the Odeon, was to close in 1983. Bingo became a popular alternative for a while. Live theatre managed to survive with Oldham Rep having 12,000 members in 1970. Public houses, far less in number as the old neighbourhoods were cleared - there were only 170 left in 1974, less than half the number of fifteen years earlier - had to change their style, offering food and often entertainment. Dance halls, previously so popular, disappeared and for a while the young went off in coach-loads to Manchester or further afield for their Saturday night-out. Oldham came back, however, and by the early Seventies there were many clubs offering live entertainment, jazz and discos.

**William Walton** receives the Freedom of Oldham in 1961. Edward Haines is Town Clerk, George Frederick Holden the Mayor.

**Football and Rugby crowds** remained huge in the post-war years. This is Watersheddings in 1956 for a home game against Wigan.

By then package holidays, Spain, Greece or farther afield, were replacing the traditional Wakes experience, while with the demise of the cotton industry the standard two-week shutdown was becoming a thing of the past.

Household appliances, changed eating habits, smaller families encouraged a rise in full-time and part-time work by women and as cotton spinning declined new occupations became available, in shops, offices, social services as well as schools and hospitals. The second income a wife's work provided augmented the new affluence. The home became a different place, generally a far more comfortable and convenient place, improved for many with hot water, a bath or shower, an indoor toilet; plenty was spent on decoration, carpets and furnishing. Neighbourhood shops disappeared by the hundred, not merely as the old streets were cleared, but as custom was attracted to the new supermarkets offering low prices and self-service although nothing like the sophistication and range of goods of a later period. Oldham's two co-operative societies could not retain their independence; they merged in 1955 and losing members and sales contracted their operations dramatically.

By the Sixties church going was becoming the practice of a small minority; for the many, churches provided little more than a sentimental retreat for marriages and funerals. Losing their congregations, churches and chapels could not maintain themselves especially when inflation quickened; many, of course were in the clearance areas. On all sides buildings were closed, sold for other uses, or demolished. The influence of organised religion was greatly diminished as was, among the young, respect for parents, for teachers, for the police, for authority in any form. As more and more parents were unable or unwilling to control their children, challenging behaviour by the young, in school, in public places, in residential neighbourhoods became widespread. Crime, vandalism, drugs became issues of concern in the Sixties. Cohabitations, divorce, single parenthood became commonplace.

Many people were not comfortable with all that was happening in this increasingly affluent consumer society. But lifestyles apart it was the changes in Oldham itself in the Sixties and Seventies that gave rise to a gloomy downbeat attitude. So many of the hopes of the post-war period had not been realised. Most seriously cotton spinning and textile engineering were now in terminal decline. If there were new jobs, many were appropriate to women rather than men, many were not well paid. The not well-off, the unemployed, the elderly were coming to depend on the welfare state for their living standards. 10,000 people received National Assistance in 1955. The new affluence was not equally shared. Thousands of Oldhamers were subject to the upheaval and trauma of the clearance of old neighbourhoods and the move to new Council accommodation. If many of the new houses and flats were a vast improvement, many of the post-war estates quickly became unpopular, some like Sholver and St Mary's the subject of scorn. Older pre-war estates like Barrowshaw and Abbeyhills were becoming no-go areas, notorious and shameful. The town centre was bare and unwelcoming. The hasty introduction of comprehensive schooling offended many parents. The town's keen swimmers awaited in vain for the large new Central Baths that had featured in many municipal election pledges. Everywhere it seemed was unsightly dereliction as old property, terrace houses, mills and warehouses were demolished. The town with its desolate areas of rubble was compared

**Royton, 1968**, derelict cleared ground before redevelopment, an ugly but unavoidable phase of transition.

to a bomb site, "a wreck of a place". At times it seemed no longer to belong to Oldhamers; many were uncomfortably aware of the growing numbers of Asian newcomers, a strong, if not predominant presence in some of the inner neighbourhoods, the staunchly Protestant and respectable Glodwick, middle-class Coppice and the poorer Westwood.

Changes for the better were scarcely acknowledged. The Clean Air legislation, for instance, was making Oldham a vastly cleaner and healthier place, free at last from the disfiguring smoke that had been such a feature of the past; atmospheric pollution, which could be measured, fell dramatically between 1959 and the mid-Seventies. Attempts were made to clear up dereliction and plant trees on vacant sites; the place was slowly greening. Many buildings were cleaned, with the help of a government scheme "Operation Eyesore"; the stonework revealed a forgotten appealing charm and certainly improved the appearance and image of the town. Scores of mill lodges, a massive nuisance and a hazard, with no useful function to perform, were filled up to find other uses. More public open space was being provided, notably 30 acres of playing fields near Boundary Park, the Clayton bequest, in 1964. Oldham then had about 1.5 acres per 1,000 people, far more than in the past but well below what was nationally recommended, namely 6 acres per 1,000; in the districts only Royton, approached the desired standard. Regarding these changes, the cynical comment was, "You can give a town a face-lift, what you can't give it back is its pride". Or, as the *Chronicle* wrote, "what Oldham needs is a transplant and all it is getting is a skin graft".

Oldham's hospital services, since 1948 the responsibility of the National Health Service and no longer dependent on charity or the rates, remained nevertheless, sadly inadequate. The Royal Infirmary in the town centre survived so long as the development of the Municipal Hospital at Boundary Park, now merged with the old Westhulme Fever Hospital and renamed Oldham and District General Hospital (ODGH), was delayed. Some extensions and provision of new facilities at ODGH occurred but there were loud complaints about waiting lists for operations and long waits in out-patients. In 1970 Oldham was told there was no hope for a new hospital for at least ten years. Much had been done to develop local health centres, however, and there were far more doctors practising throughout the district. There had been real progress in what came to be termed "Social Services"; establishing "home-helps" for the elderly and providing several residential homes, frequently mansions of the former elite. Many of the new Council estates had family centres; there were new children's homes and specialised accommodation and day centre help for those with mental handicaps.

So life in Oldham, if better in many respects, was worse in others. Certainly it was not what it had been. Brutally changed, to many the town was "going through a rough time". The Council was burdened with debt, deeply concerned about falling population, loss of rateable value and sharply increased rates, and unable to countenance any radical spending programmes. Visitors, journalists, TV pundits made unfavourable comment: this was "Lancashire's East End" said one; "it is impossible to talk about Oldham in anything but the past tense", wrote another in 1972, heading his feature *Requiem for a Mill Town*. Oldham it seemed to one visitor at the time, "had all the muck but none of the money". The Council struggled to correct the image of decline and decay, adopting the claim "Oldham, the town in the country". But at the time a bright future in the old "has-been" town was not easy to discern.

## A New Start: The Metropolitan Borough

This was the mood in Oldham when talk of a new unitary authority surfaced in the early Seventies. The more prosperous Districts, benefiting from the influx of wealthier new commuters, did not relish association with the rundown Borough with all its problems, its deprivation and its debt. They were worried at the prospect of higher rates. They feared a remote new authority would lose contact with local issues in Saddleworth, Crompton or Chadderton. They were concerned that their needs would be swamped by an authority dominated by the Borough's interests, that their resources would be usurped to spend on services and capital projects in the Borough.

Not all the leaders of the Districts shared these fears. Some saw that the merging of the separate authorities was inevitable, that there was overwhelming logic behind a merger with Oldham. They determined to throw their weight accordingly behind the change and assume leadership roles in the new authority. Above all there was a realisation that the new enlarged authority would have greatly increased resources, the scale to attract and hold professional staff of high calibre, the weight to exercise much greater influence at the regional level and with Whitehall, the muscle to get a fairer share of public spending and grant aid. The formation of the Metropolitan Borough was thus an immense opportunity for Oldham, an opportunity to address the problems that the phase of renewal had not resolved, to move on to create a modern community that could find new pride and confidence in itself. *The Economist* put it well at the time, calling for "a brave attempt to create something good and modern out of something bad and old". Loyal Oldhamers deserved that; whatever was said of the place, the majority still believed "Oldham's all reet, I wouldn't dream of living anywhere else". If creating something good and modern for them had been the challenge in 1945, to a large extent it still remained the challenge of 1974.

*Chapter XV*

# MODERN OLDHAM 1974 - 1999

The new Metropolitan Borough formally assumed its powers in April 1974; a Shadow Authority had been elected in 1973. Fears of Oldham domination were diminished by the realisation that of a total population of about 225,000, the old Borough accounted for only 102,000; of a rateable value of about £21 million, it provided £9 million. In 1973 of fifty-seven councillors elected to the new authority, thirty came from old Districts; that number was to rise to thirty-three when the Council was enlarged to sixty members in 1979. For the first time in Oldham's history there were no aldermen.

## A Difficult Start

There was argument at the time about the name of the new enlarged Metropolitan Borough. Other new unitary authorities, incorporating several old local authorities, had given themselves new names, Tameside, Trafford, Kirklees, Calderdale being examples. While there were those who argued that the name Oldham carried the image of decline, and should be replaced, sensibly the strong familiar historic name was retained. The objective was to give the Oldham name a new image; that of a lively enterprising modern community with great diversity among its parts, much of it set in attractive open Pennine countryside, rather than a decayed drab old mill town. Achieving a united common purpose was also of prime importance. If local District loyalties survived at first and, among the old especially were relinquished reluctantly, gradually a shared Oldham identity would be accepted and acknowledged with pride. Thus Saddleworth, Chadderton, Crompton, Royton, Lees and Failsworth would come to regard themselves as parts of Oldham, parts with their own history, traditions and special character, but parts of a united and coherent whole, large as the contrasts in living circumstances within the whole might be. To change the image, to create a strong united community, was the challenge that faced the leaders of the new authority.

Most of the Councillors elected in 1973 had served before; many knew each other well enough. They all wanted the new authority to succeed and there were few antagonisms. At the elections Labour took firm control with forty-two of the seats. Established and experienced Labour personalities from the old Borough as well as the Districts took the senior Council positions; J. T. "Tenny" Hilton, retired school headmaster and already on the old Borough Council for nearly thirty years, became the first Leader, Ellen Brierley, the first Mayor. Both were safe pairs of hands, well-meaning, forward-looking, concerned with the disadvantaged, and as former school teachers both looked towards education as the hope for Oldham. Another highly influential Labour figure, to many the "Kingmaker", was Arnold Tweedale; his great

**J.T. (Tenny) Hilton**, long-serving Councillor, a retired headmaster who chaired the Education Committee and then for many years was a strong Leader of the Council. Like many of his Labour colleagues he was very committed to social justice and giving the disadvantaged a good start in life; the Councils lack of financial resources was deeply frustrating in his later years. Although from the party's right wing, he held the Labour Councillors together but held onto office too long and lost their support in the end.

**Mayor Making 1974**: Ellen Brierley, first Mayor of the new Metropolitan Borough leads the churching procession. There are no top hats and frock coats, no bands or soldiers and few spectators. (Compare page 272).

interest was in modernising local industry, an issue where his influential connections outside Oldham were valuable. All three personalities were in the best traditions of the Labour party of the time.

An immediate task was the appointment of officers; inevitably there were many losers and many long serving officers retired; generally Oldham officers succeeded to the new senior posts. The Council was also busy with its procedures, harmonising terms and conditions for its staff, arranging accommodation. Along with the new unitary authorities, Government had set up new Metropolitan Councils in the major conurbations. Thus Greater Manchester Council, to which Oldham elected councillors, assumed responsibility for passenger transport, police and fire services, as well as "structural planning" throughout the conurbation. Oldham's buses had already been transferred into a new authority, SELNEC, in 1969. Oldham would raise precepts to pay for those services which it would no longer control. It was probably glad to be rid of the buses which, struggling with loss of passengers, had been a problem for years. Nor were tears shed about the loss of its police to a wider larger regional police authority.

The immediate policy task was to bring together the important services which remained the responsibility of the new Council, not least education, social services, housing and highways as well as the critical planning and economic development functions. If hitherto separate services were brought under a single control, they had also to be harmonised and equalised. That was a challenge in social services, for instance, where in the old Borough provision for the elderly or the disabled was probably as good as anywhere in the country; provision in the old Districts improved significantly as they were raised to that standard. More difficult and controversial was education where the eleven-plus and selective grammar schools had continued outside the Borough and a uniform arrangement had now to be introduced. This task was one of some difficulty and controversy.

Two other issues were immediately prominent, and neither added to the popularity of the new authority. There was the question of where it was to live. An appropriate new civic centre would house the staff, accommodate the

## A Difficult Start

**The architect's drawing of the new Civic Centre**, built on the West Street site that had been waiting "spare" for forty years.

Council but also provide much needed public halls and assembly rooms as well as create an important symbol of the new community. A modest start had been made earlier but more ambitious plans were ready early in 1974, using the central empty West Street site. The new building was costed initially at £4 million, the whole to be financed by private capital and leased to the Borough. In the event, inflation taking over, the new building cost far more, more than £9 million in the end, to be financed by asset sales and further borrowing. Inevitably, this was a minor short-lived controversy.

A second issue was cost, that is local taxes, the rates. Perhaps there were those who hoped the new authority would achieve lower costs in providing its services. That may have been one of the objectives but in the event was harshly disappointed. Formation of the Metropolitan Borough coincided with a steep rise in inflation throughout the United Kingdom. Costs - chiefly fuel related costs, salaries, interest on debt - rose sharply in 1973-74 and subsequent years. Government did not help as, with its own problems, it reduced grant support. The new Greater Manchester Council needed a large precept, partly to maintain large subsidies to the buses although fares were raised 20 per cent. From the start the new Council was struggling to save

The first meeting of Oldham Metropolitan Borough Council in the **new Council Chamber**, April 1978. Ted Lord is Mayor.

money, to constrain the increase in rates. Neither side won; in the outcome, services suffered but rates went up sharply. Thus in its first year the new Council raised domestic rates in Oldham by nearly 20 per cent. Over a five year period the rates in the old Districts, which had been a lot lower than in Oldham, had gradually to be brought into line, which meant sharper increases year by year over the period. Thus in Saddleworth, which had enjoyed the lowest rates and poorest services, the rate increase in 1974-75 was close to 40 per cent.

Things were no easier in the next few years as the Council struggled with higher costs and with overspends. Between 1974-75 and 1980-81 the Council's net expenditure rose from £26 million to £68 million, an increase of over 160 per cent; the Greater Manchester precept doubled in the same period. These changes compare with inflation over these years of about 140 per cent. Postponements of promised improvements, cuts in services, recruitment freezes were the result. In 1975-76 rates in the old Borough went up by a further 20 per cent; in Saddleworth by over 30 per cent. If the increases were smaller in subsequent years they remained substantial; rates more than doubled in the new Council's first six years. A wave of rate protests, charges of gross incompetence, bad housekeeping and high handedness were the result. The fact that the increases in Oldham were less than in many other nearby authorities was hardly seen as mitigation.

All this, of course, was the high stuff of local politics. Ellen Brierley's brave words about the new future when she became Mayor in 1974 were forgotten in a flood of criticism. Whether profligate or not, Oldham's Labour Council was hammered at the polls in 1975; the Labour vote stayed at home as turnout fell sharply and Conservatives made large gains. In the following year, 1976, on a higher poll, further Conservative gains followed, and with twenty-eight seats the Conservatives were the largest party. The following election year, 1978, saw further Tory gains giving them a large majority. The electorate clearly wanted a change in control. Not that life in Oldham grew any easier under the new Conservative administration. As unemployment in the town began to rise and the economy deteriorated in the early years of the Thatcher government in Westminster, Oldham quickly reverted to what had become its normal post-war allegiance. Labour was to return to power in 1980; it has stayed there ever since.

No doubt electoral reverses led to some rethinking among the Labour Councillors, a feeling perhaps that the leadership should pass to a new generation. If the new Borough had not got off to a good start, new ideas and new energy were called for. A changed regime was introduced in the early Eighties with the early retirement of the Chief Executive and the appointment of Colin Smith to succeed him. A new Leader of the Council, John Battye, was elected after a keen three-cornered contest. The new leadership supplied strong vision and determined drive for the modernisation task. Overcoming obstacles and meeting dissent, if upsetting not a few people along the way, it was to prove itself abundantly in the succeeding period. At the local level as at the national, good government needs good opposition to hold it to account. In modern Oldham that was no longer to be provided by the Conservative party but increasingly, as the years passed, by Liberal Democrats, commanding forty per cent of the votes cast, in recent local elections. Labour, however, remained firmly in control. The Oldham electorate which had always been willing to punish managerial failure has, presumably, remained content with its government, autocratic as it may have seemed at times, but always committed, sensible, responsible and efficient.

## Jobs in the New Oldham

Oldham had boomed for a time in the mid-Seventies; unemployment fell below 3 per cent. Courtaulds, the largest remaining employer in textiles with nine mills in the district, specialising in hosiery yarns, were installing new modern equipment and attracting more Asian immigrants to meet their labour needs on a multi-shift system. Other employers enjoyed strong demand; Slumberland, for instance, in 1975, was striving to meet a 50 per cent increase in orders. Osram in Shaw were tempting women with canteen facilities and hourly wages at 60p, or £22 weekly. There were plenty of jobs and, in conditions of high inflation, wages were rising rapidly even if still low by national standards.

The local boom notwithstanding, the new Council in 1974 charged itself to continue and intensify efforts to attract more industry to Oldham, both to secure and create jobs, and to stimulate improved employment conditions and higher earnings as demand for labour skills developed. No Council could create enterprise, nor could it encourage it by grants without Development Area status which Oldham never received. What it could do was make available sites and premises and promote the advantages of Oldham as a place to do business. And this became firm policy.

To this end the Council continued to buy old cotton mills, whether to refurbish and let them, or demolish them to create vacant land. Small derelict sites in the inner area were cleared wherever possible, often to create small nursery units for letting. But larger initiatives were taken, sometimes involving considerable expense, with the objective of creating industrial estates where aspirant firms, relocating or incomers, could lease modern standard industrial premises, or alternatively acquire sites to create their own development. Thus the old Platt site at Werneth was acquired in 1980 for over £1 million; further sums were then spent in clearance and the provision of roads, services and buildings.

**The main Platt site** in Werneth, redeveloped with modern housing and small commercial units.

**Industrial renewal**: Platt's nineteenth century offices, refurbished and converted to new uses.

**Dole queues** returned to Oldham with a period of severe unemployment in the early Eighties.

These efforts, strategic and important as they were, seemed insignificant when the local economy slumped in the early Eighties. The residual cotton and rayon spinning industry centred around Courtaulds, turned down sharply in 1980 although Courtaulds it has to be said, retained its presence in Oldham and continued to invest throughout the Eighties. But elsewhere mill closures and widespread redundancies reflected the recession in the national economy, the aftermath of high inflation and loss of competitiveness, aggravated by an over-valued pound resulting from North Sea oil. Unemployment throughout the United Kingdom doubled between 1979 and 1981 and continued to rise through 1985. That the recession was so severe in Oldham again reflected the fragile local economy, the weaknesses of many local businesses, marginal to larger concerns or small on their own. Dronsfields, the last of Oldham's textile engineers, failed in 1981. Even larger local concerns like Ferranti were in deep trouble. Oldham lost at least 10,000 manufacturing jobs during this period. Many other areas dependent on manufacturing suffered, in the North and Midlands especially, but that was of little comfort to Oldham.

The rise in local unemployment that started in late 1979 is the best index of local hardship. By February 1981 over 11,000 people were workless. Unemployment then was 11.5 per cent; at the worst point in 1982 the number

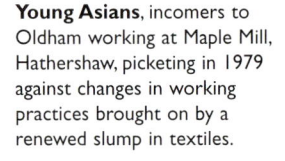

**Young Asians**, incomers to Oldham working at Maple Mill, Hathershaw, picketing in 1979 against changes in working practices brought on by a renewed slump in textiles.

## Jobs in the New Oldham

out of work reached 15,000, a rate of over 15 per cent. Those unemployed had to adjust to a sharp loss of earnings, typically for a man from £100 a week to a dole of £30 or £40. Not surprisingly, arrears of council house rents rose sharply. The situation was not helped, either for Oldhamers or local businesses, by further sharp increases in local rates including one of 22 per cent in 1981. So large an increase followed savage cuts in council services and reflected reductions in central government grants and a brief return to high inflation. Reduced housing subsidies resulted in large rises in Council rents at the same time, a double whammy for many in the town.

The only appropriate response was for the Council to redouble its efforts to attract new businesses and new employment. In 1981, controversially, it spent £2 million in acquiring and developing a site at Derker Mill to be leased to Ferranti, now a struggling enterprise relying heavily on public support. Generally in 1981 and 1982, however, there were plenty of available sites and buildings, but a lack of employers. The Government of the day were no more willing to give Oldham any special status than their predecessors. But in efforts to clear dereliction, adapt the best of the remaining mills, and develop new well-serviced sites for industrial use, the Borough was successful in attracting financial support from other public sources. It had notable success in Brussels with the European Regional Development Fund (ERDF), initially with the redevelopment of the Prince Mill site in Royton, a £2.5 million project to create a new industrial unit complex, where the Fund put up 50 per cent of the cost. The ERDF and other agencies and sources of public funding were to remain crucial in Oldham's drive to strengthen its economy and improve its appearance, image and environment. Salmon Fields at Royton was an attractive new greenfield business park, providing about 40 acres for industrial and commercial use, assisted by these agencies. Outside help notwithstanding, it cost the Borough £1.5 million in capital expenditure and encountered fierce local opposition. Strong and determined leadership to meet this resistance and overcome obstacles to the project was needed to get Salmon Fields off the drawing board. But big fights over projects of this kind had always been a feature of Oldham.

By 1985 local unemployment although well above 10 per cent and especially high for men, was falling slowly. As the national economy recovered, Oldham as a locality again came in demand by enterprises of all kinds, looking for space to expand or relocate. The Motorway links, existing to the M62 and potential, with the promised implementation of the M60

**Apprentice Presentation 1976**: efforts to develop and diversify Oldham's economy have put great emphasis on training and retraining. Jack Armitage is Mayor.

**Modern industrial premises at Salmon Fields**, developed as a business park with European Regional Development Funds.

*Above:* Oldham's link to the M62.

*Right:* **Morrison's Supermarket** in what had been Marlborough Mill, Failsworth, built in 1908.

passing through the south of the Borough and affording swift links to Manchester airport, and greatly improved access to central Manchester with the widening of the A62, were an important plus. In 1988 there was even talk of a mini-boom. The lack of large sites and suitable buildings again became a problem and land values began to rise. Industrial sites commanded values of £100,000 an acre, a figure that would compare with £400 or thereabouts a century earlier. But solutions continued to be found.

Although most of the old cotton mills had been demolished, over seventy, some of them downmarket and offering little more than cheap space, but most of them cleaned, modified and refurbished for quality occupation, remained in use. Adding to the several small industrial estates, a notable new initiative was the creation in the Nineties of Broadway Business Park on the 100 acre site of the obsolete Slacks Valley power station, Oldham and Chadderton's pride in the 1920s. Here again the Council moved to buy the whole site, at a cost of over £5 million, and develop it as a modern industrial estate. Meanwhile it did not neglect the redevelopment of older industrial areas and property. A balance had to be struck between the needs of existing Oldham firms for expansion and the desirability of attracting new enterprise from outside. Equally, the Council, with its limited resources, had to sell completed developments in order to fund the creation of further modern industrial floorspace and employment.

If the late Eighties brought a revival, there was a further setback in the early Nineties, with the number of unemployed rising again. Oldham's experience continued to parallel that of the United Kingdom; the middle and late Nineties brought renewed prosperity with reported unemployment falling back below 5 per cent. Whatever the average unemployment figure, however, the deprived parts of inner Oldham and many of the large council estates remained characterised by persistent chronic high levels of unemployment, especially among ethnic minorities.

## Jobs in the New Oldham

**The Stationery Office, Orbital Industrial Park, Chadderton**; Rugby Mill built in 1908 during the last main phase of cotton-mill building, is in the background.

There can be little doubt that attempts to stimulate, attract and accommodate new enterprise in Oldham have had considerable success. Restructuring Oldham's industry has not been without pain. Some of the former stalwarts have retreated or withdrawn. Under pressure of foreign competition Courtaulds, despite their massive investment in new technology, have had to close their yarn spinning operations in several Oldham mills. The Ferranti business finally went into liquidation but important parts of its high technology activities were continued as a result of management buyouts or the participation of international companies such as Siemens and GEC/Plessey. Other well-established Oldham businesses survived and flourished, diversifying and adapting to changed circumstances. That would be true of the Shiloh group for instance, producing quality yarns and sewing threads at Elk Mill, headed by the fourth generation of the Gartside family who were among Oldham's leading cotton entrepreneurs at the end of the nineteenth century. Another Oldham success story would be Seton Healthcare which manages a wide range of branded medical products and over-the-counter medicines from its local base. Homeshopping, as mail order has become, continues to flourish in adapted spinning mills employing about 3,000 people. British Aerospace is there with 2,000 jobs, Northern Foods with around 1,600.

**The refurbished Gorse Mill, Chadderton**, also dating from 1908, now used for warehousing and distribution of electrical fittings.

The district is now home to a large variety of manufacturing and wholesaling businesses, large and small, private or part of larger international groups, in fields as diverse as aerospace, electrical goods, electronics, engineering, food processing, catering, vehicles, furniture and clothing. All benefit from Oldham's low costs, improving communications, an available workforce with excellent attitudes and versatile skills backed by excellent training facilities, and a strongly supportive local authority. Manufacturing is not as important in Oldham as it was; it now provides only about 35 per cent of local jobs, less than half the proportion of fifty years ago, although much more than in the United Kingdom as a whole. But Oldham's manufacturing base is now a diverse one and hopefully a more robust one that will continue to find competitive status in the future.

Meanwhile jobs in the broader area of services have continued to expand, for women more than men, and part-timers in particular. Retailing, wholesale distribution, catering, hotels employ nearly one quarter of the workforce reflecting where people spend their money. A flourishing town centre has created many more jobs in services as has a developing tourist business in Saddleworth. Financial services now provide significant numbers of jobs with Sun Alliance prominent at a large data processing operation in Hollinwood,

**Modern out-of-town shopping**; in the background Elk Mill, the last cotton spinning mill to be built in Oldham in 1926.

although in this field, as in the professions, management and administration, Oldham suffers, as in the past, from the proximity of central Manchester. Local administration, education (with 5,000 jobs) and not least health care have expanded enormously to provide another quarter of all jobs. In these respects Oldham is a far kinder place of employment; the tyranny of long hours and poor working conditions in the mill has gone; a greater choice of jobs is available and work is far more congenial and secure.

If national and international businesses choose to locate and invest in Oldham, many people who work elsewhere, in Manchester, Rochdale or Tameside for instance, perhaps as many as 40,000, choose to live in the

Borough; their numbers far exceed those who work in the Borough but live outside. The residential commuter, whether Oldham born or an incomer, is attracted by convenience, comparative cost, the green environment and the quality of life available. Commuters, like the many retired people who live in Oldham, or the growing numbers of visitors who enjoy its modern shopping experience and tourist amenities, bring income and spending into the Borough and support employment in the service sector. All these are, like manufacturing, an important part of the primary base on which secondary activities depend. The Oldham economy at the end of the Twentieth Century is broad based, successful and flourishing. The claim of high prosperity had been made a century earlier, based on cotton spinning and textile engineering. If a great deal had changed in the period, a new economic base has been found. As someone had predicted, through contrivance and determination, the Oldham hive, to its credit, has been kept humming.

**Hikers in Dobcross Square**, domestic architecture, typical of the Pennines and scarcely changed from the eighteenth century.

### Oldham's Modern Education

The Metropolitan Borough in 1974 had two systems of secondary education - an imperfect comprehensive system in Oldham itself, and a selective grammar and secondary modern system in the former Districts. The Council acted without delay to "abolish the eleven-plus" and go comprehensive throughout. In selling its policy the bullet points were "No more selection or rejection. No more pressure on Junior schools to secure Grammar School passes". Existing grammar and modern schools in Failsworth and Chadderton, Crompton and Royton were merged to form comprehensives, making the best of the existing buildings and creating more split-site situations, schools in two parts. Over 6,000 children were affected, 1,200 of them in two grammar schools. In Saddleworth, the existing school was expanded to add a new sixth form and create a large comprehensive. Rather brutally Oldham now withdrew all the paid-for places that had been provided for children of ability at Hulme. So far as most Oldham children were concerned they now had a limited choice of comprehensive schools, good or bad: the alternative for those who could afford was fee-paying or a scholarship at independent schools.

All these changes did little to enamour the new authority to people living in Saddleworth or the old Districts. They contributed to the defeat of Labour Councillors in municipal elections in the mid and late Seventies. There were other problems in some of Oldham's comprehensive schools, indiscipline, falling standards and vandalism. Particular schools inevitably acquired a poor reputation; one such was the split-site Hathershaw Comprehensive where, following a series of alarming incidents in 1976, the authority had to replace the headmaster and toughen the regime to restore standards and restore a confident image. These, of course were familiar problems all over the country.

More serious was the low attainment at Oldham's eleven comprehensive schools, and to a lesser extent its four voluntary church secondary schools. GCSE results, not published by the Council, were markedly below national and regional averages. As in the past, the staying-on rate beyond sixteen was especially low, as low as one-third of the age group, about half the national average. Too many children were still leaving school as soon as they could, and inevitably lost interest in school well before they could leave. Sixth form attainment as indicated by A level performance was also one of the lowest in the country. The sixth forms were small, in many cases not viable, lacking the body of pupils needed to generate involvement and justify a broad range of subjects; they were not stimulating places, as a rule, and gave only limited opportunities; the number of Oldham children proceeding to university compared unfavourably with national averages as a result. Oldham's schools it was felt were failing local employers, failing parents, failing the children themselves.

So in the mid-Eighties Oldham began to debate the future of its post-sixteen education. It could stay as it was with its failing schools. It could take the so-called tertiary route merging all post-sixteen further education, academic, technical, vocational in an enlarged Oldham College. Or it could develop an entirely new institution, a Sixth Form College that would replace the existing sixth forms with a large central provision.

Oldham College itself was flourishing, enrolling as many as 1,400 full-time further education students a year, not merely from Oldham schools. Its site in central Oldham was taking up to 6,000 students on full and part-time courses, many adults, catering for a wide range of vocational subjects, training programmes and leisure activities. But it was outgrowing its site, its buildings were becoming dated, and the fusion of academic and technical or vocational had its drawbacks.

A long period of debate and consultation followed, finally resolved in 1989 with a decision to go the Sixth Form College route. There was some argument about the site but finally and happily a convenient central position was found,

**Oldham's Sixth Form College.**

the site of the old Oldham Royal Infirmary. At a cost of £16 million, partly financed by the Metropolitan Borough, but mainly by Whitehall, the new College was completed in 1992. It was a splendid facility of which the town could be proud; there had been nothing like it before in Oldham. Ironically, no sooner had it been opened, the Government removed Further Education from the domain of local authorities. Oldham Sixth Form College, like Oldham College of Further Education, became an independent corporate body, funded directly from the centre through the Further Education Funding Council. This was of little concern. Neither College would flourish if they were not sensitive to the needs of the local community, children, parents, employers, and serving these needs well. Each College has been a success.

Some of the comprehensives, such as North Chadderton, "the school of proven worth" as it was called, and voluntary aided Church of England schools such as Crompton House and Blue Coat School, which had large

**John Battye, Leader of Oldham MBC**, topping out the Sixth Form College in 1992.

**The main entrance to the Sixth Form College** incorporates the doorway of the old Royal Infirmary.

sixth forms and were achieving good results at that level, have retained them. Saddleworth School, although it had the best results in the Borough, lost its sixth form despite a vigourous campaign to save it. Apart from the Roman Catholic schools, all the other comprehensives supported the new College which quickly became the main provider with a sixth form of well over a thousand students. Its achievement is manifest in vastly increased participation beyond sixteen, not least from the Asian community, and significantly improved examination performance. Oldham's staying-on rate among sixteen and seventeen year olds has risen dramatically to over 60 per cent. Its Sixth Form College results are now above the national average. More and more Oldham students are now proceeding to higher education. In a potentially important initiative Oldham College and the Sixth Form College, in partnership with Manchester's universities, are developing courses leading to degrees and other qualifications in business studies, for those who want to stay on. Oldham, in the next few years, will have its Business School. All these are striking changes from the past. One outside comment in 1997 could say:

"In one of the most far-sighted acts of policy possible at the local level, the investment of the community in the development of excellence at Oldham's sixth form college has begun to pay real dividends".

Oldham's initiatives to modernise its schools were not confined to further education, important as that was. The Borough in 1974 had about one hundred primary schools; notwithstanding falling school rolls, it still has that number. School closure, parental choice, educational standards remained lively issues. Quality and performance can be influenced in many ways but not least by building and facilities. Many old inner area schools have been given up since 1974, to be replaced with new schools, continuing the pattern of the post-war years. Notably the Council has found resources to create a new primary school each year, either an entirely new building or a modern replacement for outdated premises. While there are many post war schools that now look dated and shabby, Oldham can be proud of its many new

**Alexandra Park School**, one of many Oldham primary schools rebuilt in the Nineties.

schools, models for what the remainder may become.

Meanwhile, in the inner areas of the Borough there is an overwhelming proportion of Asian children in several primary and some comprehensive schools. It is in some of the comprehensive schools, whether in the inner area or serving the large council estates where deprivation is pronounced, that the attainment of fifteen year olds in GCSE remains particularly disappointing, offering sharp contrasts to the results of the voluntary aided schools and more favoured comprehensives like Saddleworth or North Chadderton, let alone selective independent schools like Hulme. Oldham still has work to do to improve attainment in secondary education.

There is another important strand in Oldham's educational provision, namely adult and community education. Night schools, continuation schools were established before 1914 and maintained between the wars. More recently, from existing school buildings and from dedicated facilities, there is substantial provision for life-long learning, for the acquistion of relevant new skills and the development of hobbies, interests, cultural and leisure pursuits.

Meanwhile the Hulme Grammar Schools continue to flourish as independent schools. Losing their direct grant status and support from local authorities in 1976, they benefited modestly from the assisted places scheme in the Eighties and Nineties. The ending of that scheme will reduce if not remove the opportunity of children from poor or modest homes to share the traditions and standards which the Hulme Schools have maintained. But the Schools themselves are full with over 1,500 pupils, and many Oldham parents as well as those from farther afield continue to make the financial sacrifices to ensure their children receive the particular education which they provide. They remain a beacon for the Sixth Form College and Oldham's comprehensives to emulate.

## A Modern Town Centre

Already prior to 1974 the old Borough Council were preparing for a major new shopping facility in the town centre, acquiring sites and property, demolishing old buildings and planning a new enclosed shopping mall with leading national multiples as tenants and incorporating appropriate parking facilities. Such a mall, it was felt, would be a magnet that would revitalise the centre of Oldham, a modern counterpart to the traditional popular stalls of Tommyfield. As these plans matured, what in some ways had been the heart of old Oldham's "up-town", the Market Hall at Tommyfield was destroyed in a devastating fire in 1974. A further new opportunity to create modern facilities was presented.

Nothing was without controversy. Market traders, shop tenants, their business sensitive to a host of influences on the spending power and number and frequency of shopper visits, as well as rents and other operating costs, were vociferous critics of each initiative, especially if it threatened their livelihoods. The Council had to tread carefully, to consult, to respond but at the end of the day to decide.

It did not hurry with the new Tommyfield market, providing instead a makeshift temporary building. Within six months most of the tenants burnt out in the old hall were rehoused in this way. Plans for the new shopping mall, Town Square as it was eventually called, were well received when presented

**Demolition** of the unloved St. Peter's Precinct.

Oldham Brave Oldham

in 1975. Meanwhile the old Co-op buildings in King Street, long since outdated and dilapidated had been replaced with a modern superstore. With the Belgrade Hotel, opened in 1968, Oldham's town centre took another step forward.

Some years were to pass before Town Square became a reality but when it opened in 1981 it was an immediate success, both to the tenants and with the shopping public. For the Council, owner of the site, it was a fruitful partnership with a property developer who financed the building; the Council received ground rents and substantial rate revenue. Emboldened the Council saw the opportunity to go further with its drive to modernise the central area by replacing the drab decaying notoriously unsuccessful St Peter's Precinct with an extension of Town Square's enclosed mall. The plans for the Spindles Centre incorporating the latest concepts in town centre shopping, were revealed in 1986. After its acquistion in 1988 demolition of the old unloved Precinct followed and the ambitious new Centre was opened in 1991. Again it was a partnership between the Council and a specialist developer, Arlington Retail Developments. The whole Centre cost £54 million of which the Council had provided £6 million, mainly in acquiring property and site preparation, an outlay that would yield a satisfactory return in rental income. As one councillor said, "we are here to create an attractive town that is a magnet, drawing in people who want to do business here". He went on, "it is up to the skills of the business community to take advantage of the environment we have created".

Oldham now had a large enclosed modern state-of-art shopping facility,

# A Modern Town Centre

supported by extensive contiguous car parking that transformed the appeal of its central area. A pedestrianised High Street and Market Place and adjacent streets such as George Street and Curzon Street augmented the malls with traditional shops, banks, public houses and the like. Pedestrianised civic spaces such as George Square were an attractive new feature, significantly enhancing the general environment. Tommyfield, where the open stalls continued to provide look-and-choose traditional economical shopping complementing the new centre, secured its new £5 million Market Hall in 1990. The whole central area was supported by a convenient but not ideal central bus station and other bus stopping places.

These bold changes were not without their critics. Many independent shopkeepers, hostile to the "posh new centre", lost out; the peripheral shopping areas, along Yorkshire Street in particular, decayed with the completion of the new malls. There were those who pointed out the failure to attract a major flagship retailer such as Marks and Spencer. Others complained of undistinguished new buildings - the new Market Hall in particular - and the survival of tawdry shabby shop fronts and facades. The low-key cynics claimed "they are trying to make it into a city when it is only a working man's town"; their argument was that the past was "good enough for Oldham". But much had changed for the better; the new facilities were to retain trade and attract new trade from outside the district, so creating many jobs, and could only significantly enhance the image of the town. Their commercial success, the extent to which they were used, was the best measure of public appreciation.

Although so much had changed, Oldham's leaders, encouraged by the successes achieved, felt that more was needed, to refurbish or replace the remaining shabby buildings and in particular to provide additional retail development and leisure and cultural facilities to create a truly modern vibrant centre. The prospective extension of Metrolink will introduce efficient high quality modern swift public transport through the heart of the town, connecting it to central Manchester and much of the Manchester conurbation. This would be a catalyst for regeneration, offering unrivalled accessibility, so lacking in the past. The next stage, in progress as property and sites are acquired and prepared, will be a further retail mall, broadening the quality and range of available shopping, and a new cultural and leisure quarter incorporating a multiplex cinema and a new modern art gallery as well as a new library, theatre, museum and other facilities. Existing parking will be augmented; the heritage core of old Oldham preserved, refurbished and enhanced by design initiatives and new focal points, and more pedestrianised public squares created to uplift the visitor experience. Finally

*Top:* **George Square**, civic open space in Oldham's modern town centre.

*Above:* Looking down **Yorkshire Street**, 1998.

*Facing, above:* Interior of the new **Spindles Mall**; the stained glass is the work of the locally-born artist, Brian Clarke.

*Facing, below:* **Aerial view of the modern town centre**, Union Street and the Lyceum in the foreground, Town Square and Spindles in the centre, the Civic Centre in the background.

a new central bus station will provide convenient high quality facilities complementing Metrolink and connecting the centre to the entire district. All these plans are in progress, to be financed by European Regional Development Funds augmented by substantial public and private partnership funds, and attracting huge private investment in shopping and visitor facilities.

The future town centre will not correspond to the idealism of the post-war dream but will be a dramatic transformation of the old inheritance, fit to stand comparison with any in similar towns in the country. Apart from the competitive status of its shopping and visitor facilities, it will look good. Appearance and first impressions, interest and dignity, are crucially important and if that was forgotten in Oldham in the past, there is a strong awareness that they matter in the present. This will be a centre with which Oldhamers can be proud.

## Health and Leisure

Oldham waited for a long time for its much-needed new hospital. The project continued to be delayed by severe resource constraints in the Health Service. As over many years, patients complained of long delays at clinics, seemingly eternal waiting lists for operations. Oldham and District General Hospital had only 600 beds and 120 maternity beds; its acute facilities, operating theatres and the like, fell far short of modern standards and requirements. Excellent as the staff were, facilities were especially inadequate, inefficient and out-dated at the old Royal Infirmary, described in 1976 as one of the most dilapidated hospitals in the country. It continued in use until 1989; its cramped and deteriorating buildings providing a further 160 beds, mainly for accident and emergency. Backward as the town was in these respects, it could still claim some major medical advances. The world's first test-tube baby was born at ODGH in July 1978.

Eventually the promised new 1,200 bed hospital materialised. Enlargement and reconstruction of ODGH began in 1981 and was completed in 1989 at a cost of £18 million. An impressive modern hospital providing modern health care for the whole district was the result, efficient, far more effective and responsive to demand, as good as any in the region.

If the hospital came in the end, Oldham's health record has not been a good one. Death rates, although far below what they were, nonetheless have remained above national levels. Other measures of health such as the

**The Royal Oldham Hospital**, completed in 1989.

**Another view of The Royal Oldham Hospital**, incorporating part of the older Boundary Park Hospital. The design permits possible new wings to provide additional accommodation as required in the future.

incidence of limiting illness or mental disorders, to name but a few, are not encouraging. This may reflect the unhealthy working environments of the past, or more probably the extent of deprivation in the present. Unemployment, overcrowding, damp unfit houses, inadequate heating, poor diet, inadequate transport facilities all contribute to poor health, depression and stress. Certainly death rates and limiting illness are highest in the most disadvantaged neighbourhoods, in the wards with large ethnic minority populations or some of the large housing estates. Elsewhere health compares favourably with anywhere in the country.

But if there is concern about the health of the local population, there is a well-justified belief that local provision of social services compares favourably with the rest of the country. This is especially true of the care of the elderly - a numerous group in Oldham in recent decades. Domiciliary care, provision of purpose built sheltered accommodation and of residential and nursing home accommodation is generous and to a high caring standard. Similarly Oldham has always taken good care of those who are disabled, both when

**Westhulme**, built as an isolation hospital in 1877, now used for hospital administration.

337

**Schools Swimming Gala** in Oldham Sports Centre, 1998.

they are at school and throughout their lives.

Leisure facilities are important too in making Oldham a better place to live. Swimming had always been immensely popular in the district and unsurprisingly the provision of a new large modern swimming pool received high priority in post-war thinking. Certainly the old central baths on Union Street had become outdated, if not primitive by modern standards. And there were too many scattered small baths across the district. Here again there was a long delay between conception and realisation. A large modern sports centre conveniently situated in the town centre was opened in 1975.

In the past Oldham's public open space provision was poor. Post-war secondary schools had playing fields in most cases, but with restricted access; the general public has not been well-served. Not surprisingly proposals to use the Clayton playing fields for retail development in 1990, however well-

**Clayton Playing Fields**, Boundary Park in the background.

**Joe Royle, Manager of Oldham Athletic**, leads his team out at Wembley for the Littlewoods Cup Final against Nottingham Forest in 1990.

intentioned, encountered a hostile public response. Subsequently Oldham has adopted a very positive policy and is determined to create first-class arts and sporting facilities for the whole community. Following the closure of the rugby ground at Watersheddings, a new sports complex is proposed adjacent to Boundary Park, with a state-of-the-art stadium for Oldham Athletic FC and Oldham Rugby League Club and several new modern playing fields. Nearby a new athletics track is also planned. All this will be complemented by changing rooms, health and fitness facilities, bars, restaurants, even a motel, and conference and banqueting rooms. With the Council providing the land, private investment will have to meet most of the multi-million pound cost of these developments.

The town never had this kind of thing in the past. but despite poor facilities, in the world of sport as in the arts, it has produced in recent years a remarkable stream of talent. At one point, Oldham could boast both the captains of England's Football and Cricket teams, David Platt and Michael Atherton. The town has always been very musical and is well represented by Oldhamers in the contemporary classical and pop worlds. In theatre there has been a steady stream of talented Oldham performers, Eric Sykes, Dora Bryan, Bernard Cribbins among them. There are distinguished visual artists like Brian Clarke with Oldham roots.

Provision for leisure, culture and the arts now receive high priority in a community determined to be modern and compare with the best. An impressive sports complex, like cultural facilities in an attractive town centre, is seen as a gateway for investment into the entire district. Perhaps as never before, and

339

**Upper Tame, Denshaw**, traditional Pennine buildings from the domestic woollen industry period, modernised for contemporary living.

role of the local authority.

The activities of the Housing Associations apart, for many Oldham people, the huge stock of council houses, although less than it was, is the only source of an affordable dwelling, albeit frequently with the help of benefit. The Council remains, and will remain, the largest landlord in Oldham, a public rather than a private landlord; it is constantly striving to be a better, friendlier landlord. Its stated objective is to ensure for the people of Oldham a choice from a variety of affordable housing options that provide them with the opportunity to live in a home that is warm, dry, safe and secure. That objective, a physical one to provide decent housing, worded to reflect a commitment to avoid the mistakes of the past, is now at least largely met on the council estates. Provision of quality of life, in this respect the sense of pride, ownership, dignity and satisfaction an individual feels in relation to where he lives, is only partly achieved. Slowly in one way or another, Oldham's estates are being made better places to live although much more remains to be done. The larger problems of deficient housing provision remain in the inner areas of the Borough, which to a large extent have become the home of Oldham's ethnic minorities. Solving their problems of overcrowding, old unfit houses and a depressed environment, is Oldham's largest current housing challenge.

**The Inner Area and Oldham's Ethnic Minority Community**

As with its problem estates, Oldham is not alone in having an inner area problem. Decayed old urban areas have been a feature of most of the towns and cities that had mushroomed in the nineteenth century, anywhere in the world. In Oldham's case, extensive clearance had left residual old housing, some in large blocks, some fragmented, much still threatened by clearance and typically surrounded by dereliction, empty mills, old commercial premises and ill-served by amenities or community facilities. The inner area included the core of the old Borough and a corridor stretching through Hollinwood and Failsworth to the Manchester boundary. Here was ugly and depressing blight by any standards, although the blight was variable since the inner area still included blocks of residential streets such as Glodwick or Werneth Coppice, the superior nineteenth century middle class suburbs. By the late Seventies about 50,000 people were still living in this rundown area.

House property in the inner area could be rented or purchased cheaply in the post-war period. There were many places of employment nearby, and good access to public transport. Hence the area's attraction to the immigrants which Oldham continued to attract by its work opportunities. East Europeans after the war had settled in Glodwick. Afro-Caribbeans, in small numbers, had been followed by Asians, recruited by a declining cotton industry. Once a nucleus of incomers had been formed, mainly at first single men, others joined them seeking security and help from community association. The patterns of settlement which Irish immigrants had followed in the mid-nineteenth century were followed by the new immigrants. As the incomers moved in, many of the long term residents moved out. For them this was no longer the place to live. Those who remained were generally those who could not afford to move, those in poor circumstances and especially the elderly, lacking resources and clinging to a disappearing neighbourhood way of life.

Particular neighbourhoods became the home of Oldham's rapidly growing Asian population. Glodwick and Coppice, for instance, became Pakistani and to a lesser extent Indian neighbourhoods; Oldham's Bangladeshi community settled mainly in Westwood and Coldhurst. Some of these neighbourhoods, Coppice and some of the roads near Alexandra Park, for instance, were especially attractive to immigrants since they offered somewhat larger houses, well suited to multi-family or large household occupation, while being close to textile mills. Generally, Asian immigrants wanted to buy houses, as a good way of saving money and to achieve status and security; many, unable to rent, had no alternative but to buy.

From 4,500 in 1971, Oldham's Asian community had grown to 7,000 in 1981. Some of the newcomers came from Asian communities elsewhere in the United Kingdom, in Bradford or West London, for instance, but most came from well-defined districts in Pakistan and, if at a later stage, from Bangladesh; smaller numbers had come from India. Many were relatives of the early young male immigrants, or the wives and children of arranged marriages. Continued immigration and a particularly high rate of natural increase, caused the numbers to rise to close to 15,000 in 1991 and 21,000 in 1997 with a very high proportion of young children. By the Nineties, the problems of Oldham's inner area were mainly coincident with the associated problems of its Asian communities. Thus the Pakistani community in Glodwick and Coppice, close to 12,000 people in 1997, could represent up to 80 per cent of the local population in its particular neighbourhoods. In Westwood, a similar overwhelmingly Bangladeshi concentration of about 7,500 people had formed. By then the different and separate ethnic minority groups were approaching 50 per cent of the population living in the whole inner area.

Not merely were these large Asian populations living in a depressing run-down environment. As their numbers had grown, the work opportunities in textiles which had attracted them in the first place, had disappeared. A high proportion were in very poor circumstances, characterised by severely overcrowded homes, very high rates of unemployment, and large dependency on benefits to sustain a low standard of living. Here was social exclusion on a large scale, and also a tinder-box for discontent and upheaval. Thus Oldham had a dual problem: a run-down inner area, and a rapidly growing but deprived ethnic minority community living in that inner area.

The Council, like other urban authorities, chose to concentrate on the physical problem of renewal. Encouraged by central government, Oldham developed its first Inner Areas Programme for the years 1979-82. Its features included the provision of land and factory units for industry, environmental improvement and the provision of important amenities such as swimming pools, sports halls and community centres. Large expenditures were envisaged, to be financed partly by government, partly by the rates. Everything was impossibly ambitious.

**Asian Oldhamers** in Glodwick.

## Oldham Brave Oldham

The Inner Areas Programme continued, to be revised regularly, attracting what assistance it could from a large variety of Whitehall and European Union support schemes. Although the resources available have been variable, bit by bit, much was accomplished. With continuing demolition the number of people living in the inner area fell, certainly to below 40,000. With difficulty more land and premises were made available for industry, mainly in small sites. Housing renewal has continued slowly, especially in Glodwick and Westwood, and the environment has been improved mainly by clearing derelict sites, demolishing old mills and buildings, creating public open space and planting trees wherever possible. Many of the better old buildings, like Platts old offices, were refurbished and cleaned, a quick and effective way of improving appearance and image. Vandalism, litter and fly-tipping remained a problem. Concern with resentment and backlash among indigenous Oldhamers has made the Council proceed cautiously, especially with regard to provision of community facilities. Taking stock in the Nineties, however, it is apparent that whatever has been achieved, and this is substantial, there is still a long way to go to modernise the inner areas.

If something had been done to ameliorate the physical environment other problems of the minority community remained. Many Asian families had bought old houses cheaply, often with little regard to their poor physical condition. Small houses, two-up and two-down became the homes of large families, frequently three generations. Four to five, even six, children remain the norm. Only to a limited extent, have Asians become tenants of council housing; they have avoided the large estates primarily because of fears of hostility and racial harassment; allegations of discrimination in allocating

**An Asian family in Werneth Coppice**, living in a Housing Association home.

council houses have lacked substance but the issue remains a sensitive one. Housing Associations have made a modest contribution to providing suitable homes, but typically an Asian family, even if it had the resources to move, as many have, will want to remain within its own community with its places of worship, food shops and neighbours practising the same distinctive customs conferring self-esteem, identity and security. Thus, in Glodwick and Westwood, the main areas of concentration, overcrowded unfit homes remain the norm. They are often the starting point of poor health, limiting illness and tensions within the family, not least where there are growing children with rising aspirations.

Inevitably traditional religious rules with regard to customs and practices within families are being questioned and are weakening. Third generation Asians are typically developing a hybrid culture, a mixture of their own and western traditions; this can cause concern and deep pain to parents. Asian youth can easily become alienated in these circumstances and leave a crowded home to take to the streets for much of the time.

Within predominantly Asian neighbourhoods, existing schools, primary and secondary, have become dominated by Asian children, perhaps to the extent of 95 per cent of their enrolment. These schools were generally those in older, less satisfactory premises; some of them experienced teacher recruitment problems as well. As the number of pupils increased rapidly, buildings were frequently overcrowded, although new building and refurbishment is doing much to improve the situation. Many of the children had no or limited command of English at the time of joining school; language support was essential and has been provided with the use of Government Section Eleven grant aid. Cultural tradition means some Asian pupils have been handicapped in their schooling by extended absence when parents took them back on visits to family homes in Pakistan and Bangladesh. In overcrowded homes, facilities for study are often poor. Attainment at school, affected by language and cultural factors, whether at primary or secondary level was initially low, well below the average for all Oldham schools, but more recently has shown significant improvement. There is a growing recognition within the Asian community of the importance of education for personal and career advancement. The Sixth Form College in particular is an attractive and valuable facility for aspiring young Asians, anxious to improve their prospects, but bound by traditional culture to their homes and families.

The rapidly growing numbers of Asian youths have been at a disadvantage. Like many young from Oldham's other deprived areas, they have entered the employment market with poor chances. Religion and culture can inhibit young Asian women from entering many occupations. What work is available is often poor quality, some of it, for girls and women, home-work for the clothing industry, unskilled and badly paid. An address in Glodwick or in Westwood, an Asian name, will deter many employers from considering a job applicant. Advice on jobs and careers is often lacking. Asians remain poorly represented in Oldham's service industries. Where minorities are recruited to "make the numbers look right", promotion to greater responsibility is often hard to win. But some who have been able to accumulate capital, own and manage successful businesses, mainly in retailing, property, taxis and restaurants, but also in manufacturing. Oldham does not lack successful

**Waterloo Street in Glodwick, 1998**; St. Mark's church in the background.

Asian entrepreneurs, perhaps even millionaires. There are signs of an "ethnic economy" emerging and the job aspirations of many Asian school leavers will point to the developing ethnic business sector. On the bright side, a growing number are progressing through further and higher education to better jobs. Tesco, opening a new store in Westwood in 1998, will recruit over half its staff from the local Asian community. If the situation is improving in these ways, unemployment generally, and long-term unemployment and youth unemployment particularly, still remain high in the Asian neighbourhoods.

Meanwhile Oldham's Asian population continues to grow at a very high rate. It is projected to reach 39,000 in 2011 when it will approach 18 per cent of a stable total population. Distinctive communities determined to maintain their own culture, religion and languages, and more resistant to integration than other previous immigrant groups, are "here to stay", as the saying goes; Oldham is their permanent home. Achieving decent work opportunities and good, affordable housing will remain a challenge for the Asians, established as they now are.

Given the local concentration of the Pakistani and Bangladeshi communities, interaction and communication with the indigenous community remains restricted and superficial, as is understanding of the extent of deprivation. Tensions within and between the communities and circumstances of suspicion and prejudice with working class Oldham remain alive. Many in the indigenous majority resent anything in the way of special treatment they feel the minority may receive. Tensions are exacerbated by the growing activities of disaffected unemployed Asian youths, vandalism, criminal gang behaviour and drug dealing. There have been occasional racial incidents but none so far of serious proportions. Thus with the substantial growth in its Asian population, Oldham still has much to do to establish and maintain harmonious relations between its Asian communities, and its indigenous population. Equally to improve their quality of life and widen their opportunities, the Asians themselves will have to move away from some of their separateness, even intransigence, in dress, for instance, in language, in attitudes to particular occupations, adopting increasingly local customs and practices.

Pessimism can go too far. Oldham's Asians, like immigrants to Oldham in the past, will become and are becoming a hard working, successful, progressive part of a multi-cultural community. They will make their own distinctive contribution, a different but valued part of the whole.

Chapter XVI

# OLDHAM'S FUTURE

Oldham is not an old community. Not without its ups and downs, it flourished and boomed in the nineteenth century. Indeed, by the standards of that time, it was a place of high and remarkable achievements. Understandably those achievements, measured by the artefacts of the community and its industries, its houses and mills and utilities, its churches and chapels and public buildings, were a source of great pride. Oldham's ascendancy was due in large degree to an aggressive and competitive spirit of enterprise, motivated above all by a zeal to "get on" and "make some brass". Self-made men built significant private businesses among which Platts, Asa Lees, Lees and Wrigley, Collinges, Greaves and Eli Lees were the most prominent. But the town's place as "cotton spinning capital of the world" derived from the involvement of tens of thousands of working people and the success of the Oldham Limiteds in harnessing their savings to finance remarkable physical expansion and renewal of mills and machinery. A booming industry created a booming town that grew without great regard for amenity or appearance but learned to govern itself to meet its priorities at the time.

Oldham's subsequent decline as the Lancashire cotton industry and its associated engineering activities, where Oldham had been supreme, collapsed, was severe and traumatic. A period of despondency followed, a feeling that its glory had departed, that it was a "has been" town. But Oldham has reversed that decline, recreated its base and renewed itself to a remarkable degree, finding new pride and confidence. A grim decayed Victorian image has been replaced by a modern town in the countryside.

**Leesbrook Mill**, built in 1884, modernised in its green setting.

**Stoneacres**, a modern housing development near Grotton, with Oldham town centre in the distant background.

**Then and Now**: Sandy Lane, Royton in 1936 and in 1998.

The modern Borough remains distinctive; on the edge of the Manchester conurbation but not part of the city. It is a place of contrasts. Two thirds of its area is attractive Pennine hill country and meadowland. Half its population live in dormitory communities, some traditional, some modern, characterised by pleasant surroundings and comparative affluence which is reflected in low unemployment and high levels of owner occupation. But the other half of Oldham's people live in very different circumstances. On some of the large council estates and in the run-down inner areas occupied by the Asian community, unemployment, dependence on a variety of benefits, lone parenthood and other characteristics of modern poverty govern a mainly deprived lifestyle.

If much has been done to modernise Oldham in the past twenty years, large challenges still remain. Ameliorating, if not eliminating, deprivation and social exclusion is a priority task for the future, just as it has been a priority for the past decades. It will continue to demand large resources and large energy, and possibly new approaches. Thus Oldham will remain concerned with refurbishing its housing estates and with regenerating its inner areas. It will do more to advance the status of its growing ethnic minority population, to improve their homes and neighbourhoods and enhance their educational and work opportunities. The Borough will address these challenges in a balanced way without neglecting the interests of its more affluent districts, or diverting their resources unfairly. Creating a strong sense of a united whole, binding together contrasting social communities and different ethnic groups, is crucial.

These priorities are not in dispute. In addressing

them, the Borough will attract financial assistance, from central government and from the European Union, as it has in the past. The drive, determination and presentational skills of the Borough's leadership will be fundamental in this process. Oldham, in its bids to attract resources, is competing with many other places and its case has to be well-prepared and able to command attention. All this is well recognised and there can be confidence that Oldham's needs will be well-represented.

The situation of its deprived people apart, there are other priorities in securing Oldham's future. Much has been done to create an efficient and convenient town centre, with a broad range of modern shopping facilities, but that task is not yet complete. The proposed extensions to the centre, the introduction of major national retailers, and the development of new leisure and cultural provisions dedicated to relaxation and enjoyment, are crucial. Appearance and image, achieved by upgrading existing buildings or contributing new, as well as attractive civic open space, will require continuous attention. The town centre is not merely the location of key services; it is a huge place of employment. It is essential that it remains viable and competitive in a rapidly changing market. With the attraction of other centres, and particularly the new Trafford Centre in the conurbation, Oldham cannot stand still. If the centre loses its appeal, both to the local population and to visitors, the whole community will suffer.

If Oldham's employment base has been strengthened materially in the recent past, the continuing endeavour to attract new forms of business cannot be relaxed. Manufacturing activity, too often branch rather than headquarters, will remain vulnerable. The need for more sophisticated, more

**Shopping in Oldham, 1999**; inside Spindles Mall.

Young Oldhamers celebrate at the **Streets Ahead Festival**, Oldham town centre, 1998.

351

**The Huddersfield Narrow Canal** and the 1849 Railway Viaduct at Uppermill.

A popular destination for visitors and tourists, **Dove Stones Reservoir, Saddleworth**, within the Peak District National Park.

skilled, higher value added, better-paying forms of employment is only partly met. By a variety of means Oldham's economic base has to be further upgraded; in this respect, while further and potentially higher education has been re-vitalised with the Sixth Form College, continued commitment to learning, education, training and other support services is essential to ensure that the people resource can meet the challenges and demands of a developing local economy and enhance its attractiveness to incoming investment. Oldham has to further increase its accessibility; the long planned improvement to its transport links, the M60 Motorway affording swift access to Manchester Airport and the replacement of its obsolete railway by the modern Metrolink, needs urgent completion. More will be done to improve the approaches to the town, both from a traffic point-of-view and from the standpoint of image.

Professional and managerial occupations will not develop in the Borough on any scale given the proximity of Manchester. But people working in those occupations in Greater Manchester or in West Yorkshire are choosing to live in Oldham. The Borough has to remain a good place to live, not merely for those who work there, but for the commuter. There is no shame in being a sought-after commuter dormitory. An attractive and preserved environment, cultural and leisure facilities, good schools and public services generally, a wide choice of housing types, are among the many factors influencing residential choice; these factors have to be identified and nurtured. Golf courses, sports stadiums along with centres for the performing arts, are not frivolities; their availability has large implications.

## Oldham's Future

As in its past, so in its present, Oldham has no large inherent advantages of situation or local resources, other than its proximity to large populations and an attractive clean green setting. What it has above all is its particular people, the Oldhamers, drawn together over two centuries by its opportunities, and nurtured by its working and living environment.

The Oldham breed, down-to-earth, blunt and unpolished, but above all good-humoured, hard-working and self-reliant, made the place what it became. At the time, a hundred years ago, they called the place Brave Oldham because so much had been achieved, notwithstanding adversity; the breed had proved its worth. The aspiration, the perseverance and the enterprise which drove the place forward then, is needed no less today and in the future. Given that level of aspiration, as a strong brave tribe in a competitive hostile world, the people of Oldham will ensure a successful future for themselves.

**Oldham from Tandle Hill Country Park, 1998.**

# Appendix I: Past Mayors of the County Borough and Metropolitan Borough of Oldham

| | | | |
|---|---|---|---|
| William Jones, J.P. | 1849-50 | James Middleton, J.P. | 1916-17 |
| James Collinge, J.P. | 1850-51-52 | William Buckley, J.P. | 1917-18 |
| James Lees, J.P. | 1852-53-54 | John Berry, J.P. | 1918-19 |
| John Platt, J.P. | 1854-55-56  1861-62 | Charles Hardman, J.P. | 1919-20 |
| Josiah Radcliffe, J.P. | 1856-57-58  1864-65 | Frederick Houghton, J.P. | 1921-22 |
| George Barlow, J.P. | 1858-59 | William Edwin Freeman, J.P. | 1922-23 |
| Abraham Leach, J.P. | 1859-60-61 | James Kershaw Cheetham, J.P. | 1923-24 |
| John Riley, J.P. | 1862-63-64 | Fred Broadbent, J.P. | 1924-25 |
| William Knott, J.P. | 1865-66 | Frank Pollard, J.P. | 1925-26 |
| John Taylor, J.P. | 1866-67 | Samuel Frith, J.P. | 1926-27 |
| John Robinson, J.P. | 1867-68 | Edwin Heyes Shorrocks, J.P. | 1927-28 |
| William Rye, J.P. | 1868-69 | Herbert Wild Tupman | 1928-29 |
| Edmund Hartley, J.P. | 1869-70 | Isaac Crabtree, J.P. | 1929-30 |
| Edward Mayall, J.P. | 1870-71 | John Fletcher Waterhouse | 1930-31 |
| Abraham Crompton, J.P. | 1871-72 | Joseph Hague, J.P. | 1931-32 |
| William Wrigley, J.P. | 1872-73 | Elisha Bardsley, J.P. | 1932-33 |
| Emmanuel Whittataker, J.P. | 1873-74 | James Shannon, J.P. | 1933-34 |
| James Mellodew, J.P. | 1874-75 | Thomas Wrigley, J.P. | 1934-35 |
| George Wainwright, J.P. | 1875-76 | Robert William Bainbridge, J.P. | 1935-36 |
| John Wild, J.P. | 1876-77 | Frank Tweedale, J.P. | 1936-37 |
| William Bodden, J.P. | 1877-78 | Alfred James Howcroft, J.P. | 1937-38 |
| George Hamilton, J.P. | 1878-79 | James Bannon | 1938-39 |
| William Chadwick, J.P. | 1879-80 | John Robert Buckley, J.P. | 1939-40 |
| James Yates, M.D., J.P. | 1880-81-82  1904-05 | William Heaton Taylor | 1940-41 |
| Samuel Ogden, J.P. | 1882-83 | Harry Ernest Chamberlain | 1941-42 |
| Saumel Buckley, J.P. | 1883-84  1889-90-91 | Thomas Driver, J.P. | 1942-43 |
| Joshua Walmsley Radcliffe, D.L., J.P. | 1884-85-86-87 | Richard Roberts, J.P. | 1943-44 |
| Samuel Radcliffe Platt, D.L., J.P. | 1887-88-89 | Alfred Hallwood, J.P. | 1944-45 |
| Alfred Emmott, J.P. | 1891-92 | Stirling Thomas Marron, J.P. | 1945-46 |
| William Noton, J.P. | 1892-93 | Joseph Berry, J.P. | 1946-47 |
| Joseph Smith, J.P. | 1893-94 | Stott Thornton, J.P. | 1947-48-49 |
| Robert Whittaker, J.P. | 1894-95-96-97 | Alfred Marshall, J.P. | 1949-50 |
| Alfred Waddington, J.P. | 1897-98 | Ernest Kershaw, J.P. | 1950-51 |
| Jackson Brierley, J.P. | 1898-99 | Frank Lord, O.B.E., J.P. | 1951-52 |
| John Hood, J.P. | 1899-1900-01 | Henry Bradbury Whittaker | 1952-53 |
| James Eckersley, J.P. | 1901-02 | Frank Kenyon, J.P. | 1953-54 |
| George Hanson, J.P. | 1902-03 | Herbert Henry Webster, J.P. | 1954-55 |
| Horatio Chadwick, J.P. | 1903-04 | Herbert Holt, M.B.E. J.P. | 1955-56 |
| Thomas John Carson, J.P. | 1905-06 | Thomas Lyson | 1956-57 |
| Robert Gourley, J.P. | 1906-07-08 | Arnold Tweedale, J.P. | 1957-58 |
| Thomas Bolton, J.P. | 1908-09 | James Bradley | 1958-59 |
| William Schofield, J.P. | 1909-10 | Joseph Tennyson Hilton, J.P. | 1959-60 |
| Sarah Anne Lees | 1910-11 | George Frederick Holden, J.P. | 1960-61 |
| Fred Graham Isherwood, J.P. | 1911-12 | Alice Amelia Kenyon, J.P. | 1961-62 |
| Joseph Ashworth, J.P. | 1912-13 | John Shyne | 1962-63 |
| Herbert Wilde, J.P. | 1913-14 | James Herbert Broadbent | 1963-64 |
| William Lees | 1914-15  1920-21 | Edward Kenney | 1964-65 |
| James Greaves, J.P. | 1915-16 | Wilfred Clover, O.B.E. | 1965-66 |

| | | | |
|---|---|---|---|
| Henry Kenny | 1966-67 | Ethel Rothwell, J.P. | 1970-71 |
| Frank Bashforth Balson, J.P. | 1967-68 | Fred Baxter, J.P. | 1971-72 |
| Robert Bailey, J.P. | 1968-69 | David Jackson, J.P. | 1972-73 |
| Jack Warrener | 1969-70 | Malcolm Forsyth Bamford, J.P. | 1973-74 |

**Mayors of the Metropolitan Borough**

| | | | |
|---|---|---|---|
| Ellen Brierley, B.A. J.P. | 1974-75 | Arnold Tweedale | 1987-88 |
| Jack Armitage J.P. | 1975-76 | Harry Slack | 1988-89 |
| Christopher McCall | 1976-77 | Elsie Winifred Shaw | 1989-90 |
| George Edmund Lord J.P. | 1977-78 | Sidney George William Jacobs, J.P. | 1990-91 |
| Geoffrey Webb J.P. | 1978-79 | Ralph Semple, M.B.E., J.P. | 1991-92 |
| Harold Shanley | 1979-80 | Norman Edward Bennett, M.I.T.D. | 1992-93 |
| John Colin Campbell | 1980-81 | Brian John Mather | 1993-94 |
| John Raymond Crowther, J.P. | 1981-82 | Francis Heap | 1994-95 |
| Alfred Clarke, J.P. | 1982-83 | Joseph Alexander Farquhar, J.P. | 1995-96 |
| John Joseph Curran | 1983-84 | Alan Griffiths | 1996-97 |
| James Kevin Leyden, J.P. | 1984-85 | Peter Dean, J.P. | 1997-98 |
| Alwyn Bywater McConnell | 1985-86 | Margaret Riley | 1998-99 |
| Albert Banks Jowett | 1986-87 | | |

# Appendix II: Members of Parliament for Oldham

| | |
|---|---|
| 1832 | William Cobbett; John Fielden. |
| 1835 | William Cobbett; John Fielden. |
| 1835 | John Frederick Lees. |
| 1837 | General W.A. Johnson; John Fielden. |
| 1841 | General W.A. Johnson; John Fielden. |
| 1847 | William Johnson Fox; John Duncuft. |
| 1852 | John Morgan Cobbett; John Duncuft. |
| 1852 | William Johnson Fox. |
| 1857 | John Morgan Cobbett; James Platt. |
| 1857 | William Johnson Fox. |
| 1859 | William Johnson Fox; John Morgan Cobbett. |
| 1862 | John Tomlinson Hibbert. |
| 1865 | John Tomlinson Hibbert; John Platt. |
| 1868 | John Tomlinson Hibbert; John Platt. |
| 1872 | John Morgan Cobbett. |
| 1874 | Frederick Lowten Spinks; John Morgan Cobbett. |
| 1877 | John Tomlinson Hibbert. |
| 1880 | John Tomlinson Hibbert; Hon. E.L. Stanley. |
| 1885 | John Tomlinson Hibbert; James Mackenzie Maclean. |
| 1886 | James Mackenzie Maclean; Elliott Lees. |
| 1892 | Joshua Milne Cheetham; John Tomlinson Hibbert. |
| 1895 | Robert Ashcroft; James Francis Oswald Q.C. |
| 1899 | Alfred Emmott; Walter Runciman. |
| 1900 | Alfred Emmott; Winston Leonard Spencer Churchill. |
| 1906 | The Right Hon. Alfred Emmott; John Albert Bright. |
| 1910 | The Right Hon. Alfred Emmott; William Barton. |
| 1911 | Edmund Robert Bartley Denniss. |
| 1918 | Edmund Robert Bartley Denniss; William Barton. |
| 1922 | Sir Edward William Macleay Grigg, K.C.V.O.; William John Tout. |
| 1923 | William John Tout; Sir Edward William Macleay Grigg, K.C.V.O. |
| 1924 | Alfred Duff Cooper; Sir William Macleay Grigg, K.C.V.O. |

| | |
|---|---|
| 1925 | William Martin Wiggins. |
| 1929 | Rev. Gordon Lang; James Wilson. |
| 1931 | Anthony Crommelin Crossley; Hamilton William Kerr. |
| 1935 | Hamilton William Kerr; John Samuel Dodd. |
| 1945 | Frank Fairhurst; Charles Leslie Hale. |
| 1950 | Frank Fairhurst - Oldham East; Charles Leslie Hale - Oldham West. |
| 1951 | Ian Macdonald Horobin - Oldham East; Charles Leslie Hale - Oldham West. |
| 1955 | Ian Macdonald Horobin - Oldham East; Charles Leslie Hale - Oldham West. |
| 1959 | Charles Mapp - Oldham East; Charles Leslie Hale - Oldham West. |
| 1964 | Charles Mapp - Oldham East; Charles Leslie Hale - Oldham West. |
| 1966 | Charles Mapp - Oldham East; Charles Leslie Hale - Oldham West. |
| 1968 | Keith Bruce Campbell - Oldham West. |
| 1970 | James Alexander Lamond - Oldham East; Michael Hugh Meacher - Oldham West. |
| 1974 (Feb) | James Alexander Lamond - Oldham East; Michael Hugh Meacher - Oldham West. |

**October 1974 to date - Metropolitan Borough.**

| | |
|---|---|
| 1974 | Michael Hugh Meacher - Oldham West; James Alexander Lamond - Oldham East; Richard S. Wainwright - Colne Valley; Charles R. Morris - Manchester Openshaw; Joel Barnett - Heywood and Royton. |
| 1979 | Michael Hugh Meacher - Oldham West; James Alexander Lamond - Oldham East; Richard S. Wainwright - Colne Valley; Charles R. Morris - Manchester Openshaw; Rt.Hon. Joel Barnett - Heywood and Royton. |
| 1983 | Michael Hugh Meacher - Oldham West; James Alexander Lamond - Oldham Central and Royton; Geoffrey Kenneth Dickens - Littleborough and Saddleworth. |
| 1987 | Michael Hugh Meacher - Oldham West; James Alexander Lamond - Oldham Central and Royton; Geoffrey Kenneth Dickens - Littleborough and Saddleworth |
| 1992 | Michael Hugh Meacher - Oldham West; Bryan Davies - Oldham Central and Royton; Geoffrey Kenneth Dickens - Littleborough and Saddleworth. |
| 1995 | Christopher Davies - Littleborough and Saddleworth. |
| 1997 | Michael Hugh Meacher - Oldham West and Royton; Philip James Woolas - Oldham East and Saddlworth; The Rt.Hon. Robert Sheldon - Ashton-under-Lyne. |

# *Appendix III: Leaders of Oldham Metropolitan Borough Council*

| | |
|---|---|
| 1974-1981 | John T. Hilton |
| 1981-1999 | John Battye |

# Sources and further reading

The Oldham Local Studies Library has a vast and accessible collection of primary and secondary material on Oldham's history; almost all the relevant material can be found there. That having been said, the principal source of information and comment has to be the local press, the *Oldham Chronicle* from 1854, and to a lesser extent the *Oldham Standard*. I have drawn on the *Chronicle* freely; most of the quotations in the text are taken from its news reports, its leading articles and its obituaries.

Hartley Bateson, *A History of Oldham* (1974), is the standard work of reference. James Middleton, *Oldham, Past and Present* (1903) conveys the character of Oldham and its leading men at that time. John Stafford's, *Oldham as it was* (Nelson, 1973) and K. McPhillips, *Oldham, the Formative Years* (Manchester, 1981) are more recent contributions. On the general background, John Walton, *Lancashire, A Social History 1558-1939* (Manchester University Press, 1987) is excellent, as is the same author's contribution to Volume I of the Cambridge Social History of Britain (Cambridge University Press, 1990). Anthony Howe, *The Cotton Masters 1830-1860* (Oxford University Press, 1984) has much to say on the social and political activities of the new business elite in mid-nineteenth century England. Patrick Joyce, *Work, Society and Politics* (London, 1980) covers similar ground but from a different standpoint, that of factory folk rather than capitalists.

On the history and achievement of local government in Oldham the Jubilee Volume published in 1899, and *Oldham Centenary* published in 1949, in both cases by the Borough Council, are comprehensive if self-congratulatory accounts. In recent years Oldham MBC has published many reports on its programmes and on the Borough's social and economic characteristics.

To highlight particular sources, for the early nineteenth century there are valuable contemporary accounts, notably the Rowbottom Diaries in the Local Studies Library, parts of which are available in *The Most Dismal Times* (Oldham Arts and Leisure, 1996). Edwin Butterworth, *Historical Sketches of Oldham* (1856), Samuel Bamford, *Walks in South Lancashire* (1844), and Angus Reach, *Manchester and the Textile Districts in 1849* (reprinted by Helmshore Local History Society in 1972) are other descriptions of the Oldham district at or before mid-century. Benjamin Grime's "Memory Sketches", published in the *Oldham Chronicle* in 1887 and, so far as election politics go, in book form, are a vivid local record of Oldham in the second quarter of the nineteenth century. Michael Winstanley of Lancaster University has published valuable articles on Edwin Butterworth, Oldham's local government and policing, and political activity in the Borough over this period, with a full list of relevant source references. John Foster, *Class Struggle and the Industrial Revolution* (Cambridge University Press, 1974) is a well-known but unreliable analysis of Oldham radicalism, supported by a wealth of references to contemporary material. Mark Smith, *Religion in Industrial Society* (Oxford University Press, 1994) covers this aspect of Oldham and Saddleworth's history in close detail.

For the cotton industry the outstanding source is Douglas Farnie, *The Lancashire Cotton Industry and the World Market 1815-1886* (Oxford University Press, 1979), which has a detailed account of the Oldham Limiteds. Farnie's contribution to Duncan Gurr and Julian Hunt, *The Cotton Mills of Oldham* (Revised Edition 1998), is excellent and this valuable publication gives particulars of the multitude of individual mills, as well as a good account of Oldham's machine makers. On industrial relations A. Fowler and T. Wyke, *The Barefoot Aristocrats* (Littleborough, 1987), and A. Bullen and A. Fowler, *The Cardroom Worker's Union* (Manchester, 1986) are comprehensive sources. The Dictionary of Business Biography has valuable accounts of John and Samuel Platt, John Bunting, J. B. Tattersall and T. E. Gartside. William Marcroft's writings are contemporary descriptions of conditions at Platts and the affairs of the Limiteds. R. H. Eastham has published privately in 1994 a full history of *Platts Textile Machinery Makers*.

Under the aegis of Oldham Arts and Heritage, Oldham's history has been recorded in many books of old photographs supported by text. Particular mention may be made of Francis Stott's books on Crompton and Royton, Peter and Michael Fox on Saddleworth and Michael Lawson and Mark Johnson on Chadderton; more recent publications include books on Ferranti, and on the experiences of Asian immigrants in *Humlog*. Rob Magee in several booklets has brought together the facts on a multitude of Oldham and district inns and public houses; John Beever has done the same in his *History of Oldham Churches* (Manchester, 1996). There have been many other contributions to local history in recent years but especially those of Freda Millett who has drawn extensively and vividly on oral history in a succession of well-illustrated books, notably *Oldham and its People, Childhood in Oldham, Uptown, Up at Five* and several others. All of these, and other similar studies, are available at the Oldham Local Studies Library.

# *Acknowledgements*

The author would like to thank the following individuals, museums and photographic archives for permission to reproduce, or help in locating, material: Jack Armitage 325; John Battye 243, 331; Terry Berry and staff of Oldham Local Studies Library; Roger Birch for contemporary photographs 13, 16, 20, 57, 130, 131, 144, 168, 169, 178, 246, 323, 325, 327, 328, 329, 332, 334, 336, 337, 338, 342, 343, 344, 345, 348, 349, 350, 352, 353; Bodleian Library 116, 269; Helen Bradley Prints Ltd. 224; Ellen Brierley 320; Duncan Brodie (Curator, Greater Manchester Police Museum), 226; Maurice Dennett (Curator, Saddleworth Museum); Peter Fox; Duncan Gurr; Brian Holland 209; Harry Holmes 294; Hulme Grammar School 181; Arthur Kirby 164; Ted Lord 321; Michael Lawson 103, 272; Charlie Meecham 326; Freda Millett; North-West Film Archive 100; Mrs. E. Vallis and Nuffield College, Oxford 107, 111, 188; Oldham Chronicle 196, 256, 270, 278, 279, 280, 283, 286, 303, 309, 312, 315, 316, 317, 319, 320, 321, 324, 331, 339, 341, 350, 352 ; Oldham Sixth Form College 331; Royal Commission on Historical Monuments 158, 245; The staff of Royton Library; Mark Smith; Frances Stott; Ida Sutcliffe 285; Topham Picturepoint 100; Dr. Donald Walton 98, 205, 233, 274, 277, 280; Edward Webb 346; Wood Visual Communications, Bradford 289.

# Index

Abbeyhills   270, 305, 340-341
Adelphi   229
Albert Mount   131
Alexandra Park   130, 147-149, 187, 215
Alexander Skating Rink   229
Amalgamation (of Townships, Districts)   166-170, 272
Art Gallery   160-161
Asa Lees   116, 266-67, 293
Ascroft, Robert   111, 239-241
Asian Community   292-293, 317, 323, 344-348
Ashton, Thomas   106, 112, 134, 242, 251
Avro   290, 293, 327

Bamford, Samuel   44, 50-52, 68
Band of Hope   228
Bardsley, Elisha   264
Barrowshaw   220, 233, 305, 340, 342
Baths   144-145, 311, 338
Battye, John   322
Beautiful Oldham   209-211
Belle Vue   55, 220
Bent   42
Blackburne, John   208
Blackpool   56, 223, 277, 314
Bluecoat School   64, 181
Board Schools   174-179
Bodden, William   118, 248
Booth, Hesketh   137
Bradbury, Norton   273
Bradbury Sewing Machines   119
Braddocks   119
Bradley, Helen   224
Brass Bands   230
Brierley, Ellen   319-322
Brierley, Jackson   50, 136-137, 166, 251
British Aerospace   327
Broadway   263
Broadway Business Park   326
Buckley and Proctor   203
Buckley, Samuel   160, 248
Buckley and Taylor   117-118
Building Societies   119
Bunting, John   104, 212, 262, 264
Butterworth, Alfred   102, 107, 189, 207, 212-213, 251, 261
Butterworth, Edwin   18, 25, 30, 47
Butterworth Hall   141
Bye-Laws   150

Canals   21, 30
Card and Blowing Room Operatives   111-113
Castleshaw   14, 140
Cemeteries   144
Chadderton   13, 15, 17, 26, 33, 37, 81, 84, 95, 125-126; and Amalgamation 166-170; District Council 271-273, 299
Cheetham, Joshua Milne   252
Church and Chapel in Oldham and District   56-63, 210-217, 283-284, 316
Churchill, Winston   240-241, 288
Cinema   236, 279-280, 314-315
Civic Centre   269, 310-311, 313, 321
Clarksfield   15, 42 (see Lees of Clarksfield)
Clean Air   317
Cleggs of Sandy Lane   25, 83, 102, 251
Clynes, J.R.   198, 241-243, 255
Coal mining   17, 30-34, 84, 124-125, 266, 293
Cobbett, William   66, 69-70
Cobbett, John Morgan   70-71, 237-238, 240
Collinge, James   38, 42, 133, 249
Collinges Commercial Mill   25, 82-84, 101
Colne Valley by-election   243
Colosseum   229, 293
Colwyn Bay   211
Comprehensive Schools   307-308, 329-330
Conservative Party   133-136, 138, 237-243, 274, 285-287, 322
Cooperative Societies   199-201, 205, 256, 277, 316
Coppice   13, 84, 129, 187, 344-345
Cotton Industry in Oldham and district: early development   17; rapid growth after 1815   18-27; conditions in early mills   44-48; mid-Victorian boom 80-84; Cotton Famine   84-87; flotation mania   87-92; in Great Depression   92-6; manufacturing operations 99-101; industrial relations   105-112, 259-260; earnings   111, 259; numbers employed   121-123; reflotation boom   260-265; inter-war decline   262-266; calls on partly-paid shares   263-264; post-1945 boom and subsequent decline   292; conversion of mills 295
Cotton Spindles Board   265
Council Housing   268-270 (see Housing Estates)
Courtaulds   323-324, 327
Cricket   231, 279, 314
Crompton   15, 19, 21, 25-26, 42, 81, 83, 95, 102, 125-126, 166-170, 175, 215, 224-225, 260-261, 299, 304
Crompton, A and A   82-83, 102

# Index

Crossman, Richard   301
Daisy Nook   221
Davies, Richard Meredith   43, 75, 86, 174, 197, 216
Delph   (see Saddleworth)
Denshaw   (see Saddleworth)
Derker School   178
Diamond Jubilee   226
Diggle   (see Saddleworth)
Displaced persons   292, 344
Dixon, Harry   261-262, 264
Dobcross   (see Saddleworth)
Dobcross Loom Works   119
Dodd, John   114, 248
Dronsfields, of Atlas Works   118-119, 235, 248, 324
Drunkenness   142, 227, 256, 281

Economic development   323-329
Education in Oldham and district: before 1850   62-66; in later nineteenth century   172-181; in inter-war period 259, 273; in post-war period   306-310, 320; in the Metropolitan Borough   329-333, 347
Electricity   164-165, 271, 291
Elk Mill   265, 327
Emigration   86, 188
Emmott family   72, 83, 101, 250-251, 252-253; Thomas   160, 173-174, 182, 212, 251; Alfred   196, 212, 239-242, 251
Engineering   27-30, 83, 113-121, 123, 266-268, (see Platts)
ERDF   325, 336
Evening Schools   180-181

Failsworth   13, 17, 25-29, 166-170
Fawsitt, Thomas   207
Ferranti   119, 267, 290, 293, 324-325, 327
Fielden, John   69-71, 76, 237
Fields, Gracie   279-280
Fire Brigade   144
Fish and chips   205-206
Fitton Hill   298-300, 305, 342
Firwood Park   343
Football   232-233, 279
Formby, George   280
Fox, William   70-71, 173, 237
French, John Gouldie   176
Friarmere   16
Friendly Societies   48, 190
Frith, Samuel   136, 243, 285
Further education   307-309, 311, 330

Garden Suburb   211
Gartside, Thomas   105, 263
Gas   50, 72, 119, 192, 291
Gladstone   185
Glodwick   13, 38, 42, 84, 129, 150, 344-347
Going-off Clubs   222-223, 277-278, 314

Grayson, Victor   243
Greater Manchester Council   320-321
Greaves family of Derker   25, 47, 83, 101, 132, 174, 249, 261, 273
Greenfield   (see Saddleworth)
Grotton Lido   77
Grundy of Hey   61, 215, 240

Half-Time System   63, 122, 172-173, 176, 179
Hand-Loom Weaving   19, 25-26
Harrison, Maurice   307
Hartley, Edmund   114
Hat Making   17, 29-30, 84
Health   52, 152-156, 206-208, 281-282, 336-337
Henshaw Street Chapel   212-213
Hibbert family: Elijah   28; John   188, 212, 237-240, 246
Higginshaw   151
Higgs, Mary   209-211
Hill Stores   201, 281
Hilton, J.T.   307, 319
Hodgson, James   215
Hollingworth Lake   55
Hope Chapel   58, 215-216, 261
Hopwood, William   261-262, 264
Hospitals: Infirmary   208-209, 281, 318, 336; Westhulme   156, 281; Boundary Park   209, 281; Oldham and District General Hospital   318, 336-337
Housing   38-39, 42, 128-132, 149-155, 190-192, 195, 259-260, 270; after   1945 295-305, 340-344
Housing Associations   305, 342-343,
Housing Estates   268-270, 295-305, 340-343, 347
Hulme Grammar Schools   181-182, 309-310, 330, 333

Industrial Estates   295
Inner area   305, 344-348
Irish   37, 42, 197-199, 285-286

Jones family, Coal and Land Owners   30-33, 72, 75, 133, 245

Kenney, Annie   243
Knight, John   68-69
Knott, William   30, 68, 137, 146, 149-150

Labour Party   136, 242-243, 260, 284-287, 322
Lancashire Cotton Corporation   224, 265
Lancashire County Council   133, 169, 223
Lees, District of   19-21, 125-126, 166-170
Lees family of Greenbank: James Lees   25, 38, 42, 72, 75, 133; Thomas Evans Lees   174, 181, 212, 240, 249, 252-253; Elliott Lees   181, 240
Lees family of Soho: Samuel   27; Asa   27, 86-87, 116-117, 208, 248, 252-253, 266-267; Eli   28, 42, 83, 249, 252-253, 261; Charles Edward   160, 208, 249, 252-253; Sarah and Marjory   136, 209-211, 212, 216, 235,

243, 249-250, 252-253, 274
Liberal Party   133-140, 237-243
Library   158-160, 281
Limeside   269, 273, 298, 342
Lodging Houses   49, 195-196
Lyceum   64-66, 182-185

Magistrates   134
Mail order   295
Manchester   17, 21, 23-24, 33-35,
Manchester Exchange   80, 93-94
Manchester Ship Canal   121
Manchester Regiment   254
Marcroft, William   199, 251
Market Hall   147, 204
Market Place   37-38
Mason, Hugh   92
Mawdsley, James   112, 239-241
Means Test   274-275
Mechanics Institute   65-66, 185
Mellodews   83, 101, 212, 250
Mellor, Sam   264
Metrolink   335
Mill architecture   81, 91
Mill fires   81, 91
Mill lodges   152-153
Mill management   102-104
Motor transport   282-283, 290, 312, 315, 326
Motorway   325-326, 352
Mullins, William   110, 112, 134
Murphy, William   198
Music in Oldham   54-55, 229-230, 315
Music Hall   229, 281

Nelson, Horatio   72
New Industry   295
Night soil   146
Northern Foods   327

Oldham Athletic   232-233, 279, 314, 339
Oldham, Charter of Incorporation   74-75
Oldham College   307-309, 311, 330-331
Oldham Commissioners   72-74
Oldham Chronicle   235-236
Oldham Estate Co   131, 313
Oldham House and Mill Co.   191
Oldham Joint Stock Bank   94
Oldham List   106, 108-110
Oldham Master Cotton Spinners   107
Oldham Metropolitan Borough   318-323
Oldham Mission   213
Oldham Musical Society   230, 280
Oldham Operative Cotton Spinners   106
Oldham Orchestral Society   230, 280
Oldham Standard   236

Oldham Stock Exchange   261
Oldham Volunteers   234-235, 254
Oldham Way   312
O'Neill, William   103

Pauperism   196-197
Peterloo   67-68
Platt family:   Henry 28, 246, 253; James   28, 74-77, 182, 246; John   28, 74-77. 114, 133, 138; 173, 182-183. 212, 237-240. 246-248, 253; Samuel   102, 114, 134-135, 138, 169, 183, 208, 211, 229, 247. 253.
Platts (Hibbert and Platt, Platt Bros. and Co., Platt Brothers Limited)   28-29, 42-46, 70, 84, 86-87, 113-116, 133, 248, 266-267, 290, 293, 323
Playing fields   318, 338-339
P.S.A. (Pleasant Sunday Afternoon)   214
Plug Drawing Riots   67-69
Police   141-143
Poor Law Guardians   193-197, 271
Poverty in Oldham   193-197
Public park   75
Public Houses   50, 53-54, 62, 226-228, 281, 315
Public transport   161-163, 271-272, 282-283, 291

Radcliffe family   25, 42, 46, 70, 74-75, 250, 253; Josiah   133, 137; Joshua Walmsley   134-135, 169, 177, 182, 250, 253
Rates in Oldham   165-167, 263, 321-322
Religious Observance   204, 213-215, 314
Repertory Theatre   280, 315
Richardson, William   114-115, 183-184, 208, 248
Road safety   283
Robinson, William   233
Roman Catholics   198-199
Rothwell   119
Roughyeds   68
Rountree, Revd. James   177, 216
Rowbottom   47, 66
Royal Visits   284
Royton   13-19, 21, 26, 33, 42, 91-95, 125-126, 166-170, 178, 299, 304
Royton Spinning Company   88-89
Royton sports   224
Rugby   231-232, 315, 339
Runciman, Walter   240
Rushcart   221-222
Rye, William   117

Saddleworth   14-20, 27, 35, 42-43, 68, 76, 81, 84, 125-126, 170-172, 175. 221, 265, 304, 328, 343
St. Mary's   84, 149, 301-302, 305, 342
St. Peter's Precinct   296, 313
Salmon Fields   325
Salvation Army   188, 214-215
Sanitation   48-49, 146, 150-155

362

# Index

Scarlet Fever   152, 155-156
School of Science and Art   183-185
Secondary education   180
Selnec   320
Seton Healthcare   327
Sewage disposal   155
Share dealing   90-91
Shaw   15, 42, 81-83, 91-93, 95, 261-262, 343
Shaw Road   342
Shaw Singers   54
Sholver   300-301, 305, 340
Shops   201-203
Silk manufacture   17, 26
Sixth Form College   330-332
Slums   149, 154, 195-197, 269-270, 297
Smallpox   152, 156
Smethurst Street   269, 273
Smoke   153
Social Services   318, 320, 337
Spindles Centre   334
Spinks, Frederick   237-238
Stoneleigh   270-273
Strawberry Gardens   221
Street making   145-146
Strikes   106-111
Strinesdale   156, 273, 298, 340, 342
Suffragettes   243
Summerscales, John   75
Sun Mill   87-88, 103
Suthers, Elizabeth   214
Swimming   233, 338

Tame Valley   42-43
Tandle Hill   273
Tattersall, J.B.   105
Taylor, Henry   233
Technical Education   182-185, 307-309, 311
Temperance   61-62, 74, 222, 228
Theatre Royal   55, 229-231

Tommyfield   38, 50, 68, 192-194, 203, 222-224, 275, 277, 289, 333, 335
Tourism   327-328
Tout, W.J   260
Town Hall   74, 156-158, 311
Town Square   333-334
Traffic   312-313
Tripe   206
Turner, Eva   281
Turnpike Trusts   17, 21
Tweedale, Arnold   285, 320
Tweedale, Frank   284

Unemployment   260, 265, 324
Uppermill   (see Saddleworth)

Viner, Revd. A. J.   216
Voluntary Schools   172-179

Wakes   53, 221-223, 277-278, 314
Walton, William   229, 280
Ward, Samuel Ogden   104, 132, 136-137
Water closets   155, 271
Water supply   49, 72, 139-141, 271
Werneth Park   42, 130, 187, 273
Westhulme   156
West Street   37, 42
Westwood   345
Whit Walks   220, 283
Woodfield   188
Woollen industry   16, 20, 27, 81, 292
Workers Education Association   186
Working Mens Hall   74
Workhouse   189, 196-197
Worthingtons of Hollinwood   71-72, 101
Wright, Edward Abbott   83, 249
Wrigley, Edward   249
Wrigley, William   137, 239

Yates, James   136, 159-160